The
Chicago Public Library

REF

Call No F 1219.3.C75 C12

Branch McKinley

Form 178

MEXICAN INDIAN COSTUMES

THE TEXAS PAN AMERICAN SERIES

Cuicatec women of San Andrés Teotilalpan, Oaxaca. 1965

Mexican Indian Costumes

Text by Donald and Dorothy Cordry

Photographs by Donald Cordry

FOREWORD BY MIGUEL COVARRUBIAS

UNIVERSITY OF TEXAS PRESS   AUSTIN & LONDON

The Texas Pan American Series is published with the assistance of
a revolving fund established by the Pan American Sulphur Company
and other friends of Latin America in Texas.

Third Printing, 1978

FOREWORD

There have been countless books on Mexico, and almost as many albums of pictures reflecting—with greater or lesser fidelity—different aspects of Mexico's enormously varied life. Some of these productions are banal travel reports with their chief emphasis on the picturesque and the "quaint," others are serious scientific studies which have little interest for the lay public. Still others are artistic tours de force by masters of photography who take casual pictures with an eye to purely photographic values—the character of a fine head, the play of light on a gnarled tree root, the texture of a pair of earthy Indian hands, the enigma behind a child's eyes. Often published in limited expensive editions, these latter are, for the most part, outside the reach of the general public.

Donald Cordry's photographs do not belong to any of these categories; rather they partake of the best qualities of all of them. In a strictly photographic sense they rank with the best work of the modern photographers who have turned their cameras on the Mexican scene, for they are striking, dramatic, and always beautiful pictures. They possess, in addition, a direct human appeal that derives from the uncomplicated honesty of Cordry's approach. To a surprising degree they succeed in capturing the serenity, mystery, and monumental plasticity of his subjects. But more than this, they constitute an invaluable portrait of remote and little-known peoples who prefer their ancient modes and manners to a modern world about which they know little and care less, and against which their only defense is a stubborn refusal to abandon their antique ways of life.

Anyone who has traveled, if only briefly, in the Mexican interior will realize the importance of Cordry's achievement. He has visited the farthest corners of the country, the inaccessible mountain villages and the primitive communities of tropical jungles, finding Mexicans who have ancient and traditional cultures of their own—who wear, with dignity and style long lost to those who live under the standardizing influence of the hybrid cities, costumes they themselves have made. The warlike Mayos and Coras, the retiring Huichols, the unpredictable Indians of the Sierra de Puebla, the exuberant Totonacos, the elegant women of the Tehuantepec plains, the Zapotecs and Mixes of the Oaxaca mountains, the richly dressed Chinantecs, the rude Huaves of the Pacific coast, the Zoques and Chamulas of the Chiapas highlands, and many others pass in fascinating procession through the pages of this collection.

This book is thus no grab bag of animated "Mexican curios." It sets the Mexican people in true perspective against their Indian land and background. It constitutes an invaluable record of a Mexico that was, that is already—in spite of tenacious resistance—beginning to disappear, and that tomorrow may exist only as a memory and in such brilliantly realized images as Donald Cordry's photographs.

Mexico City   MIGUEL COVARRUBIAS

vii

PREFACE

The development of a study such as that presented in this book is made up of many thousands of individual situations—experienced and recorded on film and in notes and sketches, and remembered with affectionate pleasure. It also consists of many problems met and overcome (usually), many decisions made, and considerable discomfort endured.

To obtain photographs in the field we traveled by car and jeep, on foot and horseback, by oxcart, horse and wagon, and boat or dugout, and sometimes in a small airplane—which usually landed a considerable distance from the village to be visited and left us to cover the remaining miles by whatever means was available. Since we did most of our work during the dry season the weather seldom created difficulties to hamper us. Due to the cooperation of village officials we were often able to find accommodations in schools or municipal buildings, or sometimes in private homes. At other times, however, we found it necessary to sleep on the ground or—in the Huichol country—more comfortably on the sand of river beds.

For this study two Rolleiflex cameras were used (one for color and the other for black and white) and a Hasselblad 500 C equipped with a wide-angle and a telephoto lens. All film was developed commercially in Mexico, and the resulting pictures show some of the variation in quality which will be found in any commercially processed prints.

Taking the pictures produced a variety of problems —amusing and otherwise. Almost always the permission of the subject was secured before the picture was taken. Whenever possible the subject was posed: a costume photographed in motion often fails to give a correct idea of the formation of the garments or the placement or detail of design elements. Considerable time was often required to gain the subject's confidence, and sometimes we found it necessary, for diplomatic reasons, to take our pictures in locations and under condi-

tions which were photographically far from ideal. Then too, the subject's idea of the proper pose for a photograph was usually regrettable—formal and stiff, eyes fixed with a serious expression upon the camera. The subject often desired a copy of the picture, and we made it an invariable rule that this copy should be sent to him or her. Where there was no regular postal service this often entailed considerable effort on our part —sometimes even a return trip to the village.

The recording of the facts which give the pictures meaning also presented a number of problems, largely orthographic in nature. For one thing, maps, official reports, and census records of Mexico exhibit wide variations in the spelling of place names. Where records and maps conflicted we chose the spelling which seemed to be in most common use or which was used by the reference work which we regarded as most authoritative (for Oaxaca this was *Toponimia de Oaxaca*, by José María Brandomín). In some cases our first recording of a village or rancho name was a phonetic spelling based on the pronunciation of a local informant. This spelling was later revised to conform to that used in official records. A few of the places we visited, however, we have never found on any map.

Another orthographic question which we had to decide involved the use and spelling of Indian words. When a commonly used Hispanized version of the Indian word exists we have followed the Spanish spelling conventions (*huipil* and *huipiles* for the Nahuatl *huipilli*). When the word commonly used is still basically Indian we have used the uninflected Indian form (for instance, *quechquemitl* in both the singular and the plural).

Over the many years during which we have been interested in Indian costumes in Mexico, many people have helped us—so many that we could not possibly thank them all in person or list them all here. However, we wish particularly to thank the person who revealed to us, in the early days, a Mexico we might never have known—Dr. Alfonso Caso, now director of the Instituto Nacional Indigenista.

We extend gratitude to the late Dr. Eusebio Dávalos Hurtado, director of the Instituto Nacional de Antropología e Historia, who, with Lic. Joaquín Cortina, smoothed our path with village authorities; and to the late Miguel Covarrubias, and to Rosa Covarrubias, Dr. Daniel Rubín de la Borbolla, Dr. Erich Fromm, Professor Julio de la Fuente, Mr. Max Saltzman, Professor Dr. Eizi Matuda, Mr. Peter Gerhard, Mr. Donald Leonard, Mrs. Carmen Cook de Leonard, Mrs. Barbara Dahlgren de Jordán, Professor Fernando Horcasitas, Mr. Thomas A. Lee, Jr., Mr. Cayuqui Estage, and Mr. and Mrs. Felipe Teixidor, all for many favors. Mrs. Doris Heyden and Mrs. Dila Davis have both been untiring in their assistance to us. We thank Mrs. Nadia Patcévitch for many pleasant trips with her in her jeep to places difficult of access. We are also grateful to Dr. Dee Ann Story and Dr. E. Mott Davis for dating the pre-Columbian textile shown in Plate 139. Our work

has continually been facilitated in the State of Oaxaca by our friends, Dr. Juan Bustamante, Mrs. Anita Jones, Sra. María Luisa B. V. de Audiffred, and Mr. Thomas MacDougall.

In the field of textiles we particularly thank two friends who have always shared their knowledge generously with us: Miss Bodil Christensen and Mrs. Irmgard W. Johnson. We are extremely grateful to Dr. George Foster and to Dr. Isabel Kelly, who have taken great interest in our project—the latter giving much of her valuable time in our behalf.

Finally, we extend our thanks to the many Mexican Indians who received us courteously, posed for our pictures, and provided us with information. If this book succeeds in its purpose of contributing to the knowledge about and preserving a record of a vanishing aspect of Indian America, it will be because all of these people gave so generously of their time and their knowledge.

DONALD and DOROTHY CORDRY

Cuernavaca, Mexico

CONTENTS

ILLUSTRATIONS

Color Plates

Black and White Illustrations

Figures

(Drawings by Donald Cordry unless otherwise indicated.)

Maps

INTRODUCTION

"One fact alone which seemed to me of an inspired significance was that, no matter how grim the fate or circumstances, no matter how meager the scrap of living allowed to him, life was always worth it and worth fighting for to the end. Such aristocracy of spirit alone, I would have thought, should command attention in an age which, despite its advantages and comforts, has seen such a lowering in the human being's sense of the value of life that he is increasingly inclined to take his own."

(*The Heart of the Hunter*—Laurens van der Post)

THE PHOTOGRAPHS in this book are pictures of a Mexico that has disappeared or is fast disappearing. One may say that these people themselves are disappearing; for as they lose their own language, beliefs, customs, and crafts, they become another people.

We will never know what kind of culture the Mexican Indian would have developed had he not been changed by the Spaniards, by the Church, and later by land reform and industrialization. His is one of the many cultures in the world that will not crystallize, but will be absorbed.

Mexico has made wonderful progress and startling improvements through educational, economic, agricultural, and health programs. In some cases these programs have, as yet, brought little or no change in remote areas, but soon—due to the building of more roads—the lives of these Indians too will be affected.

Occasionally the building of a road through a remote village, which has been isolated for centuries, brings sorrow and tension, and divides the villagers into factions—conservatives and progressives. The conservatives want to keep their own language and their hand-spun, handwoven, embroidered costumes, which are to them a kind of symbol of their human individuality. In many cases, this poetic and conservative attitudes does not imply ignorance. They have told us of their need for doctors, hospitals, and schools; but they do not understand why to gain one good they must lose another. Op-posed to them are the progressives, who are usually in power and who are backed by power.

This is like the loom of the Indian weaver. If one thread is removed or added the whole web is affected, for better or for worse.

Worthy programs are in operation to prevent the exploitation of the Indian, and to bring him into active participation in the economic life of the country. But these programs also affect the integral part of his life which has survived against tremendous odds since the time of the Conquest. And what of his inner life which, like the outward manifestations of his character, is almost impossible for the outsider to understand? His is a temperament that ranges from gentleness to brutality, bringing to mind the ancient cult of "flowers and blood."

One hears the phrase "the sad resigned Indian, stupid and without ambition"; yet Eastern philosophies are built on a concept of acceptance—the acceptance of life and reality being an indication of maturity. Behind his placid exterior the Indian exhibits a human dignity, an inner quietness, a quality of listening, perhaps a feeling of inner security, in spite of life's insecurity. For him the line between this existence and the next is reassuringly thin.

To measure human happiness or contentment is impossible. But, in contrast to the old life in which he has had some measure of inner security, the Indian, in his new life, will have to shoulder baffling responsibilities.

He will fall heir to the anxieties and neuroses which, in the name of progress—for the first time in history—the whole world thinks it wants.

Everywhere, people want the so-called "American way of life," the embodiment of material comfort and status; but this life suppresses personal and group individuality and puts everything on the market, even one's smile. As Dr. Erich Fromm once said to me, regarding the dignity of these people who have so little of material possessions, "They are this way because they are not for sale."

The Huichols have, in the past, paid a high price to live unexploited and undisturbed by the outside world, dwelling far from water—near which most *mestizo* villages are located. But now even the Huichol Indians in the remote sierras of Nayarit and Jalisco have been persuaded—with the best intentions—to manufacture for tourist consumption their sacred "God's-Eye," a revered religious object made of sticks and yarn, which is placed in the framework of each new house and in all mountain shrines for the protection of the people—to ensure good crops and long life.

Even those of us most interested in preserving what is indigenous contribute to the breakdown. In the process of purchasing for a museum a fine handwoven headcloth from a Tzotzil who spoke no Spanish, we had the help of a Spanish storekeeper, who spoke the Indian language and conveyed our wish to the startled Indian and his wife, who were intent on their own business. When they finally understood, and decided to part with the textile, it was removed from the man's head and handed to the wife, who beat her husband across the shoulders with it—a very necessary ritual, the Spaniard explained, "To remove the spirit of the owner."

We once showed some of these photographs to a visiting New York photographer who said, "These are very interesting pictures, but it would add a great deal if the people were smiling." Soon after, he went to a village where he persuaded a group to pose for him; they were reluctant, but courteous. They were dignified and remote, and our friend tried the technique he used with children—snapping his fingers, cutting capers, saying "See the birdie!" (in English)—all to no avail. The impassive dignity remained. Our friend looked bewildered, and said on the way home, "Now I understand your pictures, but I certainly don't understand these people!"

The courtesy of the Indian is proverbial. In rural areas, where he lives in intimate contact with other members of a family group in one or two small rooms,

politeness, consideration, and patience are necessary to preserve harmony. These characteristics lead to amusing and puzzling situations. The foreign traveler (a Mexican is a foreigner too in these regions) is told what he would like to hear, instead of what is true. When he asks the distance from one village to another (after having ridden horseback for many hours) he receives the answer, "*Tras lomita* (over the hill)," with no mention of the many more hills still to be traversed.

Spanish oppression has been given as the reason for the Indian's fatalistic acceptance of what comes to him; but was he not the same before the Conquest in his acceptance of slavery to other gods and his sacrifices to them? Where there are churches now, he lives clustered around them in grass, stone, wood, or adobe huts, as formerly his ancestors lived about the magnificient stone cities or temples constructed by their rulers.

His houses, built as they are with rude natural materials, melt into the landscape, and one is conscious of a serene unity with nature. The eyes welcome the soft, broken surfaces and the blurred outlines, as the heart welcomes gentleness and kindness. Old and worn faces age and soften like ancient buildings. This harmony is a release from the tension of order that one finds in city streets and structures. The nostalgia one feels in an Indian village at dusk, smelling the acrid smoke of the small cooking fires and seeing moving shapes in the dark, seems to stir a racial memory, that is not satisfied by a barbecue in the backyard or a swimming pool that meanders through the living room. It is unfortunate that such beauty is so often associated with a poverty of material possessions. This fact does not imply, however, a poverty of spirit.

These photographs show Indians wearing their regional dress, or engaged in weaving or spinning. In groups still somewhat culturally pure, the traditional costume is among the last of the visually beautiful factors of the ancient heritage to be abandoned, and, since change will eventually come, we have felt an urgency to capture on film all we could. Taking these pictures was a great pleasure, for, although much patience was needed on the part of our subjects, we were always accepted with kindness. Our ways—which were not theirs—were looked upon with tolerance, and even when we inconvenienced them or arrived inopportunely during affairs important to them, we were received with dignity and courtesy; it was a pleasure to see "such aristocracy of spirit."

DONALD CORDRY

MEXICAN INDIAN COSTUMES

Book VI, Chapter 10, Law 15 (9 Nov. 1549):

No *encomendero* or other person shall in any case force Indian women to be shut up in corrals or elsewhere to spin and weave the clothing that they are to give as tribute, and they shall have freedom to do this in their houses so that they will not be exploited.

from *Recopilación de leyes
de los reynos de las Indias*

PART I

GROUPS VISITED

Seri	Cuicatec
Mayo	Chinantec
Huichol	Zapotec
Cora	Mixe
Tarascan	Mixtec
Mazahua	Trique
Otomí	Tlapanec
Huastec	Amusgo
Tepehua	Huave
Totonac	Zoque
Nahua	Tzotzil
Mazatec	Maya

1. Pre-Hispanic and Contemporary Costumes

 THE LIFE OF an Indian woman before the Conquest of Mexico by the Spaniards was occupied largely in weaving; weaving garments for herself and her family, and ceremonial clothes for use in the temples and for offerings; and in teaching her daughters to do fine weaving and spinning. Her status in the community depended somewhat on her skill in this activity. Even slaves who were extraordinarily proficient weavers were exempt from being sacrificed.

Women worshipped, propitiated, and were sacrificed to the goddesses Xochiquetzal and Tlazolteotl, and the god Xochipilli. Tlazolteotl, originally of Huastec origin, was represented as the goddess of dirt, and was also called Teteo Innan or mother of the gods. She was the corn, yellow and white, and everything female. She was the goddess of lust and prostitutes and, by inference, of the patient woman of the family—for she is represented as wearing about her head a cotton fillet which reaches her shoulders, and has spindles stuck in the unspun cotton (Códice Borgia 16 and 63, (fig. 1).

Xochiquetzal, the first woman, was often represented carrying a child, and was associated with rain (fertility). She was connected with the feast of Atamalqualiztli, celebrated every eight years. "In the picture of that feast in the Sahagún MSS. we observe her seated at a loom" (Spence, 1923, p. 194). She is the goddess of flowers and is the feminine counterpart of Xochipilli. Her confidants' and messengers' chief occupations were spinning and weaving. She, like Xochipilli, had an artistic significance and was patroness of weavers and artists. The invention of spinning and weaving was attributed to her.

On the feast day of Quecholli, in honor of Xochiquetzal, women sacrificial victims were burned.

And a woman burned all her womanly array—her basket, her spindle whorl, her chalk, her spinning bowl, her warping frame, her cane stalks, her batten, her heddle, her divided cord which held (up the textile), her waist band, and her

Figure 1. The pre-Hispanic goddess Tlazolteotl wears spindles stuck in the unspun-cotton fillet around her head (copies of drawings shown in the Codex Borgia).

5

1. A painted Mayan Chiptic Cave textile found in a sealed jar at Cieneguilla, Chiapas. National Museum of Mexico.

weaving stick, and her thorns, and her skeins, her shuttle, and her measuring stick. All these she burned herself.

Of these of which they disposed in this wise, it was said that they would be needed where they were going, when they went; when they died, there (these things) would await them. (Sahagún, 1951–1963, Book 2, p. 128)

When these women were about to be sacrificed, they were dressed in paper vestments, which were probably painted or stamped with elaborate designs.

Fray Toribio de Motolonía (1950, p. 59) tells us that children were given a name on the seventh day after birth and that . . . "if it was a male child, they put an arrow into his hand, and if it was a female child, a spindle and weaving stick (shuttle), as a sign that she should be diligent and housewifely, a good spinner and a better weaver." Weaving and spinning were practiced not only by the plebeian class, but also by young noble women who received instruction in the temples.

So the life of a woman from birth to death was concerned with weaving beautiful, well-made textiles. One of her obligations was to teach her daughters to weave and spin, and the Codex Mendoza shows the punishments used if the child did not work well.

Although garments were simply made—that is made from straight lengths of cloth as they were taken from the loom, without being cut—they were highly decorated. They were woven with designs (brocading, figured gauze, tapestry, warp- and weft-faced stripes), embroidered, stamped, and dyed. I. W. Johnson, says, in her "Chiptic Cave Textiles from Chiapas, Mexico" (1954, p. 140) "Two rare techniques, not previously recorded for Middle America, are represented in these comparatively few specimens: hand painting and resist dyeing (batik)" (pl. 1).

Feathers were used as adornment on cloth, and probably also for warmth. Many vegetable dyes were used. "The Indians make many colors from flowers, and when the painters wish to change from one color to another, they lick the brush clean, for the paints are made from the juice of flowers" (Motolonía, 1950, p. 220). Other vegetable dyes were made, as they are today, from roots, wood, bark, and fruit. Indigo (*Indigofera anil*, L.) gave a dye which ranged from blue to black. Brazilwood gave a red dye; a parasitic plant, orange in color, called in Nahua *zacatlaxcalli*, gave a mustard yellow and was still being used in Mitla, Oaxaca, in 1940.

Of animal dyes, one of the most famous was the shell dye. Various species of shellfish were used, usually of the rock shell family. *Purpura patula pansa* (Gould) was used on the Pacific Coast. *Thais kioskiformis* (Duclos) and species of Murex were probably also employed, as they too produce coloring matter. Francisco de Burgoa says of the Huave Indians (1934, Vol. II, p. 406), "They had time to weave cloths [*mantas*] . . . and dye them red with brazil [wood] or purple shell dye and they call these huazontecas for skirts and altar cloths [*sobre mesas*]."

Cochineal or *grana* is the female insect of the family Coccidae of the order Hemiptera, that lives on the nopal. Its dried body was an important item of tribute which the Indians (especially of Oaxaca) paid to Moctezuma in large quantities. It gave a reddish orange dye (Dahlgren, 1963).

Minerals and earth colors were also used, according to Fray Bernardino de Sahagún (1951–1963, Book 10, p. 77). Chalk was mixed with cochineal, red ochre,

2. An Otomí *ixtle* (maguey fiber) spinner on the highway near Zimapán, Hidalgo. 1940

3. An old Tepehuane bag of *pita* fiber — date unknown. Santa María, Durango.

sulfate of copper, and iron pyrites. Ochre, gypsum, and the rare mineral dumortierite were the chief coloring materials used by the Seri Indians for face painting (McGee, 1898, p. 165) (pl. I).

Cotton (*ichcatl*) was used extensively, both white and yellow (*coioichcatl*). The term *coioichcatl* is derived from two Nahua words: *ichcatl* (cotton) and *coyotl* (coyote), referring to the yellow color. Sahagún says about the cotton seller (1951–1963, Book 10, p. 75), "Separately he sells the yellow, separately the broken, the stretched." In early times cotton was probably traded and later paid in tribute to the great city of México.

Cotton was used by the nobility; and, probably, the commoners wore garments made of *nequén* (henequen or other coarser fibers. Sahagún [1951–1963], Book 10,

p. 180) tells us that, "all the Otomí women concerned themselves only with maguey fiber; [the green leaves] were toasted, dressed, scraped. They pressed the water [out of the fiber], treated it with maize dough, spun it, placed it over the shoulder, wove it" (pl. 2). Judging by the extremely fine soft Tepehuane netted bags used by men and made of *pita* fiber in times past, these garments must have been very handsome. The bags are decorated with bands in color (pl. 3).

I. W. Johnson, in her analysis of the woven textiles from the north of Mexico (from dry caves in Coahuila and Tamaulipas) found that yucca (*Yucca triculeana, Yucca carnerosana*) and the fiber of apocyna (*Apocynum cannabinum* L.) were used. These were also identified in the woven textiles from Chihuahua by Lila M. O'Neale (Johnson, letter, 1966). The excavations near Tehuacán, Puebla, under the direction of Richard Stockton MacNeish, have brought to light brocaded-gauze cotton cloth of the Venta Salada complex (MacNeish, 1961, p. 27).

Woven cotton (*Gossypium* sp.) was unknown in aboriginal Baja California at the time of European contact. A specimen described as coming from the area is a piece of pre-Columbian trade goods from the mainland of Mexico. The Seri Indians of Tiburón Island and Sonora were probably the intermediary traders. These Indians are well aware of the peninsula opposite them to the west. All of the tribes of Sonora, except the Seri, wove cotton (Massey and Osborne, 1961, p. 351).

By 1531 several attempts had been made to introduce silk culture into New Spain, and some of these, at least, had been successful (Borah, 1943, p. 8). Later, in 1541, the Convent of Santa María at Yanhuitlán was founded by the Dominicans, and they thereafter fostered sericulture in the Mixteca.

Woodrow Borah concludes, in his chapter on wild silk (1943, pp. 102–114), that oak silk (*Gloveria psiddi Sallé*) and the madroño silk cocoons (*Bombyx madroño*) were not used before the Conquest, but that this small home industry was started toward the end of the eighteenth century when mulberry silk raising was almost extinct. He goes on to say, ". . . since silk culture never was blotted out in any dramatic Jacquerie, the idea that wild silk developed to replace an extinct Mixtecan industry is not fully plausible and must be modified." Borah continues that with the diminishing of the mulberry silk industry, Indians could not get silk for their own use, and so began to use oak silk.

To say that wild silk was not used in pre-Hispanic Mexico would be difficult for us; personal observation at least admits the possibility that it was. Today it is used only in small quantities to accent a design, for narrow stripes, or in narrow belts. The fact that raw, coarse, hand-spun silk — whether wild or mulberry — used in small areas in a textile is very difficult to tell from hand-spun cotton may be one reason it was not mentioned by the chroniclers. We have shown Indian textiles of hand-spun cotton with hand-spun silk stripes to many people, and in almost all cases they would not believe that silk had been used.

In Indian Mexico weaving materials and dye plants adapted by the people for their own use are very often confined to small areas, or to one or two villages. For example, the fiber of the plant *chichicastle* is used for weaving textiles only in a small area of the state of Oaxaca. Another plant used in a special way and con-

fined, as far as we know, to only one village is the teasel. This plant serves in Hueyapan, Morelos (Nahua), for carding and for mixing black and white wool to make gray (pls. 190 & 191).

Spinning is clearly illustrated in a number of codices, and the techniques and implements used in the illustrations are still used today (pl. 229). Two types of looms were used for weaving—the backstrap or stickloom (*telar de otate*) (fig. 3) in Central and Southern Mexico; and the rigid loom which consists of a frame set on posts put into the earth. The rigid loom generally produced a ring or tubular web (for a modern example see pl. 14). The weaving implements illustrated in the Florentine Codex (Sahagún, 1951–1963, Book 8) (fig. 6) are identical with those used today.

The principal garments worn by the pre-Columbian men were the *tilmatli* or *ayate* (*ayatl*), and the *maxtlatl* (loin cloth). According to Cecilio Robelo (1904, p. 683), a *tilmatli*, when used by the nobles, was made of cotton; those of the commoners were made of *ichtli* (*ixtle*—a fiber made from the maguey plant). Today they are also made of *ixtle* and cotton, and used for carrying cloths, and also worn as in pre-Conquest times (pl. 129).

The *tilmatli* was a four-foot square of cloth, worn as a cape (Robelo, 1904, p. 683). Sometimes the extremities were knotted over one shoulder and open on the side; sometimes they were knotted and open in front like a cape. In some cases, for freedom of movement, the *tilmatli* was put under one arm and knotted over the other shoulder. This garment was made of *ixtle*, often netted in open work or of cotton cloth woven with rabbit fur. Sometimes it was completely covered with feathers in beautiful patterns; decorated with any of the many weaving techniques previously mentioned; or dyed or stamped with clay seals. It might also be decorated with shells, mother-of-pearl disks, or jade plaques. Though it was a simple garment, those worn by the nobility or the warrior class were sumptuously decorated. The *maxtlatl* was a loin cloth, also splendidly decorated.

With these basic and simple garments were worn fantastic jewels of gold, jade, semiprecious stones, rock crystal, and shell; soaring headdresses made of wood, feathers, fibers, leather, and bark paper. One has only to look at the paintings in the ruins at Bonampak to observe the incredible richness and variety of the pre-Hispanic man's costume. Although the basic costume was simple, designs were rich (Sahagún, 1951–1963, Book 8, pp. 23–25, lists fifty-four designs for men's "capes"). Sandals were elaborate — "made of ocelot skin and also embroidered" (Sahagún, 1951–1963, Book 8, p. 28), and, in the case of rulers, of gold.

The woman's dress was basically simple, but beautiful in color and adornment. The upper garment consisted of a *quechquemitl* (believed by many historians and archaeologists to have been worn only by women of the nobility and by goddesses) or a *huipilli* (*huipil*). The words *quechquemitl* and *huipil* were not always used correctly in documents of the sixteenth, seventeenth, and eighteenth centuries. The term *quechquemitl* seems to have been used less frequently than *huipil*; and often in areas where the *quechquemitl* was worn, this garment was termed a *huipil*. Why this was we do not know. Some chroniclers were probably not particularly interested in distinguishing the fine points of women's costume. With either the *quechquemitl* or the *huipil* was worn a skirt, a straight piece of cloth wrapped about the hips, and held in place by a woven belt. Sometimes a *quechquemitl* was worn over the *huipil* (fig. 9). Women's sandals were sometimes woven of *ixtle* (as they rarely are today), but in most codices women—except for women of rank—are pictured barefoot.

It is difficult for us to conceive the magnificence of the costumes and textiles in pre-Cortesian Mexico. Some idea may be had from the codices and from textile designs on sculpture of the elaborate turbans and headdresses of bark paper, cloth, and feathers. Their sheer bulk is overwhelming.

The textile industry towards the end of the fifteenth century was one of the most highly developed and richest in America, especially in Mexico. According to the Codex Mendocino and the tribute rolls, during the fourteenth century, the groups that were subjugated by the Aztec empire paid annual tribute to it of over a million pieces of cloth. This very revealing figure shows us that cotton cultivation and weaving had reached a very high level of development, probably the highest in all of pre-Hispanic history.

During the sixteenth century, it was common practice for the Indian villages to pay their "encomienda" taxes and other levies in differently woven pieces of cloth. It was also at this time that the exportation of raw cotton to Spain began as well as that of dyes, such as cochineal and log wood. Trade in cochineal reached an extraordinary volume by the end of that century. The Spaniards, for their part, introduced into America the foot loom, the spinning wheel, certain types of thread and yarn, the weaving of sheep's wool and certain articles of European wearing apparel. (Borbolla, 1963, pp. 3–9)

The Spanish Conquest brought rapid and radical change in native costume. Nevertheless, even today, one can observe evident survivals in raiment and in techniques associated with textile manufacture.

When one is absorbed with Mexican Indian costumes and textiles, the interest is consuming. There is always a mysterious new village to explore, where perhaps an unknown costume may be found—or information about one that was worn by the previous generation, in case the old regional attire has disappeared.

Some misinformation exists regarding Indian dress; and accurate data about textiles and about proper assemblage of costume parts are lacking. At times specimens in collections are mislabeled, but such mistakes can still be rectified if investigators will cooperate. We need to make correct records now, before these garments completely disappear.

One often hears from strangers to Mexico that very few indigenous costumes are to be seen (except, of course, in the splendid new National Museum of Anthropology and the Popular Art Museum), in comparison, for instance, with Guatemala—where Indians in typical dress are everywhere. One must remember that Mexico is more than fifteen times the size of Guatemala, and that one must, therefore, travel further afield to discover authentic Indian costumes. One is well rewarded for the effort. In our opinion, the costumes of conservative Mexican villages are more beautiful than those of any other Latin American country: the design is usually bolder, more indigenous, and of greater variety.

Mexico, through the work of the Instituto Nacional Indigenista, directed by Dr. Alfonso Caso, is doing a splendid job of assimilating the Indian into the life of the country. It is not an aim of the I.N.I. to take away regional dress. Dr. Caso (1962, p. 10) says, in fact, "*en muchos ocasiones el vestido indígena es mucho más adecuado a las condiciones del medio que el que nosotros pudiéramos imponerles*" (in many instances the Indian costume is much more adequate for the environment than one which we might introduce). But as people begin to feel a part of the country, they do not wish to be isolated from it by dress. So the change comes about imperceptibly, and by the wishes of the people themselves.

The Indian women's costume worn today seems to be that of the upper-class pre-Hispanic women. We read that in pre-Cortesian times the *macehuales* were obliged to wear garments of *ixtle*. This statement may have applied only to highland areas where cotton was imported, and was a luxury item, but where henequen was

9

plentiful. But in the *Papeles de Nueva España* (Paso y Troncoso, 1905, Vol. IV, pp. 170–171), in one of the *relaciones*, we find that by 1580 there was no difference between the dress of the *macehuales* (humble people) and of the *principales* (important people) among the Cuicatec and Chinantec—only that each one wore what he could afford. Later the women's beautiful *huipiles* are spoken of. We see that the men were less conservative than the women, then as they are now: they wore jackets of blue or green wool cloth, boots, breeches—and in another *relación* felt hats are mentioned. Of course, these elegant Spanish items of dress were probably given as bribes, or sold to the most important village men to help assimilate them into Spanish life.

After the Conquest, when native laws lost their power, the laws concerning dress were ignored, and the common people, most particularly the women, took over (with modifications) the sumptuous dress of the Indian aristocracy. That is what we see today—cotton so finely spun that it is like silk, with beautiful colors and designs that exhibit the woman's innate good taste, if she stays with tradition and does not copy designs from modern sources. The pre-Hispanic costume was more splendid than that of the conquerors, and the jewels and headdresses worn by Moctezuma and the nobility—so fabulous and large that they were practically architectural monuments—were comparable to the dress of oriental kings. From this heritage present-day Indians have retained a pronounced talent for craftsmanship and a deep love of beauty. With the simplest implements they are able to fashion hand-spun, hand-woven textiles, using complicated techniques that could not be duplicated on commercial looms.

Chroniclers spoke with awe of the richness of textile art. One has the impression from the *mantas* pictured in the Florentine Codex and others that design was bolder, more symbolic, and more spectacular than today—probably, to some extent, because of the separation of the religious, noble, and warrior classes, each of which had its own emblems and symbols. Sahagún mentions that the length of garments was regulated for specified ranks.

It is difficult to discover how much present-day Indian costume was influenced by Spanish costume, and how much of it was native to Mexico before the conquerors arrived. Curiously enough, many garments in use in Mexico before 1519 were also used in Spain. This fact has produced a great deal of confusion in terminology. All the *poncho*-type garments, (*jorongo, cotón, sarape,* and so forth) are often said to be Spanish, but if

we may assume that the same items of dress were used in Mexico that were used in Peru—and Mexican pre-Hispanic figurines support this assumption—we will conclude that these same garments were used before the arrival of the Spaniards, but called by other names. All are really *huipil*-like garments, some longer, some shorter, as the case may be.

The wrap-around skirt was not used in Spain, but was worn in ancient times in Mexico (fig. 13). Hats, presumably of straw, were worn in preclassic times. George M. Foster (1960, p. 98) says that there is nothing now in Spain resembling the Mexican *rebozo*. We think it possible that the *rebozo* developed in Mexico from a single *huipil* strip, or two strips sewn together lengthwise. The measurements of two *huipil* strips are about equal to the width of the present-day *rebozo*, and the latter is also woven on the backstrap loom. The length is about the same, except for the fringes. Fringes were commonly used in pre-Hispanic times on *huipiles*.

Manta is also a misleading term. It originally meant cape, cloak, or covering, and today the word is used for skirt in San Sebastián Peñoles and other places in the Mixteca Alta; however, it can also mean unbleached heavy cotton cloth, and will frequently have that meaning when used in this book.

Today special items of dress are used for the changing of office of village dignitaries, especially in certain Chiapas areas (Duby, 1961, pl. 80), and some of these items are richly decorated and are only worn for these special occasions. The Huichol puts on a fine cloth cape (pl. 163), and feather over-cape, or uses elaborate face painting for certain ceremonies (pls. 160 & 165).

The contemporary woman's costume is composed of essentially the same garments as those of ancient times. Due to climatic conditions, almost no early garments have survived in their entirety, but from codices and from archaeological figurines we can see that they were very similar. It is probable, judging by the few fragments of cloth found in dry caves, that most of the weaving techniques used in Peru were also used in Mexico; and a good many are still in use today.

The woman's garments in conservative villages consist of a *huipil* (pl. 241) or a *quechquemitl* (pl. 56) for the upper garment, a wrap-around skirt, a belt, a head covering (a *rodete*—turbanlike headdress—or a special cloth), possibly a shoulder covering of some kind, and in rare cases sandals. The *quechquemitl* was frequently worn, according to codices and figurines, by persons of rank either as the sole upper garment or on top of the *huipil*. Today one or the other only is worn, according, not to rank, but to the area in which the person lives.

All true Indian garments, except those which are actually woven in a curved technique (as pre-Hispanic Mayan *quechquemitl* were and as some *quechquemitl* are today), are fashioned of rectangular pieces of fabric, just as they are taken from the loom. In the *Columbia Encyclopedia* (1954, p. 466) we read that this was also true of Roman dress until the conquest of Rome, when trousers and the more complicated garb of the barbarian tribes quickly influenced the conquered people: "No tailoring or dressmaking in the modern sense existed, as garments were complete as they came from the loom, except for sewing up the tunic." This same thing is true of Mexican Indian dress as it has come down from pre-Hispanic times. Most webs which form *huipiles*, *quechquemitl*, and skirts have four selvages. Only occasionally are longer lengths of fabric woven, and later cut in two or more parts.

Items of women's dress which are of Spanish origin are the blouse, the gathered skirt, and possibly the *rebozo*. As Dr. Daniel F. Rubín de la Borbolla has said, the *rebozo* is of "nebulous origin." The blouse, which is being worn more and more as Indians copy their *mestizo* neighbors, will not be discussed at length in this book since our subject is indigenous dress. Women now often wear blouses under their *quechquemitl*, whereas formerly they never did. Some noteworthy blouses with delightful folkloric embroidered yokes or bands at neck and sleeves are from Atla, Puebla; San Vicente Coatlán near Ejutla, Oaxaca; and Altepexi, Puebla (pl. 184). Indian women are quite as expert with the needle as with the loom, and this was no doubt true in pre-Hispanic times, when they used needles of copper and bone.

The Indian woman has impeccable taste when she relies on her own traditional designs, instead of the "pattern sheets" now sold in all sizeable markets. These sheets, with their Dutch tulips and other nonindigenous motifs, are influencing traditional garments. In 1965 we saw monotonous modern cross-stitch being introduced even in the men's costumes of Zacatepec, Oaxaca, whereas late as 1962 the varieties of satin stitch and chain stitch traditionally used depicted only charming tiny animals on shirt and trousers (fig. 18).

Women of many Indian villages have distinctive costumes and are proud of them. One can, in most cases, recognize the provenance of a given garment, in its

ethnic group, by its general aspect, the distribution of design elements, the number of webs, the type of weave, the color and so on. Adult garments vary but little in size in a given locality, and rarely is it necessary for a weaver to change the conventional web widths or lengths for individual body differences; this may be because there is little variation in body size among Indians of a given group, or because of the deep-seated conservatism of Indian women — "*Es costumbre*" (It is the custom)—the phrase is constantly on their lips if asked about these matters.

In some states of Mexico, linguistic groups occur in more or less solid areas. Thus, in Oaxaca the costumes of many groups are easily recognized—Chinantec, Huave, Amusgo, for example—though there may be minor differences from village to village. The costumes of other Oaxaca groups, such as the Mixe, vary so much locally that unless one is familiar with them they would be difficult to place in their groups. Even more complex is the area occupied by the states of Hidalgo, Puebla, and Vera Cruz, where some villages contain as many as two or three linguistic groups, or a small area may contain Nahuas, Tepehuas, Totonacs, Huastecs, and Otomís—each with its separate costume or the same costume with small differences. Examples of a more uniform costume over a wide area are those of the Huichols, Tarahumaras, and Seris.

Why do villages in close proximity belonging to the same linguistic group sometimes have entirely different costumes? On the other hand, some villages—such as Acatlán and Mazatlán, Oaxaca (Mixe)—have almost identical *huipiles*, perhaps because one village was founded by a group that broke away from the other. In past times villages may have had different costumes so that they could recognize each other in time of war.

In the very conservative villages, women dress alike and compete with one another, not by originality of material or design, but by workmanship (expertness of execution), quality of hand-spun thread, newness and cost of ribbons and wool thread, and elaborateness of design—although the general pattern or aspect of the garment will be the same. When one shows photographs in such a village, of women from another area, reactions are mild and usually no questions are asked about the costume; but if a textile is shown, great interest is exhibited in the *technique* used to weave it.

Within villages, costumes show slight differences in social strata, usually corresponding to economic levels. The men or women who hold office (governmental or religious) often wear elaborate garments or accessories for ceremonial occasions which distinguish them from others, though in daily life they may live no better than their neighbors. In fact they may be poorer, because the expense of ceremonies and paraphernalia may put officeholders in debt for months to come. The ceremony is usually in honor of a saint who, due to these attentions, will bring prosperity, rain, and good harvests to the village. Thus the person who makes a good showing partakes of the honor.

In general, very little information concerning costume may be gathered from *mestizo* (people of mixed Spanish and Indian blood) townspeople. This may be due partly to lack of interest, and partly to their feeling of superiority to the Indian; also it is due to language barriers, and to reserve or secrecy on the part of the Indians. Mixtec and Trique Indians come to the town of Putla, Oaxaca, to buy and sell, visit the church, and get medical help. But, in 1964, storekeepers who had bought a few woolen belts, bags, and tortilla cloths from them for resale could not tell us who had made or used them, nor from what villages they came.

In Tehuantepec in 1940, before going to the Huave village of San Mateo del Mar, we inquired whether the old Huave *huipil* (vintage 1899) we had seen pictured in Starr's *Ethnography of Southern Mexico* still existed in that nearby village. No one could tell us or knew the *huipil*, though there is constant commerce between the two places. During our stay in San Mateo we found a number of examples.

The two most important Indian womens' garments used now, and in pre-Hispanic times, are the *huipil* and the *quechquemitl*, though their distribution is very different now than it was, for example, in the thirteenth century. In archaeological figurines one sees the *quechquemitl* worn over the *huipil* in the south of Mexico—Oaxaca, Yucatán, and Campeche—as well as in the north. Whether worn thus or as sole upper garment, it was always either ceremonial or worn by women of high rank. Now the *quechquemitl* is confined to north-central Mexico, and the *huipil* to the south. The *quechquemitl* is worn throughout a considerable zone today —in Nayarit and Jalisco (Huichol); Querétaro (Otomí); San Luis Potosí (Huastec and Nahua); the states of Vera Cruz, Puebla, Hidalgo (Huastec, Otomí, Nahua, Tepehua, and Totonac); and last, the state of México (Otomí, Nahua, and Mazahua).

The *huipil* is worn today, according to our knowledge, in the southeastern part of Puebla (Nahua); in Morelos (Nahua); in Oaxaca (Zapotec, Mixtec, Mixe, Huave, Amusgo, Chontal, Chinantec, Cuicatec, and Mazatec); in Guerrero (Nahua, Amusgo, Tlapanec); in Chiapas (Tzotzil, Tzeltal, Lacandón, and Zoque); and in Yucatán (Maya).

There are isolated examples of *huipiles* in *quechquemitl* areas and vice versa, but they are rare. In the town of Angahuan, Michoacán (Tarascan), a *huipil* area, the *quechquemitl* has survived as part of a dance costume, possibly another indication of its ceremonial use. Antonio García Cubas (1876, Pl. 4, Part 2) includes an engraving which shows the *quechquemitl* being worn also in Chilchota, Michoacán. The *huipil*, according to Frederick Starr (1899, p. 106), was used in the Otomí village of Huixquilucan, state of México, although the area was one of *quechquemitl*. I. W. Johnson writes (Johnson, Johnson, and Beardsley, 1962, p. 159) of *huipiles* used in Tuxpan, Jalisco. In Vera Cruz, the only *huipil* villages we know of are Amatlán, Cuautlapán, and Zongolica.

According to Robert Redfield (1930, p. 46), the *quechquemitl* was used in 1930 in Tepoztlán, Morelos, by a few old women, and had been widely used two generations before that. According to old people of Tlaltenango, a suburb of Cuernavaca, Morelos, it was also used there until about fifty years ago. The women of Tetelcingo, Morelos, not too far distant from Cuernavaca, still wear the *huipil*.

Most written material about pre-Hispanic women's costume stresses the two previously mentioned garments; but when one looks at archaeological figurines, particularly those from the Mayan area, one sees that there were an infinite variety of other garments—some of them extremely complicated and difficult of execution without cutting or fitting (*i.e.* tailoring).

Chroniclers inform us that idols were dressed with great care in pre-Hispanic times, and that their garments were changed yearly at the time of their festivities. At the present time, in a few conservative places, particularly in the Chiapas highlands, some saints are dressed in beautiful *huipiles* from the looms of the most skilled weavers instead of in conventional Biblical dress. These saints' costumes are carefully washed at the time of the titular fiesta. The water is kept in large gourds, and after the washing the authorities of the village partake of it. When they have finished, they offer the sacred water to all the people to drink (Duby, 1961, p. 27–28).

We have seen that in some conservative villages women are pleased with what is traditional, and are not looking for change or new ideas; but there are other

PLATE I. Two Seri Indian girls of Punta Chueca, Sonora, with painted faces — showing the characteristic hand-sewn blouse. 1963

villages that are particularly style conscious, and if one woman of such a group develops a new design or innovates a hair style, the whole feminine population follows suit—the younger ones at least. The Zapotec women of the Isthmus of Tehuantepec are a good example. Women of the Chinantec village of Usila also like change. Photographs taken twenty or thirty years ago, compared to those taken in 1964 or 1965, show that the excellently woven *huipil* is narrower now. Its designs are broken into smaller fussy elements (showing a decadent trend). The skirt—instead of the rather tasteful *chiapaneca corte* (skirt length) formerly used—is now fashioned of commercial cotton prints in garish patterns. Between the years 1950 and 1964 the coiffure has developed from simplicity to something stagy and fantastic (pl. 196). Usila *huipiles* are now laden with ribbons and rickrack braid, which makes them look very un-Indian.

In Santo Tomás Mazaltepec, Oaxaca (Zapotec), we noted in 1965 that at least 50 percent of the women preferred an outer skirt of orange and underskirts of white—whereas in the 1940's white on the outside and pink skirts beneath were the fashion. These women wear several skirts, but each is composed of two half skirts—in other words, two aprons, one in front and one in back. We can think of no other reason why half skirts should have been used except that these women must have seen aprons at the time of transition, when they were changing from the wrap-around skirt to the full Spanish skirt, and in some way confused the two. Conceivably, the double apron may be a survival of a very ancient style such as persisted among Great Basin peoples north of Mexico (suggestion of I. Kelly).

Another style-conscious area is Pinotepa Nacional, Oaxaca (Mixtec). Here the change means losing parts of the traditional costume in favor of non-Indian garments. In this hot region women often went nude from the waist up, for comfort. Now—because of new roads and the prevalence of cars and buses—they have put on a short apron with bib, which covers the breast and makes them less vulnerable to stares and remarks from tourists and truck drivers. This apron worn with the beautiful handwoven skirt looks peculiar indeed. Young girls here now prefer to be married in blouses rather than the old gala *huipiles* and *tlacoyales* (tasseled hair cords), though the wrap-around skirt is still worn. It was fairly easy in 1965 to buy the old silver triple cross, formerly given to each bride by her mother-in-law (pl. 117 center). It is now considered old fashioned, and a small gold or gilded cross is worn

instead. The old silver crosses used to be highly valued, and women would not part with them.

In Jamiltepec in the same area, women were eager (1965) to sell the handsome old-style handwoven men's sashes when the men were not at home. This is most unusual as often women are not allowed to sell without the consent of their husbands. Recently in Tetelcingo, Morelos, (Nahua) occurred a similar instance, indicating the right of the Indian woman to sell her own property, or more especially the work of her loom. As Calixta Guiteras-Holmes (1961, p. 51) writes of a Tzotzil village, "Womanhood is made manifest in weaving." Her loom is a powerful instrument. In a Tetelcingo compound lived two brothers in separate dwellings with their families. One brother was cooperative, and by paying for his time we were able to get the information we were seeking. The elder brother, though, was annoyed that I took photographs of his wife (with her consent) while she was weaving. In spite of his decided ill humor and lack of confidence, when we broached the subject of purchasing the loom with a partially woven woolen belt, the wife said "Yes, because it is mine."

Unfortunately style consciousness is sometimes synonymous with deterioration of the traditional costume. Jalapa de Díaz, Oaxaca (Mazatec) (pl. 4) has preserved only the form of its old *huipil*. The basic material is now cheap satin cloth, laden with inexpensive lace, garish ribbons, and rickrack, all sewn up on the sewing machine.

In Papantla, Vera Cruz, Totonac women have preserved the form of their upper garment, which is the *quechquemitl;* but for many years it and the skirt have been made of machine-embroidered organdy (pl. 5). In the past century, the costume was quite different (pl. 73), consisting of a net *quechquemitl*, bordered with imported flowered ribbon, and a wrap-around skirt of commercial cloth heavily embroidered with very good designs, probably of European origin.

All of these changes lead eventually to the disappearance of the indigenous costume, and it should be remarked here that certain showy costumes have been taken over by non-Indians, with modifications, for fancy dress. Usually more adornment is evident than when the garb is used by the Indians, and often a skirt is made to "match" an upper garment (be it *huipil*, blouse, or *quechquemitl*)—something that almost never occurs in true Indian dress. Among the most popular costumes seen in Mexico City gala balls are those from the Isth-

5. These two girls, in organdy *quechquemitl*, wear many plastic hair ornaments. Papantla, Vera Cruz (Totonac). 1939

4. Mazatec women from Jalapa de Díaz, Oaxaca, showing the deterioration of the fiesta *huipiles* of their village. Only their skirts and belts are handwoven now. *Huipiles* are fashioned of store-bought lace and artificial silks. 1964

15

mus of Tehuantepec; the state of Yucatán; the towns of Chiapa de Corzo, Chiapas; and Acatlán, Guerrero; and the *china poblana* costume (of uncertain provenance, now worn only for costume balls).

Thus everything points to the urgent need for intense, accurate, total investigation of indigenous costume before it all vanishes, and we believe that when the Indians are agreeable it is best to purchase, document, and place in museums all fine textiles still to be found. The few old people who wish to keep a *huipil* or an entire costume to be buried in are, of course, exceptions, and for the most part conditions in Indian families are not favorable for storage. Later on, young people will not be sufficiently interested, and the last trace of very interesting textiles and costumes may be lost forever.

In some instances the *presidente municipal* of a village wishes to make the settlement more progressive and exerts pressure, which may or may not help the people economically, but which often changes the costume and language. In 1965 we went to Tututepec, Oaxaca, in search of a unique and rare skirt (pl. IV d) formerly made in this village. We had seen these skirts in other Mixtecan villages—no longer worn, but saved as mementos of mothers or grandmothers who had been married in them. In the center of the town of Tututepec Indians could not be distinguished from so-called lower class *mestizos*. When we went into the Indian *barrios* (quarters) — which are incredibly beautiful, with thatched huts built on and next to tremendous boulders —we could find no trace of the old skirt, nor did we hear the Mixtec language spoken. Later, in the center of the town, a shopkeeper told us that about 1908 the town mayor had abolished the Indian costume, and had even had some of them burnt. Whether or not drastic methods were taken to prohibit the Mixtec language could not be determined. This story, in any case, is not confirmed, and may be one of the fascinating but improbable stories one hears in rural Mexico. The women of other villages difficult of access—Santa Catarina Estetla, Oaxaca (Mixtec), for example—have abandoned their beautiful costumes completely sometime between 1941 and 1960 (pls. 84, 220, & 221). Estetla, about three hard days on foot or horseback over rough mountain terrain from Oaxaca City or Etla, may have had schoolteachers who disapproved of the traditional way of dressing, and through village authorities instigated the breakdown.

This is in contrast with another remote village—Cotzocón, Oaxaca (Mixe). Cotzocón women are prolific weavers, and about three years ago Oaxaca City tourist shops were flooded with traditional *huipiles* of rather inferior workmanship. Taste has deteriorated to such extent that garments now have brocaded dates and names across the chest in large red letters. This is not even an argument for literacy as the letters are often upside down and the names misspelled, indicating that the weaver probably copied a scrap of paper written by some child.

It is difficult to say why some areas not only retain their costumes, but try to weave for economic gain also. The *huipiles* of San Pedro Amusgos, Oaxaca (Amusgo), where superb weaving is done, are coarser and less distinguished when made for tourist shops. One reason work destined to be sold away from the village is inferior is that there are no short cuts in handweaving, and no way to make a profit without saving time to the detriment of quality. One interested in making a collection of Indian costumes buys only used garments in good condition, or those obviously made for Indian use. Women are always proud of their costumes, and for a photograph put on the very best they have, like women in any part of the world.

More and more costumes are left at home when trips are made to larger towns or cities. Fear of being laughed at by *mestizos* causes the Indian to wear nondescript clothing. This state of affairs does not always hold, however—fortunately for those of us who like to see the individuality of peoples and groups in a world where everything tends to be uniform. In Putla, Oaxaca, at Christmas in 1964, Mixtecs and Triques poured in to worship in the church, and sell and purchase in the market, wearing their very best, gayest, newest indigenous costumes—both men and women. This we also observed in Tuxtepec (May 1964) when groups came from many distant settlements, speaking many tongues, on the way to a fiesta at nearby Otatitlán, Vera Cruz (El Santuario). It appears that for important religious occasions, the Indians take pride in each costume. On the other hand, if some business is to be transacted away from their village or linguistic area, they either wear ragged costumes, or simulate a *mestizo* appearance.

Some curious information relating to present-day or recently abandoned Indian costumes follows. The heavy cotton woman's costume from Mixistlán or Yacochi, Oaxaca (Mixe), together with the wool *rodete* and many strings of old trade beads (pl. 6), weighs up to 14 pounds (the beads alone weigh 3½ pounds)! This figure does not include belt or *huaraches*. These two villages are remote and difficult of access, and little in-

6. Mixe Indians in the market of Yalalag, Oaxaca. 1938

formation is available concerning the two costumes (which are similar). Both are dyed a dark greenish-blue with vegetable colorant. Plate 37 shows women from one of the two villages, wearing handwoven skirts, and blouses or shirts made of commercial cloth dyed the same dark green. This photograph was taken in 1938 in the market of the Zapotec town of Yalalag, and it was impossible to obtain the name of the village from which the subjects came. It seems from available evidence that the difference in the costumes of the two villages lies in the use of home-dyed blouses in one, and the handwoven *huipiles* in the other. Another difference is the manner of putting on the immense necklaces of trade beads, some of them extremely old. The village that wears the blouse puts the beads on with ribbons in front (pl. 37); the other, with ribbons in back and longer strands of beads in front. This may have been, in times past when both villages wore the *huipil*, practically the only means of distinguishing the two costumes, although there seems to be a difference in the way the vermillion wool *rodete* is worn. The blouse village places the wool headdress firmly on top of the hair, while the *huipil* village wraps the hair over and over the cords somewhat in the manner of the modern Huastec women of the area of Tancanhuitz, San Luis Potosí.

The two Mixe villages exhibit another feature we believe to be unique in present-day costume. That is the manner of mending holes in their skirts. In most cases, instead of patches or darns, holes have only the edges reinforced by blanket or whipping stitches in the manner of eyelets.

An examination was made of three skirts having a total of thirteen holes—five, five, and three holes respectively. The holes were round, oval, and square. Twelve holes were sewn about their edges with whipping stitches; one hole only had the edges sewn with blanket stitching. Two holes were filled in with crude darning stitching, after the holes had been bordered with whipping stitches. Only one large hole (two-by-three inches) was filled in with green-dyed cloth, after the edges of the hole were treated eyelet fashion with whipping stitches. The largest of the ten open holes was one inch in diameter, round in shape; next in size was one a bit smaller and square. Holes in two of the skirts were worked in very light-colored greenish thread as if to emphasize them, although the holes in the third skirt were sewn about with dark thread taken from the handwoven skirt itself. One small oval whip-stitched circle occurred where there was no hole, which may indicate

a memory of things pertaining to women's cults or to a growth goddess, to be touched upon later.

The manner of mending described is an ancient one, as is proved by information sent us in a letter (August 4, 1965) by I. W. Johnson. Discussing textiles dating from approximately the time of the Conquest, she comments:

Eyelets: A curious occurrence on Candelaria cloths (mantles, blankets, mummy wrappings) are the so-called "eyelets." These are rectangular, oval or pear-shaped holes, some of which are left open, and others which are filled in by a knotless netting or darning. The apertures vary in size but all have the raw edges reinforced by blanket or whipping stitches. Eyelets occur on seven specimens. One large mantle has three; two of them are filled in and the third one is left open. O'Neale [1948, pp. 132–133] describes rectangular holes, some of which are left open and others which are filled in by neat darning. They all have carefully and tightly whipped edges; none exhibited blanket stitch reinforcement. One of the Chihuahua cloths also contains three eyelets in the same piece . . . [The O'Neale reference deals with pre-Columbian Chihuahua textiles.]

That this Mixe manner of mending (unique to our knowledge) is a survival of an ancient practice is obvious from the observations of I. W. Johnson and Lila M. O'Neale. But the practice may also be a survival connected with the worship of the earth, corn, and sky goddess—Ilamatecuhtli. Alfonso Caso (1959, p. 47) says she is the "lady of the old skirt," and was also the dry ear of corn covered by the yellow wrinkled shucks. She is also referred to as Citlalinicue (Star Skirt). The holes in Mixistlán-Yacochi skirts give the impression of stars, as they were often represented in the codices—simple white disks (or holes) on a dark background—and this also suggests the "old skirt" of the goddess.

I. W. Johnson mentioned that some of the "eyelet"-mended textiles from the Candelaria cave were "mummy wrappings." Were these also dedicated to the goddess? Does the very large size of the Mixistlán-Yacochi skirts indicate that Mixe women were buried in them? The presence of one circle embroidered where there was no hole makes us feel that this practice has, or once had, more meaning than merely mending. The hit-and-miss manner of hole distribution makes any thought of decorative effect most improbable.

Many survivals of ancient practices, such as the above, concerning weaving and costume still remain in Mexico, unrecorded. But these practices will not survive for long: the old beliefs and customs are changing rapidly.

Although the young people wish to change, there are still reasons (some of them valid) why, in certain areas, the time is not ripe for change. This can be seen in the following Mixtecan mother's advice to her daughter. In southern Oaxaca, the mother of a Mixtecan Indian girl of Jamiltepec hopes that her daughter will not become a *revestida,* but will marry and proudly continue to wear her native costume. Reasons given by the mother for continuing to wear her Indian costume are (Drucker, 1963, p. 57):

(1) A "dress" (commercial cloth) is expensive, and lasts less long than the *huipil* and wrap-around skirt.
(2) The wrap-around skirt and *huipil* are prettier.
(3) The girl who wears the dress does not marry.
(4) The girl who cannot speak Spanish well or cannot read should not wear the dress.
(5) The daughter who is accustomed to wear the dress soon does not want to talk to her mother.
(6) The girl should not wear the dress, because people will talk.

Again, in about 1940 in Chan Kom, Yucatán, according to Robert Redfield (1962, pp. 39–40), the wife of a schoolteacher announced . . .

at an evening meeting that all the schoolgirls would be clothed in dresses and that their hair would be bobbed, to make them conform with the appearance of girls in civilized and cultivated communities . . . Some parents co-operated, made the dresses, and themselves cut their daughter's hair. Others strongly opposed the change. At a meeting of parents a decided majority agreed that the change would not be wise. "If our daughters wear dresses, they will not go to the *milpa* [corn field]. The huipil can stand the wear and tear of the bush; the dress cannot. And if our daughters wear dresses, who will marry them? Shall we have to bring down *dzules* from the city for them? . . . Some parents kept their girls home from school.

The whole problem is a complicated one, and for Indian girls and women to give up the traditional costume of the village is still a big step.

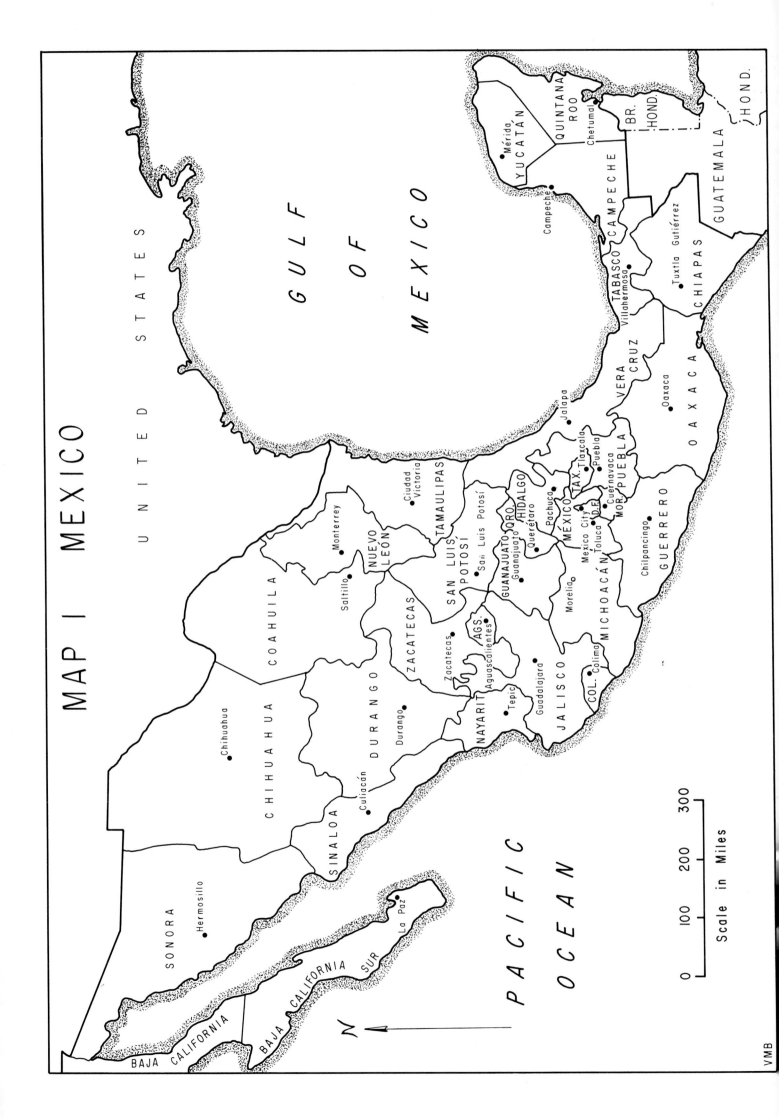

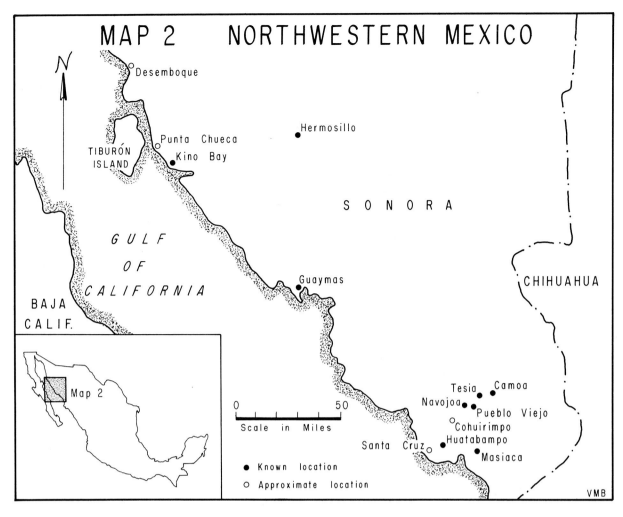

MAP 2 NORTHWESTERN MEXICO

N

Desemboque

Punta Chueca
TIBURÓN
ISLAND
Kino Bay

Hermosillo

S O N O R A

GULF
OF
CALIFORNIA

BAJA
CALIF.

Map 2

Guaymas

CHIHUAHUA

Tesia Camoa
Navojoa
Pueblo Viejo
Cohuirimpo
Santa Cruz Huatabampo
Masiaca

0   50

Scale in Miles

● Known location
○ Approximate location

VMB

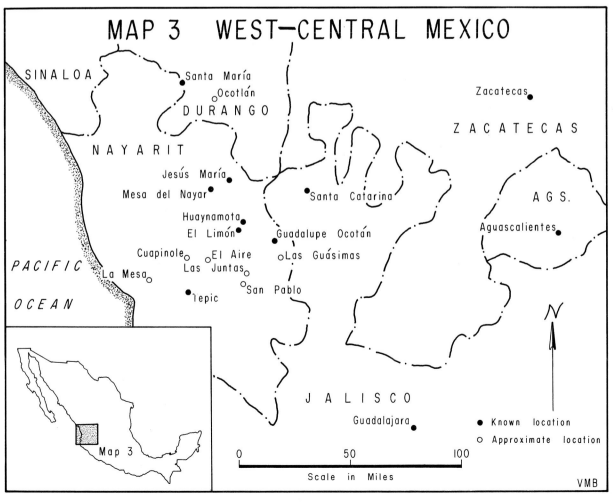

MAP 3 WEST-CENTRAL MEXICO

SINALOA
Santa María
Ocotlán
DURANGO

Zacatecas

Z A C A T E C A S

NAYARIT

Jesús María
Mesa del Nayar

Santa Catarina

A G S.

Huaynamota
El Limón
Guadalupe Ocotán

Aguascalientes

Cuapinole
El Aire
Las Guásimas
Las Juntas
La Mesa
San Pablo
Tepic

N

PACIFIC

OCEAN

Map 3

J A L I S C O

Guadalajara

● Known location
○ Approximate location

0   50   100

Scale in Miles

VMB

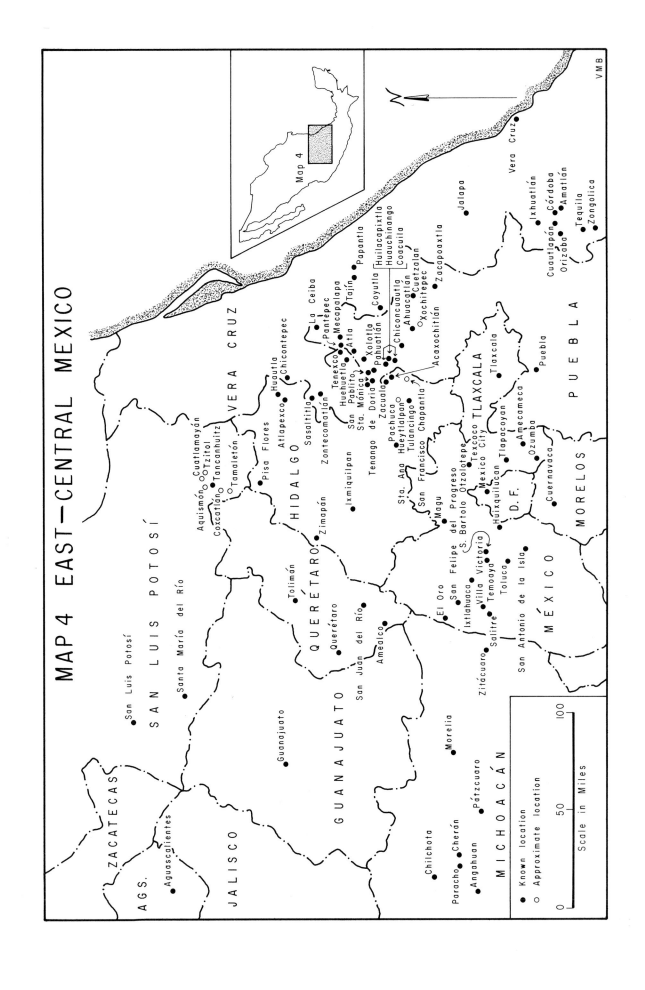

MAP 4 EAST—CENTRAL MEXICO

Map 4

VMB

ZACATECAS

A G S.

JALISCO

SAN LUIS POTOSÍ

Aguascalientes

San Luis Potosí

Santa María del Río

VERA CRUZ

Aquismón○ Cuatlamayán
Coxcatlán○ ○Tzitol
Tancanhuitz
Tamaletón

Pisa Flores

HIDALGO

Huautla
Atlapexco Chicontepec
Sasaltitla
Zontecomatlán
Zimapán

Ixmiquilpan

Tenango de Doria
Sta. Ana Hueytlalpan
San Francisco Chapantla
Tulancingo
Pachuca
Zacuala

La Ceiba
Pantepec Mecapalapa
Tenexco Atla Tajín
Huehuetla
San Pablito
Sta. Mónica
Xolotla
Pahuatlán

Papantla
Coyutla Huilacapixtla
Huauchinango
Coacuila
Ahuacatlán Cuetzalan
Xochitlán Zacapoaxtla
Chiconcuautla
Acaxochitlán

Zacapoaxtla

Jalapa

Vera Cruz

Ixhuatlán
Cuautlapán Córdoba Amatlán
Orizaba Tequila
Zongolica

PUEBLA

Tlaxcala
TLAXCALA
Texcoco
Tlapacoyan
Puebla
Mexico City
Amecameca
Huixquilucan Tlapacoyan
San Bartolo Otzolotepe
San Felipe del Progreso
Magu
Ozumba
Cuernavaca
D. F.
MORELOS

Guanajuato

GUANAJUATO

Tolimán

Querétaro
QUERÉTARO
San Juan del Río

Amealco

El Oro San Felipe del Progreso
Ixtlahuaca Villa Victoria
Salitre Temoaya
Zitácuaro Toluca
San Antonio de la Isla

MÉXICO

Chilchota
Paracho Cherán
Angahuan Pátzcuaro

Morelia

MICHOACÁN

Scale in Miles

● Known location
○ Approximate location

0   50   100

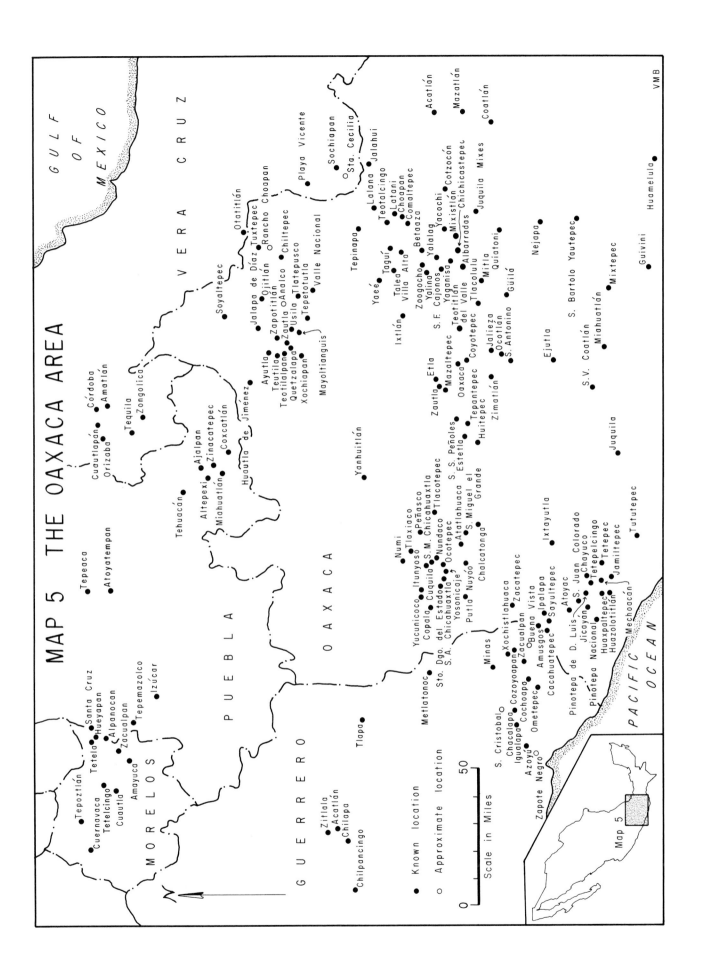

MAP 5 THE OAXACA AREA

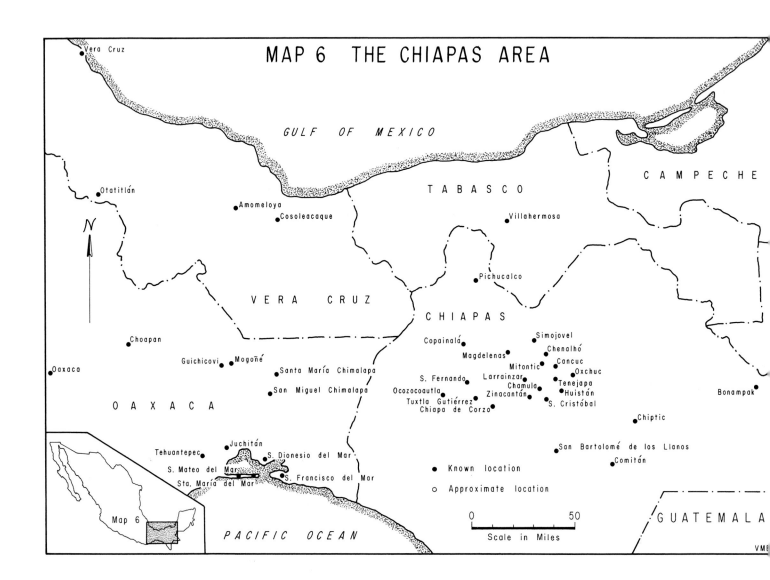

MAP 6   THE CHIAPAS AREA

Vera Cruz

GULF OF MEXICO

CAMPECHE

TABASCO

Otatitlán

Amomeloya

Cosoleacaque

Villahermosa

N

VERA CRUZ

Pichucalco

CHIAPAS

Choapan

Copainalá

Simojovel

Magdelenas

Chenalhó

Guichicovi   Mogoñé

Mitontic   Cancuc

Oaxaca

Santa María Chimalapa

S. Fernando   Larrainzar   Oxchuc

San Miguel Chimalapa

Ocozocoautla   Chamula   Tenejapa

Zinacantán   Huistán

OAXACA

Tuxtla Gutiérrez   S. Cristóbal

Chiapa de Corzo

Bonampak

Chiptic

San Bartolomé de los Llanos

Tehuantepec   Juchitán

Comitán

S. Dionesio del Mar

S. Mateo del Mar

●   Known location

Sta. María del Mar   S. Francisco del Mar

○   Approximate location

Map 6

PACIFIC OCEAN

0   50

GUATEMALA

Scale in Miles

VME

2. The Loom and Its Processes

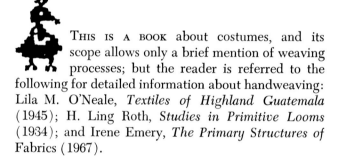

THIS IS A BOOK about costumes, and its scope allows only a brief mention of weaving processes; but the reader is referred to the following for detailed information about handweaving: Lila M. O'Neale, *Textiles of Highland Guatemala* (1945); H. Ling Roth, *Studies in Primitive Looms* (1934); and Irene Emery, *The Primary Structures of Fabrics* (1967).

Cotton

"The earliest remains of plants occurred in the El Riego phase, 7200–5200 B.C., and included a number of species later domesticated; a species of squash, *C. mixta*, chile peppers, avocados, and cotton" (Mangelsdorf, MacNeish and Willey, 1964, Vol. I, p. 444). References are frequently made in early writings to white cultivated cotton *Gossypium hirsutum* L., or, as it was called by the Aztecs, *ichcatl* (Sahagún, 1953–1961, Book 10, p. 75, Aztec text). The yellow cotton, *Gossypium mexicanum* Tod., was called *coioichcatl* (Sahagún, 1953–1961, Book 10, p. 75, Axtec text). This latter was then considered inferior to the white, though now it is widely used in some Trique and Amusgo villages for *huipiles*, and for men's clothing in the Mixteca Baja. Yellow cotton is known today in many Indian areas as *coyuche* (Santamaría, 1959, p. 54) which is derived from the word *coioichcatl*, or coyote-colored.

Under the Aztecs cotton comprised a great deal of tribute from conquered people. The old perennial cotton still grows on both the Atlantic and Pacific coasts, and in hot, humid valleys. Weavers in the highlands have to procure the fiber from traders when they go to fiestas, or from local people if the fiesta is in a locality where cotton is grown. Chiapas produces commercial cotton nowadays, but a large part of that crop is exported. Thus a Zoque informant from Tuxtla Gutiérrez told us that she always brought back cotton for her own use when she went to fiestas in San Fernando, or to the Tzotzil town of San Bartolomé de los Llanos (Cordry, 1941, p. 104).

Weavers often grow their own cotton, sometimes only three or four plants in the vicinity of their houses. I believe (though this is not verified) that the custom of having a few cotton plants nearby has some connection with rain and fertility.

The preparation of cotton for spinning is a long and laborious job. First, it must be picked over to rid it of seeds, leaves, and other debris. Careful picking over, of course, makes the finished textile free of blemishes (the Zoque say of a fine *huipil*, "How pretty, how white").

7. Beating cotton. Rancho Choapan, Oaxaca (Chinantec). 1940

Once the cotton is clean, it is then fluffed out in preparation for the next stage. A convenient amount—large or small, depending on the place or person—is spread on a deer skin or other hide, or a *petate* (palm mat), and this is placed over a thick pad made of corn husks, or other plant material.

The cotton is then beaten to form an even, smooth strip, which will be easy to spin. This operation usually is performed with the aid of two specially made sticks (sometimes only forked branches in the shape of "Y's"), one held in each hand. These are smoothed and polished, and are about eighteen inches long (fig. 3 t). The sticks used in the Chinantla are sometimes longer, and the beaters examined there consisted of from three to five sticks bound together with wire or fiber (pl. 7). In Mechoacán, Oaxaca, a Mixtecan village, four sticks are used but they are *not* fastened together. A Zoque weaver was observed using a narrow batten as a cotton beater, for lack of the appropriate sticks (Cordry, 1941, fig. 26).

The beating of the cotton may formerly have been punishment of the goddess Xochiquetzal (patroness of weavers), to make the cotton behave well on loom and spindle. This by analogy—for the particular saint concerned with rain is beaten if there is drought, and immersed in water if lands are flooded. Many references are made by Frazer to doing violence to the being who controls the weather (1936, Vol. I, pp. 296–300). On several occasions, we have observed that women were perfectly willing to spin or weave in our presence, but reluctant to beat the cotton (Mechoacán, Oaxaca [Mixtecan]; and Teotilalpan, Oaxaca [Cuicatec]). Often cotton is beaten in the late afternoon, which may be due to the fact that it is hard work and that time of the day is cooler. The rhythmic sound can be heard on a still evening for a great distance.

Spinning

The fiber (cotton, wool, silk, or *ixtle*) is spun with a simple implement, the spindle—*malacate* (from the Aztec *mal-acatl: mal* from *malina*, twist; *acatl*, cane—"cane that twists") (Robelo, 1904, p. 219). The spindle is a smooth, round stick about 11 to 17 inches long, weighted near one end with what is termed a spindle whorl (fig. 3w). The shaft may be blunt at one end, or both, or tapered to a very sharp point at one end, or both. The spindles used for wool are sometimes blunt at the end which is spun on the ground or in a container (pl. 8 a); those which are used for spinning *ixtle* (pl. 8 b) are blunt at the lower end, and terminate at the

upper end in a hook. The latter are spun, not on the ground, but in the air.

The whorl is usually made of clay (pl. 8 b & d) or wood (pl. 8 c), but among the Huichol Indians we have seen them fashioned of bone (pl. 8 e) and, strangely enough, of a thin piece of gourd about three inches in diameter (pl. 9). This would not seem heavy enough to spin wool, but it proved an efficient tool. We also observed a Huichol use a whorl made of a piece of a broken white commercial plate. Whorls vary in form and size and, in modern times, are rarely decorated. Pre-Hispanic ones were incised (fig. 2), moulded with elaborate designs, and then in some cases painted. The Otomís from the Mezquital area employ archaeological whorls—which they find in their fields, and fit with new shafts—to spin *ixtle* (pl. 2). We have observed this same custom in Hueyapan, Morelos (pl. 8 a), where wooden ones are also used.

The spindle is usually twirled in a half gourd (pl. 40), in a pottery bowl (pl. 10), or—rarely—on the ground (pl. 9). The gourds vary greatly in size, from large—six inches in diameter (pl. 40)—to small—about two and one-half inches in diameter (pl. 229). The one shown in Plate 229 was set in a twist of cloth to keep it steady. Sometimes a *rodete* of *otate* is used for this purpose. Many spinners have more than two spindles. The woman in Plate 226 has eight in the gourd in which she keeps her weaving tools (some women use a basket as a receptacle instead of a gourd). This type of spindle was used in many parts of the world (Amsden, 1964, p. 10, pl. 5). A bit of ash or lime is put on the fingers, and in the bottom of the receptacle, to make the spindle revolve more smoothly.

When the cotton is ready to be spun, a portion that can be easily handled is pulled from the beaten strip (which is sometimes rolled into a ball). The top end of the shaft is moistened and the cotton lightly applied.

The spindle shaft is held in the right hand (slanting slightly toward the spinner), between the thumb and index finger,

Figure 2. Pre-Hispanic spindle whorls.

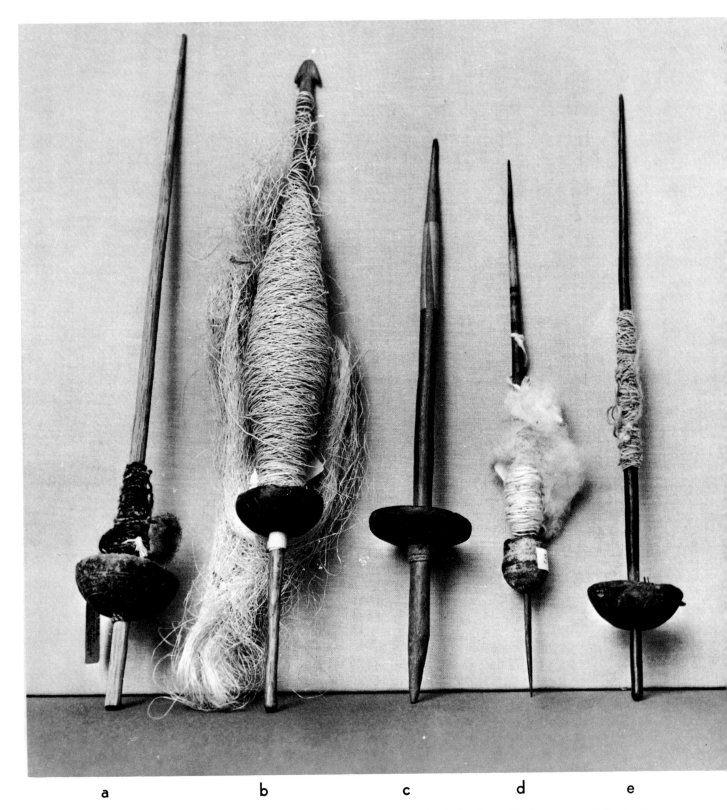

a   b   c   d   e

8. Spindles: *a.* Hueyapan, Morelos (Nahua) — archaeological clay whorl (with wool); *b.* region of Ixmiquilpan, Hidalgo (Otomí) — clay whorl (*ixtle* fiber); c. Mitla, Oaxaca (Zapotec) — a wooden whorl (for wool); d. Jamiltepec, Oaxaca (Mixtec) — a clay whorl used in Peñoles, Oaxaca (for silk); *e.* a Huichol (Nayarit) bone whorl (for wool).

9. An old Huichol woman spinning wool yarn. The spindle has a whorl made of a piece of dried gourd. Rancho El Aire, Nayarit. 1938

10. Spinning wool in Hueyapan, Morelos. (Nahua). 1963

with the second finger doing the actual twirling . . . the third and fourth fingers are placed on the same side of the shaft as the thumb, and serve as supports. While the spindle whirls, the cotton is pulled upward with the left hand, and twisted usually into a uniform thread. If there are thicker places, the spindle is again revolved and the extra thickness worked out with the left hand. (Cordry, 1941, p. 107)

Although this description is of Zoque spinning, it applies with minor differences to all cotton spinning, when the *malacate* is employed.

Sahagún says, "The bad spinner pulls [threads], leaves lumps, moistens what she grasps with her lips, twists incompetently. [She is] useless—of useless hands, negligent, slothful, neglectful—a neglectful one, lazy" (1951–1963, Book 10, p. 52).

Investigations indicate that traditionally there have been centers where spindles were made and distributed to other areas, chiefly through the medium of large religious fiestas. In 1940 the Zoques of Chiapas told us that they had always obtained their spindle whorls and weaving combs from the Tzotzil villages in the vicinity of San Cristóbal de las Casas, especially from the village of San Juan Chamula. These centers are hard to locate, because the spindles may be bought at a fiesta by traders and then distributed in distant areas. Thus the people who use the spindles frequently do not know their provenance.

Another spindle-making center is the Mixtecan village of Jamiltepec, Oaxaca. There the work is very specialized. Men make the spindle shaft, and women the whorl, which they call in Spanish *la frutita* (the little fruit). Then the shaft and whorl are painted by women. The completed spindles are sold by still other people at religious fiestas, such as the fiesta of Juquila, on December 8th; and the fiesta of Igualapa, Guerrero, on the third Friday in Lent. The Zapotecs come to Juquila from the Sierra Juárez, and take home Jamiltepec spindles. In 1940 we found these spindles as far away as San Francisco Cajonos, Oaxaca, where they were used for spinning silk.

The Jamiltepec spindles are pointed at each end, and the technique used to make them is interesting. A pole, about 4½ feet long and grooved from end to end, is held between the feet and against the shoulder, leaving the man's hands free. Bundles of squared mangrove-wood (*mangle*) sticks have been prepared in advance and are at hand. After roughly tapering one end of a stick, the spindle maker places the point in the groove and finishes it with a knife to a needlelike point. Then he finishes the other end in the same way (pl.

11. A man carving sticks from mangrove wood to be used for spindles. Jamiltepec, Oaxaca (Mixtec). 1965

11). Superstitions concerning the spindle are numerous and world-wide (see our Chapter 3).

Winding Frame or Reel

After the cotton thread is spun, it is rolled into a ball, and then sometimes put onto a winding frame. This is not to be confused with the warping frame, which certainly is of native origin.

The winding frame (fig. 3 u) is usually a shaky, home-made contrivance, a wooden frame that revolves in a base of crosspieces. The cotton thread is wound about the frame, and then reeled off onto the warping frame. The reel is more often used by people weaving on the treadle loom than the backstrap loom, and presumably is of European origin. The reel may be eliminated and—in our observation—usually is, though some Zoques used it in 1940.

31

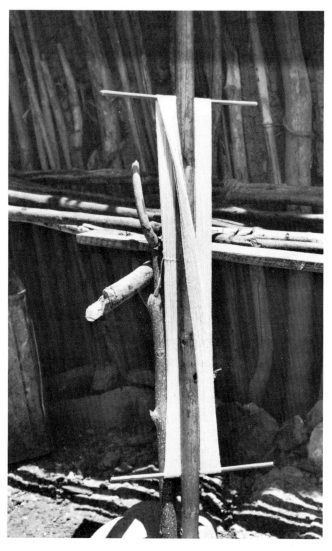

12. A Zoque warping frame showing the *corazón* (heart). Tuxtla Gutiérrez, Chiapas.

Warping Frame

Two kinds of warping frames, to our knowledge, are found in Mexico. One is a pole or rod with a crosspiece near each end. It is recorded as being used by the Nahuas of Acatlán, Guerrero (Christensen, verbal communication); the Nahuas of Tuxpan, Jalisco (Johnson, Johnson, and Beardsley, 1962, fig. 4); and the Zoques of Tuxtla Gutiérrez (Cordry, 1941, p. 110).

The second type, which seems more common in Mexico, is the warping done on stakes. If the stakes are few (two or three), they may be put directly into the ground, and if many, they are fitted into holes in a

movable frame. The stakes vary from two (Santa Ana Hueytlalpan) to fifteen (Hueyapan, Morelos). The more stakes used, the longer the textile. When there are many stakes close together (pl. 13) less walking is required by the warper than if there are few stakes very far apart for a long textile.

The purpose of warping is to establish the length of the garment, and the number of threads that form the breadth or width. In whatever method used, a cross (lease) is formed (the threads are wound on the stakes in a figure eight). This gives each thread its proper place and will form, when put on the loom, the shed—through which the bobbin passes. Before the threads are taken off the warping frame, the cross is tied to make it secure. This tied part is called by the Zoques the *corazón* (heart) (pl. 12). After the threads are taken off the warping frame, they are usually given a bath of maize water to strengthen and stiffen them, so they can be more easily handled.

Looms

Although several types of looms are employed in Mexico, most textiles are fashioned on the ancient backstrap loom (fig. 3)—also known as the girdle-back loom, the hip loom, the belt loom, the stick loom, and the waist loom. It is commonly termed in Spanish *telar de otate* (from Aztec *otlatl*—Molina, 1944, p. 78). It is well named, because when not set up with the warp threads, the loom is nothing but a bundle of sticks of various sizes, lengths, and thicknesses. These sticks are made of many kinds of woods, some hard, some soft, and some of bamboo (*otate*).

Another less common loom (pl. 14) used to weave blankets by the Mayo Indians produces what is termed ring-weaving. A similar loom is used by the Tarahumara (Bennett and Zingg, pl. VI and pp. 90–91). The posts of this loom are set in the ground, and to remove the web the threads are cut. This makes two selvages and a fringe on either end of the blanket. Ring-weaving is also done on the backstrap loom to make woolen skirts in the town of Temoaya (state of México). In this case, the sticks are pulled out, and the skirt is then one continuous web. A variation of this type of weaving is also done in San Juan Chamula, Chiapas.

The third type is the treadle loom (pl. 188) brought by the Spaniards to Mexico in the sixteenth century. Now it is used to make blankets and cloth for export and for the tourist trade—cloth used for tablecloths, napkins, *rebozos*, men's shirts, and other wearing apparel. The making of this cloth is principally a non-Indian

13. This young woman, who has married and gone to live in another village, has come for the day to use her mother's *urdidor* (warping frame). The mother, who appears in other Hueyapan photographs, wears the native costume but the daughter now dresses as a *meztiza*. Hueyapan, Morelos (Nahua). 1963

14. An excellent heavy blanket is being woven by a Mayo Indian woman of Huatabampo, Sonora, on a loom that is not common in Mexico. This loom produces ring weaving. 1938

Figure 3. A typical backstrap loom and accessories (Zoque). From Cordry, *Costumes and Weaving of the Zoque Indians of Chiapas, Mexico.* Courtesy The Southwest Museum.

a. cord fastened to a tree or post after the heading (z) is finished
b. warp beam
c. warp threads
d. comb
e. shed roll or shed stick
f. headle or heald rods
g. small batten
h. headle or heald rods
i. large batten
j. tenter
k. thorn used to fasten tenter to web
l. woven cloth or web

m. rolling stick
n. cloth beam
o. cord fastened to backstrap
p. backstrap *(mecapal)*
q. and r. bobbins
s. raw cotton
t. cotton beaters
u. winding frame
v. gourd in which spindle is spun
w. spindle
x. warping frame
y. method of applying string to heald rod
z. heading

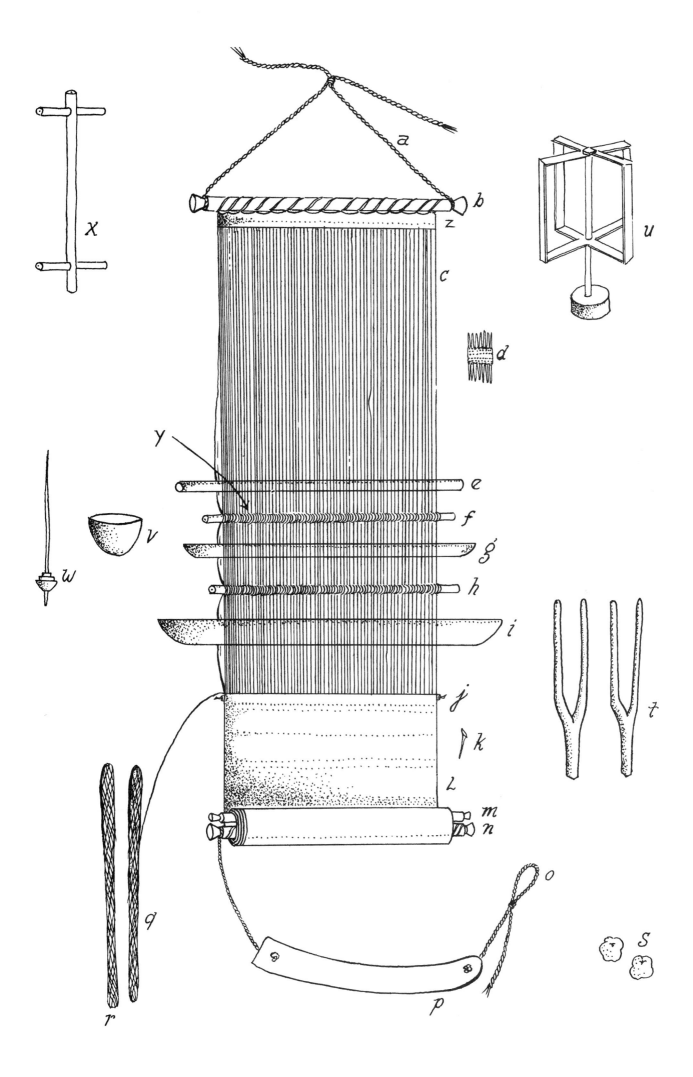

15. A detail showing the loom used particularly by men and boys in Mitla, Oaxaca. (Zapotec). 1943

industry. This loom works more quickly and produces cloth with a wider web than the backstrap loom. It is also used to weave woolen *sarapes*; and in some towns skirt lengths called *cortes* are woven for Indian women, who buy them in these centers or from itinerant traders who go into the villages.

The backstrap loom takes its name from the backstrap (*mecapal*) (fig. 3 p), which may be an old, tooled or plain, leather belt, or may be woven of maguey fiber or palm. This goes about the hips of the weaver, whether he or she stands or takes a seated position on the ground. For the most part, women weavers sit and men stand (pl. 15)—an exception is the Yalalag woman shown in Plate 199. Seated women take various positions (pls. 166 & 243), and sometimes they sit on low stools (pl. 16). Women usually kneel when working heavy cotton or woolen material, as this is a more convenient position in which to exert the considerable force necessary when opening the sheds and beating down the weft (pls. 79 & 217).

16. A Zoque skirt weaver of Tuxtla Gutiérrez, Chiapas. 1940

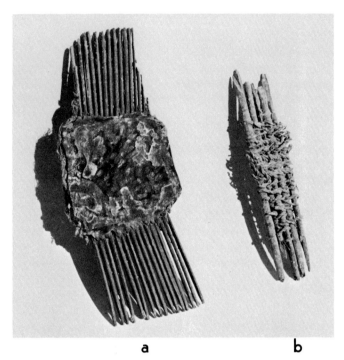

17. Possible weaving combs, both from the Tehuacán Archaeological-Botanical Project, Tehuacán, Puebla, and pictured courtesy of R. S. MacNeish: *a.* from El Riego Cave (1350–1450 A.D.); *b.* from Coxcatlán Cave (300–500 A.D.).

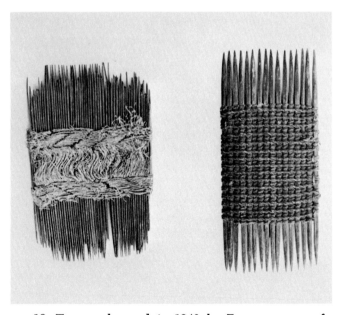

18. Two combs used in 1940 by Zoque weavers of Tuxtla Gutiérrez, Chiapas. They were made by Tzotzils of highland Chiapas and closely resemble those shown in Plate 17.

The strap has cords (fig. 3 o) attached to the cloth beam (n) and to the rolling stick (m), which lies across the web (l) and is used as the weaving progresses to roll the finished cloth on (to bring the unwoven warp closer to the weaver). The tenter (j), generally a hollow reed, is put on the under side of the cloth and fastened to the web, usually with thorns (k), to keep the width of the cloth. Sometimes the tenter is eliminated. Other loom parts include the bobbin (q & r); the batten or sword (g & i)—the word "sword" is probably used because in some primitive looms the wooden batten is made in the actual shape of a sword, with a handle at one end and a point at the other (this is illustrated clearly in a backstrap loom from Borneo shown by Ling Roth, 1934, fig. 122); the heddle or heald (f & h); the shed roll or shed stick (e); and the warp beam (b), which is fastened to a tree, post, house corner, or stake put into the ground for that purpose. This is done after the heading is finished and the loom has been reversed. Most weaving is done out of doors because interiors are dark and space is limited. Looms are sometimes put away during the rainy season, as handspun thread is believed to break due to dampness.

In addition, there are accessories to aid in putting in brocaded patterns. A smooth brocading sword or warp lifter (usually made of wood) is utilized for putting over and under counted warps, before inserting the bobbin or small ball of thread. A darning needle sometimes replaces the sword or warp lifter. In Mexico the bobbin is a slender stick wound with the weft threads (fig. 3 q & r).

An object that is sometimes used as a warp lifter—but has its particular function of straightening, evening, and pushing down certain weft threads—is the pick (pl. 43), a pointed, pencillike object made of bone, wood, or iron. These are used to even the warp threads. Beautifully fashioned combs (fig. 3 d; pl. 18) have somewhat the same function as the batten, and also push down or tighten weft threads. It is interesting to note the similarity between the archaeological combs shown in Plate 17 and the modern ones in Plate 18. When the join is too small to receive the narrowest batten, the comb is used to batten down the weft threads. We have also seen women run the comb across the loom to even the warp threads. One weaver may have all three of these tools in her weaving basket or gourd.

After the threads have had their bath of maize water, the cloth beam is put through the loop made by the threads at point A of Figure 4, the rolling stick is put through the corresponding loop at point C, and a cord

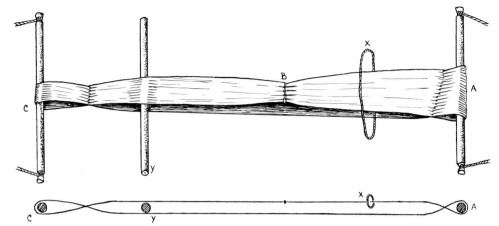

Figure 4. Setting up the loom. From Cordry, *Costumes and Weaving of the Zoque Indians of Chiapas, Mexico.* Courtesy The Southwest Museum.

or small rope is tied to each end of the cloth beam and securely fastened to a post where the weaver wishes to work. Then the rope and the *mecapal* are fastened to the rolling stick, about the weaver's waist or hips.

Next the weaver inserts the shed stick (fig. 4 y), and in some instances takes the precaution of putting a piece of string through the shed tying it so that if the shed stick should fall out the threads would not be lost. Then the string which has separated the two sets of warp threads, and among the Zoques is called the *corazón* or heart (B), is cut.

Now the weaver slides the threads along the rolling stick, carefully separating them, as they are stuck together with the corn water, and with her measuring stick she arranges the threads in the width desired for the finished cloth. At this time the threads are grouped together in small bunches about an inch apart, preparatory to changing them from the rolling stick to the warp beam. At this point the warp beam is placed on top of the upper warp threads just above the rolling stick. A piece of string of the kind called *cañamo* in Spanish (*i.e.* hemp) is tied to the end of the warp beam at the weaver's left, is passed through the shed (fig. 5-1), and looped several times around the notched end of the warp beam at the right. The same string is then looped in a spiral (fig. 5-2), over the warp beam and the upper warp threads, working back from right to left. At the same time care is taken to include, or to pass under, the string which was first put through the shed; and care is taken to leave free the lower warp threads.

The rope fastened to the *mecapal* is now transferred from the rolling stick to the warp beam and the rolling stick slipped out. The warp threads are now fastened

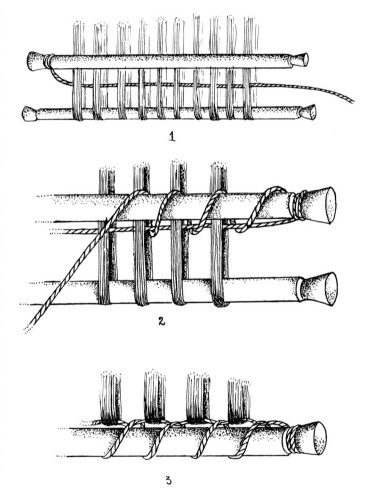

Figure 5. Details of the loom. From Cordry, *Costumes and Weaving of the Zoque Indians of Chiapas, Mexico.* Courtesy The Southwest Museum.

39

19. This Tarascan woman of Paracho, Michoacán, is weaving a *rebozo* on a wide backstrap loom. 1935.

to the piece of hemp string which in turn is fastened by the spiral string to the warp beam (fig. 5-3).

Next the weaver carefully separates the warp threads from their groups, distributing them evenly with the aid of her maguey spine to the width she wishes the cloth to be. This done, she is ready to put on the heald rod. The healds are usually made of cotton thread and contain the alternate warp threads, so that when the heald rod is lifted up, the lower shed is open.

Dr. Washington Matthews (1884, p. 380) gives an excellent description of the Navaho method of putting on the healds, which we quote in its entirety, as the Zoque method is identical (see also Cordry, 1941, pp. 117–119).

The mode of applying healds is simple: (1) the weaver sits facing the loom in the position for weaving; (2) she lays at the right (her right) side of the loom a ball of string which she knows contains more than sufficient material to make the healds; (3) she takes the end of this string and passes it to the left through the shed, leaving the ball in its original position; (4) she ties a loop at the end of the string large enough to admit the heald-rod; (5) she holds horizontally in her left hand a straightish slender rod, which is to become the heald-rod—its right extremity touching the left edge of the warp—and passes the rod through the loop until the point of the stick is even with the third (second anterior from the left) thread of the warp; (6) she puts her finger through the space between the first and third threads and draws out a fold of the heald-string; (7) she twists this once around, so as to form a loop, and pushes the point of the heald-rod on to the right through this loop; (8) she puts her finger into the next space and forms another loop; (9) and so on she continues to advance her rod and form her loops from left to right until each of the anterior (alternate) warp-threads of the lower shed is included in a loop of the heald; (10) when the last loop is made she ties the string firmly to the rod near its right end.

When the weaving is nearly done and it becomes necessary to remove the healds, the rod is drawn out of the loops, a slight pull is made at the thread, the loops fall in an instant, and the straightened string is drawn out of the shed.

The heading is a narrow strip of cloth about 1½ inches (to 6 inches on skirts) that is woven first. Then the backstrap is changed to the opposite end of the loom (the loom turned end for end), placing the heading at the top of the loom. The heading may be a substitute for laze rods, according to Ling Roth (1934, p. 20). Roth regards this as an American practice.

The weaving progresses now from the end opposite the heading. When the weaving is finished up to a point where only a small section of free warp threads remains between the two ends of the loom, a small batten has to be used instead of the large one. Finally a very narrow implement such as an umbrella rib (Zoque) with hole for threading the weft carries on the closing of the join or *rematada*. Other women use slender sticks. When the opening is too small for this implement, sometimes sewing needles are used. When the batten cannot be used to beat down the weft in the join, the comb is used. "The *rematada* in a fine new textile can hardly be distinguished from the main body of the cloth. However, with wear the threads, which are looser than the rest, will pull and become farther apart and sometimes an otherwise well-appearing garment will appear shabby in this portion" (Cordry, 1941, p. 121).

As regards the *huipil* one would think that the join, which is usually also a plainer weave than the rest of the garment, would be worn in back. This is the custom with some Chinantec *huipiles* and the old Huave *huipil* of San Mateo del Mar, whereas the join in Zoque *huipiles,* for example, and those of San Andrés Chicahuaxtla (pl. 91) are worn in front.

3. Weaving Beliefs and the Possible Meaning of the Loom

WEAVING IN MEXICO has always been closely associated with women. There are many magical beliefs and superstitions concerning the loom. The loom, the spindle, the weaving comb are all connected symbolically with hair, which in turn is connected with rain and serpents, and thus with fertility. Among the Zoque Indians of Chiapas, "many women believe that it is disastrous to weave when pregnant, as it brings bad luck to the child if it is a boy" (Cordry, 1941, p. 125). This is because weaving is a woman's occupation. We find that weapons are as closely associated with men as looms are with women. This seems to be a world-wide trait. Kelly and Palerm say that among the Tajín Totonacs (1952, p. 248), "Care is taken that no woman, irrespective of her social or physiological condition, step over a firearm. Should such a calamity occur, the aim of the weapon is ruined irrevocably."

The Zoques of Tuxtla Gutiérrez believe in women spirits, or *brujas*, that live in caves and spin but do not weave. The Tzotzils of San Bartolomé de los Llanos have the same belief, except that the women spirits (*pakinte*) live inside the rocks and sit outside and spin without weaving (Cordry, 1941, p. 127). The implication is that spinning without weaving is a futile and unproductive occupation.

The connection between hair and thread is obvious: the comb is used with both. In the loom it is used to beat down the weft threads, and in the process the warp threads are "combed." Hair has magical properties connected with the life force and with weather, crops, and fertility—"The Huichols see serpents in their own flowing hair, in one organ of the body . . ." (Lumholtz, 1902, Vol. II, p. 235). Donald Leonard says (1955, p. 5), referring to the Lacandón Indians of Chiapas, "Immediately upon death a lock of hair from each side of his head was cut and placed in his hands along with the bone of a monkey (which had been saved for this purpose)." In Aztec ceremonies, the victim's hair was cut, signifying death itself. This seems to imply that hair is a positive element directly related to the life force.

In ancient Mexico a festival was held in honor of Xilonen, the goddess of the green corn. It began at the time when the plant had attained its full growth, and fibers shooting forth from the top of the green ear indicated that the grain was fully formed. During this festival the women wore their hair unbound, shaking and tossing it in the dances which were the chief feature in the ceremony, in order that the tassels of the maize might grow in like profusion, that the grain might be correspondingly large and plentiful, and that the people might have abundance (Torquemada, 1943, Vol. II, Book 10, Chap. 19, pp. 269–270).

The serpent in Mexico was the thunderbolt and the river. Coatlicue, mother of the gods, whose monumental statue may be seen in the National Museum of Anthropology, has a head formed of two serpents. Most of the goddesses of vegetation and growth had names in "the esoteric language of sorcerers and fortune tellers" (Caso, 1959, p. 45), that included the word serpent, such as Seven Snake (Chicomecoatl), Serpent Woman (Ciuacoatl), Serpent Skirt (Coatlicue).

During the thirteenth month, which was named Tepeilhuitl in honor of the water-giving mountains, serpents were made out of the roots of trees. These sticks were overlaid with a dough made of amaranth seeds (symbol of life and immortality) (Sahagún, 1951–1963, Book 2, pp. 23, 121).

In the Huichol country, according to Lumholtz (1902, Vol. II, p. 234), when a woman was weaving a belt, the husband caught a live serpent and held it on the ground beside her while she passed her hand over its back, then over her eyes, so that when she began to weave, the design would be transferred to the belt. Lumholtz also says (1902, Vol. II, p. 214), "Girdles and ribbons, inasmuch as they are considered as rain-serpents, are in themselves prayers for rain and the results of rain, namely, good crops, health, and life; and the designs on these objects are made in imitation of the markings on the backs of the real reptiles."

When we were with the Huichols in 1937, and asked about the designs on belts, we were told that they represented serpents. Serpent belts may also be connected with protection for pregnant women. Sahagún says (1951–1963, Book 7, p. 58),

When the moon is eclipsed, he becometh almost dark . . . When this cometh to pass, women with child feared miscarriage . . . And as a remedy for this they took a piece of obsidian in the mouth or they placed it in the girdle over the belly and [did so] in order that the children [whom they carried] in the womb would not be born lipless or noseless or wry-mouthed, or cross-eyed, or that [one] might not be born monstrous.

We were told in the Mixteca Baja where women wear belts (some do not until marriageable age), that pregnant women are careful to wear belts during an eclipse, so that the unborn child will not be eaten by the moon or be deformed. We feel that the Indians are not un-aware that the belt is actually a support for the woman during pregnancy.

Xochiquetzal, the patroness of weavers, was also known as Mazateotl (deer goddess) (Spence, 1923, p. 187). The people of Tlaxcallan held a festival to Xochiquetzal in the month of Quecholli, when the Mexicans celebrated the feast of Mixcoatl, who is associated with the deer. Later we will see that this deer association is still found in present-day weavers' tools.

The weaving batten or *tzotzopaztli* may be a male fertility symbol. Its sexual implication is obvious because of the way it goes into the loom. It is also pulled toward the weaver to beat down the weft. This gesture is the common motion used today to indicate sexual intercourse (*i.e.* a pulling toward the body as when battening down weft threads on the loom with the hands closed—the only difference is that in weaving the fists are turned downward around the batten, whereas in the popular gesture the fists are turned upward).

The *tzotzopaztli* was certainly a fertility symbol as it was used in the feast of the sixteenth month called Atemoztli. Sahagún says that this feast, called "The Falling of the Water," was in honor of the gods of the mountains, and that the priests of Tlaloc (a god) made offerings to them so that they would give rain. The common people made images of the mountains (or of the mountain gods). These they made of a dough of amaranth seed. Amaranth was probably chosen because of its red color—the color of blood and fire (two symbols of life)—representing the sacrificial victim and resurrection. After offerings had been made to the figures, the priests sought weaving sticks (*tzotzopaztli*), and implanted them in the breasts of the images and took out their hearts. Then the figures were decapitated, and the guests were offered food and drink (Sahagún, 1953–1961, Book 2, pp. 139–141). This would also seem to be a symbolic opening or fertilizing of the mountains so that the streams would gush forth and wind like serpents down the mountainside, giving life to the dry valleys below.

The batten was carried by many goddesses of growth, vegetation, and fertility, and also of rain. Some also carried or wore other things connected with weaving such as emblems or badges: Coatlicue was impregnated by a ball of feathers; Xochiquetzal and Chalchihuitlicue carry both spindles and weaving battens; Chicomecoatl was identified with Xochiquetzal; Tlazolteotl has two spindles stuck in a cotton fillet on her head; Ciuacoatl, Ilamatecuhtli, and Itzpapalotl carry weaving battens.

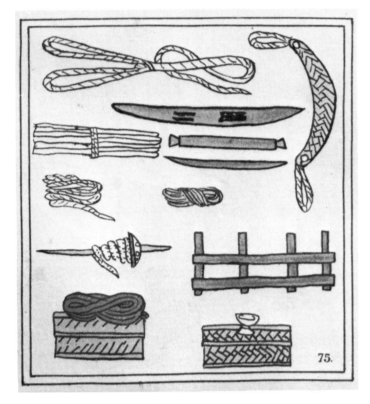

Figure 6. Weaving implements shown in the Florentine Codex.

Most goddesses had several aspects, and in some fiestas they appeared in the guise of related gods.

The *tzotzopaztli* was carried in rain ceremonies, and was sometimes translated by chroniclers as "rain rattle" or "rattle staff." I. W. Johnson (1960, pp. 75–85) describes a *tzotzopaztli* found in a cave near the city of Tehuacán, Puebla, which is slotted and has small seeds inside that rattle. She believes this *tzotzopaztli* was for ceremonial use. Sahagún (1951–1963, Book 2, p. 128) shows weaving implements, and among them is a batten with what looks like slots (fig. 6), possibly indicating objects inside.

Lila O'Neale (1945, pp. 33–34) says, concerning Guatemalan customs,

Bamboo shed rolls are used at Panajachel . . . and many other places. An old custom, to judge from the loom taken back to England by A. P. Maudslay in 1885, is still existant. Some weavers, so said a Panajachel informant, place small seeds and pebbles in the hollow bamboo and cork the ends with rags or wood. The Maudslays (1899, p. 56) write of the practice as follows: "Custom demands [at San Antonio Pa-

lopo] that the hollow reed or stick . . . should contain several round seeds or beads, which rattle up and down as it is moved for the shuttle to pass. Whatever the origin of the custom may be, one result of it is that you can always tell by the noise when the women are busy at work." At San Juan the women said "the rattle was pleasant."

The Huichol Indians of Nayarit have a rain staff which is like or similar to the shed roll spoken of by O'Neale. Robert Zingg (1934, p. 589) notes,

The Sun's wand, carried over the shoulders of the *peyote* dancers, symbolizes the rattle-snake of the Sun-father which enables the Sun-god to hear the prayers that the dancers express by their activity. The wands were commanded by the Sun-father specifically for this purpose.

These wands are a most interesting symbol of the Sun-father's snake (one of the rattlers). They are decorated with colored carvings, representing the snake's back. More significantly, they are made of a bamboo-like reed about four feet long from which the interior partitions are gouged out at either end. It is filled with a handful of small hard seed which gives a buzzing, rattling noise like that of a rattle-snake. Held on the shoulder during the dance, the seeds roll down to the other end of the staff; and while the dancers stand with heads bowed and with their wands lowered to the ground, the seeds fall back with the same buzzing sound, ready for a new round of the *peyote* dance.

Most of these prayers were for rain to water the small fields that the Huichols planted. Agriculture, weaving, and weaving tools were very closely connected, and inasmuch as these weaving implements were powerful fertility symbols, we find them used in ceremonies connected with growth.

Another instance of the magical power of the spindle and cotton thread is described by C. Guiteras-Holmes (1961, p. 43):

In order that the grains [of corn] can be easily removed from the cobs once the maize is harvested, the wife usually places her comb, her string of beads, her spindle and a ball of cotton thread in the basket with the grains that are to be planted, and leaves them there throughout the night. Some women twirl their spindle among the grains as if they were spinning.

That the things pertaining to weaving are very powerful may be further confirmed by Guiteras-Holmes (1961, p. 307), referring to Indians of Chiapas: "Nothing is believed to occur naturally . . . I have seen beans or maize fed the ball of already carefully measured thread before it is placed on the loom in order that it will be long enough."

Here we repeat that hair symbolizes the tassels of the

PLATE II. A skirt weaver. Pinotepa de Don Luis, Oaxaca (Mixtec). 1962

corn. The following quotation, aside from its particular interest, shows us how closely vegetation is connected in the minds of an agricultural people with birth:

In the seventh month of a woman's pregnancy common people of Java observe a ceremony which is plainly designed to facilitate the real birth by mimicking it. Husband and wife repair to a well or to the bank of a neighboring river. The upper part of the woman's body is bare, but young banana leaves are fastened under her arms, a small opening, or rather fold, being left in the leaves in front. Through this opening or fold in the leaves on his wife's body the husband lets fall from above a weaver's shuttle. An old woman receives the shuttle as it falls, takes it up in her arms and dandles it as if it were a baby, saying, "Oh, what a dear little child! Oh, what a beautiful little child!" (Frazer, 1963 Part I, Vol. I, pp. 72–73)

Among the loom accessories, the most interesting and varied are the picks (warp lifters) that are used in brocading or gauze weaving to separate and lift the warp threads. These are usually tough and longish thorns (Huichol) or the sharp tips of the maguey leaf (Santa Ana Hueytlalpan, Hidalgo–Otomí), but they may be fashioned of bone. In all examples seen, we were told that deer bone was used, pointed at one end. The latter were collected among the Tepehuas, Totonacs, Mixtecs, and Cuicatecs, but similar ones exist among other linguistic groups.

The Cuicatecs of San Andrés Teotilalpan, Oaxaca, make bone picks (pl. 20) which are pointed at one end, and have the small figure of a bird carved as a finial at the other. These picks vary from three to seven inches long. We examined thirty picks, some of them very old, and all exhibited the bird motif, although they showed great variety. Some looked like aquatic birds, some like perching birds with short beaks and upturned tail feathers, and others like domestic fowl.

The man in the village who made the older type has been dead for many years, but someone else now makes them. The style of carving between new and old was quite different. Although bone picks were abundant, some women seemed to prefer bright colored plastic cut in the form of a wide needle.

In Pinotepa Nacional, Oaxaca, in the Mixteca Baja, warp lifters exhibiting the same bird motif are also used, but they are made of iron by local artisans (pl. 21), and vary in length from four to five inches. Women complained (1965) that the ironworkers no longer want to bother with such small items as they formerly would make.

When we asked what bird was represented, we were

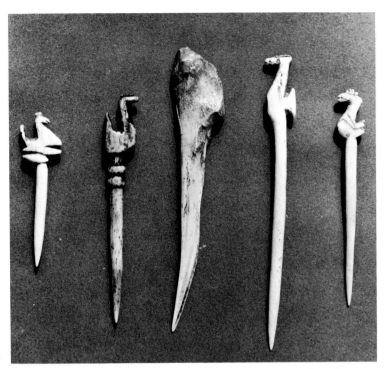

20. Cuicatec and (center only) Mixtec weaving picks of deer bone.

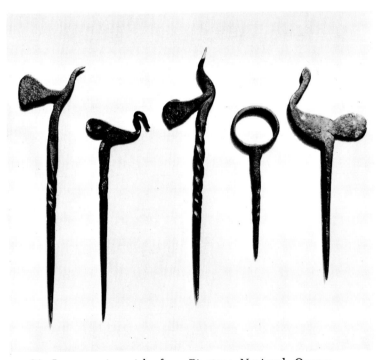

21. Iron weaving picks from Pinotepa Nacional, Oaxaca. (Mixtec).

45

22. An archaeological Mayan figurine showing a woman weaving with a bird on the end of her loom. Photograph by Irmgard Groth-Kimball.

told with what seemed like ribald laughter, that it was the *zanate* (species of grackle) (Aztec—*zanatl*) (*Quiscalus macrourus*). This bird theme used in warp-lifters is related to a myth having a wide distribution in Mexico. The myth among other things tells of the origin of the Sun and Moon (Miller, 1956, pp. 79, 86). It begins with a girl spinning, or more often weaving; a bird lights on the loom and is apparently killed by the girl with her weaving batten or sword; but when she puts the bird in her *huipil*, it revives and pecks her breast. From this she becomes pregnant and gives birth to twins, a boy and a girl, who later, after many adventures, become the Sun and the Moon.

Huitzilopochtli, one of whose aspects was the Sun God, and whose disguise as a *nahual* (sorcerer or wiz-

ard) was the hummingbird, impregnated the earth and the mountains for rain and fertility.

The "Sun and Moon" legend seems widely distributed in Indian groups all over Mexico, although it does not always have the weaving and spinning preface. This may be due to variations as told by informants, and also to the lack of published material. Plate 22 shows a clay figure from Jaina, Campeche, from the "late-classic" period, now in the National Museum of Anthropology in Mexico City. This figure we believe illustrates the same legend, although the legend itself does not seem to be reported from Campeche.

Eduard Seler (1963, Vol. I, fig. 386) reproduces a plate from Sahagún of the fiesta of Atamalqualiztli, showing the goddess Xochiquetzal at a loom on which a bird is perched. In this plate, the goddess has her loom attached to a flowering tree about which birds are flying, one of them a hummingbird dipping into a flower.

A variation of the "Sun and Moon" legend is given by G. de Cicco and F. Horcasitas (1962, pp. 74–79). This is Chatino, and has many of the elements of the Mixe one. In this, however, the mother of the Sun and Moon is *"tejiendo para vestir al ganado, las bestias y los tejones y todos los animales que hay en el mundo"* (weaving to clothe the cattle, the beasts and the *tejones* [small carniverous animals] and all the animals there are in the world). She does not finish the armadillo, because the thread gives out and he remains rough (or unfinished). Although Xochiquetzal was the goddess of love and beauty and the patroness of weavers, in this legend we would identify her as the mother goddess, and thus she would also be a deity of creation.

There is a strong connection between Coatlicue and Tlazolteotl, Xochiquetzal, Ciuacoatl, Chicomecoatl, and the ancient goddess of creation Tonacacihuatl. In the Codex Telleriano-Remensis and Codex Vaticanus A, Tonacacihuatl is identified with Xochiquetzal, and the pictures shown under the nineteenth week of Codex Telleriano-Remensis picture her with precisely the same dress and emblems as Xochiquetzal (Spence, 1923, p. 148).

Identification is difficult as one goddess was associated with another and took her attributes, and names were changed as they passed from one area to another. Many Christian elements have confused original concepts, as we see in the Cuicatec weaving picks or warp lifters which display a bird that appears to be a cock, one of the symbols of the Passion.

The Bird-Sun-Moon motif is found on earrings from

23. Pre-Hispanic green stone objects. The one on the left, resembling a weaving pick, is from the state of Guerrero. The one on the right, from the state of Colima, is possibly a weaving comb: height — 4⅞ inches; width — 2¾ inches (both in the Leof private collection, courtesy Dr. Arno Leof).

Jicayán, Oaxaca; and silver birds and combs occur on old necklaces from the Sierra Juárez in Oaxaca.

Plate 23 shows two very interesting objects—a stone comb and a stone pick, both archaeological specimens. These humble utilitarian objects, made in stone and perforated so that they could be hung or worn, were probably used ceremonially. The teeth of the comb are of a peculiar shape, almost identical to those of combs formerly made by Chamula Indians and sold to the Zoques (fig. 7 c). An informant from San Juan Chamula, Chiapas—Salvador López Calixto—told us that the fine end of the Chamula comb was used for combing

the hair, and the short blunt teeth, resembling the archaeological specimen, for weaving.

The stone pick with the hummingbird finial from Guerrero is about the same size as those of bone used today by the Cuicatecs (pl. 20). These stone objects have often been called "blood letters." However, it seems improbable that these blunt stone objects were used for this purpose. A sharpened bone would be much more efficient, and in most codices "blood-letters" (used in autosacrifice—blood offered to the gods) were pictured as made of bone. Weaving combs for daily use would probably not have been made of stone

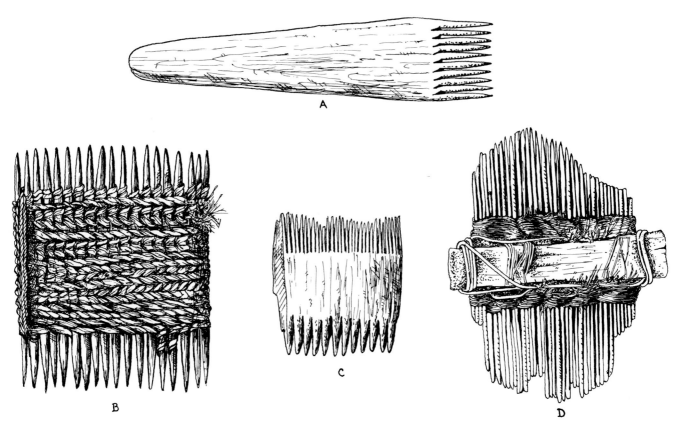

Figure 7. Combs used in Tzotzil and Zoque weaving: *a.* Tzotzil, from San Bartolomé de los Llanos; *b, d.* Old types formerly used by the Zoques; *c.* A type now commonly used by the Zoques. From Cordry, *Costumes and Weaving of the Zoque Indians of Chiapas, Mexico.* Courtesy The Southwest Museum.

either; it is too heavy and difficult to work and use. Stone was a precious material, and such objects would only have been intended for ceremonial use. In our opinion, the weaving picks of deer bone, in ancient times, probably played this dual role—as blood-letter to propitiate the goddess of weaving, Xochiquetzal, and as a weaving implement dedicated to her. These stone picks and combs indicate the probable existence of important women's cults in which stone weaving implements replaced the bone ones ordinarily used, and in whose ceremonies weaving and weaving implements played an important role.

In summing up, we may say that true weaving on the backstrap loom, using cotton or other fiber, probably came into existence after agriculture, when settled or semisettled communities were possible. Some leisure is necessary for women who weave, and that leisure was only possible when there was a fairly certain food supply from plant cultivation, to supplement hunting and gathering.

The agricultural existence must have seemed a life of prosperity, especially if these people were still in contact with hunting tribes that lived from hand to mouth and covered themselves with skins—which when damp took a long time to dry and which were uncomfortable, hot, stiff, and heavy. In contrast, even the coarsest woven fiber must have seemed almost miraculous.

With agriculture came the greater need for rain and for ceremonies to secure it. The loom, rain, and hair—all associated with women—became magical symbols, which in turn came to symbolize a settled family life, with secret women's cults connected with fertility. These cults were probably of great importance, as they were among the Mendi of Africa up until the early nineteenth century, and woman and loom became rain symbols. These cults were absorbed gradually into the religious life as society became more complex.

In these early communities, the sun (usually masculine) was less important than the moon (usually feminine) of the lunar calendar. Gradually the sun took on more significance, and in most groups was represented by a bird. Survivals of this belief remain to this day in decorations on weaving implements.

A bird, as we have seen, came to drink the blood of sacrifice to the sun, and also, in some legends, impregnated the moon. Xochiquetzal, earth and moon goddess, had characteristics of the ancient hunting god, including his association with the deer. This goddess also became the patroness of weavers, and that is probably why we find representations of deer on the ends of some loom sticks, and also why the weaving picks are made of deer bone. The birds carved on weaving picks would seem to represent the sun god, Huitzilopochtli or Piltzintecutli, husband of Xochiquetzal, who was also the sun god who impregnated her to give birth to the sun and the moon. As in many other mythologies and religions, this makes the solar deity both father and son, and represents both birth and rebirth.

As we have seen, the loom and products of the loom are powerful fertility symbols in many parts of the world. In Mexico the shed rolls and battens which rattled like the soft sound of rain or the warning of a rattlesnake, made the loom a constant prayer for rain; and the loom's association with hair made it a positive life-giving force, in contrast to the negative aspects of the cut hair of the dead or those about to die. Woman's hair also had a direct relationship to agriculture.

Over the millennia, the loom—aside from its association with fertility and rain—possibly came to represent the family: the loom, female; the batten, male; and the shuttle, a child connected by the umbilical cord to the loom.

49

4. The Huipil

from the Aztec, *huipilli* — Santamaría, 1959, p. 608.

The *huipil* is a simple garment that appears under other names in other parts of the world, notably in Africa and India. It is sacklike with openings for the head and arms and is made from rectangular strips of cloth as they are taken off the backstrap loom (not shaped or fitted by cutting). It may be long or short, narrow or wide. It may be woven of heavy wool (pl. 257), coarse and rough; but cotton is the most common fiber used. Sometimes the cotton is heavy and coarse, sometimes so finely spun as to be filmy and semitransparent (pl. 24). When the cloth is woven with a gauze technique, it is frequently netlike (pl. 136). Other fibers are also used, such as the bark of a tree or shrub called *chichicastle* (from the Aztec *tzitzicaztli*) (Robelo, 1904, p. 542), which is treated and utilized for weaving. The use of *chichicastle* has almost disappeared. It was or is used in a small area in the state of Oaxaca, the center of which is San Juan Guivini, in the district of Miahuatlán.

The use of heavy or light materials, of course, varies according to climatic conditions. Thus, heavy feltlike wool *huipiles* are worn in San Juan Chamula, Chiapas (pl. 256), (altitude 7,546 feet), and filmy cotton ones in San Bartolomé de los Llanos (pl. 251) (at a much lower altitude), also in Chiapas, and in the hot country of the Pacific coast. This rule is not uniform because

the nights in the coastal foothills may be cool, and the *huipil* is often used as a night garment or covering. The solution may be to shed the *huipil* entirely during the day in these hot regions (pl. II). In this area the *huipil* is more likely to be a ceremonial garment (pl. 230). Its substitute (pl. 227) is worn for modesty or warmth. Both types of upper garments are put on in many ways according to the occasion (see Chapter 32).

In Mexico the *huipil* is worn only by women, with the exception—to our knowledge—of the Lacandón men of Chiapas, who, as well as their women, wore *huipiles* of bark cloth until recently, sometimes decorated with crude designs painted with *achiote* (*Bixa orellana*—a tree, the seeds of which are used for red coloring matter). Gertrude Duby de Blom says (letter, August 16, 1965), "I saw in 1943 one child with a bark cloth shirt. One of the other Lacandón had a shirt for religious use at that time. After that they disappeared rapidly."

Huipiles are composed of one, two, or three loom webs (fig. 8 c, d, & g), sewn together lengthwise, folded transversely, with the neck opening cut—a vertical slit, or square or round hole (fig. 8 h, i, & g). *Huipil* strips are sewn up the sides to leave either very tiny arm openings, (fig. 8 a, c, & e), or very large ones (g), depending upon the geographic area. The sides of some *huipiles* are sewn up only for a few inches from the

24. A Mixtec woman of Chacalapa, Guerrero, wearing an exceptionally finely spun and woven *huipil*. 1965

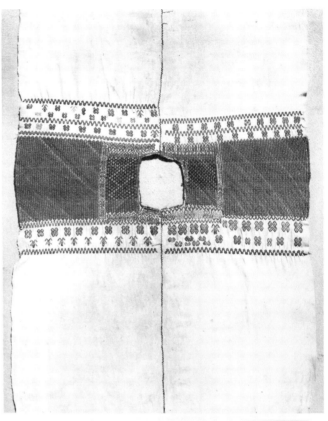

25. An open-sided *huipil* from San Miguel Mitontic, Chiapas, showing the square-cut neck more prevalent in Chiapas than elsewhere in Mexico. (Tzotzil).

bottom, to allow greater freedom of movement, in particular for nursing babies and keeping them warm or out of the sun as the case may be (pl. 236). Some *huipiles* are left open altogether at the sides (fig. 8 d), as in Tetelcingo, Morelos (pl. 86), and often in Santa María Cuquila, Oaxaca (pl. 27).

In a document which probably dates from the sixteenth century (Galicia Chimalpopoca, 1947, p. 10), we read that *huipiles* open down the front, *como bata* (like a dressing gown), were among the items of tribute. Open garments such as these are seen in Mayan figurines. These presumably would have been fashioned of two woven webs, joined at the back and sides, and left open down the front. This fashion we have not seen in modern times.

One quite different *huipil* is that of Tuxpan, Jalisco. It consists of a single rectangle doubled horizontally (fig. 8 a) making a wide, rather short garment joined across the shoulders with space left unsewn for the

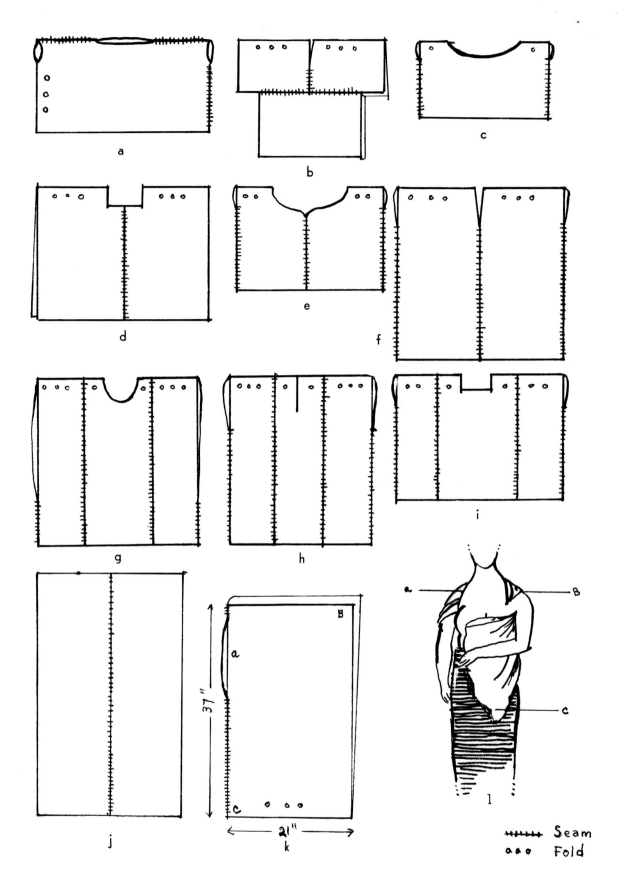

Figure 8. *Huipiles* — diagrams of various forms.

a. Tuxpan, Jalisco (Nahua) after Johnson, Johnson, and Beardsley, 1962, pp. 149–217
b. Temoaya, state of México (Otomí)
c. San Bartolomé de los Llanos, Chiapas (Tzotzil)
d. San Miguel Mitontic, Chiapas (Tzotzil)
e. Tuxtla Gutiérrez, Chiapas (Zoque)
f. Yalalag, Oaxaca (Zapotec)
g. San Andrés Chicahuaxtla, Oaxaca (Trique)
h. Santiago Nuyóo, Oaxaca (Mixtec)
i. Magdalenas, Chiapas (Tzotzil)

j. Mechoacán, Oaxaca (Mixtec) — a garment commonly called a *tralla*
k. and l. Tetepec, Oaxaca (Mixtec). A very unusual upper garment, termed a *tralla*, woven in one piece — 21 by 74 inches — and folded as in k, with one side sewn together leaving a 13-inch arm hole (a). According to Lucila Franco, the right arm is inserted and the garment pulled across the back and held to cover the chest. A carrying pocket is formed at (c).

26. A Mixtec girl weaving. Note her open-sided *huipil.* Santa María Cuquila, Oaxaca. 1943

27. A mother and daughter of Cuquila, Oaxaca, in everyday *huipiles*. (Mixtec). 1943

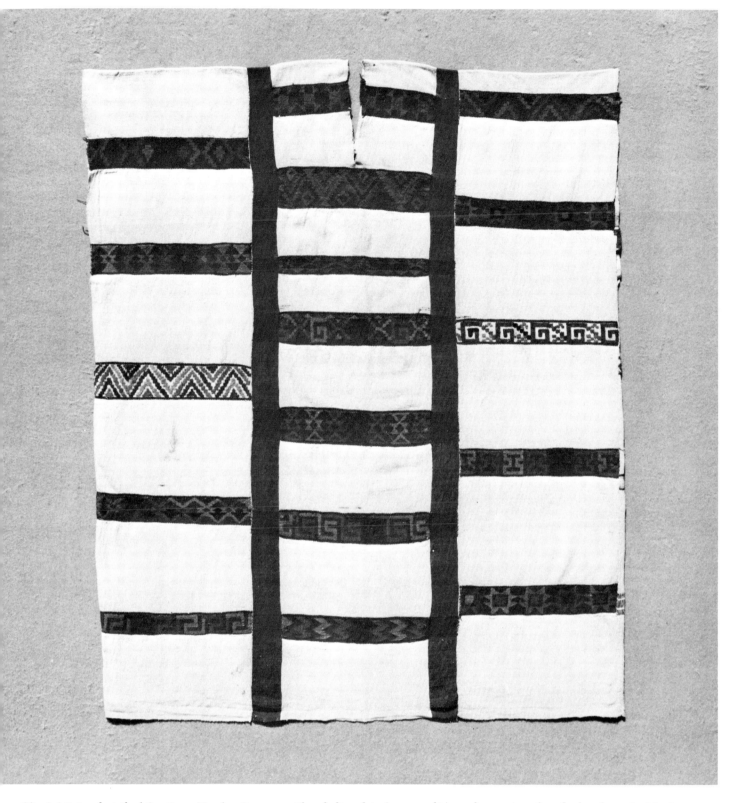

28. A Mixtec *huipil* of Santiago Nuyóo, Oaxaca, with a kelim slot (woven slit) neck opening, found elsewhere in Mexico, to our knowledge, only in old Santa Catarina Estetla *huipiles*.

neck (in boat neck style). One side of the garment is sewn up, leaving one small armhole. The second armhole is cut, and is reinforced with decorative stitching like the other above-mentioned joinings. An almost identical garment is used as a head covering, and is called a *joloton* (Johnson, Johnson, and Beardsley, 1962, p. 159).

Huipil webs are fastened together in many instances with carefully executed embroidery stitches, which constitute an important decorative element in the garment; thread colors often change every few inches (pl. 137). Effects vary from delicate small whipping and buttonhole stitches to handsome wide satin-stitch joinings (pl. 41). When a colored stripe is woven in on the edge of the center web selvages, simple over and over hand sewing is usually used for joining (pl. 241). The center web is wider than the other two when such stripes are woven in.

A third and increasingly popular way of joining *huipil* strips is the insertion of 1¾-inch-wide commercial rayon ribbon in bright colors, often red or strong blue, sewn in with machine stitching (pl. IV c). Many yards of ribbon—easily ten—are required for these *huipiles*, apart from the long decorative ribbons which hang either as neck trimming or from the many strings of beads worn for gala wear. Ribbon is an expensive item.

The two-web Choapan *huipil* is joined with sewing down the sides, but the center front has an insert of ¾-inch white lace in the join, both in front and in back, below the neck slit (pl. 201).

Some fine old *huipiles* may still be found with remains of imported pure-silk ribbon entirely sewn in by hand along the web joinings (for example, see pl. 42), and it is known that embroidered flower-patterned multicolored ribbons imported from Europe were brought into Mexico and used perhaps up until World War I. The well-to-do Nahuas of Amatlán, Vera Cruz, were fond of these ribbons, as were the Zapotecs of San Pedro Quiatoni, Oaxaca (pl. 46).

In most two-strip *huipiles*, the neck opening is simply a section left unsewn between the two strips (fig. 8 f; pl. 48). An exception is the Zoque two-web *huipil*, which has a large round neck opening (fig. 8 e; pl. 250). The center strip of a three-web *huipil* may have a vertical opening put in during the weaving. This is termed a kelim slot and was common in ancient Peru. It is an unusual technique in contemporary Mexican weaving: the only modern examples we know are from Santa Catarina Estetla and Santiago Nuyóo (pls. 84 & 28), both Mixtecan villages in Oaxaca. This technique was an ancient practice in Mexico, judging from the fact that small *huipiles* of cotton with kelim-slot neck openings have been found in caves in the Mixteca Alta, and were probably left there as offerings (Johnson, letter, October 14, 1965).

Neck and sleeve openings are finished in many ways, and usually the reinforcement serves also as adornment. When an everyday *huipil* has a selvage neck slit, a binding or trimming is seldom added. The finishing also depends on the financial status of the woman. Usually girls of marriageable age are better dressed than older women, whether married or not. Old women who are left alone to live with married children and help out with household tasks, but who are not able to contribute in other ways, are often dressed in rags. This may be in part because their weaving days are over, due to failing eyesight.

All cut neck openings have sturdy bindings, either of plain tape or cloth, to prevent fraying (see the Ojitlán everyday *huipil* in Plate 195); of ribbon reinforced with rickrack braid (pl. 33); of ribbon reinforced with embroidery (pls. 39 & 216); or of embroidery alone—usually blanket or buttonhole stitch (pl. 259). Sometimes the embroidery used about the neck opening is the only embellishment of an everyday *huipil*.

We had the opportunity of seeing a round neck opening cut by a Cuicatec woman of San Andrés Teotilalpan, Oaxaca. She folded the center *huipil* length to find the middle, and then, "freehand," took a generous swipe with her scissors and cut an opening; then she tried it on and cut it larger until she was satisfied. In the end it barely went over her head. Most neck openings of Mexican *huipiles* are so small that non-Indian women cannot get them on. Some Zapotec villages (Santa Cecilia, Vera Cruz) and eastern Chinantec villages (Teotalcingo and Lalana, both in Oaxaca) in hot, humid climates, are the only areas we know where an exceedingly long neck slit is customary.

Selvage arm openings are usually decorated or reinforced. Sometimes lace is used (pls. 29 & 194). Usila *huipiles* made in 1964 were laden with ribbons and lace at the armholes, almost creating a short sleeve, capped by ribbon rosettes on each shoulder (pl. 196), whereas earlier Usila *huipiles* were without these modern trimmings. The Usila *huipiles* made before 1940 had brocading of wool; now commercial embroidery cotton is used. Some *huipil* arm openings are left simply with their web selvage edges (pl. 30); others have blanket or buttonhole stitching (pl. 49).

Huipil strips are usually woven with four selvages.

29. A group of Chinantec women of San Felipe Usila, Oaxaca, with the river and mountain in the background. 1964

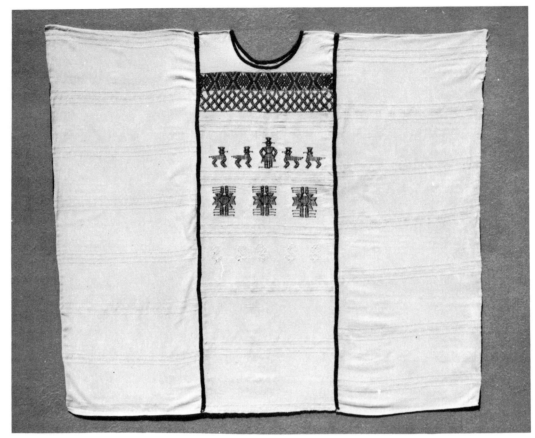

30. A characteristic *huipil* from the prolific weaving village of San Juan Cotzocón, Oaxaca. (Mixe).

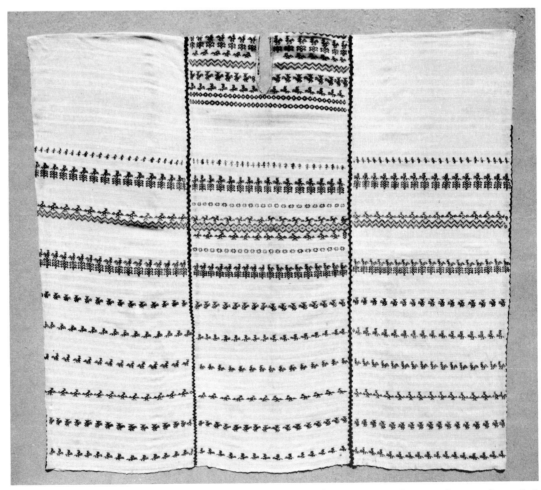

31. An example of the now extinct *huipil* of San Bartolo Yautepec, Oaxaca, having brocaded design rows worked in cochineal-dyed silk. (Zapotec).

32. A *huipil* from Buena Vista, Guerrero (group not known), having a gay and originally conceived yoke design in strong colors.

This means that the loom is set up separately for each of the two or three webs or lengths that make a garment. Occasionally, however, more than one length is woven at a time in which case the cloth is cut in appropriate lengths afterward. This means that one notices hems at the bottoms of some webs instead of selvages, as, for example, in San Sebastián Zinacatepec, Pinotepa Nacional, and San Andrés Teotilalpan. When the center strip is wider than the two side strips (pl. 50), the loom must be set up at least twice. Naturally it is easier to set up the loom for one length that will do for all three *huipil* webs, thus avoiding two or three separate loom setups. The Amusgo *huipil* weavers of Xochistlahuaca, Guerrero, follow this method, which calls

for skillful handling. The length required for the three-web adult Xochistlahuaca *huipil* totals some 234 inches.

The following are a few *huipil* measurements after strips are joined and folded transversely at the shoulder. Some *huipiles* are wider than they are long (pl. 50), and vice versa (pl. 44). Many others are almost square (pls. 31, 32 & 134). The shortest adult *huipil* measured (pl. 251) was 13 inches from the shoulder fold to the bottom of the garment; the longest was one 60 inches in length (not pictured), from San Miguel Chicahuaxtla, Oaxaca (Mixtec). On an Indian woman this garment would drag on the ground. This *huipil* and even those 50 inches long are tucked up or made into rolls about the waists to make them shorter, although

33. A man and wife of Santa Cruz Nundaco, Oaxaca. Except for very special occasions the woman's *huipil* would be gathered up and rolled about her waist. (Mixtec). 1943

34. A Zapotec family. Yalalag, Oaxaca. 1938

35. People bathing in the river and washing clothes. Usila, Oaxaca (Chinantec). 1964

they are sometimes allowed to fall loose for fiestas and ceremonial occasions (pl. 33).

The widest *huipil* examined was a wedding *huipil* of Huazolotitlán, Oaxaca, measuring 54 inches across (pl. 147). This garment had wide ribbon insertions between webs, adding to the total width. The widest *huipil*—considering actual woven width joined with embroidery stitching only—measured 51 inches and came from San Bartolo Yautepec, Oaxaca (pl. 31). Very wide *huipiles* hang over the arms to the wrists, whereas very narrow ones barely cap the shoulders.

The narrowest example seen, woven in one web, was 18 inches wide (pl. 251). *Huipiles* from the high Mixteca villages in the region of Tlaxiaco, Oaxaca, are very long and usually do not have corresponding great width (pls. 44 & 45). The San Miguel Chicahuaxtla *huipil* mentioned above, which was 60 inches long, measured only 37 inches in width, making it the most extremely proportioned *huipil* we have seen.

Huipiles are worn many ways. Some of moderate length hang loose outside the skirt (pl. 34), or hang free when no skirt is worn (pl. 240). In some areas, when worn with a skirt, the *huipil* is gathered or folded up about the waist, for freedom of movement, or to protect a newish garment from soiling when sitting on the ground. For such times a heavy skirt is adequate. Obviously, whether a skirt is worn or not depends on numerous factors. Skirts are worn in many cases for ceremonial occasions, or when it is cold, or simply when the woman has the cash to buy or weave one. *Huipiles*

36. Country people on the merry-go-round. Papantla, Vera Cruz (Totonac). 1946

folded up about the waist serve for carrying small objects (pl. 237).

Some *huipiles*, even big heavy ones, are worn tucked inside the skirt as in Mixistlán (or Yacochi?), Oaxaca, although in one or both villages a man's shirt has now largely replaced the handwoven *huipil* (pl. 37). In San Juan Chamula, Chiapas, the heavy wool *huipil*, still commonly used, is sometimes tucked inside the skirt.

Early chroniclers state that Indian women of the noble classes wore several *huipiles* at one time, each one long enough to be seen beneath the upper ones, and each surpassing the next in beauty. Today two *hui-*

piles may be worn for warmth (if a woman is fortunate enough to own more than one), a newer one over a ragged one. Often the outer one is pulled up over the head as protection from sun or rain. At times *huipiles* put on as usual, with the head through the neck opening, may be worn with the wearer's arms inside rather than out through the armholes—a wonderfully adaptable garment! In the Pinotepa Nacional and Jamiltepec area in southwest Oaxaca, the old wedding or fiesta *huipiles*, and the many ways of wearing them for different occasions, are disappearing.

To save *huipiles* they are sometimes worn wrong side

37. Mixe women from the village of Mixistlán or of Yacochi—Yalalag market. 1938

out; and very often, when the owner must travel on foot to a distant market, fair, or fiesta, an old ragged garment is worn during the dusty or wet journey, and the new one carried in a flour sack or a basket to be put on for the big occasion. We have bought *huipiles* beautifully woven but so grey with dirt as to be almost impossible to clean or wash. This is usually the case only in areas where water is exceedingly scarce, due to the village location or the season. On the whole Indian women are very clean, and bathe or wash clothes several times a day in rivers not always near and convenient to their villages. A beautiful sight, known to travelers in Mexico, is that of handsome Zapotec women bathing and washing their clothes in the Tehuantepec River. Another wide river, the Santa Rosa, which flows by the northern Chinantec town of Usila (pl. 35), presents a picture of women with bright commercial, patterned skirts tied above the breast as they bathe and wash their multicolored handwoven *huipiles*.

One observes how clean the people are in coastal villages where much white is worn (pls. 36 & 225). Farther north in Yalalag, sparkling white *huipiles* are most noticeable on the Tuesday market day (pl. 37), when they contrast strikingly with the dress of their exotic neighbors, the Mixe women of Mixistlán and Yacochi, who come in on that day wearing dusky, dark-green costumes with vermillion wool-cord headdresses and many strings of old glass trade beads. The white-costumed woman in Plate 94 was photographed after her long trip afoot to Oaxaca City from the Sierra Juárez, before she changed into clean white clothing.

Because of economic pressure *huipiles* have to last a long time. An interesting garment in this respect is the *huipil* of San José Miahuatlán, Puebla (pl. 179), of heavy unbleached commercial muslin which has deep embroidered bands of decoration. These bands outlast three *huipiles*. We were told that they are cut out from the original garment, and appliquéd on new ones over and over for a period of ten years. The rich dark red of the thick-piled bands (a color used much in Indian Mexico to simulate cochineal-dyed yarns) is worked in commercial yarn which fades, and when the third *huipil* is worn to shreds, the once dark-red bands have been faded by sun and washings to a pale yellow.

We have observed other instances of garments being used until they are very old. One Cuicatec *huipil* has been worn for many years (pl. 38), and is made of parts of at least three garments. At the bottom right-hand edge one sees the remains of the original neck opening. The old center strip has been cut in two, and

38. Parts of several garments comprise this old Cuicatec *huipil*. The right-hand strip contains very good traditional brocaded designs. San Andrés Teotilalpan, Oaxaca.

the other half has been put on the left of the rear (not seen in the photograph). Either a new neck has been cut at its proper place or a piece of another *huipil* with old worn opening has been utilized. Parts of a third old white everyday *huipil* with gauze-weave bands has been introduced in many patches.

Every bit of material must be used until it no longer exists. A piece of a *huipil* to wrap a baby or a loom finally is reduced to a mere scrap. In 1963 in Peñoles, Oaxaca, where today a *huipil* of store muslin has taken the place of the handwoven one, we searched endlessly for a scrap of an old handwoven one said not to have been used for many years. We found a very small piece in a remote *rancho* which verified our belief that the *huipil* (unrecorded and unknown to our knowledge) did resemble that of Santa Catarina Estetla. The handwoven *huipil* has also disappeared from the latter village, but we had seen and photographed a few rare examples in 1941 (pls. 84, 220, & 221).

When attempting in 1963 to reach the villages of

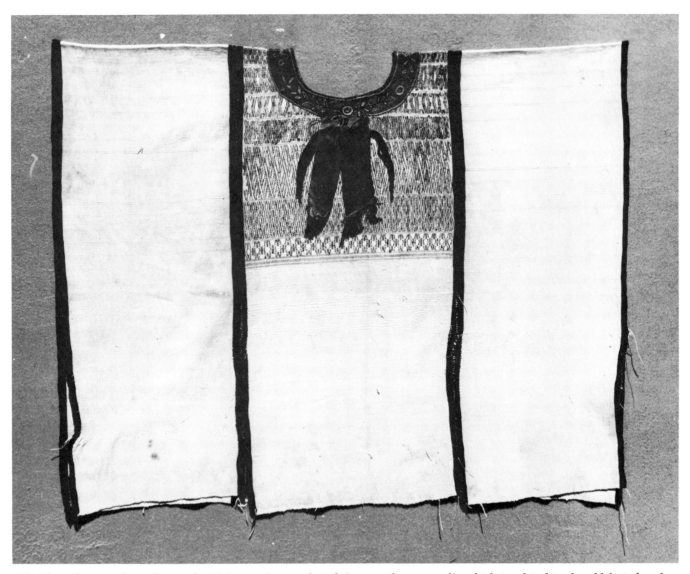

39. The only example we know of a Huitepec, Oaxaca, *huipil* (now no longer used), which is related to the old *huipiles* of Santa Catarina Estetla. (Mixtec).

Peñoles and Estetla via Zimatlán, Oaxaca, (later we entered further north from Etla) we were told that the village of Huitepec formerly had a *huipil* very similar to the famous Estetla one. In 1965 Cayuqui Estage went to investigate Huitepec textiles for us, and we obtained another link with the past from this little-known part of the Mixteca Alta; a wonderful brocaded textile, large and very old (pl. 141), with vegetable-dyed silk designs (similar to the "white-on-white" old brocaded weaving of San Esteban (Atatlahuaca, Oaxaca—also Mixtecan), and a Huitepec *huipil* (pl. 39), one of the last examples extant (which shows a similarity to old Estetla *huipiles*).

Very neat in their eating habits (with few implements of any kind), exceedingly agile until very late in life, Indian women mysteriously avoid burns from sparks of open cooking fires. One finds very few holes, save the breaks that finally come through age. Well-woven handspun cloth does not easily tear. The dirt one finds is apt to be earth grime and fruit stains, perhaps resulting partly from carrying leaf-lined string bags of fruit to distant markets.

We have found very few *huipiles*—always gala ones —put away before they disintegrated completely. Those which were kept were either kept to be buried in or to be given to a daughter (who usually is no longer inter-

40. A Chinantec girl spinning. She wears an everyday *huipil*, with designs probably of pre-Hispanic origin. Rancho Choapan, Oaxaca. 1940

41. An Ojitlán woman from Rancho Choapan, Oaxaca, showing the old manner of wearing the characteristic head-cloth and the fiesta *huipil*. (Chinantec). 1940

ested and prefers a shiny rayon dress). Unfortunately, some old *huipiles* have been damaged by cockroaches or rats. Only in Pinotepa Nacional (pl. 42), in Amatlán (pl. 175), in San Mateo del Mar (pl. 93), in San Sebastián Zinacatepec (pl. 189), and in Ocozocoautla (pl. 47), have we found *huipiles* from twenty to sixty years old being saved in a moderate state of preservation. In some villages in the Mixteca Baja (example: Pinotepa de Don Luis, Oaxaca), *huipiles* are worn only twice by the owners. First, at their wedding; and again, when they are buried. But sometimes the *huipiles* which we purchased were dirty and ragged. This was because the men wear them for *carnaval,* and they get rough treatment in the horseplay that goes with this fiesta (verbal information—Lucila Franco). The *quechquemitl* is likewise worn by men for certain dances during *carnaval* in areas where this garment and not the *huipil* is used.

Many pueblos have more than one type of *huipil*—one for everyday, and another for weddings and fiestas, and sometimes a third, exceedingly simple in style, worn only by old women. The everyday *huipil* is less complex than the fiesta one in surface design and color, which means that it is less expensive in store-bought ribbons and thread or yarns (frontispiece). The Ojitlán everyday *huipil* is exceptional (pl. 40). We find it more beautiful—with its large red embroidered designs on heavily textured whitish ground—than the rather garish all-red fiesta *huipil* trimmed with sequins and lace (pl. 41).

The extraordinary wedding *huipiles* which we found in 1964 in Pinotepa Nacional had been kept by a few old women to be buried in. These are brocaded "white-on-white," and show anthropomorphic, zoomorphic, and geometric designs (pl. 42). The cloth itself was not woven in Pinotepa Nacional, but was purchased many years ago (we believe not later than 1920) in the great fair of Igualapa, Guerrero, on the third Friday of Lent.

We also found a curious *huipil* which had been worn with the old skirt shown in Plate IV d. It was made from a patterned lace curtain and was obviously admired for its imagined resemblance to the wonderful white-on-white brocaded *huipiles* formerly worn in the area of Pinotepa Nacional. The example we found was trimmed with pink satin ribbon.

Another notable gala *huipil*, the wedding garment of Zinacantán, Chiapas, with feathers worked into its decoration (pl. 259), is the last reminder of the all-over feather capes and other garments of pre-Conquest times. Another pre-Conquest feature of this *huipil* (aside from the rectangle in front and back below the

42. An old white-on-white brocaded wedding *huipil,* purchased in Pinotepa Nacional, Oaxaca, and believed, at this writing, to have possibly been woven some twenty-five years ago or more, in San Esteban Atatlahuaca, in the Mixteca Alta Tlaxiaco region, Oaxaca. The woven dimensions of this garment and the so-called wedding *rebozo* in Plate 141 are identical, and many of the same design elements are found in both textiles.

neck, and the use of feathers), is the wide decorative border around the bottom of the garment. Codices picture both *huipiles* and skirts of early times with borders (figs. 9 & 13). Few *huipiles* today (or skirts either) display this feature; they tend to have design areas about the neck and shoulders, and in all-over horizontal stripes. *Huipiles* of Santa María Zacatepec, Oaxaca, have two woven red stripes around the bottom, and very rarely, a row of brocaded animals.

The Cuicatec village of San Andrés Teotilalpan, Oaxaca, near the border of the Chinantec territory, has three *huipil* types (pl. 43 & frontispiece), all but the white one showing distinct influence of bolder Chinantec designs. The third type (not shown) is a white *huipil* with a single wide red brocaded band across the chest below the neck opening. In Teotilalpan we saw traders from the Chinantec town of Analco, who had come to sell *huipil* lengths, adding to the admixture of styles.

Several types of *huipiles* are woven in Santiago Nuyóo, but due to insufficient data some of these are often confused with other Mixtec garments: it is not impossible to see, for instance, that garments such as those shown in Plate 44 (from Nuyóo) and Plate 45

43. Weaving a white gauze *huipil* strip in San Andrés Teotilalpan, Oaxaca. The weaver is using a deer-bone pick. (Cuicatec). 1965

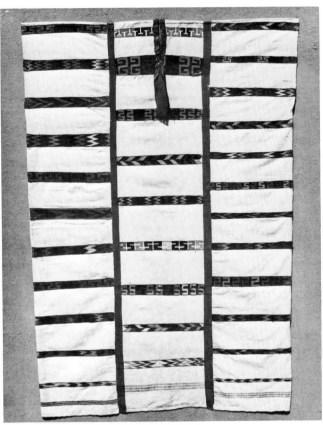

44. A *huipil* of Santiago Nuyóo, Oaxaca (Mixteca Alta), where the women are excellent weavers. (Mixtec).

Figure 9. The *quechque-mitl* worn over the *huipil* (a copy of a drawing shown in the Florentine Codex).

(from Yucunicoco) might be thought to come from the same village.

Because Nuyóo is difficult to get to, and because at present any number of Mixteca Alta *huipiles* are mistakenly said to be from Nuyóo, there is a mystery in the name. We went at Christmas to Putla, where people from Nuyóo come into market. At that time we saw only manta *huipiles* from there; yet in the past they have made unique and beautifully fashioned *huipiles*, with kelim-slot necks and wide completely reversible, horizontal, multicolor bands in a tapestry weave with *greca* designs (pl. 44).

In San Pedro Quiatoni, Oaxaca, where the very individual woman's costume has almost disappeared, there existed a very wide, heavy, white cotton *huipil* of two strips, and another type, for gala wear, more finely spun in three widths (pl. 46). Purple thread in embroidery around the neck of our two-strip *huipil* proved to have been shellfish dyed (Saltzman; analysis, letter, January 9, 1964), although this village is farther

45. A Mixteca Alta *huipil*, with characteristic richly brocaded yoke and dark-blue woven vertical bands between *huipil* webs. Yucunicoco, Oaxaca (Mixtec).

46. A San Pedro Quiatoni, Oaxaca, girl, wearing a fiesta *huipil*, with old ribbon, and a necklace of old trade beads. Her earrings in the shape of stylized birds are typical of the village and are hammered out of silver coins. (Zapotec). 1964

47. An extraordinary old white-on-white Zoque *huipil*. This and the white garments in Plates 42, 56, and 201 were photographed in front of dark paper or against the light. Ocozocoautla, Chiapas.

from the coast than areas where this dye was commonly used.

High cold settlements may have both wool and cotton *huipiles*—as in Cuquila, Oaxaca; where a simple woolen one is fashioned of two woven webs (pls. 26 & 27). Because of the two vertical stripes, these garments appear to be woven in three webs. Upon examination of the photographs one sees that they are two-web *huipiles*. The cotton one (not pictured) has three. The cotton *huipil* must be uncomfortable to wear in the cold highlands, but perhaps it is a mark of prestige. It is larger than the wool one, although cotton—which comes from coastal regions—is harder to come by than wool. These cotton garments, which are used for weddings and fiestas, show more care in execution, more decoration, and more ribbon than everyday ones. Santo Tomás Ocotepec, also in the high Mixtec Tlaxiaco area, also has a wool and a cotton *huipil*, both made of three webs. From examples seen, the wool garments in Ocotepec seem quite as highly decorated as the cotton ones.

Probably, however, the cotton one is the gala garment.

The *huipil* depends for its beauty on its surface decoration, rather than on its simple though graceful and uniform lines. A variety of weaves in the white web often provides ample decorative effect. One of the most common is gauze, and its variations (pl. 250) are combined with plain weaves. White brocading on white is common in the hot country, such as Oaxaca, Chiapas, and parts of the state of Puebla, where thin webs are used. An old type of all-white *huipil*, that depended for its beauty on weave and design rather than color, is the much-admired one from Choapan (pl. 201), covered with intricate woven patterns with no colored stitching or ribbon added. Each web of this intricately patterned garment took four months to finish; the whole *huipil*, eight months. We have been told by the Zoques, the Mixtecs, and the people of San Bartolomé de los Llanos that weavers, who have spent their lives weaving complicated brocading of white on white (pls. 47 & 254) frequently go blind in middle age.

73

48. Four Yalalag girls in fiesta costumes at the Oaxaca Indian State Fair in Oaxaca City. (Zapotec). 1941

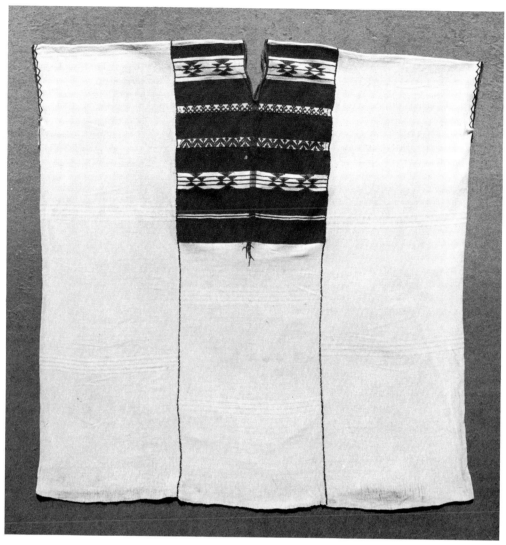

49. This excellently woven red and white Mixe *huipil* from San Juan Mazatlán, Oaxaca, is similar to those woven and worn in San Pedro Acatlán.

The Yalalag white *huipil* combines plain weave with heavy white ribbing on a finer web. This heavy ribbing occurs over the shoulders and constitutes the chief decoration apart from the twined horizontal motif directly below the neck slit, which ends in long tassels (pl. 48). The latter decoration is fashioned today of colored artificial silk threads, and is often not worked in during the weaving as formerly, but made separately and sewn on after each washing—because the colors used to dye commercial threads sometimes run. Other *huipiles* having two or three webs with a vertical unsewn section for a neck opening, like the Yalalag *huipil*, tend to have for reinforcement and decoration a similar though smaller twined horizontal ornament worked in during the weaving, and always centered below the neck slit both in front and in back. Other examples come from Santa Catarina Estetla, Mixistlán, Zinacantán. Tepinapa, Chinantec (Bevan, 1938, Pl. 11 [21]), may be added to these.

Pre-Conquest *huipiles* pictured in codices depict rectangular shapes below neck openings (fig. 13). An example of a similar decoration is the modern Zinacantán wedding *huipil* (pl. 259), and the tradition is carried into the modern Chinantec *huipiles* of Ojitlán (pl. 41). Some of these have rectangles—approximately 1½ by 3 inches—of black or colored ribbon sewn horizontally some 10 inches below the round neck, with no relation to the all-over design of the garment—an ugly addition to these barbaric, splendid garments, even though it is related to pre-Hispanic *huipil* design. *Huipiles* from some other regions have sections of ribbon sewn horizontally below the neck with long ribbon streamers—

75

50. A beautifully woven brocaded *huipil* from Larrainzar, Chiapas. (Tzotzil).

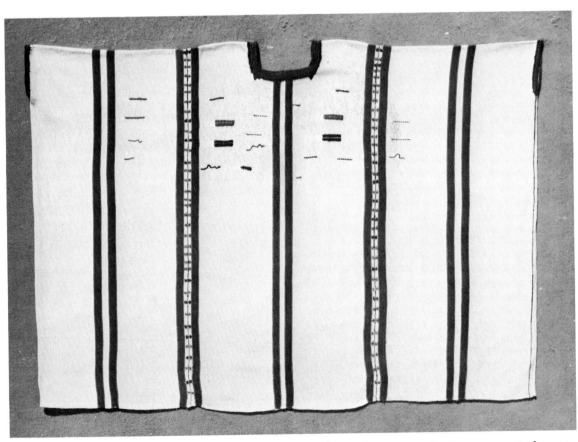

51. A Tzeltal *huipil* from Santo Tomás Oxchuc, Chiapas, unusual in its motif of strong vertical warp stripes relieved only by free horizontal embroidered spottings.

this element is better integrated into the yoke design of the *huipil* (pl. 189).

Three-strip *huipiles* often have a solid area of woven or embroidered design in the center web about the neck and extending almost halfway down the *huipil* both in front and in back (pl. 49). Some *huipiles* with this central yoke have similar solid decorative areas over the shoulders in the side webs as well. The wedding *huipil* of Ixtayutla, Oaxaca, shown in Plate IV c, is an outstanding example of this, and such placement of design areas is particularly characteristic of certain Chiapas *huipiles* (pl. 50).

A large design area in front below the neck, and a somewhat smaller one in back, may be combined with other horizontal elements (pls. 45 & 234).This horizontal element is strong in many *huipiles*, but particularly in those of the Trique and Mixtec villages of the Mixteca Alta surrounding Tlaxiaco, Oaxaca. Unfortunately, we have insufficient data concerning these Mixtec and Trique textiles. In the first place, the *huipiles* are similar and, in the second, one village is more and more apt to copy the design of another. Therefore, unless *huipiles* from this area are actually collected in a given settlement, much confusion develops concerning their origin. Horizontal multicolored woven bands, red predominating, combined with horizontal broken lines of geometric patterns, occur in infinite variety in the three-web *huipiles* of this area, always with a wider, more-solid decorative design section directly below the neck in the center web.

By far the most sumptuous *huipiles* of this type are from Itunyoso, (pl. 234) and Yucunicoco (pl. 45), Oaxaca. *Huipiles* from these two villages are often confused because both have far wider horizontal brocaded bands than others. They are distinguishable one from the other in that there is almost no plain woven background at all in Itunyoso *huipiles*. Another area with *huipiles* having strong horizontal feeling is the Mazatec in northwestern Oaxaca (Jalapa de Díaz, among others) (pl. 4). These garments are now sadly degenerated.

Vertical emphasis in Mexican *huipiles*, apart from decorative web joinings or a single colored stripe woven on both selvage edges of some center webs, is rare. Woven vertical red stripes occur, however, in some Chiapas garments (pl. 51).

Usually there are similarities of costume within a linguistic group if villages are relatively close geographically, although there may be points of difference.

Yalalag market day (pl. 52) shows many varieties of white *huipiles* from outlying Zapotec settlements. In Ometepec, Guerrero, a town which like Tlaxiaco is surrounded by Indian villages, it is fascinating to observe the many variations of Amusgo *huipiles* seen on market days.

Neighboring pueblos may show common factors, especially if the same language is spoken, but sometimes they differ drastically. Two Nahua neighboring villages in Guerrero—Acatlán and Zitlala (the latter buying their costumes from the former)—wear identical costumes except for a single string of beads, yellow in the former and red in the latter. On the other hand, three Nahua towns in the neighborhood of Tehuacán, Puebla, wear costumes which have no relation whatsoever to each other (pls. 179, 185 & 189).

Materials to make *huipiles* are secured from a variety of sources. Villages of the eastern Oaxaca Chinantec (Bevan, 1938, Pl. 10, No. 19) purchase simple white *huipil* cloth from enterprising nearby Zapotec weavers. Zapotec women of Choapan, who used to weave one of the most remarkable *huipiles* in Mexico (pl. 201), today do not—to our knowledge—weave at all; at present a few old women purchase a plain white *huipil* from the village of Taguí, such as they themselves used to weave for everyday wear.

Silk thread dyed with cochineal is purchased by the weavers of Ixtayutla three times a year on fiesta days in the town of Pinotepa de Don Luis, two days distant by foot. The silk thread has, in turn, been brought from a distant town in the Mixteca Alta—one of the villages named Peñasco. Silk thread that was used in *huipil* yokes of San Sebastián Zinacatepec (pl. 189) came a long distance from the high Mixteca in the days when silk raising flourished. Cotton is raised in many southern areas, and *huipil* thread still is usually hand spun, but commercial thread is also being used. *Huipiles* woven with it are inferior in quality, texture, and durability. Commercial weaving and embroidery threads are brought in by animal train today to the most remote weaving areas.

In many parts of southern Mexico the *huipil*, as previously mentioned, is used as a ceremonial garment. For daily use on the street, only a square or rectangle of cloth is worn as a shawl to cover the head and breasts. This may be made of artificial silk (Nahua of Cosoleacaque, Vera Cruz). In the Mixteca Baja these cloths are usually hand spun, and woven in two strips (Chapter 32). Those of Mechoacán (pl. 227; fig. 8 j)

52. Market day (Tuesday) in Yalalag, Oaxaca, showing the variety of white Zapotec

costumes of the region, and dark-skirted Mixe women in the foreground. 1938

and Tetepec (pl. 142; fig. 8 k & l) have a woven colored band on one side of each web, which meet when the pieces are sewn together and form a decorative stripe down the center. On finer examples, the thread for stripes is dyed with a colorant made from the shellfish *Purpura patula pansa*. These cloths are called *trallas*. In many lower Mixtecan settlements they are inexplicably called *huipiles*. It is this nomenclature which brings them into this section.

The *huipil* and the *quechquemitl* are the most important of the decorative textiles belonging to costume in Indian Mexico. Textile decorative elements, including *huipil* design motifs, will be discussed elsewhere.

5. The Quechquemitl

from the Nahuatl, *quechtli* (neck) and *quemitl* (garment)
—Professor Fernando Horcasitas,
verbal communication.

THE *quechquemitl* (pls. 62, 64; fig. 10) is a woman's upper garment and is usually described as capelike. In our opinion this gives a totally wrong impression, as it has no opening except the aperture for the head, while a cape has a vertical opening at the front, back, or side. The term shawllike is equally misleading.

It is also wrongly described as triangular. Regardless of its construction (fig. 10), when the two points are placed one on top of the other, a square of two layers of cloth is formed—with a V for the neck. However, when the garment is put on, it gives somewhat the impression of a triangle due to the horizontal shoulders of the wearer. The *quechquemitl* may be worn with points in front and back or over the shoulders, depending upon the custom in a given village. It is true that the artists who depicted *quechquemitl* in the codices have sometimes drawn small garments, very narrow across the shoulders with narrow long points, suggesting that they were not essentially squares. But artistic license is to be taken into consideration; it is also possible that these early garments were constructed differently. We know that different weaves change the appearance (pl. 53). A gauze weave stretches and is apt to give a long narrow impression, similar to *quechquemitl* in the codices.

We know of three types of *quechquemitl* construction. Type No. 1 is simple, but Nos. 2 and 3 are so ingenious that one wonders how the fashions were initiated and when. Type No. 1, the simplest (fig. 10), is fashioned of two squares of cloth sewn up on two adjacent sides with a neck opening left between. More commonly, a calculated rectangle is folded over to form a square, only one side needing to be sewn together, and a neck opening is left between the two closed adjacent sides.

Type No. 2, the most common, is used in many areas and made of many materials and weaves—usually handwoven. Two rectangles are woven of calculated width and length. The dimensions seem quite standard in each village, but as a general rule have been getting smaller in the last twenty years. The narrow end of each rectangle (fig. 10, type No. 2, a) is sewn to the long side (b) of the other rectangle, with the desired size V neck opening left when points are placed center front.

Of type No. 3 we know only one specimen—a finger gauze-weave silk *quechquemitl* in our collection, probably from the latter part of the last century (pl. 53), and presumably from the state of Puebla. Diagrams of this rare garment have been published by Christensen (1947, p. 135) and Johnson (1953, p. 244). This *quech-*

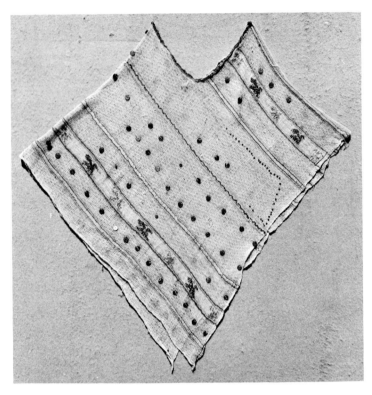

53. A very rare gauze-weave silk *quechquemitl* — age unknown. State of Puebla (Otomí?).

quemitl is fashioned of a single rectangle, 12 by 38 inches. In the center of one long side has been cut a rectangle 6 by 12 inches. To form the garment, the piece is folded over at (c) (fig. 10, type No. 3) so that sides (a) and (b) are joined, the selvage edges of the fragile material sewn with almost invisible stitching of the natural silk. The small piece of clothing forms a 19-inch square, and was probably worn with points center front and back, although we have no data concerning this *quechquemitl*. This garment brings to mind the possibility that *quechquemitl* depicted in the Selden and Bodley Mixtec codices, which have long narrowish points, may have been woven of particular gauze weaves which stretch when hung on the bias.

Russel Davis says (1961, pp. 1–4) a *quechquemitl* was used in pre-Hispanic times that, to our knowledge, is not used today. His conclusion is drawn from observations made on "three fragments of Middle pre-Classic types D I figurines. These feminine figures were said to be from Tlapacoyan, district of Chalco, state of México." The fragments show jacketlike upper gar-

ments which Davis considers to be *quechquemitl*. These he says, are fashioned of two rectangles (as in fig. 10, type No. 2) each twisted once before being sewn together. It is suggested also that rectangles of longer proportion, worn differently, could form a sling for carrying a baby.

Walter Krickeberg (1933, p. 51) says that only noble women used the *quechquemitl* in pre-Conquest times. He also states that this garment was esteemed as very precious in the eyes of the tribes of the Mesa Central.

In Sahagún (1951–1963, Book 10, p. 184) we read of the Totonacs, "They were quite elegant. And since they wove like Huaxteca women, they were wearers of varicolored skirts, varicolored shoulder shawls. Their shoulder shawls were of netting." In this paragraph we see that *quechquemeque* has been translated as shoulder shawl. From what is said in this chapter, it seems probable that the Huastec women were known for their *quechquemitl*, and it may have been that the Totonacs took over the *quechquemitl* from them.

The *quechquemitl* was probably a ceremonial garment. The figures in the Codex Selden are shown wearing this garment sometimes alone and sometimes over a *huipil*. The Codex Selden was painted in the sixteenth or seventeenth century, but depicted events and personages from 794 to 1556. We see very little change in the attire of these personages, and this may be because the artist drew them in the costume of his own time—as did the artists of the Renaissance, who pictured biblical characters in Renaissance dress. Obviously the codices may not be a reliable source for dating costumes. In going over the interpretation of the Codex Selden 3135 (A.2) (Caso, 1964), and the Codex Bodley 2858 (Caso, 1960), both Mixtec, an interesting fact came to light. In the names of noble Mixtec women the word *quechquemitl* often appeared: 2 House "Jeweled Quechquemitl," 4 House "Eagle Quechquemitl," 3 Tiger "War Quechquemitl," 1 Monkey "Quechquemitl Jewel." Although they also wore the *huipil*, this word did not once appear in the names. This would seem to indicate that the *quechquemitl* had to do with rank, and that examining other codices along these lines might be rewarding.

Laurette Séjourné (1962, pl. 4l) pictures a figurine clearly wearing a *quechquemitl* beneath a cape. *Quechquemitl* with exceptionally large neck openings may be seen on archaeological figurines from the Maya area (see pl. 22)—some much larger than in the plate cited. One suspects that this *quechquemitl* is woven in the "curved-weave" technique, as it is definitely rounded in

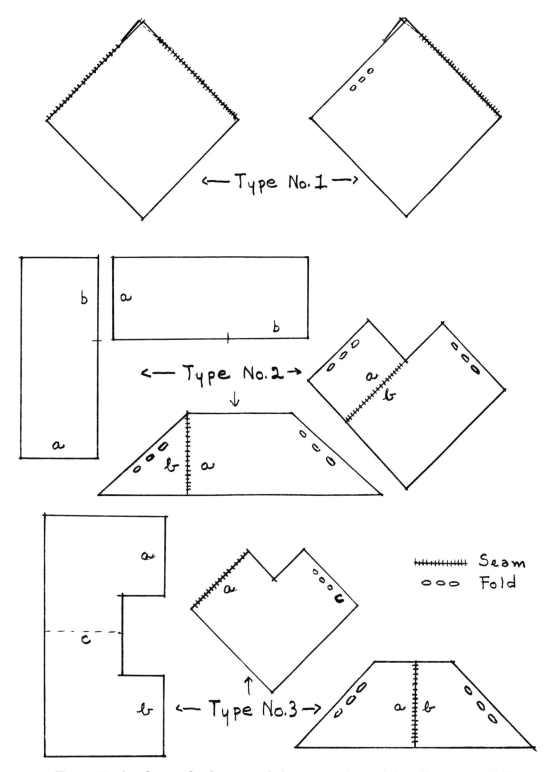

Figure 10. *Quechquemitl* — diagrams of the various forms (after Christensen, 1947, p. 135).

54. A white cotton *quechquemitl* from Xolotla, Puebla, a handsome dark-red wool brocaded band. (Nahua).

front. Some *quechquemitl* on Totonac figurines are so long that they reach the ankles, but these long garments seem to be unusual.

We think of *quechquemitl* as being woven garments, and the statement quoted above, "Their shoulder shawls were of netting," suggests gauze weave. It is possible that—in remote times—garments were netted of fiber and may have been made before the advent of the backstrap loom. We know that netted *tilmatli* were covered with feathers (Sahagún, 1953–1961, Book 9, pp. 91–92), and it is quite possible that *quechquemitl* were also.

The woven cotton *quechquemitl*, to our knowledge, appeared first in classic or pre-classic times. In William Spratling's book (1960, p. 22) we read, "Characteristics of the following, the Classic Epoch, in this early phase differ from the preceding and at the same time show evolution . . . female attire became richer, more ornamental; the quechquemitl was used . . ." "Master Works of Mexican Art" (Gamboa, 1963) shows a beautiful figure of Xilonen, goddess of maize, dressed in a *quechquemitl.* This is Huastec, Pánuco, A.D. 1000–1250 from Tuxpan, Vera Cruz. Frederick Dockstader

(1964, pl. 69) shows a figure of a young Totonac girl wearing a *quechquemitl,* which he dates "300–600."

The *quechquemitl* seems to be a garment originally worn in warm or temperate regions, and then probably taken over by people of the Valley of México from the Totonacs or Huastecs. Before the Conquest these smallish garments were not made of wool, and were therefore not as warm as the long cotton *huipiles.* The women, with some exceptions, now wear blouses under the *quechquemitl,* and take off the latter garments when they get too warm.

In the *Interpretatión del Códice Seldon 3135* (A.2) (Caso, 1964, p. 81 of the commentaries—pp. 6–IV and 87–I of the Códice Selden 3135 [A.2]), we see a princess whose name is 6 Monkey "Serpent Quechquemitl," who goes to make an offering before the goddess 9 Grass. The offering consists of a number of precious objects, including a *huipil,* a skirt, and a *quechquemitl.* The latter garment is adorned with a border of "white Xonecuillis [see Chapter 11] on a black ground, the same as the one worn by the goddess ♀ 9 Grass." *Xonecuillis* are her characteristic symbol. Later the princess 6 Monkey appears wearing a *quechquemitl* with multi-

PLATE III. A Huastec Indian cheese vendor. Tancanhuitz (Ciudad Santos), San Luis Potosí. 1965

colored chevrons—symbols of war. So we observe, according to Caso, that Mixtec royalty wore the *quechquemitl*, and that designs had definite significance and meaning.

Although non-Indian women may buy some *huipiles* to be worn, they are not as easily used with modern clothes as is the *quechquemitl*. In fact, the latter garment has become so popular that it has been taken out of its natural area (north-central Mexico) to Oaxaca, where it has not been worn since pre-Hispanic times, there to be copied in wool by the expert and commercial Zapotecs of Mitla. One of the common sights of Oaxaca City is a Mitla woman with a huge pile of *quechquemitl* on her head, tempting tourists who sit in sidewalk cafes around the plaza. *Quechquemitl* are thus worn all over the world at times, instead of sweaters. Some are black with silver or gold threads, and would surprise and puzzle Indians from the true *quechquemitl* areas of Mexico. However, Sahagún (1951–1963, Book 10, p. 52) mentions that the weaver "provides a metal weft . . ." There is some doubt in our minds about the translation of the word *Tlateputzpaciotia"* (*tepoz*, metal; and *tepotz*, reverse). It is possible that this may refer to "reverse weft"—a weaving technique. Gold and silver threads were apparently used in weaving in Guatemala in pre-Hispanic times (Osborne, 1965, p. 19).

The *quechquemitl* is worn either with points to the front and back (pl. 58), or with the points hanging from the shoulders of the wearer (pl. 63). Although it is smaller than a *huipil*, it is an adaptable garment and serves also as a head covering; or a baby may be wrapped in it or put under it to be fed (we see in the Codex Borgia [1963, pl. 17], Xochiquetzal as a solar goddess suckling a small nude figure).

Smallish objects are sometimes twisted or tied into it, but it does not seem to be as versatile as the *huipil*. Thus one can easily imagine that it functioned as a ceremonial garment, conveying prestige on the person wearing it. However, its chief use now—aside from being worn over the shoulders—is to cover the head. The curved weave *quechquemitl* of Santa Ana Hueytlapan (Otomí) is small, and is put over the head in two distinct ways (pls. 173 & 174). The garment may also be put on the head, and a straw hat worn over it (Huichol, Otomí). In Plate 173 we see the *quechquemitl* worn in a very strange fashion. The ends and sides are turned up into the neck opening, and when it is put on it gives the impression of a child's newspaper soldier's hat (it seems quite un-Indian, perhaps be-

55. This old Huichol woman is wearing a *quechquemitl* as a head covering in the characteristic Huichol manner. Las Guásimas, Nayarit. 1937

cause one does not associate hats with Indian women). Sahagún says (1951–1963, Book 10, p.178), that "the Otomí were very gaudy dressers . . . vain people; that is to say, what there were of capes, of clothing, which were one's special privilege, they took all, they wore all, to be vain people."

The Santa Ana *quechquemitl* is small and rather stiff, which allows it to be worn as in Plate 174, with the curved part over the forehead. With a larger, thinner garment such as that of Tolimán, Querétaro, this is not so feasible, and the longer side is worn over the forehead (pl. 60). The Huichol women sometimes wear this garment as a head covering in a unique way. Their manta (unbleached commercial cloth) *quechquemitl* have small neck openings that go over the head tightly. The garment is put on, and then pulled back over the face (wrong side out), until it hangs over the back of the head (pl. 55).

Quechquemitl are also worn as head coverings in

56. A *quechquemitl* woven in white gauze-patterned weave, from Atla, Puebla. (Nahua).

Huehuetla, Hidalgo, among the Tepehua; but it is a thin gauze garment, and can be tied about the head pirate style, as some of the heavier brocaded garments—such as those embroidered in wool—cannot. The women of this town wear the *quechquemitl* with the points in front, but the weaver in Plate 67 has turned hers somewhat to the side so the points do not interfere with her loom. In Xolotla and Atla, in Puebla (Nahua), the garment is worn three ways—as a head covering, and as a body covering with points either to the front and back, or to the sides. We have been told that among the Tepehuas and Nahuas a married woman wears the garment one way, and an unmarried girl another. We are inclined *not* to believe this (although it was reported by an Indian) until more data are obtained from reliable informants. George M. Foster says (1960, p. 139),

speaking of Spanish costume, that in Largatera the mantilla is removed from the bride and replaced with the handkerchief, which she will wear on her head to mark her as a married woman. He also states that, "In the Basque provinces until recent times women always wore handkerchiefs on their heads as a sign of their status. Only unmarried girls would go bareheaded." These customs, although they may have been common in Mexico, are rapidly dying out. It is difficult, without living for a long time in an area, to obtain information about usages that are obsolete.

Bodil Christensen (verbal information) has seen old Otomí women in San Pablito, Puebla, without any blouses underneath their *quechquemitl*. This same usage has been observed among Totonac and Nahuas in the market at Ahuacatlán, Puebla (information from

Dr. Isabel Kelly). It also is usual in the Nahua village of Chiconcuautla, Puebla, where little girls wear *only* the *quechquemitl*. The custom of wearing no blouse was also common (1960) in the village of Coyutla, Vera Cruz.

As has been mentioned, the *quechquemitl* is sometimes an extra garment, and one may go into a village where it is commonly worn and not see even one. The casual observer would think that it was now obsolete, but if he returned in cool or rainy weather, or at the time of a fiesta, he probably would find many women wearing them. The seasonal aspect, of vital importance, is seldom sufficiently stressed by investigators.

Atla, Puebla, has three types of *quechquemitl:* one a lacy figured gauze weave (pl. 56), and the other two, also of gauze, one brocaded with dark-red wool yarn. On the whole, Indian women are well acclimated and seem to feel cold less than do their *mestizo* neighbors. A Virgin from the church of Alta was photographed being carried in a procession (Montoya Briones, 1964, Pl. XL, p. 146), dressed in a beautiful adult-sized *quechquemitl* of the gauze type, with a wide wool brocaded band down the front. In this photograph, points of the garment are worn at the sides, and the small figure is completely covered. The custom of dressing church saints with indigenous garments is now very rarely seen in Mexico.

In Cuetzalan, Puebla, where women wear the huge *rodete* of green and purple wool, a special gauze-weave *quechquemitl* is worn over this (pl. 177). We were told in Cuetzalan in 1939 that one *quechquemitl* was worn over another by young girls, but according to our own observation this is not a common practice in other villages. However, Eduard Seler says (n.d., Vol. 3, Part 3, p. 3) of Huichol women at the early part of this century, before blouses were worn, that they "are accustomed to wear as many of these *quechquemitl* one over the other as the means or fondness of their husbands permit." Even in pre-Hispanic times the *quechquemitl* was often worn over a *huipil*, though we have not seen it pictured over another *quechquemitl*.

A rich woman may own as many as four *quechquemitl* (Huastec), and a poor one only one, or—sadly enough—none, as we found out from a Huastec woman who sold hers to us. When we returned to her house to take photographs, she requested that we bring the garment, whereupon we realized that she had sold her last one. She then informed us that with what we had paid, "I'm going to get a new and better one, and have some *centavos* left over."

The *quechquemitl* seems to have survived more nearly in its original state than has the *huipil*. It retains its Indian character to a greater degree, so that—with a few exceptions, it is not laden with commercial ribbons, lace and rickrack as are some *huipiles* today. Now, it is usually worn over a blouse, and the blouse is often highly adorned. *Quechquemitl* from some villages such as Papantla, Vera Cruz, and La Ceiba, Puebla, are made of commercial cloth.

Worn today over a blouse, the *quechquemitl* is a secondary garment. For this reason, we believe it has tended to disappear more rapidly than the *huipil*. It is worn for custom, for warmth, and for beauty. But the tradition is dying out, as are many old customs. Because of the blouse, it is not needed for modesty; and for warmth the *rebozo* may be substituted, and makes the woman feel more comfortable in an acculturated community.

In size the *quechquemitl* varies less than does the *huipil*, for it is always worn with a skirt. The *huipil*, in contrast, may reach only to the waist, or may fall from shoulder to calf, to toes, or to the ground—and in many cases may be worn without a skirt.

Handwoven *quechquemitl* weaves and materials vary as with the *huipil;* but in one important *quechquemitl* area (to be mentioned below) garments are woven half of cotton and half of wool. This never occurs to our knowledge with *huipiles*. Cotton *huipiles* may be brocaded or embroidered with wool. *Huipiles* of wool are apt to be decorated with wool, but *huipiles* woven of either material do not have large background areas woven of the opposite material.

Quechquemitl from San Pablito, Puebla (Otomí) (pl. 63); Santa Ana Hueytlalpan, Hidalgo (Otomí) (pl. 170; Chapter 16); and Zontecomatlán, Vera Cruz (Nahua), though woven of heavy white cotton, contain near the lower border very wide bands of red wool, put in with the "curved-weave" technique.

On the whole the *quechquemitl*, although it is a smaller garment than the *huipil*, has a fantastic variety of surface decoration. The surfaces of a good many *quechquemitl* are covered almost in their entirety with embroidery (pls. 144 & 146), whereas *huipiles* have more woven brocaded decoration.

Out of the forty-five *quechquemitl* which we examined, from twenty-five villages or areas, all but three were of type No. 2 (fig. 10). In this predominant group, sizes were found to vary surprisingly little. Below are some detailed observations with respect to the *quechquemitl*.

57. A rare narrow *quechquemitl* from Sasaltitla, Vera Cruz. (Nahua). Collection of Bodil Christensen.

For the convenience of the reader, we are giving measurements of *quechquemitl* (regardless of manner of wearing) when laid out as in type No. 2, where they form a square (this method seems to give the clearest impression of the garment). If the reader wishes to find the length of rectangles used to form a given *quechquemitl*, it is obviously only necessary to add the length of one side of the total square to the length of one side of the neck opening.

Of peoples we know, only two have *quechquemitl* fashioned as in type No. 1. These are the Huichol (pl. 163), and the Nahua-speaking village of Cuatlamayán, San Luis Potosí (pl. VII). Probably other northern *quechquemitl*, now extinct (Cora, Tepehuane, Tarahumara, for instance), were formed thus also. All traditional Huichol *quechquemitl* known to us since 1937 have been type No. 1, either of two squares of *manta*, each side averaging 28–31 inches, or a rectangle folded over to form such a square (sometimes two square bandana handkerchiefs are used).

Of two equal-sized Cuatlamayán *quechquemitl* in our collection (squares, 26½ inches on each side), one is formed of a folded *manta* rectangle. The other—a particularly fine example—is of heavy plain-weave handwoven white cotton (pl. VII). It is formed essentially as type No. 1 is, although the material is curiously pieced—not as a system of construction, but because of a shortage of cloth at hand. Almost always

garments are quite exactly calculated, but occasionally one finds piecing needed to complete the two squares (type No. 1) or two rectangles (type No. 2). The two rectangles (type No. 2) of one fine old handwoven Tepehua garment from Pisa Flores, Hidalgo, are pieced at each end with *manta,* and the all-over embroidery is carefully continued throughout (pl. IV a).

Garments of type No. 1 construction are apt to be considerably larger than those of type No. 2; Plate 163 shows how large a 29-inch square looks when worn by an Indian woman. Of some forty-five *quechquemitl* we have examined, only one of type No. 2 is larger than this one, and most are decidedly smaller. A very beautiful handwoven, solidly brocaded *quechquemitl,* said to be used only in a dance in Angahuan, Michoacán (not a *quechquemitl* area), forms a 35-inch square, the largest we have seen. Antonio García Cubas (1876, Pl. 4, Part 2) shows a *quechquemitl* from Chilchota, Michoacán (referred to in our Chapter 1). We know of no existing example, so cannot say whether the garment was large or small, or whether it was used in combination with the *huipil.* Of type No. 2 construction the second largest we have seen, a dark-blue wool garment with small white stripes, forms a 24-inch square, and is from Santa Anita Zacuala, Hidalgo. Although the village belongs to the municipality of Acaxochitlán, one sees Santa Anita women busily spinning while they sit in front of their little mounds of foodstuffs in the market of Tulancingo.

The most unusual *quechquemitl* we have seen (type No. 2) is a curious garment from Sasaltitla, Vera Cruz (Nahua), (pl. 57) deeply covered with red-wool looped stitches on the outer surface, and showing a geometric pattern on the reverse. (collection of B. Christensen) It is formed of two 24-by-4¾-inch rectangles joined end-to-side, forming a 14½-inch square. This very narrow neckpiece is more a piece of decoration than a garment. One would think it was meant to be a border attached to strips of plain material perhaps, but according to the collector, it is complete as it stands. The next in size (a 17½-inch square) is from Ixmiquilpan, Hidalgo (Otomí), a modest dark-blue cotton garment, points worn over the shoulders. This is ikat dyed.

In some cases we have been able to study as many as four garments from a given village, and we find that the adult *quechquemitl* measurements are surprisingly standard for each locality—in other words, the size of the rectangle is known to produce the desired garment and size of neck opening. However, in some areas *quechquemitl* are made smaller than they were twenty-

58. A Huastec woman of Tamaletón, San Luis Potosí, with an embroidered *quechquemitl*. 1964

lapa and Pantepec (both Puebla) wear their very richly brocaded and embroidered handwoven *quechquemitl* as upper garments—head through the neck opening, points front and back (pl. 133). Many Otomí villages, those of the Hidalgo Ixmiquilpan and Mezquital area and the Sierra de Puebla, wear the points over the shoulders, although their garments are extremely different from each other in every other respect.

The beautiful Otomí white cotton and red wool, curved-weave and embroidered *quechquemitl* of San Pablito, Puebla (pl. 63), and the very small unadorned ones—also woven in the "round-shoulder technique"—from Santa Ana Hueytlalpan, Hidalgo—are worn rounded points to the sides. Yet some Otomí areas, far removed from the above, wear their very different *quechquemitl* with points front and back—among them the nearly extinct ikat-dyed silk or artificial silk handwoven garments of Tolimán, Querétaro (pl. 62), and the fine large wool ones of Amealco, in the same state.

The Nahua-speaking peoples who wear *quechquemitl* are found chiefly in the states of San Luis Potosí Hidalgo, Puebla, and Vera Cruz. To our knowledge, most Nahua villages wear their *quechquemitl* with points front and back. Exceptions may be Atla and Xolotla, Puebla—villages each having two or three types of garments, which in itself is most unusual. Bodil Christensen gives this verbal information, saying that she has seen garments with points worn in the front and garments with points worn on the sides in both villages. Some *quechquemitl* having particularly large neck openings tend to shift about to some extent, or may be temporarily shifted for convenience while engaging in a particular task.

The Huastecs of San Luis Potosí in the area of Tancanhuitz, Aquismón, Tamaletón, and Tzitol wear their *quechquemitl* with the points center front (pl. 58). Mazahua *quechquemitl* we saw in 1939–1940 in the area of Ixtlahuaca and San Felipe del Progreso, both state of México (pl. 59), were worn with points over the shoulders.

Quechquemitl are woven today of wool, of artificial silk, or of cotton—cotton ones predominating. The all wool *quechquemitl* from cold high regions in the state of México have been going out of style for some years, in favor of sleezy commercial cotton *rebozos*. Mazahua Indian women from the northeastern part of the state (El Oro, San Felipe del Progreso, and other villages) had splendid wool costumes up into the 1940's, but

59. A Mazahua mother and daughter from near San Felipe del Progreso, state of México. 1938

five years ago. This is also true of *huipiles.* The reasons may be simply change of fashion, but a more apt reason is the saving of time and materials. In Santa Ana Hueytlalpan, Hidalgo (Chapter 16), *quechquemitl* are truly "neck garments," whereas specimens collected some years ago were much larger. Probably no blouse was worn under the earlier ones.

In the *quechquemitl* areas that we know, the greater number of garments are worn with points front and back. One cannot say that each linguistic group always wears its *quechquemitl* in the same manner. In the Papantla, Vera Cruz (Totonac) area, the head is not put through the neck opening of the large organdie *quechquemitl* (to our knowledge); instead it is casually thrown over the head or doubled over the shoulders (pl. 5). On the other hand, the Totonacs of Mecapa-

judging from the present-day attire of Mazahua women seated on sidewalks in downtown Mexico City, selling small foodstuffs, only fine handwoven wool patterned belts are still worn. In place of the old costume, one sees several layers of brilliant artificial silk skirts and ruffled Victorian style blouses worn one on top of another for warmth.

A handwoven wool *quechquemitl* of hand-spun yarns in our collection—of the type seen in Plate 59 (region of San Felipe Progreso, México, 1940), type No. 2 construction—contains handsome 1-to-1½-inch white-edged warp stripes of dark-blue, purple, and pink wool. It is formed of two rectangles, 20 by 28 inches, worn with the points off the shoulders—44 inches from point to point.

Encouraging to relate, we saw quite a group of women from Amealco, Querétaro (Otomí) in the Sunday market of San Juan del Río in 1964, dressed in fine wool *quechquemitl* and skirts. The upper garments were of black wool with small white stripes, multicolored embroidery about the neck, and a multicolored fringe; the garments were type No. 2, with the points worn center front. We were unable to purchase such a *quechquemitl*—the women were very shy, and very serious, and busy buying piles of *ixtle ayates* to take elsewhere to sell.

Further north in Querétaro, we visited in the same year the Otomí village of Tolimán, to study the tie-dyed silk (now artificial silk) *quechquemitl* which used to be made there. We found very few weavers left, although some good wool bags are still made. Formerly a fine costume was worn in this village—which had no road reaching it. A road was under construction in 1964, off the Mexico City-Querétaro Highway to the north, but even before this venture was initiated, the costume had virtually vanished. We found only a very old woman and her middle-aged daughter who still wove the tie-dyed silk (now artificial silk) *quechquemitl* and belts, which were distinctive of this locality. Some tie-dyed cotton *quechquemitl* and belts are still woven. Plates 60 and 61 show the preparing of a skein of cotton warp thread for tie-dyeing. Rings of light *ixtle* fiber are wrapped closely around the skein every ½ inch. The spot covered by the *ixtle* resists dye, and the belt pattern results (*sale pinto* [spotted]—white where the strings are tied).

An old *quechquemitl* and a modern one, both from Tolimán, were compared (pl. 62 shows the old one); the chief differences were the far greater clarity of the tie-dyed designs in the old garment (probably made forty to fifty years ago), and the quality of the real silk thread. The old garment is fashioned of two rectangular, backstrap-woven strips (one long strip has been cut in two), 14 by 31 inches, forming a 22-inch square. The 14-inch cloth width has a predominance of *solferino* (strong purplish-pink color) warp stripes, broken by small stripes of red and white with one ⅞-inch yellow stripe, and a bright green tie-dyed design, near the outer edge of the two woven rectangles. In the body of the predominate *solferino*, some bright blue and white tie-dyed stripes occur. The weft is red cotton thread, the warp comprising the tie-dyed silk. The modern *quechquemitl* has similar color arrangements, but poorer workmanship and thread; it is made of two pieces, 12 by 30 inches, making a 21-inch square garment, somewhat smaller than the old *quechquemitl*. In the new garment, a well-worked ¾-inch wide *randa* (decorative joining) unites the two pieces. This in itself represents an immense amount of work with needle and orange artificial-silk thread.

The Tolimán *quechquemitl* are worn with the point in the center front, over a white cotton blouse with a plain gathered medium-low round neck. They are also worn loosely over the head for protection from the sun (pl. 60).

Elsewhere cotton *quechquemitl* are common, and range from heavy white plain weaves, either brocaded or embroidered (or both within a single garment), to lace like gauze weaves. Of the heavy white cotton garments, some of the handsomest are those of San Pablito, Puebla (pls. 63 & 64), and Santa Ana Hueytlalpan, Hidalgo (pls. 170, 173 & 174)—fashioned in the "round-shoulder technique" with wide red wool border bands. The former (Christensen, 1947, p. 128) "may be divided into two main groups: (1) Those with a broad woolen band . . . always a brilliant red," 6 to 9½ inches wide, "and (2) those with a narrow woolen band," the narrow ones being purple or dull purplish red. Plate 63 shows a group 1 garment, which has four design areas worked in black and purplish-red wool cross-stitch, in conventionalized bisymmetric patterns of large eight-sided star-shaped flowers, and other flower forms and decorative stem patterns. Plate 64 shows an example of group 2 with narrow (2⅜-inch) purple band with a center stripe made up of two orange wool warp threads. The large white areas above the wool band are here decorated quite at random with bold black and red motifs (monkey, double-headed eagle, deer, domestic

60. An Otomí woman with a handwoven *quechquemitl* of artificial silk over her head. She is tying threads to be used in the tie-dye process. Tolimán, Querétaro. 1963

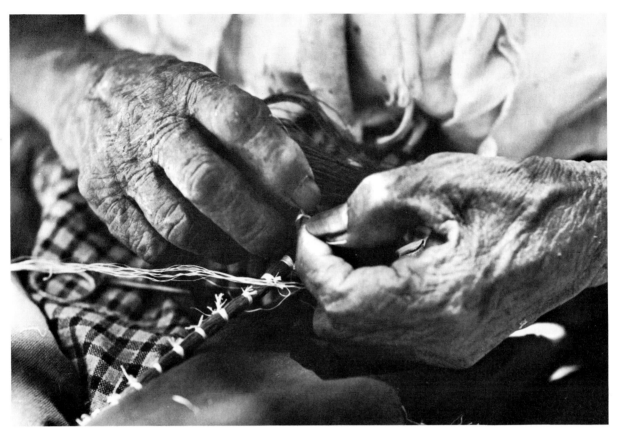

61. A close up of the thread-tying process, preparatory to making a cotton belt. Tolíman, Querétaro (Otomí). 1963

62. An old tie-dyed silk *quechquemitl* from Tolimán, Querétaro — made in 1920 or earlier; largely *solferino* in color. (Otomí).

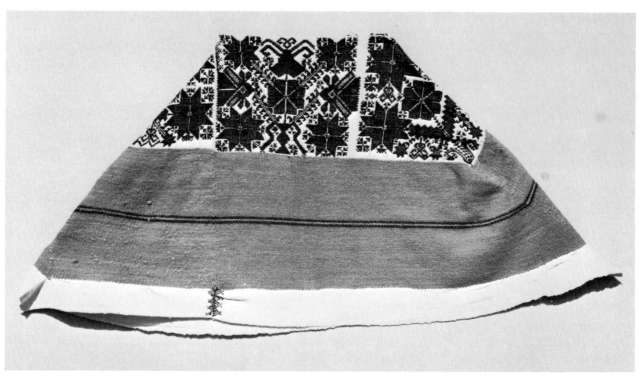

63. A curved-weave *quechquemitl* from San Pablito, Puebla, with a wide red wool band at the bottom and conventionalized plant designs embroidered about the neck opening. (Otomí).

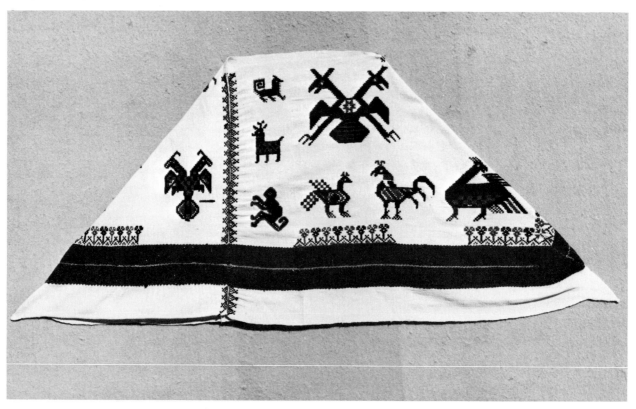

64. A *quechquemitl* from San Pablito, Puebla, having a narrow wool band and prominently executed double-headed birds, monkeys, and other embroidered elements freely placed. (Otomí).

65. An ancient clay figurine (Oaxaca), showing a *rodete* and a *quechquemitl.*

66. A woman, in a handwoven white *quechquemitl,* who came into the large town of Huauchinango from Huilacapixtla, Puebla. (Nahua). 1963

fowl), and a handsome joining stitch embroidery between the rectangular construction lines. We wonder whether the *quechquemitl* shown on the Oaxaca clay figure (pl. 65) must not have been woven in a curved technique.

Some other groups have a heavy white cotton *quechquemitl* with a very narrow dark red wool "curved weave" border, plus some other corner decoration (see Chapter 18). Others—like that of Cuatlamayán, San Luis Potosí (pl. VII); San Francisco Chapantla, Hidalgo (pl. 144); or an old handwoven one from the region of Tancanhuitz, San Luis Potosí (pl. 146)—all rely on multicolored embroidered areas or all-over embroidery for decoration, rather than decoration fashioned as brocading during the weaving proper.

We have already mentioned that women in Cuetzalan use gauze-weave *quechquemitl* (see also Chapter 18). In the Nahua region of Huauchinango, Puebla

(northwest of Cuetzalan), are other villages where gauze weaves bearing a resemblance to those of Cuetzalan may be seen. An example from Coacuila, Puebla, however has no extra adornment or edging of any kind.

From Huilacapixtla, Puebla, comes a heavier white *quechquemitl* with ¼-inch plain-weave weft stripes of a contrasting thread, which when washed puckers to give a seersucker effect (pl. 66). The effect is achieved by putting weft stripes in loosely in certain areas, to contrast with more tightly pulled threads in other areas.

From Atla, Puebla, comes a *quechquemitl* finely woven in "figured gauze." It is described by Laura E. Start (1963, p. 62) as containing "several types of gauze weave . . . plain gauze, checkered tabby, and plain, with Peruvian and ogee weaves for chevron, horse, and figure motifs." Our example contains 3½-inch rows of animals, humans on horseback, and double-headed birds—the work resembling, though not identical to, that on the heavier Zapotec Choapan *huipil.*

The processes used to decorate present-day *quechquemitl* include embroidery, brocading, and figured gauze. As far as we know, direct painting is not used at present (1965) on any *quechquemitl* as it is on the *huipiles* of Usila, Oaxaca (Chinantec). There is, however, a present-day method of color stamping for textile decoration, known to us from two places only: Peñoles, Oaxaca (pl. 219); and Huehuetla, Hidalgo. The process in the latter village is used on the *quechquemitl*, and will be described here.

We have no information concerning the antiquity of this technique, which we can only describe as a form of stamping, although it does not entail pressing with a rigid object (*i.e.* one of clay or wood). The Huehuetla process consists of impressing the color from areas of brocading and embroidery, worked in nonfast yarns, onto plain background parts through folding and steaming (pls. 68 & 69).

The process has been photographed, and a description of the steps follows: Our informant, who is seen at her loom in Plate 67, fortunately for us had two recently completed *quechquemitl* rectangles (fig. 10, type No. 2) ready for the stamping process. We wished one web to be kept, for comparison, in its natural state, and our Tepehua friend demonstrated with the second web. In Plate 68 a we see her at the river washing the textile thoroughly with both powdered and bar soap. After two washings and rinsings, she gives it a third soaping and leaves the soap in the cloth. Plate 68 b shows her carefully folding the woven rectangle, so that the deep-red wool brocaded areas are placed directly on top of the plain background spaces. In Plate 68 c she is pushing the damp neatly folded web into a dried corn husk (such as is used for wrapping *tamales*). She uses two or more husks, which very adequately cover the folded web. In Plate 68 d we see her tying two narrow strips of fiber torn from another husk around the package. In Plate 68 e she has taken the wrapped textile into her house, and placed it in the center of the clay *comal* under which are coals from a wood fire set between stones. The heat steams the wrapped textile, and causes the dark-red color to stamp itself unclearly on plain light areas. She turns it over a number of times with her hand, leaving it altogether about ten minutes or a bit less. We were told that some women place a half gourd over the "*tamal*" to hold in the steam.

67. A Tepehua woman weaving a *quechquemitl* strip. Huehuetla, Hidalgo, 1965.

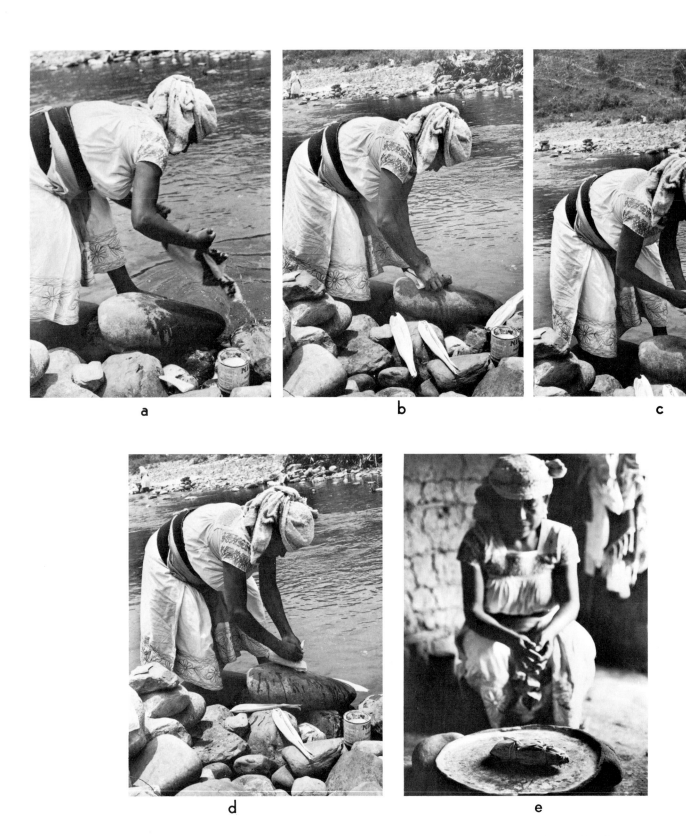

68. Preparing the *quechquemitl* strip for stamping (a dyeing process). Huehuetla, Hidalgo (Tepehua). 1965

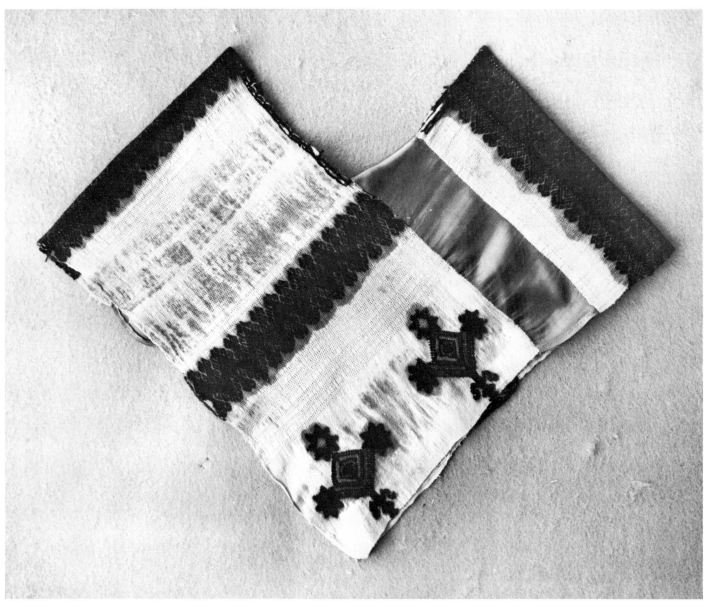

69. A finished Huehuetla *quechquemitl* showing the irregular markings resulting from the stamping process. Huehuetla, Hidalgo (Tepehua). 1965

6. The Skirt

THE TRUE INDIAN SKIRT of pre-Conquest origin is the "wrap-around," formed of a long hand-woven rectangle of cloth wound about the bare limbs, fastened with a sash or secured by simply tucking in one corner. The rectangle may consist of one, two, three, and occasionally more loom lengths sewn side by side. In some areas the long rectangle is left open, and in others it is sewn together end to end to form a tube. We term both as "wrap-around," because each is arranged about the body for each wearing. One should remember that the loom length of the skirt becomes what is usually known as skirt width when worn, and the width on the loom is actually the length on the wearer (fig. 12). Skirt measurements given in the following discussion are average adult sizes—as several sizes may be woven in a village, and two or more styles of skirts.

There are as many weaves, colors, sizes, and modes of wearing these often very graceful skirts as there are names for them—*manta, lia, costal, sábana, enredo,* are some of the Spanish terms. Each linguistic group has also one or more Indian name (*chincuete, posahuanco, cuelpachuet,* for example). Zoque women living on the outskirts of Tuxtla Gutiérrez, Chiapas, where customs were changing rapidly some years ago (1940), said of themselves, *"Ella es de costal"* (she is of—wears—the wrap-around skirt), or *"Ella es de enagua"* (she wears a gathered skirt of commercial cloth, or treadle-loomed cloth from Comitán, Chiapas).

Out of some thirty-five wrap-around-skirt villages we have visited, with another fifteen we know about, at least twenty-five still (1965) wear backstrap-loomed material for skirts; whereas as long ago as 1936 Lila O'Neale says of Guatemalan skirts (1945, p. 163), "They are practically all woven on treadle looms by professionals." Some villages in Mexico weave their own skirt webs; others purchase them from weaving centers; still others wear wrap-around skirts of treadle-loomed material or of commercial cloth.

Skirts are woven in plain weaves, basket weaves, rep weaves, and some wool skirts in diagonal weaves. Some fine old cochineal-dyed skirts from the valley of Oaxaca contained lozenge patterns. Fibers in use today are cotton and wool, although some *ixtle* and other fibers have been used until recent years. For some backstrap-loomed cotton skirts, hand-spun thread is employed; but more and more commercial material is replacing it. When wool is used it is likely to be hand-spun, and sheep abound in many of the colder areas (Mixteca Alta, Oaxaca; villages surrounding San Cristóbal de las Casas, Chiapas; Toluca, state of México; and some high Morelos areas).

Wool skirts are apt to be dark in color, usually natural black, or brown, or mixed (Hueyapan, Morelos

a. A Tepéhua *quechquemitl* from Pisa Flores, Hidalgo, showing the same design over the shoulders as is used in Huehuetla (Tepéhua), *quechquemitl*, and the same general wide lower band pattern as is used in certain Totonac *quechquemitl*.

b. A detail of a brocaded woman's *huipil* from San Bartolomé de los Llanos, Chiapas (Tzotzil). Here the white and colored brocading is pulled up to give strong raised patterns.

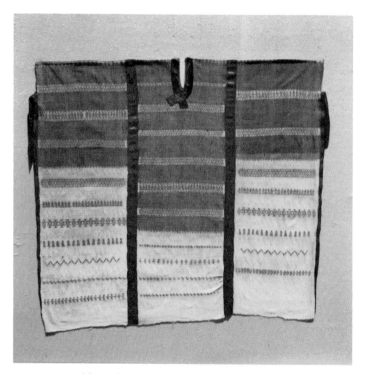

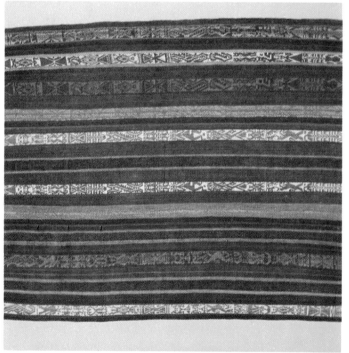

c. A wedding *huipil* brocaded with cochineal-dyed silk. Within the solid red-purple areas, and in horizontal rows below, a few other colors are introduced very delicately in the brocaded rows of human figures and bird designs. Ixtayutla, Oaxaca (Mixtec).

d. A very old and rare striped skirt from Tututepec, Oaxaca (Mixtec), displaying shellfish-dyed warp stripes and many beltlike elaborately patterned bands throughout.

PLATE IV

—pl. 70); or anil-dyed dark blue; white wool is rare (San Pablito, Puebla). Wool skirts have less pattern today than cotton ones, but a few are striped (Temoaya, state of México, and other villages in the Toluca area). In wool skirts in collections made twenty to forty years ago, stripes occur in garments from the Oaxaca villages of Yalalag, San Pedro Quiatoni, and Mitla. But such skirts are no longer woven. The most striking old wool skirt with stripes was the deep rose cochineal-red one from Mitla, in handsome warp-face patterned weave with ¼-inch solid greenish-black stripes containing zigzag and curvilinear running designs on a red background. A very few coarsely woven Mitla skirt lengths of commercially dyed red wool are still seen in tourist shops for use as couch covers.

Cotton wrap-around skirts sometimes are white (Amatlán, Vera Cruz; Cuatlamayán, San Luis Potosí; Cuetzalan, Puebla; Jamiltepec, Oaxaca); natural-tan cotton (or imitation) with white stripes (Yalalag, San Pedro Quiatoni, Yaeé, all Oaxaca); or dark blue (Copala, Oaxaca, and Oxchuc, Chiapas, among others). All the black cotton wrap-around skirts we know are of commercial cloth (Tancanhuitz, San Luis Potosí; San José Miahuatlán, Puebla). Colored stripe patterns bring to mind first of all, (1) the many variations of blue, purple, and red warp-striped skirts woven in Pinotepa de Don Luis, Huaxpaltepec, and other villages in the Mixteca Baja; (2) the handwoven multicolored striped *refajos* (wrap-around skirt) of some Popoluca villages in Vera Cruz— for example, Amomeloya (Foster, 1940, fig. 6); (3) the firmly woven yellow, red, green, and white striped skirts of Cosoleacaque, Vera Cruz (Nahua)—which are still very much in evidence, as we witnessed at the early May fiesta of Otatitlán, Vera Cruz (1964); and finally (4) the herb-dyed green striped skirt (almost extinct) of the Mixe villages of Mixistlán and Yacochi, Oaxaca.

Of skirts in pre-Conquest times and after, we read in the Florentine Codex (Sahagún, 1951–1963, Book 2, p. 93), "some had [designs of] hearts, some were [embroidered] with a mat design like birds' gizzards, some were ornamented like coverlets, some had spiral or leaf [designs], some were of plain, fine weave. All had borders and fringes; all [the women] wore skirts with borders." Whereas skirts in early times contained painted designs, complicated woven patterns, embroidery, and so forth, very few skirts today are as elaborate as the *huipil* and the *quechquemitl*, or contain as many decorative elements.

The shellfish-dyed purple cotton skirt (which has a dark-blue warp and a discreet yellow stripe), so prized along the Isthmus of Tehuantepec, is now almost a thing of the past; completely gone is the multicolored Tututepec skirt (pl. IV d), with its elaborate beltlike bands containing animal and plant designs with *caracol*-purple and cochineal-dyed silk. According to informants in the Mixteca Baja area, similar fiesta *posahuancos* were woven and worn in both Mechoacán and Huazolotitlán, Oaxaca, up to perhaps forty or fifty years ago. We obtained the example shown in Plate IV d in the village of San Pedro Atoyac, although it was said to have been purchased in Tututepec. Today some wraparound skirts are embroidered, but for patterned weaving one thinks chiefly of the white Jamiltepec skirts (called *sábanas*) with raised single-faced multicolored weft stripes (brocaded) of zigzag and chevron patterns in wool or commercial embroidery cotton (pl. 225).

Both a wool skirt and a cotton one may be worn in the same village (Copala, Oaxaca; San Pablito, Puebla). Often the skirt for gala wear is larger and, in temperate climates, is of wool for greater show, as the wool may be brought in from afar (Yalalag, Oaxaca; Cuetzalan, Puebla; San Pedro Quiatoni, Oaxaca). Skirts are still woven for little girls in only a few localities that we know of (Ojitlán, Jamiltepec, and San Andrés Chicahuaxtla, Oaxaca; and Chamula, Chiapas), but where small girls are still dressed in semi-indigenous costume usually commercial *manta* is used (Cuetzalan, Puebla; Temoaya, state of México).

Women who wear skirts at ankle length need at least 36–38 inches of cloth, in spite of short stature, because skirts are brought up high on the figure, well above the waistline, and usually surplus cloth is turned down several inches inside or outside over the belt. For a ruff standing up about the waist, above the belt and in front only, see the women from San José Miahuatlán, Puebla, in Plate 179. Women and little girls of Oxchuc, Chiapas (Tzeltal), also wear large ruffs in front, and their *huipiles* hang over on the outside. They pride themselves on looking, indeed, very pregnant, all of the time.

One-web skirts are rather rare (unless the single width is sewn on to a section of *manta* or other fabric at the top), because backstrap-loom weaving does not prove manageable in more than 30-inch widths, and about 22 inches is average. An old single-web dark-red wool skirt in our collection has a 36-inch loom width— a most unusual backstrap-loom width, no doubt woven

70. A market scene with women in *ixtle* shoes; one woman is in a dark-brown wool costume, another in blue. Hueyapan, Morelos (Nahua). 1963

by a man (in Tlacolula, Mitla, or Teotitlán del Valle—all Oaxaca). Its four selvages prove the loom type used.

Anil-dyed blue or black wool skirts woven by the prolific women weavers of Santa Ana Hueytlalpan, Hidalgo (pl. 170) are also single web, up to 36 inches or more in loom width. San Andrés Chicahuaxtla, Oaxaca (pl. 235), has the smallest single-web wrap-around skirt, reaching usually only to the knees and measuring 25–26 by 61–62 inches.

Most other one-web skirts we know have a top section of *manta* to add sufficient length to bring the skirts to the instep, ankle, or calf. Usually the top section is not meant to show in the assembled costume, and is worn (as in Yalalag, Oaxaca, and Amatlán, Vera Cruz) with a longish *huipil*, only the handwoven skirt web showing below it. In Temoaya and other Toluca-area Otomí villages, the *manta* upper section shows in the assembled costume, because short upper garments are worn (pl. 169, fig. 8 b).

Two-web skirts predominate, because, obviously, two convenient loom widths of 19–24 inches sewn side by side make an average ankle-length skirt, regardless of mode of wearing in whatever village or area. Examples have been found in wool (Ocotepec, Cuquila, Peñoles, and Copala, Oaxaca; Cuetzalan, Puebla; Hueyapan, Morelos) and in cotton (Sayultepec, Santiago Nuyóo, Yalalag—all Oaxaca).

Some two-web skirts are of great size, because of unusual modes of wearing them. For example, see the large old Tuxtla Gutiérrez (Zoque) skirt (*coastal—sack*) (pl. 248); the San Bartolomé de los Llanos (Tzotzil) skirt (pl. 71), and that of Mixistlán or Yacochi, Oaxaca (Mixe), (pl. 37). The first mentioned skirt measures 64 inches in width (wearer's length) and requires the aid of another person to arrange, with its unusual *bolsa* (bag) (fig. 12.) One Zoque weaver said some years ago that the *bolsa* is only for show (*lujo*), but her husband laughingly remarked that it is provided in order that when women go to a fiesta, they can steal whatever they wish, hide it in the *bolsa*, and not be discovered! (Cordry, 1941, p. 84). The old handwoven herb-dyed Mixe skirt, is worn with the 16–18 inches of surplus material folded over on the outside. This skirt is formed of two 28-inch webs. We read in O'Neale (1949, p. 113) that a long tubular skirt is the South American "tipoy," worn to make a double section over the hips, Mixe fashion, or with the upper section pulled up about the shoulders.

Another two-web skirt of exceptional size (woven width) in our collection is a diagonal-weave black wool garment from Ocotepec, Oaxaca, (Mixtec). We have not seen it worn, but judge that the extra cloth of its unusual 56-inch width is turned down inside. Very large skirts may be used in very cold climates for extra warmth, and also for show. The wealth of the wearer is thus made apparent. Lengths and widths of woven skirts are not always standardized within a village. Sometimes they are made large to allow for growth.

In towns where middle length or long *huipiles* are worn, a skirt is used only for fiesta or gala wear (Amusgos and Zacatepec, Oaxaca). On the other hand, *quechquemitl* villagers must always wear skirts, as do women of hot coastal villages where no upper garment is worn a great deal of the time.

The three-web skirts are chiefly the many-patterned striped cotton ones of the Mixteca Baja, made principally in Pinotepa de Don Luis and Huaxpaltepec, both in the district of Jamiltepec, Oaxaca. These have anil-dyed blue backgrounds with purple stripes. Thread for the purple stripes is dyed with shellfish or with analine dye. These skirts also have stripes of cochineal-dyed dark-red silk thread called *hiladillo*. Each combination is for a particular kind of skirt (everyday or wedding), and each village has its own patterns. Every Sunday in the market of Pinotepa Nacional, one sees a row of seated women from Pinotepa de Don Luis with a number of skirts neatly piled on the ground for sale. Usually these are everyday skirts; finer gala ones are usually made to order. In plate XIII at the Jamiltepec New Year's Day fiesta, women of several villages are looking at skirts from Pinotepa de Don Luis. These handsome rectangles, fashioned of three loom webs approximately 15 by 70 inches, sewn together lengthwise, are a pleasure to see. They are worn in a dozen or more villages. When at home these women wear only skirts (with no pleats or extra fullness) and belts; and no upper garment. Unfortunately, self-consciousness is coming into the picture, and in several villages very ugly aprons with bibs are now being worn by young girls—or blouses of a sort.

Mysteriously, these saronglike skirts seem always to allow ease of movement in the many positions assumed by people who live close to the ground—largely without chairs, benches, or stools. Whether kneeling to spin or weave, squatting on haunches by household fires, or seated by mounds of produce in a market, these women

71. San Bartolomé de los Llanos women by the fountain in their village. (Tzotzil). 1940

display a grace comparable to that of the women of Bali and Sumatra.

The skirts of the Mixteca Baja will probably not die out for many years, even though the thread will be neither hand-spun nor dyed by hand. Already a few *mestizos* born in the region who speak Mixtec are bringing in commercial threads, (and giving permanents to young Indian girls anxious to follow *mestizo* ways). These are means of making friends and cajoling the older Indian women into parting with fine textiles to sell to collectors and museums. The weavers can produce more and earn more by using commercial threads, but results invariably bear the mark of the machine age, though webs are still handwoven.

The only skirt we know made up of more than three handwoven webs sewn side by side is the gala tube skirt of wool (and the everyday one of cotton) of San Pablito, Puebla (Otomí) — both following the same form. The bottom of the 40-inch gala skirt has an 8-inch dark-blue wool band followed by three white wool webs of the same width, and an equal width of blue plaid cotton *chiapaneca*, (*manta*-lined) at the top. Formerly these white wool skirts for very special wear had a curious 11-inch bottom web of a tapestry-like purple and black wool, said to have been especially woven in the city of Puebla, and used chiefly in the village of Santa Monica, near San Pablito.

Some backstrap-loomed skirts are made in the villages where they are worn (Yalalag, Peñoles, and Cuquila, Oaxaca; Santa Ana Hueytlalpan, Hidalgo; Temoaya, state of México; Acatlán, Guerrero; Cosoleacaque, Vera Cruz). Certain villages purchase skirt webs from other villages where the same Indian language is spoken. There are exceptions—for example, Zacatepec, Oaxaca (Mixtec) buys from Sayultepec, Oaxaca (Mixtec); but so do the women of Amusgos, Oaxaca, who speak a different tongue. Some San Pablito (Otomí) skirt strips are woven by the industrious Otomí weavers of Santa Ana Hueytlalpan. Many villages of the Mixteca Alta Tlaxiaco region buy black wool skirts from Magdelena de los Comales, Oaxaca (Mixtec).

Before discussing wrap-around skirts of treadle-loomed or commercial cloth further and indicating where they are used, it might be well to analyze a few of the many ways wrap-around skirts are worn, whatever fabric is employed. For the purpose of clarity in these descriptions, only the length will be mentioned. The accompanying figures do not indicate (1) whether surplus material about the waist is turned in next to the body, (2) whether it is turned down outside over the belt, or (3) whether it stands up as a ruff. See the plates and PART II for these details, and for types of materials used in each skirt, and measurement from waist to knee, calf, ankle, instep, or ground—as the custom may be.

Fig. 11 a.

Saronglike fashion. Open-ended rectangles of various lengths, wrapped about the limbs without fullness or pleats.

1. The single diagram presented for this classification gives the manner of wrapping the striped skirts (*posahuancos*) of many villages in the Mixteca Baja: Pinotepa Nacional, Pinotepa de Don Luis, Huazolotitlán, Huaxpaltepec, Atoyac, San Juan Colorado, Mechoacán, Jicayán, and many others. Loom Length: 61 to 68 inches. In wrapping, the final end seems invariably to terminate on the wearer's left side facing toward the front. The initial end is doubled slightly inwards as wrapping begins (pl. 226).

2. Some other villages or regions have types of saronglike skirts, each with a slight variation: The Isthmus of Tehuantepec, Oaxaca (including some Zapotec, Mixe, Huave, and Chontal settlements)—length: 90 to 98 inches. Jamiltepec, Oaxaca (Mixtec)—length: 56 to 66 inches. San Andres Chicahauxtla (Trique)—length: 62 inches. Cosoleacaque, Vera Cruz (Nahua)—length: 85 inches.

Figure 11 b.

Small tube skirts. Three examples.

1. Copala, Oaxaca (Trique)—circumference: 76 to 78 inches. Extra loom length is arranged into three neat pleats on each side of the wearer facing toward the front.

2. Cuatalmayán, San Luis Potosí (Nahua)—circumference: 75 inches. Extra loom length is formed into a single inverted box pleat, at the center front.

3. San Juan Chamula, Chiapas (Tzotzil)—circumference: 60 to 76 inches (variation of No. 2).

Figure 11 c.

A longer tube skirt. With consequently more complicated handling of extra circumference.

Tetelcingo, Morelos (Nahua)—circumference: 84 to 102 inches. Skirt measurements vary exceedingly, because several types of commercial cloth are used today, and the amount purchased depends upon the wearer's pocketbook. The wear-

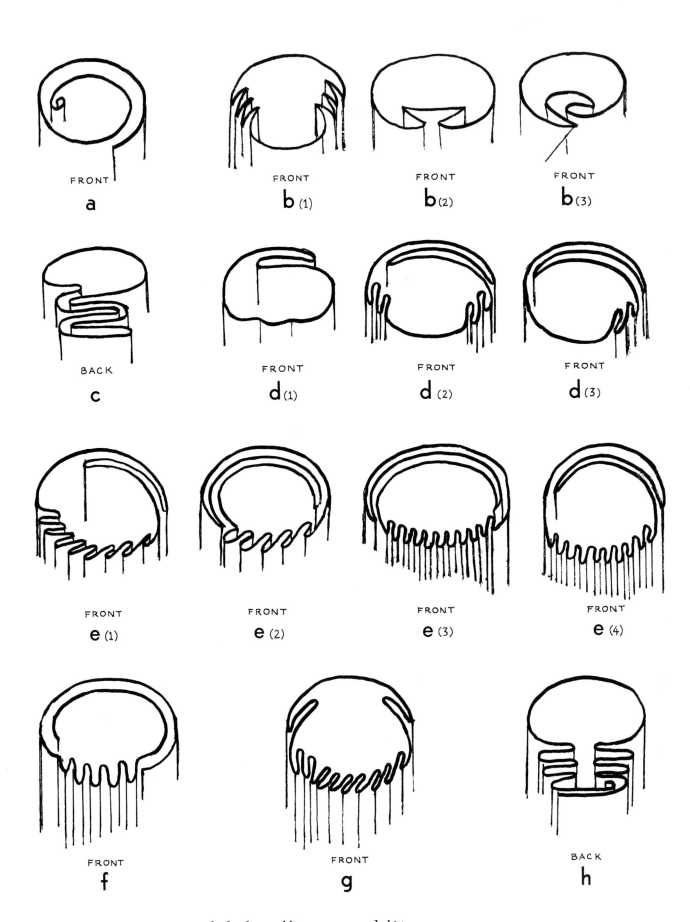

Figure 11. Various methods of assembling wrap-around skirts.

a. A skirt wrapped in sarong fashion.
b. Small tube skirts.
c. A longer tube skirt.
d. Tube skirts put on with triple thickness across the back.
e. Longer tube skirts put on with triple thickness across the back.
f. A long open-ended skirt.
g. A very-long tube skirt, not triple across the back.
h. A long open-ended skirt with all extra material arranged at the back.

er steps into the tube, extends in front of her all extra cloth. She begins folding it back and forth into pleats approximately 12 inches wide, one on top of the next, which she switches to the center back when formed, before securing the skirt with her two wool belts.

Figure 11 d.

Tube skirts which are put on with triple thickness across the back.

1. San Pablito, Puebla (Otomí)—circumference: approximately 92 inches. This skirt is put on with one wide pleat across the back ending on the left side of the wearer. Some San Pablito skirts show in addition a little soft fullness across the front.

2. Amatlán de los Reyes, Vera Cruz (Nahua)—circumference: approximately 118 inches. The tube is doubled to make three thicknesses across the back. The remaining cloth is formed into several pleats on each side facing the front.

3. Santa Ana Hueytlalpan, Hidalgo (Otomí)—circumference: 132 to 140 inches. The triple thickness is brought very far forward on the left side, after which several deep pleats are formed on the left side facing front.

Figure 11 e.

Longer tube skirts put on with triple thickness across the back.

1. Temoaya, state of México (Otomí)—Circumference: 125 to 152 inches. The skirt is worn with a triple thickness from the center back to the left front side of the wearer, with all remaining cloth laid in about nine deep pleats working from left to right.

2. Cuetzalan, Puebla (Nahua)—circumference: approximately 152 inches. Triple thicknesses are brought very far around the sides toward the front, after which the remaining material is formed into five deep pleats folded from left to right in front.

3. Huehuetla, Hidalgo (Tepehua)—circumference: approximately 168 inches. A triple thickness of material is worn across the back and quite far around toward the front, with the remaining material gathered across the front.

4. San José Miahuatlán, Puebla (Nahua)—circumference: 156 inches. This skirt is of black commercial cotton cloth. The wearer steps into the tube, leaving a triple thickness across the back,

and arranging all remaining material in many pleats across the front.

Figure 11 f.

Long open-ended skirt.

San Juan Yalalag (Villa Hidalgo), Oaxaca (Zapotec)—length: 116 to 144 inches. Beginning on the right side, the skirt length is wrapped across the back and around the body a second time (when a 144 in. skirt is used) with the final end finishing at the left side. Deep pleats of the remaining material are formed across the front.

Figure 11 g.

Very long tube skirt, not triple across back.

Hueyapan, Morelos (Nahua)—circumference: 168 to 235 inches. A wide *tabla* (box-pleat) is formed across the back, after which six or seven very deep pleats are formed on the left working across the front. Two or three such pleats are then formed on the right side, facing forward.

Figure 11 h.

Long open-ended skirt with all extra material arranged at the back of the wearer.

San Sebastián Peñoles and Santa Catarina Estetla, Oaxaca (Mixtec), and formerly other villages in the eastern Mixteca Alta-Etla area. The skirt arrangements are very similar, subject to skirt size: Peñoles—length: approximately 150 inches. Santa Catarina Estetla—length: approximately 106 inches. All fullness is pulled to the back of the wearer and evenly divided. On the left side three or four pleats are made, and partially held with a belt or with the assistance of another person. Next the right hand pleats are formed, and the final end laps over the final pleat on the left. This arrangement results in a series of box pleats as seen in Plate 216.

Figure 12

Very large skirt arranged with a bolsa.

The following is a description of the putting on of the old Zoque skirt of Tuxtla Gutiérrez (Cordry, 1941, pp. 83–84)—circumference: 64 by 125 inches.

Women customarily require the aid of another person in order to put on the large skirt. First the woman steps into the skirt, arranging it so that the middle of the cross (A) comes on her right hip, and gathering the extra width into a roll about the waist. Her assistant pulls the extra length out to point (B) with her right hand [fig.12–2] and with her left hand gathers

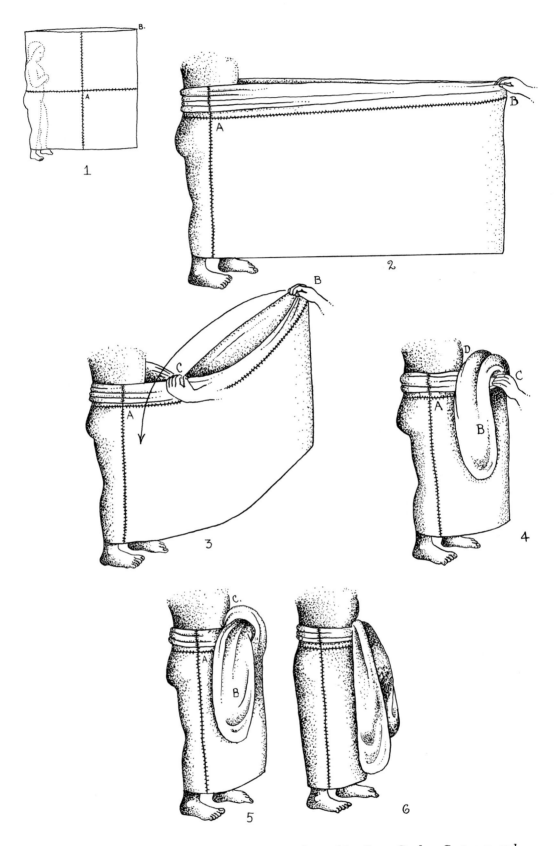

Figure 12. The Zoque manner of putting on a large skirt. From Cordry, *Costumes and Weaving of the Zoque Indians of Chiapas, Mexico*. Courtesy The Southwest Museum.

the cloth together near the body of the wearer at point C [fig. 12–3] . . . Then the material from C to B (which will form the *bolsa* or pocket) is thrown over the cloth between C and the body of the wearer [fig. 12–4] . . . and C is tucked into the waist at D. This holds the skirt firmly in place, so that no belt of any sort is used or needed [fig. 12–5] . . . Next the *bolsa* is arranged so that it hangs evenly toward the right side of the front [fig. 12–6] (pl. 248).

Women of San Bartolomé de los Llanos, Chiapas (Tzotzil), arrange their skirts in a similar manner (pl. 71).

For a long time there have been centers, usually in larger non-Indian towns, where treadle-loomed skirt lengths are woven. In some cases these skirt *cortes* (lengths) travel considerable distances—even into neighboring states. Old women of San Sebastián Zinacatepec, Puebla, wear blue gathered pleated skirts fashioned of *cortes* made in or near Oaxaca City. This state capital is a treadle-loom weaving center.

The red cotton *cortes* (pieces approximately 31 by 110 inches) called *chiapaneca* are woven in several patterns. The weft pinstriped ones, called *tachón* (fine stripe) and *rayadillo* (striped) (Jones, letter, October 20, 1965), have two groups of from three to seven black pinstripes, with small spaces between, alternating with background spaces. We know these pinstripe patterns to be worn in the Choapan, Oaxaca (Zapotec), area (including the villages of Latani and Comaltepec), and in Chichicastepec (Mixe). Other *chiapaneca cortes* have delicate plaid designs in black on a red ground. These are worn in Usila, Oaxaca, and other western Chinantec villages—also in San Andrés Teotilalpan, Oaxaca (Cuicatec), and San Juan Mazatlán, Oaxaca (Mixe).

These *cortes* are now rarely seen for sale in Oaxaca City on market day, but are taken out into the villages by *commerciantes*. *Chiapaneca* cloth is rather sleazy, and is usually worn gathered onto a band rather than as a wrap-around. A few old women in Usila still arrange their skirts with each wearing.

We have been unable to discover the origin and meaning of the word *chiapaneca*. Some informants think that cloth woven in the past in Comitán or Chiapa de Corzo, Chiapas, may have given this association. The word *chapaneco* is frequently mentioned in documents from the eighteenth century. We read, for example, that women in villages under the jurisdiction of Santo Domingo Nexapam, Oaxaca, "wear skirts which they call chapaneco . . ." (Paso y Troncoso, 1950, p. 21).

72. A Zoque woman of Copainalá, Chiapas, wearing a skirt of Guatemalan material arranged with a *bolsa*. 1940

Juchitán in the Isthmus of Tehuantepec makes a firmer, much superior weave of *cortes* (well suited for wrap-around skirts); some of dark blue were formerly sold to the Chontals of Huamelula, to Huave Indian villages, and to the Zapotecs of San Bartolo Yautepec, all in Oaxaca. Still popular and much used today are the red *cortes* with a widely spaced ¼-or-⅛-inch white, yellow, or blue stripe. Two 21-by-90–94-inch loom webs are sewn together lengthwise. Skirts are worn sarong fashion by old women of Tehuantepec and Juchitán, and by many Zapotec and Huave women of Isthmus villages (pls. 93 & 205). Farther north in Oaxaca, Mixe women use this material—in Cotzocón, Mogoñé (pl. 206), and Acatlán.

Within our memory Zoque women of Copainalá, Chiapas, wore treadle-loomed skirt materials of ikat patterns (pl. 72) brought all the way from Guatemala

109

73. An old-style costume, no longer used. Here and in Plates 5 and 127 we see that the Papantla *quechquemitl* is folded and worn over the shoulders as a cape. The neck opening is not used. Papantla, Vera Cruz (Totonac). 1939

for gala wear. Everyday skirts were of red or blue cloth with bold-colored stripes. This material was woven on upright looms in Comitán de las Flores, Chiapas.

San Cristóbal de las Casas, in the cold Chiapas highlands, is surrounded by many Tzotzil and Tzeltal villages which retain to greater or lesser degree both men's and women's distinctive handwoven costumes. Many costume parts are made in the villages actually using them; a good many items of leather and wool are furnished other villages by the industrious craftsmen of San Juan Chamula—a variety of both men's and women's wool belts, *sarapes,* and *cotones* of different pat-

terns for different settlements. Although Chamula women weave heavy, black wool skirts for themselves and a wool skirt for women of Zinacantán (Tzotzil) nearby, to our knowledge, women of other cold-country Tzotzil and Tzeltal villages wear wrap-around skirts of dark-blue cotton cloth, treadle-loomed and woven in San Cristóbal de las Casas. In the villages of San Andrés Chamula, now called Larrainzar, and Oxchuc (Tzotzil and Tzeltal respectively), the two loom lengths (21 by 80 inches), sewn side by side and end to end to form a tube, each have different painstakingly embroidered multicolored joinings, so that the skirts—though of the same loom cloth—have a village identity.

The webs of a great many skirts woven on the backstrap-loom are sewn side by side (and end to end if they are tube style) with firm undecorative whipping stitches in the same colored thread or yarn as the skirt. Others, however, have handsome joinings in a variety of embroidery stitches, some wide, some narrow. Those of San Bartolomé de los Llanos, Chiapas (Tzotzil), are the most exaggerated. These dark-blue cotton skirts have 1½-inch satin-stitch joinings, using wool, yarn, and artificial-silk thread in pink, blue, green, and yellow. Embroidered tendrils and flower forms and other motifs embellish other areas of the skirt (pl. 251; Chapter 37).

Emphasis on a bottom border is clear in pre-Hispanic and sixteenth-century skirts as depicted in the codices, especially those of the Mixteca; but on the whole this is not the case with present-day skirts of the old wrap-around type. At the Indian State Fair of Oaxaca (1941) a woman of Santa María Zacatepec, Oaxaca, had embroidered small animal designs along the lower edge of her striped (Sayultepec-woven) skirt, which were barely visible beneath her very long *huipil* (Zacatepec and Amusgos are among the towns where women wear no skirts except for gala occasions).

Maya women of Yucatán, although their *huipiles* and skirts have been fashioned of commercial cotton, lace, and artificial silk fabric for many years, do retain the feeling of border decoration on the lower edge of both *huipil* and skirt. Another skirt with border embroidery is the highly individual gala one of Huautla de Jiménez, Oaxaca (Mazatec). This heavy white, single-strip wrap-around skirt (of handwoven or commercial cloth) contains a distinctive 2⅜-inch solid dark-red wool embroidered band around the bottom, broken by four curious black triangles. Free embroidered motifs are scattered along on the white ground above the solid band (a man leading a horse and conventionalized flower or leaf patterns alternating). The yarn used in this border was formerly dyed with cochineal.

A fine embroidered skirt not in use even twenty-five years ago was the white *manta* wrap-around Totonac skirt with a border, and large flowering tree and bird designs carried out in red or blue thread, some in cross-stitch (pl. 73), others in satin stitch. Isabel Kelly and Angel Palerm (1952, p. 238) state that "of the embroidered skirts only one appears to have survived in Tajín; we were allowed to photograph it (pl. 32, a–d), but the owner refused to sell, inasmuch as she planned to be buried in the garment." As early as 1940 we found it impossible to obtain one of the old Totonac skirts in Papantla. We saw only white-organdy gathered skirts, machine embroidered. (pl. 127).

Skirts of some Nahua villages in the states of Hidalgo and Vera Cruz (Chicontepec, Vera Cruz; and Izocal, Atlapexco, and Huautla—all Hidalgo) have handsome heavy deep-pile embroidered borders. These skirts are gathered on a band, not wrap-around (Christensen, verbal).

Some white commercial-cloth wrap-around skirts—Huehuetla, Hidalgo (Tepehua) (pl. 68), and Pantepec, Puebla (Totonac) (pl. 133)—have wide flower pattern and line borders of machine embroidery in several colors of cotton thread.

To complete this survey of Indian skirts with due emphasis upon the ancient wrap-around form, we mention the wrap-around skirt areas where the mode of wearing continues, though materials are no longer handwoven, on either the backstrap or treadle loom. Commercial cloth has long since taken over in Tetelcingo, Morelos (Nahua) (pl. 86); black commercial poplin or other cloth in San José Miahuatlán, Puebla (Nahua) (pl. 179), and in the Huastec area around Tancanhuitz (Ciudad Santos), San Luis Potosí. Cotton cloth purchased in Oaxaca City, having very large blue and white or green and white checks, has been used for many years by the Zapotec women of Mitla, Tlacolula, Teotitlán del Valle, Ocotlán, all of Oaxaca, for wrap-around skirts. The 1941 Indian Fair delegations from these valley towns wore old-style dark-red wool skirts, but for everyday the cottons had already superceded hand-loomed skirt lengths. The only exceptions in the early 1940's were thin old women to be seen at the Sunday Tlacolula market with frayed wool striped *sarapes* from nearby Santo Domingo Albarradas wrapped around for skirts. Wrap-around skirts of *man-*

74. A Tarascan woman in the Pátzcuaro, Michoacán, market, wearing a very high-backed skirt, held in place by numerous handwoven belts. 1936

111

75. The side and back views of an old-style Tarascan skirt. Cherán, Michoacán. 1935

76. Rancho Zapote Negro, Guerrero. Inside a shelter used by people who have come to settle here from San Miguel Metlatonoc. The women wear everyday *huipiles* and ruffled skirts. (Mixtec). 1965

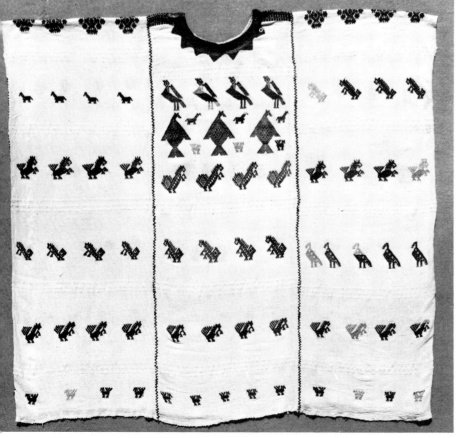

77. A gala *huipil* purchased from the women at Rancho Zapote Negro, formerly from Metlatonoc, Guerrero. (Mixtec). 1965

78. A girl of Xochistlahuaca, Guerrero, showing the old manner of wearing the skirt in this village. (Amusgo). 1965

ta are worn for everyday in areas where handwoven white used to be worn, as in Cuetzalan, Puebla, and Cuatlamayán, San Luis Potosí (Nahua).

A unique skirt, which is almost extinct, is the high-backed, pleated, Tarascan skirt, handwoven of dark-blue wool (pl. 74). According to Frederick Starr (1901, p. 112), a skirt he obtained was composed of fourteen webs (38-inch lengths) sewn side by side vertically to form a pleated tube 22 feet in circumference—arranged about the body with each wearing, and held with many handwoven patterned belts worn at one time. Plate 75 shows side and back views of a less extreme style Tarascan skirt (Cherán, Michoacán).

Skirts gathered into a band are rarely of material woven on the backstrap-loom. These fabrics are apt to be too heavy for such use. A handsome exception is the San Pablo Yaganisa skirt from the white-costumed Villa Alta, Oaxaca (Zapotec), area, gathered into a hand-woven narrow ribbed band with long ties—though in the wearing this is covered by a raw-silk sash of *solferino* color (the white *huipil* is tucked inside).

To finish this skirt survey—European-style skirts gathered into a band have and will be touched upon, but only when worn in conjunction with the true Indian *huipil* or *quechquemitl*. The *chiapaneca* skirt *cortes* of Oaxaca City, which are usually gathered at the waist, are decorated in Choapan, Latani, Comaltepec (all Oaxaca), and Santa Cecilia (Vera Cruz), with wide lower borders of appliquéd ribbons cut into points, combined with rickrack braid, in yellow, green, and blue (pl. 81).

In many Amusgo and Mixtec villages in southern Guerrero, where superb handwoven *huipiles* are worn, only gathered commercial-cotton skirts are seen, some of checked or flowered materials, some with gathered tiers of flounces (pls. 76 & 24). The most original one is that of Xochistlahuaca, Guerrero (Amusgo), of *solferino*, chartreuse, or white Indian-head cotton, open at one side, and worn under one arm and tied over the opposite shoulder (pl. 78). It is used about the house as an only garment, and is charmingly decorated with a wide lower border suggestive of the ribbon appliqué treatment described above, but carried out in one color only in a contrasting colored cotton cloth, well turned under and machine sewn.

7. Hairdresses and Head Coverings

 THE DARK HAIR of the Indian woman is a pleasure to see. It is almost always clean (where there is enough water), and gleaming with *mamey* (mammee) or other oil.

As recently as 1940 hair was combed with handmade combs, some of which were also used in weaving processes (pl. 18). Although plastic combs are the rule today, one still sees these wooden combs for sale in markets, and some of the combs of horn from San Antonio de la Isla, state of México, which are embellished with animal and bird forms. Brushes made of fiber are still sold in rural areas for various uses, including the brushing of hair. Such brushes were formerly used in many parts of Mexico, and W. J. McGee pictures one (1898, pp. 226–227, and fig. 29) which he says is "made of yucca fiber bound into cylindrical form . . ."

There are many modes of hairdressing. Usually a more complicated fashion is used for fiestas and ceremonies—with ribbons, tape, handwoven cords, flowers, plastic combs—than for everyday. Although hair traditionally is never curled, some older Indian women dye their hair black, and many dislike greying hair. In Michoacán a type of organ cactus is used for dye.

In some villages, there are several ways of dressing the hair. It is often worn falling loose over the shoulders; for example, in Yalalag, Oaxaca (Zapotec) (pl.

198); Ixtayutla, Oaxaca (Mixtec); Metlatonoc, Guerrero (Mixtec); by Huichol Indians in Nayarit and Jalisco; and Lacandón Indians in Chiapas.

Women's hair is almost never cut in any way, and as far as we know, in Indian Mexico today only Huichol women cut long bangs over their eyes (pl. 163). We read in Sahagún (1951–1963, Book 10, p. 179) that in pre-Hispanic times hair was sometimes cut, "and as gaudy dressers, as vain as the [other] Otomí, were the old women, who still cut the hair over the forehead: who still also cut the hair on one side, leaving the other side long . . ."

A few of the villages where hair is worn in one braid down the back are Tetelcingo, Morelos (Nahua); Copala, Oaxaca (Trique); Amusgos, Oaxaca (Amusgo); and San Pablito, Puebla (Otomí). An example is seen in Plate 192.

It seems to us that the majority of women wear their hair parted in the center with two braids down the back—the ends often tied together with a ribbon, tape, or string, as in Plates 79 and 174, to keep the braids from falling forward and getting in the way when work is being done. When the hair is worn in two braids, it is often worn another way also—wrapped about the head in some fashion (pl. 252).

We have seen it worn in two braids by women in the

115

79. A weaver of blue cotton *rebozos*. Acatlán, Guerrero (Nahua). 1964

a   b   c   d   e

80. Women's hair cords: *a*. Huazolotitlán, Oaxaca (Mixtec), fashioned of human hair; *b*. San Pablito, Puebla (Otomí), of wool yarn and beads; *c*. Ocotlán, Oaxaca (Zapotec), of green cotton and silk thread; *d*. Ixtayutla, Oaxaca (Mixtec), of black wool cords; *e*. Pinotepa Nacional, Oaxaca (Mixtec), of wool and artificial silk.

117

following areas: Punta Chueca, Sonora (Seri); Cherán, Michoacán (Tarascan); the area of San Felipe del Progreso, state of México (Mazahua); Tolimán, Querétaro (Otomí); Temoaya, state of México (Otomí); Santa Ana Hueytlalpan, Hidalgo (Otomí); San José Miahuatlán, Altepexi, and San Sebastián Zinacatepec, all in Puebla (Nahua); Acatlán, Guerrero (Nahua); Peñoles, Santa Catarina Estetla, and Cuquila, all in Oaxaca (Mixtec); Chacalapa, Guerrero (Mixtec); Santo Tomás Mazaltepec, San Pedro Quiatoni and Tehuantepec, all in Oaxaca (Zapotec); San Andrés Teotilalpan, Oaxaca (Cuicatec); Usila and Ojitlán, both in Oaxaca (Chinantec); San Mateo del Mar, Oaxaca (Huave); San Andrés Chicahuaxtla, Oaxaca (Trique); Jalapa de Díaz and Ayutla, both in Oaxaca (Mazatec); Tuxtla Gutiérrez, Copainalá, and Ocozocoautla, all in Chiapas (Zoque); and Chamula and San Bartolomé de los Llanos, Chiapas (Tzotzil).

When spending a short time in a village, one may be confused by the fact that some of the women are always seen with loose flowing hair. This is because they have washed it and are letting it dry, and not because it is the custom to wear it this way.

Alfred M. Tozzer says (1907, p. 25), "The Lacandone men as well as the women wear their hair long. It thus serves as a protection for the neck and shoulders." During the last twenty years, certain groups have sometimes worn the hair gathered together at the nape of the neck and tied rather than loose. Huichol women and men sometimes tie the hair with a specially woven ribbon, making a twist around the hair at the nape of the neck with the ribbon, and then bringing it up front on top of the head, and knotting it there (pl. 163). Tozzer tells us (1907, p. 30) that "The Lancandone women wear a bunch of gayly colored bird feathers and the breasts of small birds hanging from the back of the hair where it is tied."

Women who wear their hair in one braid do not always tie it at the end of the braid (Tetelcingo, Morelos —Nahua). In San Pablito, Puebla (Otomí), a colored woolen cord (50–80 inches long including decorative ends) is wrapped around the single braid. In the one examined, there are four decorative ends (two to each end of the main cord). These ends vary but are about 6 inches long and contain variegated colored balls of wool, three to each of the four decorative ends. The balls are separated by tubes of beadwork which closely encircle the cord—each end terminates in a woolen tassel (pl. 80 b). These ends hang below the tip of the braid. To our knowledge, a finely made green hair cord

from the valley of Oaxaca (pl. 80 c) has not been made or worn for at least twenty years.

For the most part, ribbons are now used braided into the two braids, and at times these are twisted up about the head. This style is very general in the valley of Oaxaca, the Isthmus of Tehuantepec, and other coastal areas, and was probably adopted partly for coolness (pl. 245). Sahagún (1951–1963, Book 10, p. 184) says of the Totonacs, "Their hair strands were braided with varicolored [strips of cloth] wrapped with feathers. In the market place they were well bedight with flowers." We read in *Mexico South* (Covarrubias, 1947, p. 44) of the women of a delightful village in the state of Vera Cruz—Cosoleacaque (Nahua), "They wear their hair in two braids intertwined with red ribbon, crossed in the back around the head and tied in front with a bow; and they invariably wear large fresh flowers in their braids."

In certain areas the hair is divided into two parts, rolled instead of braided, crossed in back and brought forward above the ears, and knotted once or twice in front (pl. 226); the ends are then tucked into the roll at the sides. This mode is common in the Mixteca Baja. In some of the eastern Chinantec villages in northern Oaxaca, the hair is rolled very low across the forehead with largish buns over the ears. Bernard Bevan (1938, pl. 15–31) shows this fashion from Lalana, Oaxaca.

On one journey (1964) to Choapan, Oaxaca (Zapotec), we took with us a photograph we had taken at the Indian State Fair of Oaxaca (1941), to which event had come numerous delegations from the region of Choapan. The photograph depicted a group of girls in the Choapan costume (pl. 81), but when we showed it to old Choapan women they looked puzzled, and said that the girls were not from Choapan proper but a little village nearby, because—"They have ribbons in their hair, and we don't." Except for this distinguishing feature, the costumes—now almost extinct—were identical.

In posed, postcard photographs of the Jamiltepec, Oaxaca (Mixteca Baja), costume, one sees a sort of diadem made of many spindles stuck into the hair and radiating out fan wise. This is some romantic invention probably springing from the fact that spindles are made in this village. Indian women anywhere, when working with several spindles, may stick one in the hair just to get it out of the way, but no headdress is made with them today.

Among old-style hairdresses now going out of use is the one for brides in Pinotepa Nacional, Oaxaca (Mixtec), which has counterparts in fashions seen on pre-

81. Zapotec girls from a small village near Santiago Choapan, Oaxaca, whose costume can be distinguished from that of the larger village only by their hair ribbons. 1941

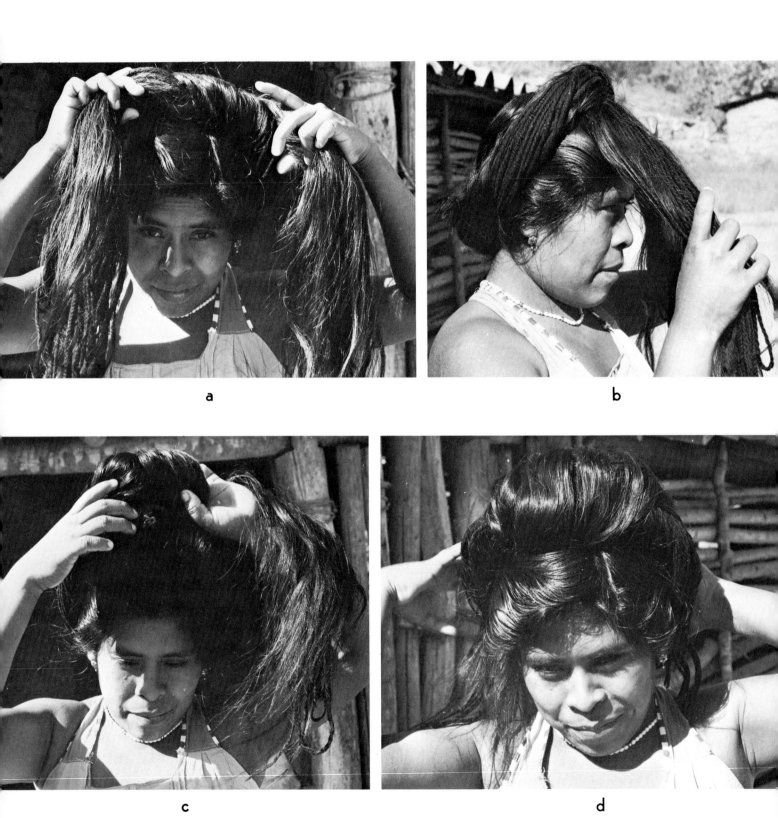

a

b

c

d

82. The hairdress of Huazolotitlán, Oaxaca. (Mixtec). 1965

83. A girl with the exaggerated hairdress of Huazolotitlán, Oaxaca. (Mixtec). 1965

Figure 13. *Huipiles* shown in the Florentine Codex, displaying the use of borders. The drawings also show bordered skirts and typical styles of hair-dressing.

Conquest figurines. It consists of wool cords (*tlacoyales*) with handsome long varicolored silk tassels arranged in the hair so that they fall forward over the shoulders (pls. 80 e & 230). Another custom, now extinct, is the use of silver hair ornaments to decorate the hair arrangement in Choapan, Oaxaca (pl. 124; Chapter 9).

There has come to us recently a set of special multi-braided black cords (pl. 80 d) 80 inches long including 10-inch fringes at both ends, said to be worn for fiestas by only one woman—the *Mandona* (who watches the fiesta food and distributes it to those who have contributed firewood for its preparation) in Ixtayutla, Oaxaca (Mixtec) (verbal communication, Lucila Franco).

Hair fashions change, and girls and young women are always the innovators. In Usila, Oaxaca (Chinantec), a particularly exotic hair style has become popular (pl. 196); but older women continue to wear their hair in two braids down the back or wound simply about the head, sometimes with a small knot in front.

Women of Huazolotitlán in the Mixtec district of Jamiltepec, Oaxaca, have a unique hairdress, but it may be that young women of neighboring villages are now copying it in a modified way: a mass of from twelve to sixteen dark-brown wool cords (length about 40 inches) tied by several threads at the center point, are placed at the back of the neck after the parted hair has been divided. From each side the hair is brought forward, wrapped about the cords (which are used as filling and are not supposed to show). The girl who demonstrated the technique for us was nervous and performed too rapidly. In Plate 82 a she has tied a knot of hair and cords in the center front, well above her forehead. In Plate 82 b the knot has been tucked under the cords, and all hair brought forward in preparation for the next step. In Plate 82 c she throws the hair back over the cords to make a high puff or mound. Plate 82d shows the finished hairdress (though the ends are not well tucked in). A conservative young woman from the same village is shown in Plate 83 with a more exagger-

121

84. Mixtec girls from Estetla, showing braids tightly bound (*cuernos*) and *papelillo* beads. Oaxaca City, Oaxaca. 1941

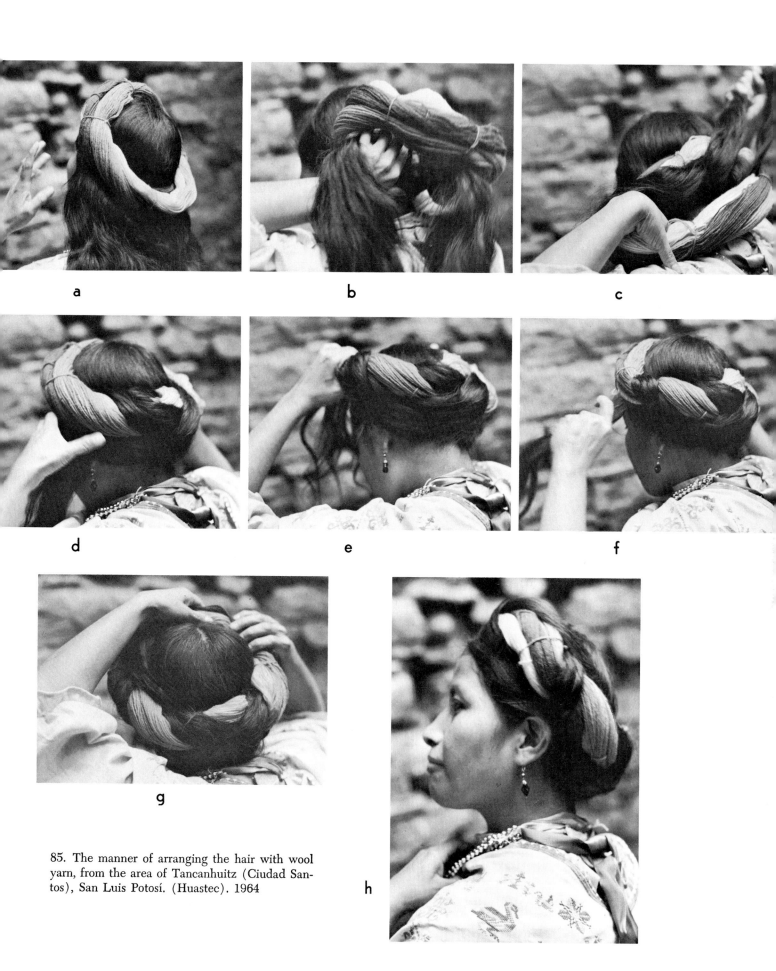

a

b

c

d

e

f

g

85. The manner of arranging the hair with wool yarn, from the area of Tancanhuitz (Ciudad Santos), San Luis Potosí. (Huastec). 1964

h

a

b

c

d

e

86. Dyeing the hair green in Tetelcingo, Morelos. (Nahua). 1966

124

PLATE V. A Nahua woman of Tetelcingo, Morelos, dyeing her hair green. 1966

ated hairdress. She was very shy, and refused to remove her head covering for the photograph.

An old custom in this village, as in many primitive communities, is the saving of hair that is combed out over the years in a special jar reserved for the purpose. Calixta Guiteras-Holmes (1961, p. 113) says, for example, of the Tzotzil Indians of San Pedro Chenalhó, Chiapas, "This custom of preserving . . . pertains to any hair that is combed out or cut off, with the exception of a man's when he goes to a barber. These precautions spare the soul, because otherwise after death it would become exhausted seeking these parts of the body: the whole must go to the Hereafter."

Hair is also saved for another purpose. We have in our possession from Huazolotitlán a set of sixteen spun cords, fashioned of carefully rolled, cleaned, and brushed combings of human hair (showing tiny knots occasionally to aid in joinings), tied together at a center point like the sets of wool ones, and formerly used for the same purpose (pl. 80 a). This set of hair cords came to us after our visit (1965) to Huazolotitlán. When we were there, we were told that the old custom was on the wane, and no old woman could be located who owned such a set of cords.

In pre-Conquest and post-Conquest codices one notes a prevailing everyday hairstyle on women who wear the *huipil*. The curious stiffly bound or doubled ends of hair, which turn upward at either side toward the front like short horns, are difficult to explain, and do not occur in Indian hairdresses today (fig. 13, the two women on the bottom row at the right).

Most unusual are certain other hairdresses which have endured since pre-Conquest times. The following are samples: the *cuernos* (horns) of Santa Catarina Estetla, Oaxaca (Mixtec) (pl. 84); and *rodetes* of Yalalag, Oaxaca (Zapotec) (pl. 48), of Mixistlán and other Mixe villages, Oaxaca (pl. 37), and of Cuetzalan, Puebla (Nahua), (pl. 177). All of these are formed of heavy woolen cords. A variant was noted (1940) in the hairdresses of women from Huistán, Chiapas, seen in San Cristóbal de las Casas, who wore a headdress of red woven-wool ribbons.

Huastec women of the area around Tancanhuitz, San Luis Potosí, today commonly wear a *rodete* (*petob*) fashioned of four or five different colored skeins of commercial wool yarn. These skeins are of a suitable circumference to fit the head, and women choose the colors they wish from venders in Sunday market stalls, who tie the skeins lightly together ready to be worn. They are placed upon the head with the hair falling loose (pl. 85 a). The wearer then flips the yarn skeins backward, and divides her hair into equal parts at the center back (pl. 85 b). She crosses the two equal divisions of hair, and pulls them up over the yarn headdress at left and right (pl. 85 c). Then she replaces the *petob* in its original position and we see the hair crossed at center back (pl. 85 d). Now she begins to cross the hair over the *petob* at each side (pl. 85 e) and pulls the crossings tight over the ears (pl. 85 f). Next the hair is crossed over the yarn at center front and secured, the ends of the hair being tucked neatly out of sight (pl. 85 g). Finally, we see a side view of the finished hairdress in Plate 85 h.

It is obvious from codices and pre-Columbian figurines (pl. 88) that many types of *rodete* headdresses were common before the introduction of wool into Mexico. Many of the cord-type headdresses depicted could have been made of cotton; others showing flat striplike elements could have been formed of leather. The idea of the present-day *rodete*, used for decoration, may have come from the utilitarian need for making a base of cloth or fiber to aid in carrying round-bottomed jars or gourds upon the head.

Recently the writers have observed and photographed a probable link with other materials used to make pre-Conquest *rodetes*. As previously described, the Huastec women commonly wind their hair at the present time around a *rodete* of multicolored yarns. We observed, however, that at home or in the fields, a *rodete* made of vine is sometimes used, particularly by old women. For coolness and economy the vine seems ideal. In Tamaletón near Tancanhuitz we were told that many years ago all *petob* were of vine.

The variety of vine traditionally employed in Tamaletón, *Philodendron radiatum* Schott-Araceas (identified by Professor Dr. Eizi Matuda, Instituto de Biologia, U.N.A.M.), adapts itself well—having long round smooth even tendrils, which remain pliable for a considerable period. Tendrils may be cut in the mountain at any time of the year, according to informants. The green vine is called *Yash-tam-nic*. Photographs show the formation of the Huastec *petob*, as seen in March 1965. A crown of vine loops is shaped to head size, then carefully and evenly bound transversely with an additional tendril. Plates 87 a and 87 b show the vine and the making of a *petob*. Plates 87 c through 87 f show the same wrapping of the hair as with wool-yarn *rodete* described above. The plastic result strongly suggests early headdresses (pl. 88).

Also interesting was the simultaneous finding of a

87. An old Huastec hair arrangement, using a vine instead of wool yarn: *a* shows the woman with the vine to be used; in *b* the husband forms a *petob*; *c–f* show the manner of arranging the hair with the *petob*. Tamaletón, San Luis Potosí. 1965

88. A Zapotec clay burial urn from Monte Albán 3 B (400–700 A.D.). This figure shows a hairdress which resembles the Huastec *petob* fashioned of vine. Courtesy of Howard Leigh, Mitla, Oaxaca.

different plant in use in the Nahua village of Cuatla-mayán in the same area where today a smooth sausage-like headdress some 1½ inches in diameter is seen (pl. VII). This tubular crown is wrapped with colored cotton cloth and/or commercial colored-wool tape, but it was found that the interior core is fashioned of *mecate de platano* (strips of banana-tree bark). This *rodete* was not seen worn without the cloth wrapping, but cotton cloth may have bound these smooth hard rolls in pre-Columbian times too.

Sahagún says, speaking of women (1951–1963, Book 8, p. 47 & 48), "[so] did they place importance upon their heads; it was dyed with indigo, so that their hair shown." Also (Book 10, p. 185), speaking of Huastec women, "Behold their array . . . they dyed their hair diverse colors . . . Some yellow, some red."

On one occasion when we went to Tetelcingo, Morelos, in March, 1961, we found that the custom of dyeing the hair green was currently practiced by a few women; but due to the conservative attitude of the people, very little information was garnered. On a subsequent trip with Miss Christensen, an effort was made to pursue this investigation. At that time the taking of photographs was prohibited, although information was gathered about costume. In December, 1965, and early January, 1966, the new *presidente-municipal* was cooperative, and allowed photographs to be taken. We were, on three occasions, accompanied by Mrs. Carmen Cook de Leonard. In the following I am simply describing my own photographs shown in Plates 86 and V.

This dyeing process may prove with more research to be associated with agriculture (dyeing the hair red, yellow, green, or blue to simulate the color of the corn or corn silk). As has been previously mentioned, hair was dyed in pre-Hispanic times, either green, yellow, or red. Sahagún has been quoted concerning the fiesta of the eighth month, but Fray Juan de Torquemada's description (1943, Vol. II, Book X, Chap. 19, pp. 269–270) is more complete. He says, speaking of the Nahuas, that they gave (in the eighth month) a fiesta for the goddess Xilonen, patroness of the *elotes* (*xilotes*) or green corn. In this fiesta the women danced wearing their hair loose over the shoulders. They believed that their long hair simulated the corn silk—as though wishing to say, "as the hair is long and plentiful, thus the maize will be."

The dye used in Tetelcingo was extracted from the leaves of a shrub (pl. 86 a) identified as *Euparium albicaule* Schultz, Bip. by Dr. Eizi Matuda of the National University of Mexico. Plate 86 b shows the leaves which have been soaking in water, being ground on a *metate* (stone on which corn is ground). The vivid green liquid produced partly fills a brown clay bowl placed close in front of the *metate*. We were requested to return three days later because the liquid had to stand for that length of time before being used. When we returned the color had darkened somewhat. The subject first washed her hair with clean water (pl. 86 c), pulled it all forward, and dipped it in the brown bowl of dye several times (pl. V). When the hair was taken out of the dye, it was knotted in front (pl. 86 d), and the knot thrown back on top of the head (pl. 86 e) and left to dry. This seems to be the characteristic technique for hair drying in Tetelcingo, unlike the usual method of letting it flow down over the shoulders.

With reference to the hair of the Indian men in Mexico today, we may say that besides the Lacandóns, those who still wear their hair long are the conservative men among the Seris, Tarahumaras, and Huichols. Some young Seri men were seen in 1964 in Punta Chueca, Sonora, with hair long and completely unconfined (pl. 89). Some older Seri men wore a single braid. The Tarahumaras wear headbands to hold their loosely flowing hair. Huichol men who still follow old traditions sometimes have their long hair dressed by their women, put up in a braided bun at the back of the head. In Plate 106 we see two Huichol men with long hair confined only by handwoven bands about the crowns of their heads.

Other Huichols and some Indians of the Chiapas highlands display a sort of bowl-shaped haircut (pl. 97), but more and more Indian communities have a Sunday barber, and men and boys line up for so-called "civilized" haircuts.

A few hats are seen on archaic figurines, but hats on the whole were adopted by Indian men in the early sixteenth century, soon after the arrival of the Spaniards. Some ceremonial ones of felt decorated with ribbons, which show decided Spanish influence, are still seen today (pl. 260), though hats are commonly of straw. Indian women cover their heads in a number of ways, and not all of them are of early Mexican origin. In some areas they have even adopted men's straw hats.

In our observation, especially woven head coverings are not worn in *quechquemitl* areas (unless it be an extra *quechquemitl*). The women of these groups are more apt to adopt the commercial *rebozo*. This generally applies to the Huastecs, Totonacs, Otomís, Maza-

89. A group of Seri women and children by the community store, drinking bottled drinks. Their clothes show a marked nineteenth-century influence; the girls at the right have their faces painted. Punta Chueca, Sonora. 1963

huas, and Nahuas who are found within the *quechque-mitl* province. Only in *huipil* areas, to our knowledge, does one find specially woven head coverings.

Whether the *rebozo* was adopted with the edict of 1582, issued by the Real Audiencia, compelling creoles not to dress in Indian garb; or whether it developed—as has been stated elsewhere—from the dictates of priests that the converted Indian women cover their heads in church; or whether they may have adopted the woven *huipil* strips in some areas, is not certain. We have noticed that Indian women today do not always cover the head when entering church—in some Chiapas villages; in Amatlán, Vera Cruz; and in Tetelcingo, Morelos, for example. Fray Francisco Ajofrín (1964, Vol. II, p. 50), who wrote in the eighteenth century of his travels to the Cuicatec village of Teutila, Oaxaca, says that the women did not cover their heads in church; and—as an aside—he states that apparently when the Apostle had commanded women not to enter the church bareheaded, he had not spoken to the Indian women.

Women's covering the head with a length of draped cloth, as protection from the sun, does not seem to us to have been a pre-Hispanic Indian custom. In figurines one sees elaborate headdresses used for ceremonies, or to indicate rank, or *rodetes* used for everyday to keep the hair in order and for adornment. Objects are seen on the heads of figurines which resemble the half gourds used by Indian women today (pls. 84 & 236).

George M. Foster (1960, p. 98) indicates that the *rebozo* in Spain is usually a small square cloth, sometimes no larger than a handkerchief, usually not similar to the long-fringed Mexican *rebozo*. This latter item of women's dress, in our opinion, may be of Mexican origin. The fact that the *rebozo* is almost always ikat dyed is an interesting point. Ikat is not common in present-day Indian garments, but was used in pre-Hispanic times in Peru and almost certainly in Mexico. There is the possibility that the *rebozo* was introduced from Southeast Asia, where ikat was well developed, and skirts and *rebozo*-like garments were common. According to Foster's data, the smaller cloths used in Mexico (pl. 200) would possibly be more Spanish than the *rebozo*.

As to *rebozos* today, there are two general types; (1) those of ikat-dyed commercial cotton, which are worn by *mestizas* and by Indian women also—for example, in the valley of Oaxaca (pls. 186 & 202) or in the market of Zimapán, Hidalgo (pl. 111); (2) the many types

of backstrap-loomed *rebozos* which are not ikat dyed. These are made either of wool or of cotton, are either plain or striped, light or dark in color, but with natural color and white predominating. All usually have handsome fringes. Only the Altepexi *rebozo* terminates in round tufts, and is woven on a treadle loom.

Some villages we know that have special handwoven *rebozo*-sized head coverings are Altepexi, Puebla (Nahua) (pl. 184); San Pedro Quiatoni and Yalalag, Oaxaca (Zapotec) (pl. 48); Paracho, Michoacán (Tarascan) (pl. 19); Santa Cruz Nundaco (pl. 33) and Cuquila, Oaxaca (Mixtec); Acatlán, Guerrero, (on the loom in pl. 79), Hueyapan, Morelos, Santa Anita Zacuala, Hidalgo, and Hueyapan, Puebla (all Nahua). Some villages having special handwoven non-*rebozo*-sized head coverings are Choapan, Oaxaca (Zapotec) (pl. 124); Ojitlán (pl. 41) and Usila, Oaxaca (Chinantec) (pl. 194); Cotzocón, Oaxaca (Mixe); Chamula (pl. 256) and San Bartolomé de los Llanos, Chiapas (Tzotzil) (pl. 251).

Some villages wearing close-fitting half gourds as head coverings, chiefly in the Mixteca Alta region, are Santa Catarina Estetla (pl. 84), Cuquila, and Ixtayutla, Oaxaca (all Mixtec); and Copala, Oaxaca (Trique) (pl. 90). At the fiesta of Igualapa, Guerrero in 1965, we observed some old women wearing large inverted gourds of irregular shape, making no pretense at fitting the head but serving as protection from the sun. In Plate 90 one Trique girl wears a painted gourd from the famous town of Olinalá, Guerrero. Gourds are worn alone or sometimes over a cloth which covers the head. Whereas the half-gourd head covering is confined to women's use today, we read (Ajofrín, 1964, Vol. II, p. 63) that in the eighteenth century, in the vicinity of Soyaltepec, Oaxaca (Mazatec), both men and women wore "very elaborately decorated" half gourds upon their heads—for protection from the sun and for use as cups from which to drink water or *posole* (a drink made of cooked ground corn).

The *huipil grande* of the Isthmus of Tehuantepec (pl. 210) is a special festive head covering, more complicated than *rebozos* or *cloths*, as are the identical garments made of simpler materials in Huamelula, Oaxaca (Chontal), and the *huipil de tapar* of the Zoques of Tuxtla Gutiérrez, Chiapas, probably now extinct (pl. 250).

Some special handwoven, sometimes decorative, coverings, which serve both head and shoulders, should be mentioned—such as special blankets used by Trique

90. Trique girls from San Juan Copala at the Indian State Fair, wearing many *papelillo* beads; one wears a lacquered gourd from Olinalá, Guerrero. Oaxaca City, Oaxaca. 1941

91. Trique women and children wrapped in diagonal-weave blankets. San Andrés Chicahuaxtla, Oaxaca. 1943

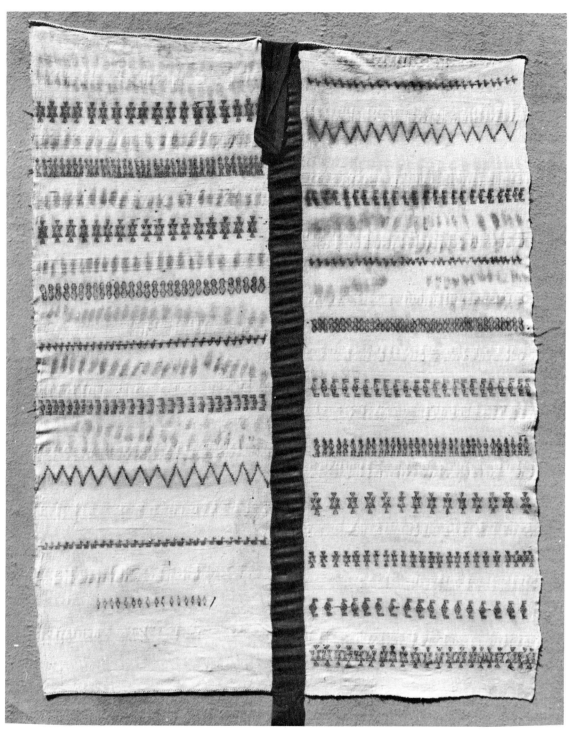

92. A *tralla* or cape worn as a sole upper garment, as a shawl, or as a cape over a fiesta *huipil*. Between brocaded design rows are indications of finger painting. Cactus fruit (*pitaya*) juice (according to our informant) was formerly used for such painting, but only *fuchina* is employed today. This technique differs from other painting or stamping processes of recent times in Mexico in that the extra color in white areas is applied freely with fingers or thumbs. Ixtayutla, Oaxaca (Mixtec).

93. Drying fish in San Mateo del Mar, Oaxaca. (Huave). 1940

women of San Andrés Chicahuaxtla, Oaxaca (pls. 91 & 235), and handwoven straight pieces of cloth used as capes in a few villages, as in pre-Conquest times. We have only seen capes used in *huipil* villages—San Juan Chamula and several villages in the Chiapas highlands, and elsewhere only in the Mixtec village of Ixtayutla in the district of Jamiltepec (pl. 92); the latter, in warm country, is only for ceremonial use.

Not all head coverings used today are decorative, very special, or handwoven. For relief from the sun, the Huave women of San Mateo del Mar (pl. 93; Chapter 35) tie a square of commercial white cloth pirate-style about the head. Thus one can spot them for a consider-able distance in the Tehuantepec market among con-servative Isthmus women who dress quite similarly to-day. The common commercial thin bath towel is seen upon heads almost everywhere for protection from rain or sun. Even where handweaving is done, one may be used to save a *quechquemitl* while the wearer is work-ing. In Huehuetla, where the *quechquemitl* is common-ly used as a head covering, the bath towel may be sub-stituted (pl. 68). For protection from rain, a large banana leaf is far more picturesque, as is the old-style straw raincoat with its Far Eastern look—now largely replaced by squares of brilliant colored plastic, sold everywhere before and during the rainy season.

8. Belts, Tortilla Cloths, and Bags

 COMPARATIVELY LITTLE INFORMATON is available concerning the centers where women's belts are made today. This is due to several difficulties in investigation. Very often belts are woven in one village or center, and carried long distances over mountain trails to be sold to women of another region. Sometimes belts are sold only once a year at large fairs where trader meets buyer. Often the merchant and his client do not speak the same language, or they may speak different dialects. The woman wants a new belt, the same kind of belt that she, her mother, and her grandmother have always worn, but she is not greatly interested in where it comes from.

There are a number of belt-weaving centers in the Mixteca Alta, in the vicinity of the villages of Peñasco. These supply the western Mixteca Alta and the Mixteca Baja as well; and until recently these weaving centers did business with towns in the state of Puebla. This region, as far as textiles are concerned, is not well known or documented; and the gruelling task of going from village to village on horseback will be necessary before the story is complete. This situation exists in many parts of Mexico.

Belts have always been an important element in both men's and women's costumes; but women's belt styles will far outlast those of men (which are being replaced little by little by commercial leather or plastic ones), because they are essential to secure the wrap-around skirt. Also many beliefs and superstitiions surround the binding of the stomach for the protection of the unborn child against evil influences. We were told by a doctor who had worked in the area that the Chinantec women of Ojitlán, Oaxaca, bind themselves tightly with their belts to avoid a palpitation of the diaphragm which frightens them. The truth of the matter is, he said, that the tightness of the binding itself causes the sensation.

Elsie Clews Parsons says about Mitla, Oaxaca (1936, p. 38), that "Women sleep in their chemise. Over the chemise is drawn very tightly a belt woven of maguey fiber, the ordinary matting which is four fingers wide, wrapped double and tied with cotton strings. Women wear this stiff belt because they think it keeps them from having the dark blotches on the skin called *paño*." An unusual aspect of this interesting finding is the use of an undergarment and extra belt. (Zapotec women of Mitla still wear *solferino* wool belts to hold their wrap-around skirts.) Most of the blotched skin disorders, either white or dark, are called *pinto* elsewhere.

Once, in Tuxtepec, Oaxaca, while talking to two Mazatec women (pl. 4) from Jalapa de Díaz, we noticed a belt tied about a basket to keep the contents from overflowing. It proved to be the one worn by these

135

94. A Zapotec woman of Betaaza, Oaxaca, who has traveled far to the Saturday market in Oaxaca City. She wears a *solferino*-colored silk sash — now rare. 1942

women. When we wanted to buy the belt they laughingly pulled up their *huipiles* to show us that their wrap-around skirts were held up by pieces of frayed rope!

The belt is usually a decorative feature in a costume

(pl. VI a). When visible belts contribute color and design interest, but sometimes they are covered by long *huipiles* or have the skirts folded over them about the waist. This concealment makes it difficult to get information about them. In Tetelcingo, Morelos, a very plain costume is enhanced by a colorful wide wool belt which has a narrow belt sewn on to it. The gay colored belts show on each side of the wearers, for the long *huipiles* are completely open. An all-white costume like that of Zoogocho or Betaaza, Oaxaca (Zapotec) (pl. 94), with the *huipil* tucked inside the skirt is enlivened by a wide handwoven natural-silk sash dyed *solferino* color.

Some villages we know where women's belts are home woven are Betaaza, Oaxaca (Zapotec); Ojitlán, Oaxaca (Chinantec); Tetelcingo, Morelos (Nahua); Altepexi, Puebla (Nahua); San Juan Chamula, Chiapas (Tzotzil); Jalapa de Díaz, Oaxaca (Mazatec); Santa Ana Hueytlalpan, Hidalgo (Otomí); Huehuetla, Hidalgo (Tepehua); Temoaya, state of México (Otomí); Hueyapan, Morelos (Nahua); and Cosoleacaque, Vera Cruz (Nahua). Some villages we know where women's belts are not made, but are purchased from outside centers: Pinotepa Nacional, and surrounding villages, Oaxaca (Mixtec); Jamiltepec, and surrounding villages Oaxaca (Mixtec); San José Miahuatlán, Puebla (Nahua); San Sebastián Zinacatepec, Puebla (Nahua).

Women's belts often have to support a very heavy skirt, and for this reason are usually 100 inches or more in length, and are wrapped several times around the body. The measurement includes the *soyate* (*zoyate* [Aztec]=palm; this refers to the textile material—Robelo, 1904, p. 466), when one is used. These diagonal-weave tubes of palm are extraordinarily functional, flexible, and rough to grip the cloth of the skirt. When the belt is attached to a *soyate* (pl. VI a), only one end of the woven belt has a fringe. The opposite (selvage) end is sewn to one end of the *soyate*.

Some belts worn with *soyate* are those from San Sebastián Peñoles, Oaxaca (Mixtec); Santa Catarina Estetla, Oaxaca (Mixtec); Santa María Cuquila, Oaxaca (Mixtec); Pinotepa Nacional, Oaxaca (Mixtec); Pinotepa de Don Luis, Oaxaca (Mixtec); San José Miahuatlán, Puebla (Nahua); Ixtayutla, Oaxaca (Mixtec); Altepexi, Puebla (Nahua); San Sebastián Zinacatepec, Puebla (Nahua); Santo Tomás Mazaltepec, Oaxaca (Zapotec). Some belts worn without *soyate* are those from San Andrés Chicahuaxtlá, Oaxaca (Trique); Cuetzalan, Puebla (Nahua); Chiapas highlands villages (Tzotzil, Tzeltal); Tetelcingo, Morelos (Nahua);

Temoaya, state of México (Otomí); Tolimán, Querétaro (Otomí); Huehuetla, Hildalgo (Tepehua); Santa Ana Hueytlalpan, Puebla (Otomí); Cosoleacaque, Vera Cruz (Nahua); Jamiltepec, Oaxaca (Mixtec).

In Jamiltepec and Ixtayutla, Oaxaca, the same women's belt is used, brought in from the Mixteca Alta. The belt is short (47 inches, including the fringe at one end). In Ixtayutla, where a heavier skirt is worn, the belt is sewn to a substantial *soyate*. Jamiltepec women wear smaller, lighter-weight skirts (pl. 225), and they choose to buy two of these same 47-inch woven-cotton belts, and sew the two unfringed ends together, dispensing with the *soyate*.

Weaves, patterns, colors, materials, widths, and lengths of a number of women's belts are described in Part 2, and some may be seen in Plate VI a. In size alone there is a wide variety—all the way from the narrow, short, cotton and artificial-silk one of Altepexi (pl. 185; Chapter 20), to the wide, long wool belt of Santa Ana Hueytlalpan (pl. X; Chapter 16).

The exact provenance of the women's belts of Pinotepa Nacional and Jamiltepec, both in the state of Oaxaca, remains a mystery. The first, a belt of red wool, and the second, a belt of dark-blue cotton, are brought in to the big regional fairs in the area, and may be bought only at these times—unless a lone trader comes in between fiestas. In neither area could we find a woman who could give us the name of the towns in which they were made. The women said, "They come from the Mixteca Alta." In Susana Drucker's book on Jamiltepec (1963, p. 27) we read, "The belt is bought from the Mixtecos of the zona alta, and is woven of thick blue thread with geometric designs and costs twenty pesos." Some large wool belts cost as much as 150 pesos today ($12.00 U.S.).

Often when a new belt is needed, there is a very long wait before vendors appear. Recently the able weavers of San Juan Colorado, north of the Pinotepas, have taken to copying the red wool Mixteca Alta belt used in a number of villages nearby, so as not to have to depend upon the itinerant Mixteca Alta source.

Some women of Nuyóo, Oaxaca, in the Mixteca Alta, wear a very distinctive orange and black belt (pl. VI a), which we were told was woven in the village of San Juan Numi. This will bear investigation: that town may prove to be another belt-weaving center. Numi and Nuyóo are not near each other, but between them is the market town of Tlaxiaco where Indians meet to buy and sell.

Some of these belts from the Mixteca Alta are ex-

ceedingly similar to belts made in the important Zapotec weaving center of Santo Tomás Jalieza (pl. VI a), but Mixteca Alta examples (probably from the region of the Peñascos) near Tlaxiaco are generally coarser, contain more wool, and vary in design. Some of the wider ones, however, contain variations of the Jalieza plumed-dancer motif.

When we went to the big religious fiesta and fair of Igualapa, Guerrero, the third Friday of Lent in 1965, we looked in vain for the belts or belt sellers of the Mixteca Alta. Whether they had been there, sold their merchandise, and left, or whether they had not come at all, we could not find out.

Since writing the above, we have received information from Bodil Christensen (verbal) that she and I. W. Johnson found belts from the Mixteca Alta at the fair in Pinotepa de Don Luis in 1958. They were told by the men who sold them that they were made in San Agustín Tlacotepec, Oaxaca, near the villages of Peñasco. These included the blue cotton belts worn in Ixtayutla and Jamiltepec, both in Oaxaca, and the wool belts worn in other villages in the Mixteca Baja. Further investigation may prove that the cotton and the wool belts come from different, but nearby, villages—usually one place makes only one general type of belt.

Villages in the eastern part of the Mixteca Alta (Peñoles, Santa Catarina Estetla, and others), in the district of Etla, trade more directly with Oaxaca City. They wear Santo Tomás Jalieza belts and purchase them on trips to their state capital.

It is probable that Jalieza belts travel farther than any others in Mexico. Tourists from everywhere buy them either in the village, in Oaxaca City, or in Mexico City; and Indians of Guatemala used to wear them and perhaps still do so today. Lilly de Jongh Osborne (1935, p. 67) says, "The Pokoman Indian women of Mixco have special belts which they buy from traders who come once a year, during the dry season, from distant Oaxaca (Mexico). The Mixqueñas will wait all year to acquire one of these new belts, despite the fact that they weave other textiles in their village. A Mixco woman, 30 years ago would not consider wearing any other kind of belt but those" (referring to Jalieza belts with plumed dancers.)

Dolores Morgadanes (1940, p. 361) says that women from Yalalag wear "belts identical to those worn by Mixco women." There is some misunderstanding about this. The traditional Yalalag belt for both men and women, before 1940, was a wide, white, cotton one. Those of the women were sometimes dyed pink, and

95. Zapotec women weaving around a tree. Note the belts hanging for sale. Santo Tomás Jalieza, Oaxaca. 1960

were sewn to a *soyate*. A woman may marry into a Yalalag family, and use part of her own raiment. The belt in question may have been worn by a woman just passing through Yalalag. Santo Tomás Jalieza belts began to be used in Yalalag about 1950. Actually, the belts Morgadanes saw used in Guatemala were no doubt made in Jalieza, for the traditional plumed-dancer patterns and colors are described.

Whether these belts are still taken into Guatemala we do not know, anymore than we can say whether Zoque women of Copainalá, Chiapas, still make pilgrimages to Esquipulas in Guatemala, and bring back

red ikat-dyed treadle-loomed skirt *cortes* for gala wear as they did as late as 1940.

In Mitla, Oaxaca, a finely woven wide *solferino* wool belt with very nice fringes has been used for a good many years by women, who wear wrap-around skirts. Elsie Clews Parsons (1936, p. 41) wrote that, "About fifteen years ago the uniform rosy belt took the place of a narrow belt diversely figured with animal and geometric designs. La Conquista dancer was also figured." This again no doubt refers to belts woven in Santo Tomás Jalieza, the not too distant weaving center in the valley of Oaxaca.

A Zapotec Indian from Mitla told us very recently that the *solferino* sash, used only by conservative older women who still wear the wrap-around skirt, is no longer woven in Mitla proper (weavers are too busy with commercial weaving), but is purchased from the nearby village of San Pablo Güilá. So there are many changes, as breakdowns occur everywhere, inevitably and gradually.

In 1942 we purchased very beautiful patterned silk belts from San Francisco Cajonos. They seem to have been the product of a very small local industry, and are now (1966) almost impossible to get. They were usually white, green, and yellow, with *solferino* predominating; and had designs of deer, corn, female figures, and geometric designs. Most of the few belts woven today in Cajonos are patterned, but all in white; they are rarely sold now in Oaxaca City.

The question of belts becomes very complicated in areas where a number of linguistic groups reside in the same village, or in close proximity. In Huehuetla, Hidalgo, populated by Tepehuas, women weave and wear an exceedingly handsome geometric-patterned belt of heavy black wool and white cotton. Measuring 6 inches wide by 98 inches in length (including 17-inch braided fringes at both ends), the belt encircles the body of the wearer twice, and must—according to tradition—end on the left side with the long fringe crossing in front from right to left. These belts they weave for themselves (pls. VI a & 68).

We had previously visited the Totonac village of Mecapalapa, Puebla, in the same general area; we found some women there wearing the Tepehua belt, whereas conservative Totonac women wore the red wool belt used also in the Totonac village of Pantepec, Puebla. Only by their different *quechquemitl*, not by their belts, could one be certain of correctly identifying the linguistic groups in this particular area.

Women commonly are the belt weavers (pl. 95), but in Altepexi, Puebla, men weave women's belts as well as men's (pl. 96). There are very few belt weavers left in this village. In the village of Tetelcingo, Morelos—where many women still wear their traditional dress—there remain but three or four belt weavers. We observed that the teenaged daughter of our belt-weaving informant, a woman about thirty-five years old (pl. 192), had never learned her mother's craft and clearly never would. One wonders whether the costume will have to disappear when there are no more belt weavers in this village—where the ring-weaving technique is employed and two belts are worn one over the other.

96. A loom for belt weaving, with a rigid heald. Altepexi, Puebla (Nahua). 1963

Materials used to make these belts are obtained in a laborious manner. The white spool thread (used in the warp) is purchased in the nearby town of Cuautla, but the blue, green, and red wool (afterwards respun) comes from Texcoco, state of México, and must be purchased on market days in Ozumba, state of México.

In the Puebla villages of San José Miahuatlán and San Sebastián Zinacatepec, the women were very vague as to where their belts came from. But the *mestizo* owner of a Miahuatlán corner store named the village where the belts in his town were made (Chapter 19). In Zinacatepec no one knew where their very different red wool belt was woven, and there were considerable complaints that no belts came in anymore. Here the costume is disappearing rapidly, and no doubt it is not worth the trader's time to journey a long distance to sell so few belts.

Isabel Kelly and Angel Palerm (1952, Pl. e, f, p. 364) in their study of Tajín, Vera Cruz (Totonac), mention

139

the red and white woven women's sash, "purchased in former times from traders from the highlands; precise provenience unknown to informants. No longer available, but a few such belts are still found in Tajín and are worn exclusively by elderly women." We, also, do not know who made these belts, but the same belt is still used today in the more conservative Totonac villages of Pantepec and Mecapalapa, both in Puebla. We have noted that the red wool belt used by Cuetzalan, Puebla (Nahua), women (pl. VI a; Chapter 18) is exceedingly similar, and is said to be woven in Xalacapa, Puebla.

In the Huastec area of Tancanhuitz (Ciudad Santos), San Luis Potosí, we were surprised to find Huastec and Nahua women wearing cotton ikat-dyed belts from Tolimán, Querétaro. Though it is a long distance from Tolimán to Tancanhuitz, there is a bad road of sorts, and a single enterprising *mestizo* woman keeps the entire trade to herself, selling belts each Sunday in the Tancanhuitz market. Plate VI a shows a very fine old silk belt purchased in Tolimán.

Another belt-weaving village is San Juan Chamula, Chiapas (Tzotzil). Here the weavers make their own wide women's belts (pl. VI a); and the women's belts for a number of other villages, including Larrainzar. The particularly fine men's belt (pl. VI b) of Larrainzar is woven in Larrainzar, which gives some idea of the difficulties of finding the provenance of woven articles in the Chiapas highlands. In this area more ceremonial garments exist today than in any other part of Mexico. Whereas *huipiles* and *quechquemitl* are almost always woven in the conservative villages where they are used, skirts and belts are not.

The same belt is sometimes used for both men and women: for example, the beautiful silk cochineal-dyed belts from San Juan Mixtepec, Oaxaca, and the Chontal cotton belts from Huamelula, Oaxaca. The latter are dyed with shellfish dye, but now the color is being copied with a mixture of commercial *fuchina* dye (According to Santamaría, 1959, p. 538, *fuchina* was a colorant extracted from varieties of the fuchsia plant; today in Mexico it is an aniline dye of fuchsia color.) and brazilwood dye (verbal communication, Don Francisco Bartolo). Very nice belts for men are made in Usila, Oaxaca—brocaded designs on a red ground (pl. VI b) —but they are going out of fashion, and only a very few old men now own them.

Men's handwoven belts and sashes are becoming rare, as has been stated. The Huichol men's double cloth, patterned sashes, woven of natural-colored wools,

are the finest in Mexico (pls. 97 & VI b). True to their serpent association, they are very long, up to 130 inches or more. The longest men's belt we examined is one from Santa María Zacatepec, Oaxaca, measuring 14 inches wide by 146 inches long (pl. VI b).

Occasionally a ceremonial belt is worn by men. A very handsome one is worn by an official (*mandón*) in Ixtayutla, Oaxaca (Mixtec). It is very different from the everyday belt. The latter is dark blue, and is worn in Ixtayutla and dyed in Pinotepa de Don Luis, Oaxaca. The ceremonial belt, handed down from one official to another, and only replaced when it is ragged (verbal communication, Lucila Franco), is 102 inches long without the fringe, and 14 inches wide. It has white cotton warps; the wefts are of blue cotton, with the exception of four bands, 3 to 4 inches wide, of cochineal-dyed silk. These bands alternate with the background blue. The warp fringe is dyed with cochineal.

When we collected narrow figured silk belts from San Francisco Cajonos in the Sierra Juárez, Oaxaca (Zapotec), in the early 1940's we were puzzled that no one seemed to wear them, and that the industry seemed very small. We did not go to the village ourselves. In 1966 we wrote to Mrs. Anita Jones of Oaxaca City and told her the story. At first she thought these belts might have been made for tourists, but we decided that at that time there were too few foreigners interested, and the village was too remote. Mrs. Jones then found, through contacts we had made in 1942, that these belts (usually measuring about 58 inches in length including fringe) were made for what appears now to be a very special use: to hold up the *huipil* "sleeves." Women resorted to this measure while cooking or grinding—especially during fiestas. Cotton belts were normally worn, but the silk ones were favored by richer women (or for special occasions)—see Figure 14 (drawn from photographs courtesy of Anita Jones).

Mrs. Jones has also recorded this custom from San Antonino Castillo Velasco, Oaxaca (Zapotec) (letters, April 19, 1966 and March 10, 1967), and from Asunción Ocotlán. These valley of Oaxaca villages no longer commonly wear the *huipil*, but a few of the older women demonstrated the old custom of holding in *huipil* "sleeves." For this purpose these and other valley villages formerly used Santo Tomás Jalieza belts, measuring 1 inch in width by 67+ inches in length including fringes. As seen in Figure 14, there were distinctly different fashions for this belt use in different villages. These findings are especially interesting because the same custom is recorded by Lilly de Jongh Osborne

a. Some women's belts and where they are worn: (left to right) Huehuetla, Hidalgo (Tepéhua); Tolimán, Querétaro (Otomí); Cosoleacaque, Vera Cruz (Nahua); San Sebastián Peñoles, Oaxaca (Mixtec), but made in Santo Tomás Jalieza, Oaxaca (Zapotec): Pinotepa Nacional, Oaxaca (Mixtec); Cuetzalan, Puebla (Nahua); Larrainzar (San Andrés Chamula), Chiapas (Tzotzil); Temoaya, state of México (Otomí): Santiago Nuyóo, Oaxaca (Mixtec).

b. Some men's belts and where they are worn: (left to right) Santo Domingo Chicahuaxtla (Santo Domingo del Estado), Oaxaca (Trique); Santa María Zacatepec, Oaxaca (Mixtec); Santa Catarina, Jalisco (Huichol); Rancho El Limón, Nayarit (Huichol); Rancho El Limón, Nayarit (Huichol); San Juan Copala, Oaxaca (Trique); Jamiltepec, Oaxaca (Mixtec); Usila, Oaxaca (Chinantec); Larráinzar (San Andrés Chamula); Chiapas (Tzotzil).

c. A Huichol man's double-cloth bag — natural tan and brown wool, containing a design showing dogs, and probably woven between 1925 and 1935. Guadalupe Ocotán, Nayarit.

d. An old Chinantec man's headcloth from Usila, Oaxaca — no longer woven in the village or worn, unless possibly by one or two of the elders for ceremonial occasions.

PLATE VI

97. A Huichol man from Las Guásimas, Nayarit, at the Chapalagana River, Nayarit, demonstrating the use of the bow and arrow. 1937

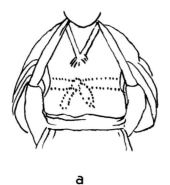 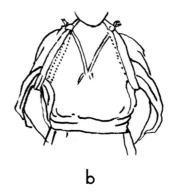 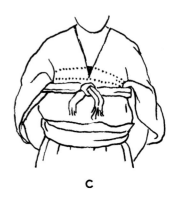

a   b   c

Figure 14. A special use of women's handwoven belts, to hold in excess width of *huipiles*, leaving hands free. Based on photographs and letters by Anita Jones.
a. Asunción Ocotlán, Oaxaca (Zapotec); *b*. San Antonino Castillo Velasco, Oaxaca (Zapotec); *c*. San Francisco Cajones, Oaxaca (Zapotec).

(1935, p. 19), who reports the surplus of the wide *huipiles* of Mixco, Guatemala as being "held up from the arms" by a woolen cord. Japanese women had the same custom and used *tasuki* cords.

Servilletas and Bags

Tortilla cloths (*servilletas*) of many sizes and proportions are greatly admired by Indians, and in most weaving villages either *servilletas* or beautifully woven bags were made for carrying purposes. Many are still made today in some areas, although like all handweaving the custom is decreasing.

Although *servilletas* and bags in most cases are not strictly a part of the women's or men's costume, one cannot ignore these items, which have always displayed some of the nicest free expression in design and color of all weaving done in this country.

Rarely does a village weave both *servilletas* and bags, although from Ixtayutla, Oaxaca (Mixtec), where *servilletas* are made, one very large white brocaded bag was acquired by us recently—it was said to be used for carrying candles to the church. Bags on the whole come from the northern and central areas—Tepehuas, Huichols, Coras, Otomís, Huastecs, Mazahuas, and Nahuas (but they are also made in the Chiapas highlands). *Servilleta* villages, for the most part, those of southern Oaxaca and southern Guerrero—comprising the Mixteca Baja, the Chontals, Huaves, Mixtecs, and the Amusgos of Guerrero.

In the large area of the Mixteca Alta, customs among both Triques and Mixtecs are mixed. Indians of the eastern Mixteca Alta, particularly from the Peñoles area, weave bags—large grey wool ones and cotton ones with natural-silk stripes dyed with *fuchina* (pl. 219; Chapter 29). More and more today, in the Oaxaca City market, when one peers into the great net bags of fruits brought by vendors from this high cold area, one sees that cheap Oaxaca City treadle-loomed *servilletas* are taking the place of home-woven bags.

On the western side of the Mixteca Alta, in the Tlaxiaco area, one finds both *servilleta* and bag villages. The Trique villages of San Andrés Chicahuaxtla and San Martín Itunyoso make beautiful *servilletas* (pls. 98 & 99; Chapter 33) as carefully worked as their *huipiles* are. Now that there are so many more possibilities of traveling part of a long trip by bus, we have seen women from San Andrés Chicahuaxtla as far away as Tehuacán, Puebla, seated quietly on the sidewalk, each with one of her large *servilletas* tied twice from corner to corner keeping the *tortillas* clean, that must serve as food for several people on an entire journey.

Another Trique village, that of Copala, Oaxaca, is famous for its red-striped bags of many sizes, with fine fringes and very well executed multicolored joinings at the sides (pl. 238).

Usually neither *servilletas* nor bags are actual costume accessories, but there are a few exceptions. One cannot say that certain small headcloths, such as the tan cotton one of San Juan Cotzocón, Oaxaca—used to top the headdress of woolen cords—may not also be used to wrap up *tortillas* or top a basket on the road. In San Bartolomé de los Llanos, Chiapas, the gay brocaded *servilletas* definitely serve both as head coverings

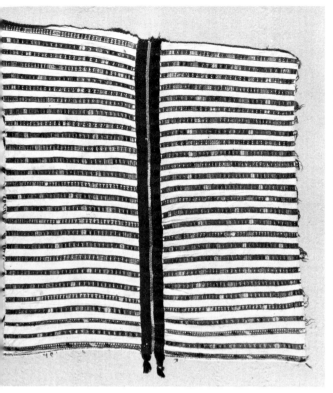

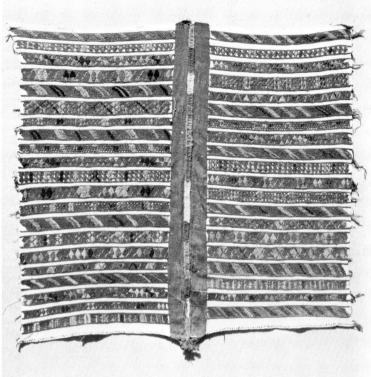

08. A *servilleta*. San Andrés Chicahuaxtla, Oaxaca (Trique).

99. A *servilleta*. San Martín Itunyoso, Oaxaca (Trique).

100. A Huastec woman's bag, embroidered on *manta*. Coxcatlán, San Luis Potosí.

101. A very old bag of soft-red wool and white cotton (provenance unknown – possibly Otomí, and possibly from Santa María del Río, San Luis Potosí, according to Bodil Christensen).

102. A Nahua bag from Atla, Puebla. Dark-red wool embroidery on *manta*.

103. A *servilleta* – front and reverse side. Xochistlahuaca, Guerrero (Amusgo).

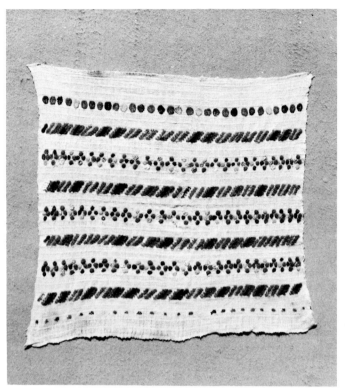

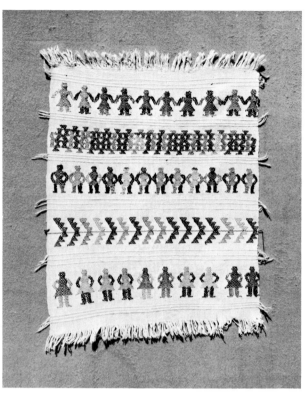

104. A white *servilleta* with multicolored brocaded designs. San Bartolomé de los Llanos, Chiapas (Tzotzil).

105. A *servilleta*. San Juan Colorado, Oaxaca (Mixtec).

and as *tortilla* cloths (pls. 104 & 251; Chapter 37). The Huastec woman who wears an embroidered *quechquemitl* almost always wears an embroidered bag (pl. 100) over one shoulder.

In the Sierra de Puebla one finds both bags and *servilletas*. In San Pablito, Otomí women make very nice white cloths with white looped designs; whereas from Atla (Nahua) we have seen *manta* bags embroidered in dark-red wool (pl. 102). The latter have a nice woven tape attached, and are worn over the shoulder. Bags which have no element for hanging are folded into baskets, or small ones—for money and small treasures—are twisted into men's or women's belts (Cordry, 1940, p. 60).

Servilletas for *tortillas* are not often exactly square—including fringes they average from 17 by 21 inches (pl. 103, Xochistlahuaca, Guerrero—Amusgo), to 26 by 33 inches (pl. 149, San Mateo del Mar, Oaxaca—Huave).

The few exactly square ones in our own collection are 23 inches square (pl. 104, San Bartolomé de los Llanos, Chiapas—Tzotzil); 27 inches square (pl. 98, San Andrés Chicahuaxtla, Oaxaca—Trique); and 29½

inches square (pl. 247, San Mateo del Mar, Oaxaca—Huave).

Servilletas are made for other purposes: in very small sizes to hold in the hand beneath a ceremonial, thinly scraped gourd for drinking *posol de cacao* at fiestas in Tuxtla Gutiérrez, Chiapas—Zoque (Cordry, 1941, pp. 98–99); in larger rectangles to cover crude home altars, or to cover tables for fiestas (Pinotepa Nacional, Oaxaca—Mixtec). Some San Pablito, Puebla, cloths—judging by their size and proportion—are intended for the latter use.

Servilletas in the Mixteca Baja are notably attractive, and are used not only for *tortillas* or topping baskets, but for display beneath breads or sweets being sold in the market of Pinotepa Nacional. Here one may recognize the village of the vendor by her skirt, her *huipil* or *tralla*, her jewelry, and her *servilletta*.

Many techniques and patterns are found in *servilletas*. They may contain all-over single-faced brocaded designs in red and white cotton (San Mateo del Mar —pl. 149; Chapter 35); colored stripes or simple arrowhead patterns alternating with corded white weft stripes (Atoyac, Oaxaca); or they may contain multicolored

106. A Huichol man, with long hair and head-band, weaving a large bag of *ixtle* fiber. Rancho Cuapinole, Nayarit. 1937

107. A Mazahua bag, handwoven and embroidered, from San Simón, near Zitácuaro, Michoacán. Collection of Bodil Christensen.

108. A Mazahua bag embroidered on *manta*, in two values of blue. Collection of Bodil Christensen. Villa Victoria, state of México.

109. An Otomí *solferino* and white wool bag. Tolimán, Querétaro.

110. An Otomí wool bag — vermillion, dark blue, and white. Collection of Bodil Christensen. Puerta del Salitre, Querétaro.

111. Otomí women with woven bags, at the Sunday market of Zimapán, Hidalgo. 1940

112. An Otomí woman carrying a characteristic bag. Zimapán, Hidalgo. 1940

rows of single-faced brocaded motifs of male and female figures alternating with geometric patterns (San Juan Colorado, Oaxaca—pl. 105). San Juan Colorado weavers are particularly prolific and weave many items. They are wont to set up their *servilleta* looms for as many as six cloths at one time, leaving distance for the fringes between, and cutting them apart when they take them off the loom.

Formerly, just before Christmas, large handwoven *servilletas* were brought into Oaxaca City to be sold. These came from the important December 8th fiesta of Juquila, further south in the same state. Townspeople looked eagerly for these cloths that had come from the great religious fair, and it was quite an event to buy one of the heavily fringed white *servilletas* with pulled-up designs in red.

The Indians of the Chiapas highlands, to our knowledge, make more bags than *servilletas*. All over Mexico bags of *ixtle* (called *morales*) are used by men, and these are woven in many highland areas, where the material is available (pl. 106). Finer bags of *pita* (twine made from agave) used to be made by the Tepehuane in northern Mexico (pl. 3); and the Tzotzils of San Juan Chamula make excellent small fiber netted pouches,

which may serve as money bags tucked into a sash. Very beautiful white cotton bags, brocaded in wool, used to be made in Tenejapa, Chiapas (Tzeltal).

The bags pictured in this book are fine old ones. Besides the patterned bags of the Huichols and Coras—the most wonderful embroidered and brocaded bags in Mexico (which have now either disappeared entirely, or greatly deteriorated in workmanship)—are those of the Otomís and the Mazahuas shown in Plates 108 & 110. In many instances bags were carried by both men and women. The Zimapán Otomí bags seen in Plates 111, 112, and 148 date from 1940 when work was still of excellent quality.

Bags which may be said to be actually a part of the costume are those of the Huastec women of the Tancanhuitz area, San Luis Potosí. One may say that a set of embroidered *quechquemitl* and bag to match is essential, for each woman wears a single bag (pl. 100) over one shoulder, and it serves as a receptacle for her small belongings and purchases. The rows of small hip bags, tiny neck bags, and large woven or embroidered bags (pl. 163; Chapter 14) worn by Huichol men are definitely part of the costume.

9. Jewelry

 In Mexico before the coming of the Spaniards beautiful jewelry was made by highly developed craftsmen. They used gold, silver, jade, shell, and various kinds of precious and semiprecious stones, to laboriously fashion their intricate creations.

The simpler marginal groups used seeds, berries, and feathers. We find groups today, such as the Seris, Huichols, Lacandóns, and Huaves, who use shells, seeds, and even fish vertebrae (Huave) as adornment—possibly because these natural objects have magical or symbolic significance. They usually wear glass beads also and these are highly prized, especially when the region is difficult of access. When the Spaniards came, they brought with them glass beads which they used for barter. The Indians were attracted to these glittering new things, and they passed from hand to hand, penetrating into the most remote areas of the country.

When we were with the Huichols in 1937–1938, they much preferred to exchange the things we wanted to buy for beads, yarn, mirrors, and salt, than to sell them for money. At that time they wore sections of sweet-smelling twigs—perforated and strung like necklaces. We were told that these were worn for the pleasant odor, but they may have had another significance. The Huichols also string buttons and thimbles into their necklaces along with shells and seeds. However, small beads are greatly valued; those of glass—blue and white —are strung and twisted into ropes for both men and women (pls. 164 & 165). The Huichols have a greater love of adornment than any other group we have encountered in Mexico. Among them one of the most startling things we saw were puppies with pierced ears, and small tufts of wool hanging from the perforations, like earrings (pl. 113). At a fiesta we also noted dogs with necklaces of seeds.

The Seris still adorn themselves with shell necklaces, although they also sell them to tourists. We saw one old woman in Punta Chueca with half a pair of scissors hanging on a cord about her neck. This doubtless served a dual purpose as, aside from its decorative value, it was a useful instrument in the making of baskets. On another occasion the keys to our jeep were lost in the sand; after much searching we finally spotted them on a string about a woman's neck. They were returned with good grace.

Necklaces, rings, and earrings seem to be preferred to bracelets. The patterned bead bracelets of the Huichol men are well known, but other bracelets are rare. An unusual form of woman's bracelet has been observed, to our knowledge, in only three investigations: by Frederick Starr (in 1899); Johnson, Johnson and

151

113. Even the Huichol dogs are decorated. This one has a small earring made of a tuft of wool. Rancho El Limón, Nayarit. 1938

Beardsley (in 1962); and by ourselves (in 1937–1938, and in 1965). The bracelet referred to is a long string of glass or coral beads which may measure up to 110 inches or more. Those observed by Starr (1899, pl. XCV) are pictured on two Mixe women from Coatlán, Oaxaca. Each woman wears two of these bracelets, one on each wrist. According to our informant in 1965 in Cuatlamayán, San Luis Potosí, it was the custom for a girl to be given by her mother-in-law two long strings of beads, which were wrapped around both wrists. The Cuatlamayán woman in Plate VII wears them. These are very small black glass beads, and each string measures 110 inches in length. In 1937 we saw Huichol women with long single strands of beads wrapped about the wrists, but no special information was gathered about them.

Johnson, Johnson, and Beardsley (1962, p. 162) observed bracelets like the above, fashioned of highly polished coral beads interspersed with a few silver and glass beads. The beads were much larger than those of Cuatlamayán, and the strands measured 70–100 centimeters, making 6–10 revolutions about the wrist. These authors had the coral examined, and found that it was probably imported from the Philippines. These bracelets, according to photographs, were worn on one wrist only—the left or the right.

Probably a great deal of coral came into Mexico on the Manila galleons. It has always been highly valued in Indian Mexico. In Pinotepa Nacional in 1961 we found that one string of coral beads, about 23 inches long and of moderate size, was of value equal to one good native skirt with caracol stripes.

The long glass beads from San Pedro Quiatoni, Oaxaca, are interspersed with half-inch handmade polychrome beads with raised designs (pl. 46). These are pictured by William Orchard (1929, pl. XIII), and he says about them (pp. 89–90), that they are all of Venetian origin, and were not made in a factory, but were fashioned by families in their homes; this fact accounts for the great range in shape and decorative patterns. These beads, he says, have been collected from the Crows of Montana, the Blackfeet, the Comanche, and the Sioux Indians.

The necklaces from San Pedro Quiatoni were prized by the Indians in 1941–1942, and they usually did not wish to part with them. There is still no car or bus road to this village, but—isolated as they are—they have in recent years almost completely abandoned their old costume. Because of this, these necklaces are now more frequently found for sale in Mitla and Oaxaca City.

Another type of glass bead pictured by Orchard (1929, p. 87, fig. 84) is found especially in Oaxaca, and is described by him as also of Venetian origin. The bead is known to the trade as "Cornaline d'Aleppo," and is found widely distributed throughout the North American continent. According to Orchard these beads were received by the Indians through the Hudson Bay Company's trading posts. Orchard goes on to say that a more recent variety of the same general kind was the bead having yellow or white centers of opaque glass, with an outside covering of red transparent glass. These are of particular interest to us because they are widely found today in Mexico, especially in Oaxaca. They are strung with small birds, combs, and other small objects—all made of silver.

In the two Mixe villages of Mixistlán and Yacochi, women until recently wore 3½ pounds of beads (pl. 37). These had obviously been treasured, and handed down from one member of the family to another, although, in some cases, the women had been buried in them.

Such beads range from large to small, and many are extremely old; especially a type of crude opaque blue glass bead, that may date from the late seventeenth or early eighteenth century. In these strings are many white opaque glass beads which may have come from China on the Manila galleons. These necklaces are usually composed of twenty or more strands.

The fashion in beads varies as do other fashions. In Usila, Oaxaca (Chinantec), in 1964 many strings of capsule-shaped modern red glass beads were worn with medals or with small gold crosses (pl. 114). In San José Miahuatlán, when they can afford them, women now wear strings of black glass beads—imitating the black jet beads formerly worn with silver medals.

On our last trip to San Mateo del Mar, Oaxaca (Huave), in 1963, we observed that most women wore only a single string of small glass beads. Women of Acatlán and Zitlala, Guerrero (Nahua), neighboring villages, wear the same costume, but may be distinguished by their beads. Acatlán women (1964) wear a single string of imitation yellow amber (pl. 115), and in Zitlala they wear a single string of red beads.

Silver was worked for decorative church objects as soon as the Spaniards came to Mexico and brought silversmiths. The imported craftsmen taught the Indians their own techniques. However, ancient traditions inherited by the Indians from their ancestors were apparent in designs executed for the many churches founded by religious orders. The following three districts of Oaxaca formerly had silver mines: the district of Ixtlán de Juárez; the district of Villa Alta; and the district of Choapan. These mines contributed to the production and popularity of silver objects, jewelry, and crosses in this region.

In Colonial times silver objects were supposed to be marked, and to contain a certain silver content; but in workshops in remote mountain villages sometimes a low grade of silver was used, and as far as we have seen there were no markings on small pieces—especially jewelry.

One of the important large centers which worked silver was the Sierra Juárez in Oaxaca, and from this region came the so-called Yalalag crosses. Julio de la Fuente (1949, p. 74, and footnote 17) gives three names for the crosses: (1) *Krus Yun* (Zapotec); (2) "Three Marys"; and (3) "Of Choapan"; the latter implying that the crosses were made in Choapan. These crosses have been well described (Davis and Pack, 1963, pp.

114. A Chinantec girl of Usila, Oaxaca, showing the striking hairdress and jewelry. 1964

103–106), but we add some additional notes. In our opinion, the crosses were made in many centers. One of the most important was in and around the Zapotec villages of Choapan, Latani, and Comaltepec (all in Oaxaca)—in the Sierra Madre del Sur.

When we were in Yalalag in 1938, the triple silver crosses (pls. 116 & 117) were seldom worn. Already small gilt crosses had superseded them. It was not difficult, however, to find or purchase old crosses; today they are practically nonexistent. At the Oaxaca Indian State Fair of 1941, only one Yalalag girl in a delegation

115. Nahua women of Acatlán, Guerrero, in characteristic embroidered handwoven skirts. 1964

116. Triple crosses from Oaxaca (both Zapotec): left, Choapan cross; right, Yalalag cross.

117. Triple crosses: left and right, Sierra Juárez (Zapotec); center, Pinotepa Nacional (Mixtec).

of six (on the left in pl. 48), wore an old-style silver cross.

We have consulted many books about the history of the church in Oaxaca and of silver in Oaxaca, but these small items are rarely mentioned. We know that early European Christian crosses were sometimes made with a jewel hanging from either arm of the cross. We have in our possession a Macedonian cross (pl. 118), which probably dates from the late eighteenth or early nineteenth century. The earliest representation we know of in Mexico of a cross with small pendant objects is seen in a portrait of Fray Gregorio Beteta, *"ministro Zapoteco"* (pl. 119). The legend on this painting bears the date of his death, 1562, but from its style the painting may date from a later century. It hangs in the church of Santo Domingo in Oaxaca City. The cross with pendants, as we see from the painting of the illustrious

friar, is a rosary; and the pendant crosses in the mountain villages of the Sierra Juárez are still called *rosarios*.

A cross with small crosses and medals is pictured worn by peasant women of Salamanca, Spain (Ortiz Echagüe, 1950, p. 129), (pl. 120). In the early sixteenth century, soon after the Conquest, friars went to the mountain area of Oaxaca, and the crosses may have been brought from Spain, and copied in a direct, simplified fashion—with Indian interpretation.

Santiago was the patron of Spain in the sixteenth century, and he was frequently invoked in the battle cries of the Spaniards against the Indians during the Conquest. Walter Starkie (1957, p. 44) describes how, "on the march towards the mysterious city of Moctezuma, when the small force of Cortez was attacked ceaselessly by the Indians in overwhelming numbers,

155

118. A silver cross with pendants, from Macedonia.

119. Fray Gregorio Beteta — a painting in the great church of Santo Domingo in Oaxaca City, Oaxaca.

Cortez shouted the war-cry, *Santiago y a ellos* (St. James and at 'em), and with the help of the Apostle the Indians were driven back with great slaughter." Many other instances of appeal to Santiago for aid during battle are cited.

Many villages were given the prefix of Santiago. In Santiago Choapan, the crosses often have pendant medals instead of crosses (pl. 116). Usually one or two of the medals depict a man on horseback with a lance killing a dragon or serpent. Santiago is conventionally depicted on horseback with a Moor beneath the horse's hooves, but the medals in Santiago Choapan do not follow this pattern. That there was some confusion on the part of the Indians when the moulds were brought from

Spain seems possible, for the saint killing the dragon is actually Saint George, who had a very small following in Mexico in comparison to other saints.

The triple crosses of Choapan and Yalalag vary in overall size from 3½ to 7 inches in height; and they vary considerably in the design of the large cross and the small pendant crosses. Most old crosses which one buys in a center like Oaxaca City have been restrung. In Yalalag in 1938 most old crosses were sold with no beads of any kind, whereas in Choapan in 1964 and 1965 the few remaining had been kept with beads. Crosses were not worn, as they are seen today, with complete necklaces. The Indians wore them with a long string or ribbon across the back and a section of beads on each side

120. Triple crosses from Salamanca, Spain. From José Ortiz Echagüe, *España: tipos y trajes.*

121. A large cross and silver ornaments from the Choapan, Oaxaca, area. (Zapotec).

in front near the cross (pl. 200). Indeed the sharp edges of the small silver objects in some of these *rosarios* are exceedingly uncomfortable close about the neck.

The provenance of another type of cross is uncertain, due to age and the fact that it is no longer used (pl. 121). This large, flat, etched cross measures 6⅝ inches in height, and was found in Choapan, but possibly came from the eastern Chinantla where some silver jewelry was also used. We have been told by Jerónimo Quero

of Mitla, a Zapotec who buys and sells in these roadless mountain villages, that the latter crosses—due to their size and value—were owned by only a few people, and were rented to be used at funerals where they were worn by the person officiating. After the funeral they were placed standing upright at the head of the deceased until time for burial. These crosses probably date back to the eighteenth century.

Another type of cross, peculiar to the region of Talea de Castro (an old Oaxaca mining center), and Yaeé, Oaxaca, is pictured in Davis and Pack (1963, p. 19). This is a much smaller flat cross, etched with the symbols of the Passion. Although many have been sold, these crosses are still worn infrequently in the Zapotec village of Yalina, Oaxaca, on the "Dia de la Cruz," May 3rd.

Most of these villages in the eighteenth century used *relicarios* (reliquaries), with cases of silver or silver gilt, containing pictures of saints usually painted on tin, bone, or ivory. As *relicarios* were generally about ½ inch in thickness, one finds pieces of old documents or religious printed matter used as filling. If a date is found on the old paper, it is usually from the middle of the eighteenth century. The case of one *relicario* in our collection is decorated with enamel. The Choapan girl in Plate 200 wears a similar one, without enamel.

We have a necklace almost identical to one pictured in Davis and Pack (1963), p. 83), strung with silver beads, coins of the eighteenth century, small keys, musical instruments, combs, and birds—objects which may have to do with old beliefs concerning women.

On one occasion in Choapan, Oaxaca (Zapotec), we were shown a large silver cross hanging from a necklace of old trade beads. Strung with these was a curious ornament, 2⅝ inches long, also made of silver. This was a bird, not at all like an eagle but with a crest; in its talons it held a knifelike object. When we asked the owner about it, she said, "It is an eagle holding a jaguar's claw." Later we found more of these ornaments in the town, not always on necklaces, but saved as mementos of grandmothers. These were all more or less the same size. One was a lizard, and there were several birds— all of whose tails terminated in a knifelike form (pl. 121).

Later, in the Mixteca Baja we discovered necklaces (pl. 122), worn by the old women called *mandonas* (who serve in official capacities). These necklaces also contained silver birds and animals. One ornament was a bird whose tail terminated in an enormous claw (the claw was one symbol of Ciuacoatl, who was sometimes

158

called Quauhciuatl—"Woman-eagle"—and was connected with childbirth). Another was an alligator (*cipactli?*), the tail of which also terminated in a knifelike form, as do those of the Sierra Juárez and the Sierra Madre del Sur.

We see in the Codex Borgia a bird with a clawlike object in its talons (fig. 15 a). In his *Comentarios al Códice Borgia*, Eduard Seler (1963, Vol. I, p. 84) says, referring to this plate, that the quetzal bird holds a curved pointed object like a thorn or spine. He goes on to say that in Plate 30 of the Codex Vaticanus, we see the same bird holding in its claws the same object, which contains streaks of blood. The extreme point of the object is finished with a small yellow disk (or ball?), which has two short protruding ends (fig. 15 b). Seler wonders if this drawing alludes to the umbilical cord, which was buried in the place of the future activities of the child: if a boy, in the battlefield in territory of his enemies; and if a girl, near the hearth.

We wonder if the object held by the bird could be the knife (claw or talon) with which a child's umbilical cord was cut. Could the bird holding it be the *tona*, or guardian animal, associated with the child? It seemed to us that the yellow object into which the knife is thrust (fig. 15 b) might represent cotton, although José Luis Franco (verbal) feels it may be *copal* (incense made of gum resin), not cotton. In any case, *copal* burned on the *brasero* (brazier) suggests some sort of ceremony; and, as Seler says, a girl's umbilical cord buried near the hearth would point out her future activities, which would include spinning and weaving.

So the small silver ornaments or charms from the Choapan and Mixteca Baja areas may be an interesting survival of pre-Hispanic beliefs carried over into Colonial times, and still existing today.

A very strange pair of silver ornaments were found in Santa Fe, New Mexico, a number of years ago. We were told that these came from Oaxaca, Mexico, and that they were very old (pl. 123 a). We did not believe the provenance given, as they were a type of large ornament which seemed more South American than Mexican, and which we had never seen. However, we purchased the pair of pins for further investigation. In 1964 we went to Oaxaca, and Choapan was one of the villages we visited. We showed the pins to a number of old people, and some of them remembered that they had heard about the silver *clavos* (nails), as they were called. Later from a trader in Mitla, who buys and sells in the Choapan region, we bought a second type of pin (pl. 123 b). This is a 5–5½-inch pin with a disk about

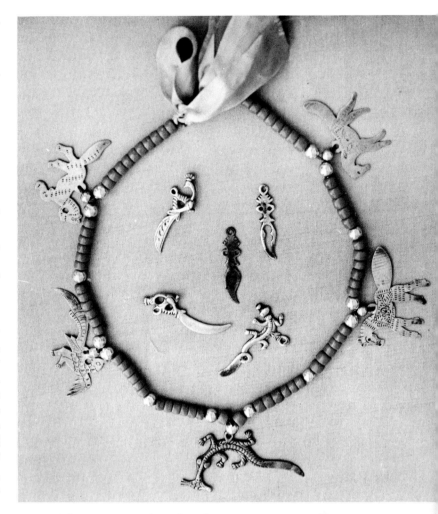

122. Silver ornaments from the Choapan, Oaxaca, area (Zapotec), surrounded by a necklace with similar silver objects from Pinotepa Nacional, Oaxaca (Mixtec).

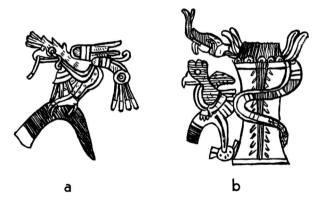

a   b

Figure 15. Bird and knife designs (copies of drawings from Codex Borgia).

159

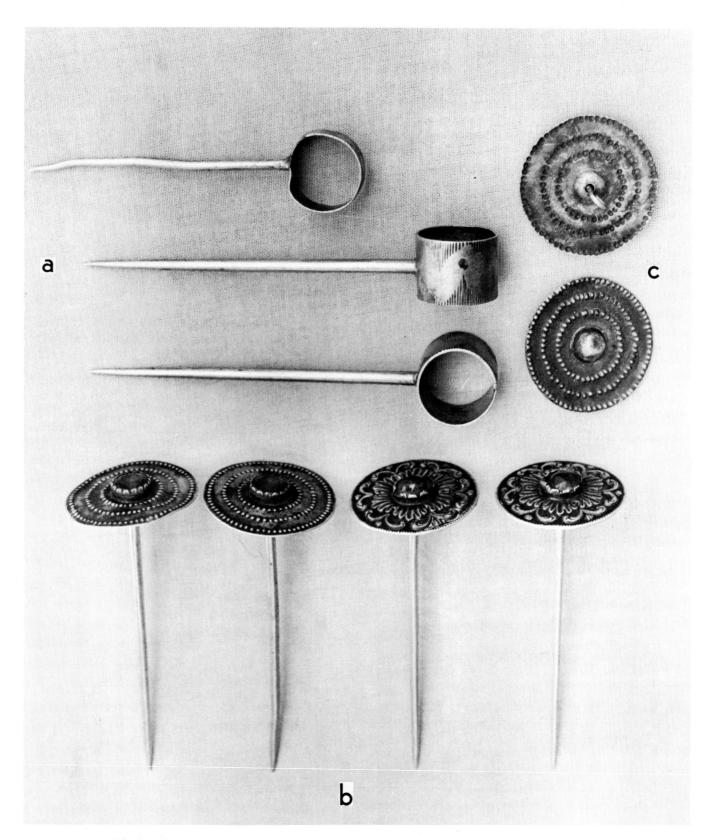

123. Old silver hair ornaments from the Choapan, Oaxaca, area. (Zapotec).

2 inches in diameter. Sometimes the disk is cast, and has designs, and sometimes the designs are in *repoussé*. On a later trip to Choapan we took this single pin with us, and people remembered more about it than the first type. They produced several pairs, and showed us how they were worn. The *clavos* had been worn by the grandmothers of women forty or fifty years old. A third variety (pl. 123 c) was also worn, but seems to have been worn in some Chinantec as well as Zapotec villages in the Choapan area.

These old hair ornaments seem to have been undocumented previous to this writing. The following gives meager information about them, gathered in Choapan and from commercial travelers of the region. Type (a) was so old that it was remembered but vaguely. Manuela Jerónimo (about fifty years old) remembered that she had heard of the *clavos* as a child, and thought that both of the types having pins (pl. 123 a & b) were put on as in Plate 124. In the case of type (a) (pl. 123 a) the rolled or twisted hair may actually have passed through the ring, although we have one example that measures less than one inch in diameter. According to informants, type (a) *clavos* were also hung about the bride's neck. A ribbon was tied to each ring, and they hung forward on her breast. This type uses simple incised linear designs as decoration.

Type (b) was remembered more clearly, especially by Isauro Martínez, whose wife had worn *clavos* on her wedding day in 1910. Even at this time the ornaments were old, and had been handed from mother to daughter. They were finally either sold or lost.

Type (c) is a disk without the long pin, but with a shank; and according to Martínez one was tied on either side of the front of the *huipil* just below the shoulders, for festive occasions. Both Jerónimo Quero and Francisco Bartolo had seen and purchased this type. Sr. Bartolo said that he had seen them used in a different manner by a woman from the eastern Chinantla in the 1950's. In this region, a bun of hair is worn over the ears, and the *clavos* were placed over this, and held in place by putting nails through the hair and through the rings at the back of the ornaments.

There is no doubt that this type of ornament was widely used, and that examples remain, jealously guarded as heirlooms. Sr. Martínez said that long ago silver was piled on the ground in the village square on Sundays "like tomatoes." But with the Revolution customs changed. Old people in Choapan knew where crosses still existed as family treasures, and where rare examples were kept as mementos, throughout this re-

124. A woman wearing a characteristic red headcloth and a pair of very old silver hair ornaments. Santiago Choapan, Oaxaca (Zapotec). 1964

gion, including the villages of Jalahui, Latani, Comaltepec, and probably those of the nearby Chinantec. Due to the upheavals during the Revolution, many of these silver ornaments were sold, hidden, or lost.

In the valley of Oaxaca in 1939, Tlacolula women could be seen wearing a silver ornament for special occasions, a custom undoubtedly taken over from the silver chains and keys formerly worn by nuns. The Indian women of Tlacolula wore such chains, with large silver clips fastened at one side of their *solferino* wool belts, worn with cochineal-dyed dark-red skirts. We have not seen these characteristic ornaments for many years.

In 1961, while on a visit to Pinotepa Nacional, Oaxaca, we were startled to see a silver cross showing the influence of the Sierra Juárez cross, made in moulds and having three small cut-out low-relief silver virgins hanging from the extremities. We found the son of the silversmith whose workshop was called "La Roca de Oro." The father, Don Felipe Ruiz, long before his death in 1920 had imported a silversmith from Oaxaca City and set to work making crosses, which were given to brides in a number of Mixteca Baja villages by their mothers-in-law. We have determined after considerable research that the silver pendants represent the Virgin of Juquila, although the son of Don Felipe Ruiz, who still owns the moulds for the crosses, said they were the Virgin of the Soledad.

The great fiesta of Juquila in southern Oaxaca on December 8th is a meeting place for Indians from all parts of Oaxaca. In former years Zapotec Indians of the Sierra Juárez could be seen wearing their triple crosses. The Mixtecs of the coast probably saw these crosses and subsequently adopted them with variations and changes for their own use (pl. 117). Each village strung its cross differently—with balls of wool, silver animal cut outs, beads, or corals. Today the silver crosses are being sold by many women, for the fashion has changed and they are no longer worn. A small gilt cross is used instead.

Many Indian women today wear the beads called *papelillo* (paperlike), which are made of very thin glass painted in brilliant colors in the fashion of Christmas-tree ornaments. These are used at times in great masses, the ends of the strands fastened together with ten or fifteen long ribbon streamers. *Papelillo* are worn by many groups, as seen in (pls. 40, 84 & 90). Many styles of inexpensive tin, brass, or thin silver earrings set with colored glass are sold at the big religious fairs. Fashions change, and we noted that in 1964 some Usila girls were discreet and favored simple gilded hoops, an inch or more in diameter. In Jamiltepec, Oaxaca (Drucker, 1963, p. 29), adult women never wear earrings; they are used only by young girls. In Cuetzalan, Puebla, we were told that young girls might wear many strings of *papelillo* beads tied with as many ribbons as they could afford, but older women must wear few beads, and only the minimum number of ribbons needed to tie them.

Other Indian silver manufacturing centers besides the Sierra de Juárez, Oaxaca, used to be the region of Toluca, state of México, where particularly large earrings were made; and the lake region of Pátzcuaro, Michoacán (Davis and Pack, 1963, pl. 50), famous for both earrings and necklaces with fish and shell motifs.

Gold jewelry is still worked for Indian consumption in various centers. Some of these are Iguala and Ometepec, Guerrero; Oaxaca City, Oaxaca; Tehuantepec, Oaxaca; Tuxtla Gutiérrez, Chiapas; Papantla, Vera Cruz; and the state of Yucatán.

In 1941 and in 1965 we noted that women of two neighboring villages speaking different tongues—Amusgos, Oaxaca (Amusgo), and Zacatepec, Oaxaca (Mixtec)—have different tastes in jewelry. For fiestas the former wear very few strings of *papelillo* beads and small earrings; whereas the Zacatepec women, whose *huipiles* show greater freedom of embroidered and brocaded designs, favor dozens of strings of *papelillo* very high about the neck, and more flamboyant earrings.

Before the advent of better communication, and of commercial earrings of brass, tin, and thin silver, doubtless many villages made jewelry of things at hand. From Xolotla, Puebla (Nahua), we recently acquired an old pair of earrings showing decided ingenuity. These are fashioned of a circular disk, and three cones of fine, skillfully woven, yellow grass, to which are sewn pendants of old tubular beads.

We have concentrated here upon the old silver jewelry of the Sierra Juárez and Choapan region of Oaxaca. Links with the past are almost lost, but we hope that some clues given here may serve as a basis for the work of future investigators.

10. Men's Costumes

INDIAN MEN's garments today bear little resemblance to ancient costumes, except in minor detail. This is because the man leaves his village to go into centers where Indian dress is a curiosity. He changes partly to avoid stares and comments, and partly because his economic level has been raised and he can afford to purchase town garments.

The principal items of men's apparel which have retained to some degree their ancient character are belts and sandals (pls. 126 & VI b; fig. 16 d) and at times a hip-cloth (pl. 188). The elaborately worked handwoven belt may have its origin in the pre-Cortesian *maxtlatl* or loincloth, but it is also possibly Spanish. It is worn today over other clothing. Often handsome belts are hidden from view by a shirt worn loose outside the trousers. Belts may be knotted center front in a manner reminiscent of the *maxtlatl*, as in Magdalenas, Chiapas, or with ribboned ends hanging halfway to the knee as in Copala, Oaxaca, or more commonly knotted at one side as in Cuetzalan, Puebla. In Huistán, Chiapas, after belts are wrapped around the body, the ends are tucked in and hang down, one end on each side of the wearer (Chapter 38). The dark-blue cotton fringed belt ends of Ixtayutla, Oaxaca, hang center back, showing below the loose shirts (pl. 224).

In modern times a handwoven square or rectangle of cloth, varying greatly in measurement, is used by men for many purposes, The survival of the *ayate* (*tilmatli*) will be touched upon elsewhere. Among the headcloths the most decorative and the largest we know is the headcloth of San Bartolomé de los Llanos, Chiapas (pl. 125; Chapter 37). Some fine head and shoulder coverings are still worn in villages of the Chiapas highlands, and often indicate rank or social position. Fine examples, now rarely seen, are from San Bartolo Yautepec (Zapotec), Huautla de Jiménez (Mazatec), and Usila (Chinantec) (pl. VI d)—all in Oaxaca.

The costume of Tarahumara men (Chihuahua and Durango) although it is changing rapidly, is probably more like pre-Conquest fashion than that of any other group today. The Tarahumara man folds a large square of cloth triangularly about the hips, over the loincloth, and ties it in front with the points falling at the rear. A home-woven blanket is wrapped about the body for cold weather, in North American Indian style, with no hole for the head. Now a shirt is worn, or at times trousers, but the hip-cloth remains, and in *Unknown Mexico*, by Carl Lumholtz we observe that other northern groups dressed in this same manner (1902, Vol. I, p. 124 shows a Pima with hip-cloth over trousers, no shirt; p. 133 shows a Tarahumara with neither trousers nor shirt

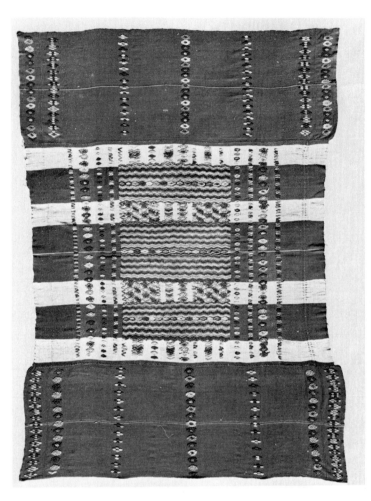

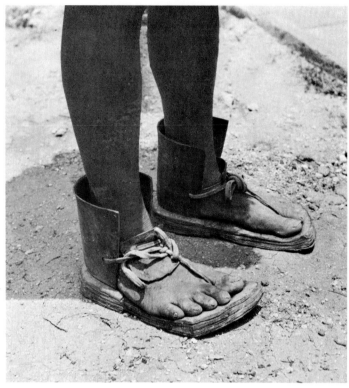

126. Sandals of ancient design — called *caites*. Zinacantán, Chiapas (Tzotzil). 1942

125. A San Bartolomé de los Llanos, Chiapas, man's head-cloth. (Tzotzil).

in the manner of some pre-Columbian sculpture; p. 426 shows Tepehuane men with shirt, trousers, and hip-cloths).

Curiously, the now extinct traditional man's costume from a very different area, that of Altepexi, Puebla, near Tehuacán, displays this same square cloth triangularly folded about the hips and knotted in front, over other clothing (pl. 188). Possibly these cloths were taken off at times for use as head or shoulder coverings, or as wrappings in which to tie belongings. This 45-inch-square Altepexi hip-cloth reaches about the body like those in the Lumholtz photographs. All these cloths were probably used in many ways, like the woman's accessories: most women's headcloths, shoulder capes, *mamales*, (cloth used as sling for carrying babies), *rebozos*, even *servilletas* serve many purposes.

In the Chiapas highlands a special type of high-backed sandals of ancient origin—called *caites*—are worn, especially for ceremonial occasions. Plate 126 shows a Chiapas Tzotzil sandal with a medium high heel-piece. Special ceremonial ones are more extreme, and reach upwards to the calf of the leg. See the list, at the end of this chapter of villages where men retain indigenous dress today, though in large part the dress is not of pre-Conquest origin.

We know of no other group except the Huichols in which the man is more decoratively and elaborately arrayed than the woman. The Huichol woman has such skill with both needle and loom that her man is greedy for more and more beautiful embroidered garments, woven bags, and the long double-cloth wool sashes with which he decorates himself (pl. 165). Perhaps because of this the woman has no time to weave the cloth used to make men's and women's clothes. They have used *manta* since before 1900. Before that, wool shirts were used by the men, and woolen *quechquemitl* by the women, but these were not elaborately decorated.

PLATE VII. A Nahua woman of Cuatlamayán, San Luis Potosí. 1965

Although the man's *manta* costume remains highly decorated to this day, even when we visited the group in 1937–1938 some women were already using two red flowered bandana handkerchiefs to make their *quechquemitl*. The men, however, still proudly wear their elaborate costume on visits to Mexico City.

Robert Zingg, in his report on the Huichols (1934, pp. 701–703), speaks of the mythological context of the costume: an important contribution because in very few reports is costume considered in this manner. The costumes of other Mexican groups, now acculturated, may once have had a mythological and symbolic meaning. Zingg says that a dirty costume on a woman is a sign of sexual impurity, but that this fact does not seem to cause the women to wash their clothes (in our observation, one reason they do not wash their clothes is a lack of water). More important is the mythological injunction of the Sun-father that the Huichols have a neat appearance. Zingg's informant added that a lazy indifferent Huichol who does not comply will be reduced to eating wild roots and animals like the rat. The good Huichol, however, who wears fine clothes, will have cattle and cheese as well as chiles and *tortillas*. Zingg goes on to say,

Indeed, a fine Huichol man's costume is what first enabled the Sun-father to rise into the sky and shine. There is so much mystical power involved in the man's costume that the Deer-people could not change Duck-boy into a deer-person until they had taken off his Huichol finery. Duck-boy was the father of the Huichols. This mystical power of the costume is again seen when the Sun-father asks *Kauymáli* if he has weapons and regalia with which to defend himself. *Kauymáli* replies, "No, I have only ordinary clothes and they are worn out."

Another reference shows that a fine costume aids the singing-shaman in the power of his singing.

The Huichols, according to Eduard Seler (n.d., Vol. 3, Part 3, p. 1), were persuaded by the early Jesuit priests to wear shirts. In those times the shirt was worn with only a loincloth; we saw a few instances of a survival of this custom in 1937–1938. The majority now wear white *manta calzones* (long trousers) of the type seen in Plate 163. Today the Huichol men's attire is beginning to change. We have seen that some shirts are now being made of blue flowered cloth, although still in the traditional style, and still worn with bags and belts.

Most men's costumes have been influenced by outside pressures or by the appeal of items seen in travels

127. A family from out of town in modern Sunday costume. Papantla, Vera Cruz (Totonac). 1939

in the outside world. Carl Lumholtz tells us (1902, Vol. II, p. 289–290) that the Huichols were required to wear trousers when entering Tepic, capital of Nayarit. Even the wide loose drawers (pl. 163) which are still worn today, were prohibited by law, and trousers were rented out by enterprising Mexicans in a supposed effort to "promote culture." Later the "commander of the territory" allowed the Indian drawers.

The Papantla, Vera Cruz (Totonac), men's costume (pl. 127) is said to have come about through the in-

Clerical influence has been pointed out in our description of the long-extinct costume of San José Miahuatlán (Chapter 19); and the origin of the ballooned trousers of San Bartolomé de los Llanos, Chiapas (Tzotzil) is unknown (pl. 254). The men of San Bartolomé wear wonderful large brocaded headcloths (pl. 128) which have counterparts in Guatemala and are possibly of Spanish origin. Cloths tied about the head occur in pre-Columbian codices and sculptures, and one must remember that probably not all garments or ways of wearing them were depicted.

Hats need not be designated as wholly Spanish in origin. Hats that appear to be of straw are worn by nude male and female figurines pictured in *Masterworks of Mexican Art* (Gamboa, 1963, Cat. 1–101). These figurines are dated from 1500 to 1000 B.C. The fanciful tiny crown of the Huichol hat, with its balls of colored wool and madrona leaves hanging from the brim, and the Chiapas Tzotzil pointed crowns, with many ribbons, may be suggestions of the flights of imagination seen in wonderful ancient Mayan hats and headdresses, both male and female.

The Indian wool blanket—of many sizes, weaves, and patterns—goes by many names and has many forms, all open down the sides: a two-web garment with an unsewn slit for the neck; a one-web garment with a woven selvage kelim slot for the neck; the *poncho* form with round or square-cut neck, and straight small sleeves set in. These are all commonly said to be of Spanish origin; yet like the *huipil* they are straight woven webs and have counterparts in ancient times.

As late as 1940 and after, Otomí men in the state of México still wore the *ayate* of woven *ixtle*, sometimes brocaded or embroidered, tied over one shoulder in the fashion of the pre-Conquest *tilmatli*, when it is not being used as a carrying cloth (pl. 129).

There are also a few surviving elements in Mexico of aboriginal men's clothing. The Seri Indian who wore a knee-length rectangle wrapped about his limbs (and still sometimes wears a suggestion of this garment over trousers today) must have kept warm with animal skins, and his pelican-skin robes—as no doubt did the northern groups (previously described wearing loincloth and hip-cloth) before the advent of wool for blankets.

There is uncertainty about the appearance of some formerly used men's costumes, because many have disappeared completely in the last twenty-five years. Unfortunately, in some places people with good intentions, but not enough knowledge, are trying to revive cos-

128. Tzotzil men of San Bartolomé de los Llanos in dance costume. Their headcloths resemble certain Guatemalan examples. Tuxtla Gutiérrez, Chiapas. 1942

fluence of French sailors seen on the Vera Cruz coast (Dr. Isabel Kelly, quoting M. Stresser Paen,—verbal communication); most shirts we saw (1939) had large sailor collars and silk scarves, and most unusual were the high-laced black shoes that we saw being worn on Sundays the same year—probably a status symbol; the area was rich in vanilla plantations.

129. Otomí men from Zacamulpa, in the region of San Bartolo Otzolotepec, state of México, wearing brocaded *ayates* woven of *ixtle*. 1937. Photograph by Bodil Christensen.

Costumes which may soon disappear, due to the breakdown occasioned by the new highways in southwestern Oaxaca are those of Santa María Zacatepec, Oaxaca (Mixtec) (pl. 223), and of the Pinotepas. In the large town of Pinotepa Nacional with its several sizeable Indian *barrios*, both shirts and trousers were woven until recently by the women on the backstrap loom. Today trousers are still handwoven, but only elderly men wear the entire handwoven costume. Young men prefer a commercial blue denim jacket with metal buttons.

Other handwoven costumes which cannot hold on much longer—from southern Oaxaca Mixtec villages—are white handwoven shirts with bright-colored stripes. Usually the trousers are white, though they too are sometimes striped. All have similar woven sashes with fringed ends, that are embroidered by men. Some of the villages where these are worn are Atoyac, San Pedro Jicayán, San Pedro Tetepelcingo (pl. 232), and San Juan Colorado. Also included in this list are the natural-brown cotton shirt and brown or white trousers of Mechoacán, near Jamiltepec (pl. 227), where a fine handwoven sash is still worn. The young husband in Plate 131 wears an all-white costume with a short shirt, slightly flared for coolness (Pinotepa de Don Luis).

These villages in the south of Mexico, where some handwoven men's apparel still exists to some extent, may be said to follow, as to general pattern, the now nearly extinct Zoque handwoven man's costume (fig. 16): shirt, trousers, belt, and sandals (the Zoque Spanish-style short leather over-trousers excluded). Straw hats in Mexico today, regardless of type and area, have lower crowns than formerly. Sandals vary, the majority having leather straps across the toes and soles made of old rubber tires. We have never seen the Huichol wooden clogs mentioned by Zingg (1938, p. 700). Proportions of garments vary; some have no buttons; neck openings vary; sleeves are made from straight loom lengths; some trousers have no ties, but rely on the handwoven sashes to hold them up.

Pockets are almost always absent in handwoven indigenous clothing, and for this reason all sorts of bags are used—made of leather or woven of wool, cotton, or *ixtle*, and worn in many ways. Men's bags of modern times have an interesting history, and were important before the advent of trousers. Besides serving to carry small belongings, they were worn below the waist center front by the Huichols to hold in place their shirtlike garments worn without trousers. A survival of the old custom is the wearing of a fine handwoven bag by the

130. A Tzeltal Indian of Cancuc, in San Cristóbal de las Casas, Chiapas. 1940

tumes which have already vanished. This is an admirable effort if a sample of the old costume remains to copy, but the attempt can cause great confusion if it does not.

The man's costume, shirt and trousers, of San Bartolo Yautepec, Oaxaca (Zapotec), brocaded with cochineal-dyed silk, observed though not still in use by 1952 (by Bodil Christensen and I. W. Johnson); and that of the Chontals of Huamelula, Oaxaca, have not been worn since 1940 or before. Gertrude Duby (1961, pl. 87) tells us that the man's costume of Oxchuc (Tzeltal), a town difficult of access in the Chiapas highlands, is now but little used. Plate 130 shows a Tzeltal from the related village of Cancuc (San Cristóbal de las Casas, 1940) where the same form of garment is worn—really a narrow *huipil*-like garment with sleeves, held in by a sash or belt.

131. A wedding group of Pinotepa de Don Luis, Oaxaca. (Mixtec). 1962

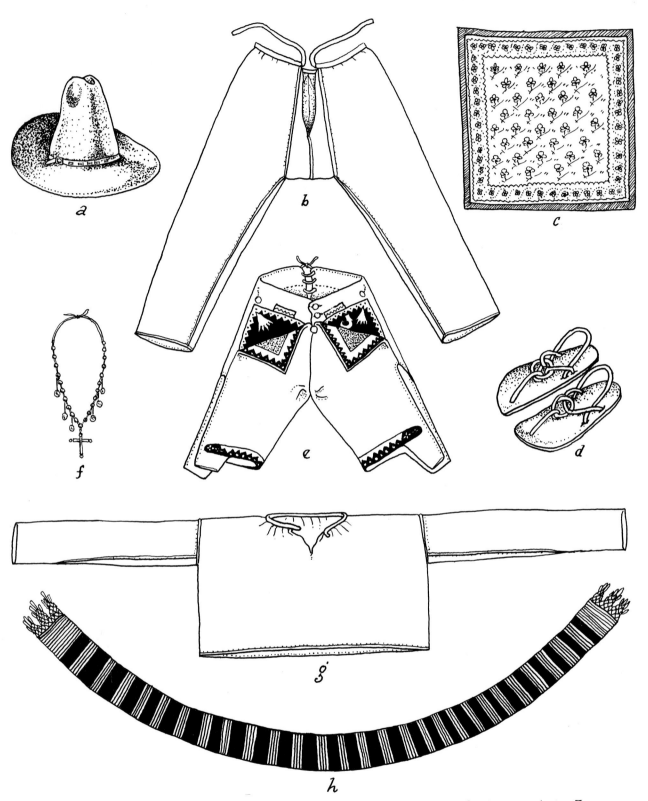

Figure 16. The old-style Zoque men's costume. From Cordry, *Costumes and Weaving of the Zoque Indians of Chiapas, Mexico.* Courtesy The Southwest Museum.

a. hat
b. trousers
c. large handkerchief
d. sandals

e. leather trousers
f. rosary
g. shirt
h. belt

Huichol shrimp fisherman seen in Plate 132. This bag serves two purposes—as a place in which to put the shrimp and as a body covering. Pedro Hendrichs Pérez (1945, Vol. I, p. 109) describes Nahua men of the hot country near the river Balsas in Guerrero as having no pockets in their *manta* shirts and trousers, and as being distinguishable from "men of the Sierra" by a semicircular wool bag (*huicho*) worn below the belt center front. In 1938 the mountain Mixe with their black felt hats usually wore small shoulder bags of fur.

Today the men of Copala, Oaxaca (Trique), instead of adopting nondescript modern dress, are using extremely colorful shirts. When seen in numbers in the Putla, Oaxaca, market at Christmas time (1964), every man had a satin shirt in different brilliant colors—pink, *solferino*, bright blue, yellow, green, purple.

Of course it must be made clear that even the handwoven men's costumes, consisting of shirt and trousers with or without stripes and brocaded or embroidered decoration, are only folk costumes. That is, they are native interpretations of foreign garments, such as trousers, fashioned from backstrap-loom webs of cloth. Men's folk or regional costumes of distinct and individual character still to be found today, or until recent times, are described in Part 2: Chapters 12, Seri; 14, Huichol; 17, Amatlán; 18, Cuetzalan; 19, San José Miahuátlán; 20, Altepexi; 31, Santa María Zacatepec; 32, the Mixteca Baja; 34, Amusgo; 36, Zoque; 37, San Bartolomé de los Llanos; 38, some highland Chiapas villages.

The fact remains that the parade has been fascinating in Mexico—one of endless variety and many influences; but with his ever increasing contact with modern ways, the man's costume is disappearing much more rapidly than those of the Indian woman.

132. An old Huichol shrimp fisherman. Chapalagana River, Nayarit. 1937

11. Design

TEXTILE PATTERNS are of two types: (1) inwoven during the actual construction on the loom; and (2) applied after the material has been taken off the loom. The first includes plain-weave of striped and checked patterns, and brocaded or otherwise woven motifs. Applied decoration includes painted and stamped patterns, embroidery, affixed beads, metal ornaments, *etc.* This classification is extended to include fringes and tassels. In any patterning, color plays an effective role. (O'Neale, 1949, p. 119)

Designs woven into textiles are limited by the horizontal weft and vertical warp threads. This means that no curved lines can be executed, although a good weaver will give the illusion of curved lines by the delicacy of her work.

Embroidered designs are completely free of the vertical and horizontal restrictions of woven patterns. In Mexican textiles, however, very little more freedom is shown in embroidered designs than in woven ones, because the threads of the textiles are—in most cases—carefully counted. Sometimes it is not easy to discern which technique (embroidery or brocading) has been used. Examples may be cited, such as the reverse side of the embroidered San José Miahuatlán *huipil* (pl. 181), or certain areas of a Mecapalapa or Pantepec

quechquemitl. The latter garments display both woven and embroidered areas (pl. 133). The wide outer border is brocaded, and the area near the neck is embroidered with a plant emerging from a small vase. An old Santa Cruz Tepetotutla *huipil* pictured in Plate 134 contains both embroidery and woven patterns. The *huipil* of the Chinantec girl pictured in Plate 40 is entirely decorated with embroidery worked in horizontal stitches by the counting of warp threads. These restrictions, imposed either by the loom or, in embroidery, by tradition, influences designs to some extent.

Designs on textiles in ancient times were not always represented in weaving or embroidery techniques. Many of them were as freely painted on cloth as on pottery.

It seems to us that designs may be classified in four groups: (1) designs showing pre-Hispanic influence, whether or not the original symbolism is remembered; (2) designs of European origin; (3) designs drawn from nature (which sometimes have a wide distribution); (4) embroidery-sheet patterns mixed with European or indigenous design. Designs on textiles showing survivals of pre-Hispanic influence that can actually be named seem few. It is possible that in the sixteenth century many designs were changed slightly (enough

172

133. Two girls of Pantepec, Puebla, wearing their beautiful heavy handwoven *quechquemitl*, brocaded and embroidered in brilliant colored wool yarns. (Totonac). 1965

134. A very fine Chinantec *huipil* from Santa Cruz Tepetotutla, Oaxaca, in which the color red predominates — woven in 1939.

135. A beautifully woven Cora Indian bag of dark-blue wool and white cotton. The design is a variation of the stepped-fret pattern. Jesús María, Nayarit.

to make them unrecognizable now) to meet the approval of the Spaniards. These may in some cases still have a secret significance for the Indian.

One of the most widely used Indian designs was the stepped *greca*, or stepped fret. The ruins of Mitla have over twenty varities of this pattern on the stone walls. Basically it was a design that was used especially to decorate gourds, and was called *xicalcoliuhqui*. Hermann Beyer (1965, pp. 53–104), writing of the stepped fret, says that if it had any symbolism, it signified beauty, gaiety, and abundance; that it is found on decorations of temples, and also vestments, and can represent many things—cloud, serpent, whirlwind, or whirlpool. We see a variation of the latter on the outer borders of a Tepehua *quechquemitl* (pl. IV a). Here the figures are not strictly "frets," but six-sided elements carried one to the next, as is the stepped fret; therefore, speaking in the broadest terms, it is one.

We see the stepped fret on an old "white-on-white" *huipil* shown in Plate 42; on a Huichol men's sash (pl. VI b), where it assumes the aspect of a plumed serpent; and on a Cora Indian bag (pl. 135). Beyer believes the design to be late, and to have predominated in "Mexicano Nahuatl" areas. Miguel Covarrubias (1947 p. 188) speaks of this design thus: "Perhaps the most characteristic motif of Middle American aboriginal art . . . derived from stylization of the sky-serpent . . . thus a symbol of Quetzalcoatl."

A variation of the stepped fret (according to Enciso) is found in *Sellos del antiguo México* (Enciso, 1947, p. 26). The name of this design was given to us by a Nahua woman of Cuatlamayán, San Luis Potosí, who called it *pato de tigre* or "tiger foot" (footprint). Her *quechquemitl* design (shoulder pattern in pl. VII) varies slightly from the seal motif in Enciso's book, probably because it is embroidered. Another interpre-

136. An Amusgo lace-type elaborately brocaded *huipil* from Xochistlahuaca, Guerrero.

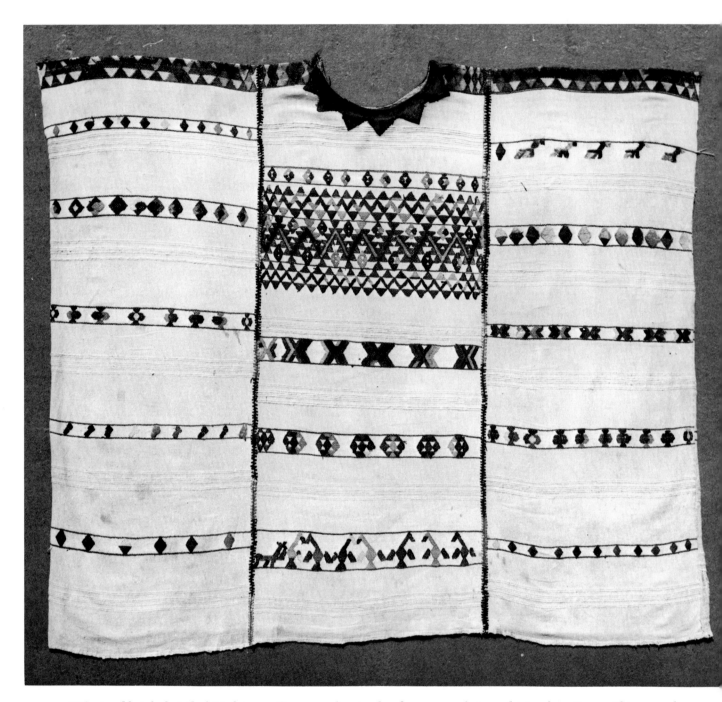

137. An old-style *huipil* of Metlatonoc, Guerrero, showing handsome use of stepped-triangle patterns. This example was woven before animal and bird designs took over in this village (pl. 77). (Mixtec).

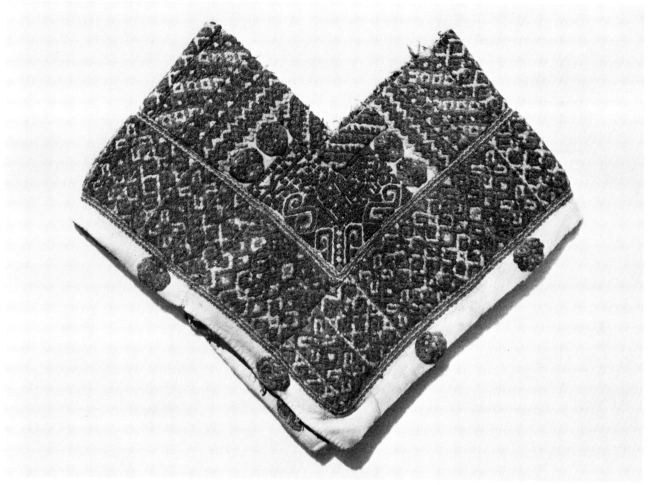

138. A rare *quechquemitl* woven and embroidered in dark wools which now, after washings, has a blackish-orange overall tone. From Tenexco (Municipio de Pantepec), Puebla. (Otomí). Collection of I. W. Johnson.

tation of the same pattern is found on the dark brocaded band of the Xolotla, Puebla (Nahua), *quechquemitl* (pl. 54).

Other old designs given names in *Sellos del antiguo México* (Enciso, 1947, pp. 2–3) are a running triangular motif (pl. 136) called "solar ray" or "fire serpent," and the "banded triangular motifs" which we find in some textiles today (pl. 137, chest and shoulders).

Another ancient design seen on modern textiles is called *Xonecuilli* or the "blue worm." It is usually an "S" reversed, standing or lying sideways, and used in running pattern. On each of the outer webs of the *huipil* in Plate 42 we see one row strongly suggesting the ancient *Xonecuilli* design. In the Florentine Codex (Sahagún, 1951–1963, Book 7, p. 66), we read,

The stars which are in the Little Bear these people call Citlalxonecuilli. They represent them in the shape of an S, backwards, (of seven stars). They say they are by themselves, apart from the others, and that they are brilliant. They call them Citlalxonecuilli because they resemble a certain kind of bread which they make like an S, which they call Xonecuilli, which bread was eaten in all the houses each year on the day named Xochilhuitl.

This design is seen on Huichol, Huastec, and Chinantec garments, as well as those specifically mentioned. The "blue worm" is prominent in the center area below the neck, on the interesting dark, heavily woven Otomí *quechquemitl* from Tenexco, Puebla, shown in Plate 138.

Alfonso Caso points out (1964, p. 81, referring to pp.

177

139. Part of an elaborately patterned pre-Columbian red *huipil* from Chilapa, Guerrero. The red color comes from an iron-oxide pigment. A radiocarbon test of this textile indicates that it dates about A.D. 1290±80 (Radiocarbon Dating Laboratory, The University of Texas at Austin, sample number Tx-441). The textile will be described and analyzed by I. W. Johnson and José Luis Franco in a forthcoming article. Photograph courtesy of Dr. Dee Ann Story.

140. A woman's red headcloth with both warp and weft colored stripes and brocaded double-headed birds, from Usila, Oaxaca. (Chinantec).

6-IV and 7-I of the Codex) that the goddess named 9 Grass "Death" wears a *quechquemitl* with a border of *Xonecuillis*. The prince and princess are making an offering to the goddess 9 Grass "Death," among which is "a complete dress, skirt and quechquemitl. The latter is adorned with a fringe of white *Xonecuillis* on a black ground, the same as the one worn by the goddess ♀ 9 Grass, which is a characteristic symbol of her."

Lilly de Jongh Osborne (1935, p. 66) pictures a Guatemalan design, which she identifies with the ancient glyph signifying movement ⬡. A similar design is worked on the front of a Chinantec *huipil* ◈ from Santa Cruz Tepetotula, Oaxaca. The pattern, somewhat changed over the centuries, is still recognizable on some *huipiles* from Metlatonoc, Guerrero (Mixtec).

There are bird, animal, and insect designs which—

either by their subject or execution—may have early origins. Some motifs, notably the insect representations in Plate IV d, have the character of ancient seal designs (Enciso, 1947, pp. 63 and 70). The monkey (*ozomatli*) was a popular subject in ancient Mexico, as shown by Jorge Enciso (1947, pp. 117–121). This was one of the "day signs." The motif is still used (pls. 47 & 64), as are many other animal designs.

A decorative unit, fascinating in the infinite variety of its interpretations and its popularity in Mexico today (and long ago), is the double-headed bird. Although it is usually thought to have stemmed from the post-conquest Hapsburg eagle, the same theme was employed in ancient Mexico—on seals, spindle whorls, and pottery. Whatever the origin, one finds it used by the Huichols in the north, by the Indians in the Mixteca Alta, by the

Chinantecs, by the Zapotecs of the area of Choapan, and by ethnic groups on down to the coast of Oaxaca (pls. 64, 129 & 140). The most impressively elaborate interpretations we know are to be found on a very old textile (pl. 141) found in Huitepec, Oaxaca (Mixtec), and believed to have been woven more than fifty years ago in San Esteban Atatlahuaca, Oaxaca (Mixtec); and on the *huipil* shown in Plate 42.

The use of the double-headed bird by the Huichols may have come about through their observation of the motif used on coins in Guadalajara or Tepic in early times. Carl Lumholtz' opinion differs (1904, p. 302, Design No. 15). He says, "This design and the double-headed heraldic eagle of Europe have no connection with each other. The front view of the eagle is not considered perfect unless both sides of the head are shown. This bird is associated with the God of Fire, and its plumes are highly valued." Whatever the origin of this design may be, the double-headed bird offers a wonderful solution for the filling of square or rectangular spaces, and can be adapted to many uses and weaving techniques.

Sacred animals which depicted the ancient glyphs or day signs are still used today, but for the most part have lost their significance completely. Some of the animals are the crocodile, lizard, deer, rabbit, dog, monkey, jaguar, eagle, and vulture. Besides animals, there were flower (*xochitl*), and movement (*ollin*) designs. Both the animals and flowers may have originally been copied from nature, and patterns may have been handed down for their decorative quality, with no thought of any other meaning. Some investigators find that weavers will give a name to each design in a woven textile, but if those designs are shown to four other weavers in the same village, each may name them differently. One design that usually retains the same name is the "fishbone," commonly used in many areas (pl. IV b).

Geometric patterns, which have sprung from all sorts of sources, are known in Mexico by many names; and are variations of chevrons, squares, triangles, frets, and so on. In the *Interpretación del Códice Selden* (Caso, 1964, p. 83) we read, regarding page 8-III of the Codex, "The princess assumes a humble attitude and, for the first time in this Codex, she appears wearing the quechquemitl decorated with multicolored chevrons, which are the symbols of war . . ." In Plate 142 the second repeat design row suggests the chevron.

Most Trique and Mixtec villages we know in the high Tlaxiaco region use only horizontal bands in their *huipiles*, with repetition of geometric patterns to the ex-

clusion of bird, animal, plant, and human forms (pls. 45 & 143). This tradition obviously does not stem entirely from painted designs on ancient Mixtec pottery, some of which contains wonderful free zoomorphic and anthropomorphic decoration. Santiago Nuyóo is the only village we know in this rich weaving area which introduces suggestions of formalized flower shapes (pl. 28).

We see that textile designs of the Mixteca Alta were not much affected by the coming of the Spaniards. The motifs used are probably the result of working with brocading technique within many narrow bands. Many of these simple design elements have a world-wide distribution, and some may be found as far back as the time of the Sumerians.

Areas and villages where designs are more European in character are those where embroidery is the predominant technique used. A great many textiles showing European character have for their central theme some sort of vase from which spring conventionalized flowers (pl. IV a), or a large eight-pointed star (pl. 144). The latter widely distributed design, Lumholtz designates as the *toto* flower (among the Huichols) (pls. 97, 145, 163), but it has many meanings. In Cuatlamayán (pl. VII) we were told it represented both star and sun. In the San Pablito *quechquemitl* shown in Plate 63, star designs are used on stems as flowers, and in the lower corners to fill in.

In an old San Francisco Chapantla *quechquemitl* (pl. 144) the corner design is essentially European, probably of peasant origin, and it terminates below the neck in the same star design. Fill-in elements are other smaller symmetrical plant designs, and many animals and birds. This samplerlike execution does not seem Indian in character. The influence of coats of arms or coins is seen along the upper left edge. The handwoven embroidered Huastec *quechquemitl* in Plate 146 has similar characteristics.

Besides an admixture within a single textile of both woven and embroidered designs, one may also find combinations of pre-Conquest and European motifs. An example is the Tepehua *quechquemitl* in Plate IV a from Pisa Flores, Hidalgo, with its border of the old *remolino* (whirlwind or whirlpool) pattern and flower and vase patterns (designs in this *quechquemitl* are both woven and embroidered).

The third classification (designs drawn from nature) refers to motifs which are comparatively free of influences—old or new. They are motifs which show use of flowers, birds, and animals depicted from knowledge

PLATE VIII. A weaver of women's sashes, Santa Ana Hueytlalpan, Hidalgo (Otomí).
1963.

141. An old textile which was termed a wedding *rebozo* — purchased in Huitepec, Oaxaca — of vegetable-dyed silk brocaded designs and designs of soft colors. We think, at this writing, that this old textile may have been woven fifty to seventy-five years ago or more in San Esteban Atatlahuaca in the Mixteca Alta, Oaxaca. (Mixtec).

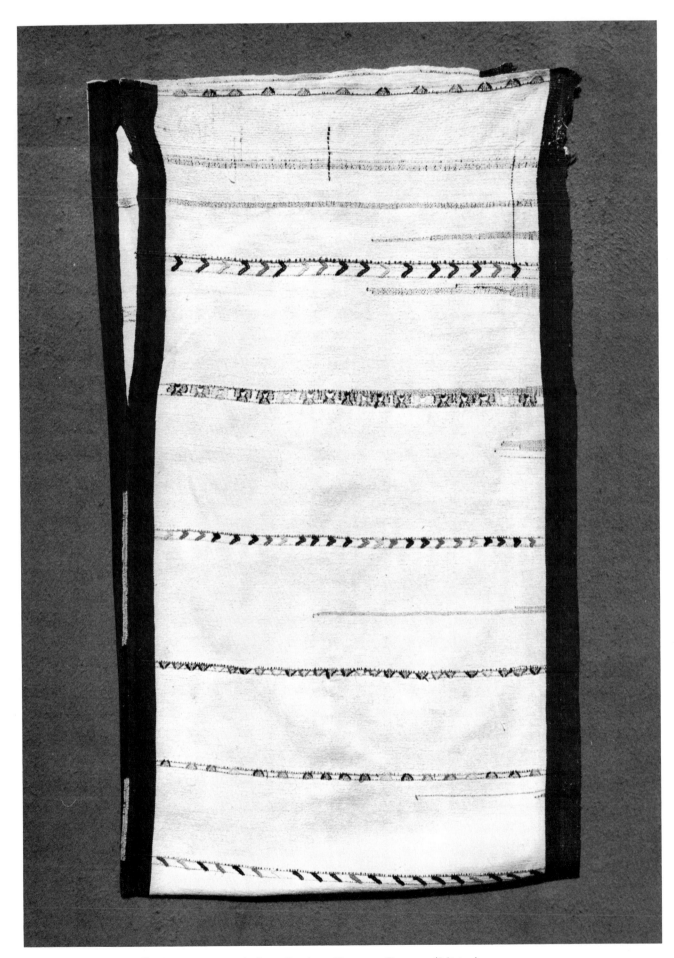

142. A unique *tralla* (upper garment) from Santiago Tetepec, Oaxaca. (Mixtec).

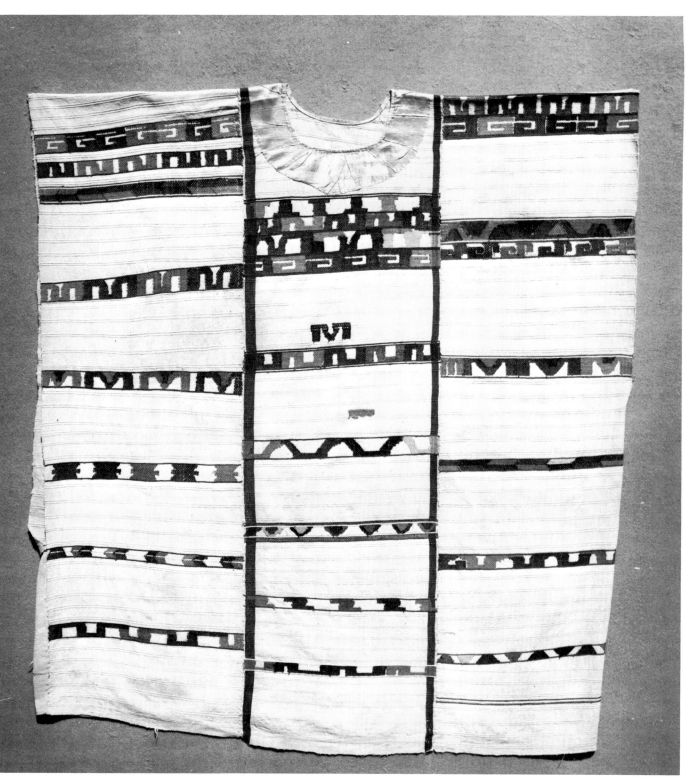

143. A Yosonicaje, Oaxaca *huipil*, with design elements which differentiate the garment from other *huipiles* of the area. (Mixtec).

144. An old *quechquemitl* from the region of San Francisco Chapantla, Hidalgo, showing a large star and many intricate embroidered designs in soft colors of wool yarn on a handwoven ground. (Otomí or Nahua?)

145. A Huichol woman from Las Guásimas, Nayarit. Her face is painted vermillion, and she is embroidering a small bag. Note the beaded earrings. 1937

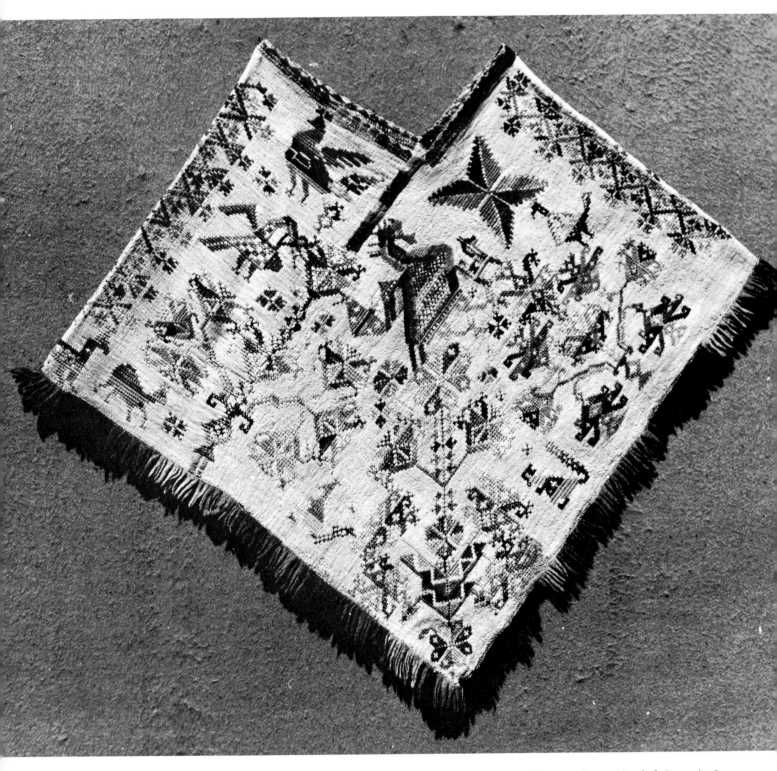

146. An old handwoven embroidered Huastec *quechquemitl* from the region of Tancanhuitz (Ciudad Santos), San Luis Potosí. Today, the *quechquemitl* we have seen from this area are embroidered on *manta* (pls. 58 & III).

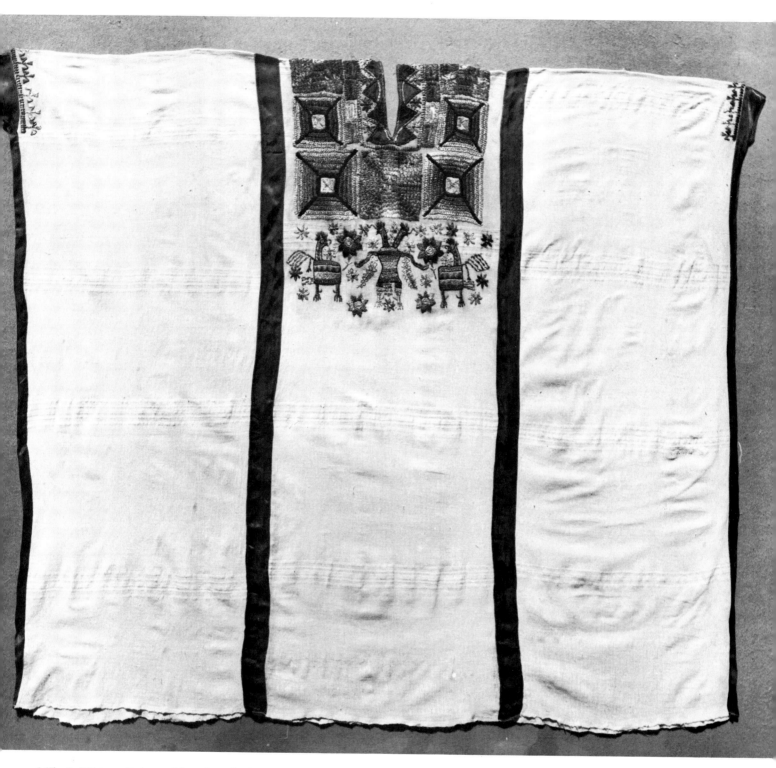

147. A Mixteca Baja wedding *huipil* of Huazolotitlán, Oaxaca, which has an embroidered neck yoke worked in artificial silk in many colors. Below the squared-off geometric elements one notes two folkloric birds with a double-headed bird between. (Mixtec).

Figure 17. Huave Indian designs, from an old *huipil*.

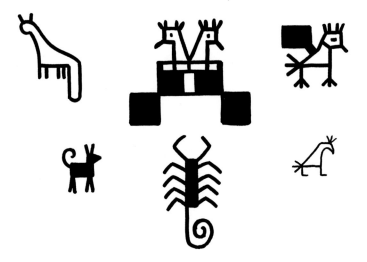

Figure 18. Animal embroidery motifs used on the men's costume of Santa María Zacatepec.

the people have of these nature forms through observation in their daily life. Sometimes fantasy or a designer's imagination is inspired by the need to fill a space: a Choapan *huipil* (pl. 201) shows a turkey and a carefully drawn goat, or other domestic animal, with a bird atop its tail and a small dog beneath its hooves. Designs such as these may refer to legend, but it is doubtful; the turkey's tail is imaginatively stylized.

The embroidered birds on the front of the Huazolotitlán wedding *huipil* in Plate 147 display a certain childlike freedom of expression, whereas the embroidered squares higher about the neck follow careful thread count, and are therefore conventional and ordered.

It is not easy to determine design origins for some of the more folkloric textiles of Mexico. The varieties of brush-tailed horses in a Metlatonoc *huipil* (pl. 77) may have come from elsewhere, but the strange birds in the central panel seem to be the product of pure imagination, as does the delightful cat on an Otomí bag (pl. 148).

Animals most definitely drawn from nature are those worked in shellfish-dyed purple thread in old *huipiles* from San Mateo del Mar, Oaxaca (Huave) (pl. 246; fig. 17). Seagulls, pelicans, ducks, deer, and goats are close at hand and best known, as companion creatures living on the wide sandy stretches and lagoons. These are carefully and faithfully drawn without exaggerations; they are filled out for variety by changes in scale, and a few discreet abstract representations of shells and flowers among the birds and animals. The *servilleta* in Plate 149 also shows carefully drawn deer, seagulls, and spotted donkeys, in red brocading on a white ground divided horizontally by geometric running patterns, and vertically by delicate stylized plants. The embroidered animals and scorpions of the traditional Zacatepec men's costume (fig. 18) are freshly conceived.

In the photographs we have avoided textiles with designs copied from the pattern sheets which are now being sold in markets. One *huipil* has excellent European-style designs of star flowers about the upper area, but mixed with designs of naturalistic green leaves and flowers further down below, the latter obviously non-Indian (pl. 175).

148. An old Otomí blue and white cotton bag with a cat design, from the region of Zimapán, Hidalgo.

189

149. A *servilleta*. San Mateo del Mar, Oaxaca (Huave).

PART II

12. Punta Chueca, Sonora (Seri)

 PLATE 150 shows the arid coastal region occupied by the Seris of Punta Chueca, whom we visited in 1963. From Punta Chueca one sees Tiburón Island, the former home of the Seris, now not used as a permanent settlement. The entire Seri nomadic population in 1959 was given as 242 (Wm. B. Griffen, 1959, p. 6), but more recently in the area the figure of 270 was quoted to us. The Seris move up and down the Sonora coast opposite Tiburón. Their most permanent village is Desemboque, north of Hermosillo. Punta Chueca is a settlement difficult of access, approachable through sandy terrain from the Mexican fishing village of Kino Bay, and consists of some twenty people and five or six crude houses, which bear little or no resemblance to old style Seri dwellings. These people live chiefly by fishing for turtle, which they sell to Mexican middlemen. Existing on the fringes of civilization, they are now dependent upon Mexican fishing merchants who come at appointed times to purchase their turtle or fish; they bring drinking water and supplies for a small store which they open only at these times (pl. 89). No longer subsisting on plants, roots, and fish, the Seris prefer to trade their catch for such items as canned food, potatoes, and salt. Having lost their own customs and religious beliefs, they need much more time for any true assimilation into modern life.

Their language is related to Yuman, according to A. L. Kroeber (1931, p. 5). According to their own legend, the Seris came originally from Baja California. Professor Jiménez Moreno describes the Seris linguistically as Sioux-Hokano, related to the family Humana of California.

The Seri Indians suffer from five eye maladies or abnormal eye conditions, including the dreaded trachoma (Cano, 1960, p. 51). The degeneration of the pigment in the retina gives a light bluish tone to most Seris' eyes, noticeable to even the casual observer. Although the woman in Plate 151 was the only entirely blind person we saw in Punta Chueca, the right eye of the young man with long hair in Plate 89 is affected, and the woman at the left in Plate 150 told us that she also had "the disease."

Women's Costume

Whereas Seri women once wore a pelican skin "robe," today their dress consists of a high-necked long-sleeved buttoned bodice with a gathered frill hanging below the waist, a long full skirt, and a store kerchief tied under the chin (pl. 89). Among the Indians of Mexico, the Cora women and those of certain Nahua and Otomí groups also wear variations of Victorian blouses, originating in mission influence before 1900. Very notice-

193

150. Seri women. The surroundings show the sandy desert in which these Indians live. Punta Chueca, Sonora. 1963

able was the fine condition and general newness of clothing worn in Punta Chueca. This denoted a considerable pride in personal appearance; yet these people live with no furnishing or conveniences of any kind amidst an incredible accumulation of debris piled about in complete disorder.

BLOUSE AND SKIRT. The semi-Victorian style blouse possibly shows a military influence. The example measured was of dark-blue Indian-head cotton, with double hand-sewn pipings of white and red cloth—each approximately ¼ inch in width—used for trimming at cuff, yoke, top of pockets, and waist, and in a vertical band at each side of the center-front opening. Seven buttons are used, often of different colors—with crude buttonholes.

A full, gathered, Indian-head skirt of a solid contrasting color is formed of three lengths of cloth, 41 inches wide, cut and finished into a 1¾-inch double band at the waist. The length of the skirt, including the band and a narrow hem at the bottom, is about 37 inches. The skirt is worn ankle length (pl. 150). The Seris are reputed to be unusually tall.

Although in Punta Chueca women's apparel was cut and sewn by hand, patterned commercial scarves were used as head coverings, tied under the chin, particularly by young girls. A few matrons, only, were seen without head coverings.

FACE PAINTING. The Punta Chueca group is isolated, and therefore conservative. The main Seri settlement, Desemboque, shows in all ways more influence of civilization. We were told in Hermosillo that girls in Desemboque will no longer paint their faces in the old Seri fashion. In Punta Chueca several older women and young girls had simplified markings on the cheekbones and bridge of the nose (pls. 89, 151, & I), not much resembling W. J. McGee's descriptions (1898) of beautifully executed designs radiating over the cheeks in sprays of spiral dots. Three colors were then chiefly used (McGee, 1898, p. 165): (1) white (gypsum); (2) shades of yellow, pink, and brown with ochre; and (3) blue (dumortierite–a rare mineral). The colors we saw in Punta Chueca in 1963 were white, a red brown, and blue. The white and brown were made from soft stones rubbed with saliva on another stone. The blue seemed to be store-bought powdered paint mixed in a shell. Colors were applied with a bunch of human hairs knotted together to form a brush.

Face painting is confined to women and young girls, although male infants are also thus decorated. Designs were originally insignia of totemic character denoting,

151. An old blind Seri woman with a painted face. Punta Chueca, Sonora. 1963

according to McGee, "the clans of which the tribe is composed."

JEWELRY. Necklaces of shells only were seen here, although cords of human hair and necklaces of serpent's skins and of seeds were reportedly still used.

Baskets

We found two women who still engaged in basket making in the tradition of the Southwestern basket makers. Seri baskets, according to Kroeber (1931, p. 19), are similar to Papago, Pima, and Apache baskets. Material used in Punta Chueca comes from the *torote prieto* tree (*Bursera laxiflora*—McGee, 1898, p. 208). Handsome geometric designs, following old traditions, are worked in browns from plant dyes. Seri baskets are called *coritas*. One of the basket makers shown in Plate 152 is working in her hut of sticks and mud. In the pot in the foreground are *torote* strips being soaked before use. In her right hand is an awl, made from the bone of a mule deer. Such bones have been used since ancient times.

195

152. A Seri woman basketmaker of Punta Chueca, Sonora. The instrument she uses is made of deer bone. 1963

Men's Costume

Although the Seri men wear store-bought shirts and dark cotton trousers (no footgear), some still wear their hair long. Older men wear a braid down the back; young men wear the hair long and loose (pl. 89), falling free and very well cared for. When two young men took a trip by truck to the fishing village of Kino Bay, they added to their costume of bright shirt, dark trousers, and white straw hat a straight short saronglike garment of bright-colored store-bought cloth. This cloth was tied under the loose shirts in the center back and reached almost to the knees.

This garment is a remnant of the skirtlike garment once worn as sole clothing by both Seri men and women. Although the men of Punta Chueca were conservative, many men of the large settlement of Desemboque are said to have short hair. We were told that when the hair is cut short, men no longer use the saronglike garment.

Plate 89 shows the marks of contact with civilization in Punta Chueca: wooden boards, bottles of soft drinks, and the clothing of the young Seri man—who still has long hair as did his ancestors. Other more primitive Indian groups in Mexico who do not cut the hair are the Huichols and the Lacandóns, but these latter have not abandoned their indigenous clothing as have the Seris.

13. The Environs of Navajoa, Sonora (Mayo)

THE MAYO INDIANS today are found, not only in their original homelands along the lower Yaqui and Mayo rivers, "but all the way from southern Arizona to central Sinaloa" (Beals, 1945, p. 1). On the Mayo River, the towns of Camoa, Tesia, Navajoa, Cohuirimpo, and Santa Cruz date from mission times. Our photographs and observations were made in the region of Navajoa in 1938 and 1963. Mayo Indians work for others, or rent or own small plots of land. The area is agricultural, principally in the hands of large landowners, and dependent upon overall irrigation—Sonora having barely two inches of rain annually. Crops are corn, wheat, chickpeas, squash, tomatoes, and cotton. The Yaquis and the Mayos engaged in rebellions and civil wars in 1740 and 1865, but the last serious uprising (Beals, 1945, p. 4) in which the Mayos took part was in 1887; and in 1936 a Mayo Indian was elected governor of Sonora.

Everyday Costume

The everyday costume of Mayo men and women has been like that of the rural Mexican for many years, although there are reports of Mayos seen nearly naked or men in breechclouts in more remote areas today. Commercial leather belts have largely replaced the men's wool belts of brown or blue (occasionally with stripes or floral patterns), woven by the Mayo women. Horsehair belts made by the men, and fine, heavy wool blankets woven in tube form by the women (pl. 14) are sold for supplementary income. Many good blankets are to be found in the central market of Navajoa. A very sturdy type of market basket of peeled willow twigs, and mats of woven palm are also made and sold.

Pascola Dancer's Costume

Many Indian dance costumes—due to historical and religious themes—are not of great interest from an indigenous standpoint; others, however, are decidedly noteworthy (pls. 153, 154, & 178). The Mayo *pascola* dancer and the Yaqui deer dancer are in a class apart, truly indigenous.

Pascolas (termed "fiesta dancers") perform one at a time, chiefly at Easter, at fiestas of San Juan Bautista and Espiritu Santo, and at funerals—particularly the funerals of little children.

The costume of the *pascola* dancer (pl. 155) consists of a wide, tooled-leather belt from which hang a dozen or so copper or brass bells, and a curious arrangement of a long, narrow handwoven sash with fringed ends attached to the waist, and extending down to wind about

153. A *mestizo* dancer of San Pablo, Nayarit, resting between movements of the dance of the "Bows [and Arrows]." This is a non-Indian dance done by natives of Nayarit who reside on the fringe of the Huichol area. 1938

154. A man with headdress and mask for the dance of the "Para-Chicos." Chiapa de Corzo, Chiapas (Chiapaneca?). 1940

155. This Mayo Indian *pascola* dancer wears the typical mask and costume, with leggings made of cocoons filled with small pebbles that rattle. Masiaca, Sonora. 1938

and hold in place the dancer's white clothing about the knees. Each lower leg is wound with a long double string, which has been sewn through a series of cocoons, the ends of which have been clipped off, and the hollows filled with small pebbles to make a whishing sound. These strings of cocoons are called *tenovares*. In his right hand the dancer holds a wooden rattle in which clashing metal disks are secured by a metal pin.

The carved-wood, painted mask, though related to the Yaqui *pascola* masks, is otherwise unique in Mexico and artistically finer than other Mexican masks. A grotesque interpretation of human or animal faces, these masks are painted black with some white, and have red lips or tongues. Usually an incised cross may be found on the upper edge, and some small pieces of mirror are inlaid in the wood. These masks are easily distinguished from other Mexican masks by the ring of horsehair fastened around the edge with wooden pegs. The dancers' feet are always bare. There are two forms of *pascola* dance: one performed to the indigenous music of drum and flute, with the mask worn directly over the face; and one, danced to the nonindigenous music of harp and violin, in which the mask is worn tipped back on top or to one side of the head. In 1963 we found but little deterioration in the excellent craftsmanship and design of these Mayo masks, save that a shiny commercial paint is now sometimes used instead of mat hand-ground colors.

156. The head of a Mayo *pascola* dancer. Masiaca, Sonora. 1938

14. The Huichols of Nayarit

The Huichol Indians of Nayarit and Jalisco were supposedly "conquered" in 1722, at which time the Franciscans built five churches in their territory, now all in ruins. Before this conquest—throughout the rise and fall of Moctezuma's empire—the Huichols remained aloof in their almost inaccessible mountain fastness and their culture remains remarkably intact today. Even their very old system of punishment existed in 1937 (pl. 157). The Christian church of Guadalupe Ocotán, Nayarit, in 1938 was occupied by a Mexican blacksmith who did work for the entire area. The altar was used by Huichols for their own indigenous religious paraphernalia—small clay figures, "god's eyes" (pl. 158), curing arrows (pl. 159), and incense burners of the type seen in Plate 162. In Plate 160 a Huichol treasures also a Christian painting on tin, and one finds that the Huichol is not averse to seeking the help of Christian deities along with his supplications to his nature gods who must furnish crops, rain, or good hunting.

Although there are five principal Huichol settlements, with Santa Catarina, Jalisco, as the true religious center, the greater part of the Huichols (now totaling some seven thousand) live in small family groups. Some 150 ranchos or isolated elements consisting of but a few houses account for a large part of these natives. The entire life of the Huichol is built around an endless series of symbolic, mystic, religious beliefs and enactments pertaining to his many gods who reside in natural elements—rain, sun, fire, and so forth. All plant and animal life has deep significance and all material things represent some nature form—i.e. the Huichol stool represents the flower of the century plant (sotol) the drum, a large-leaved oak tree (Lumholtz, 1902, Vol. II, p. 30). Designs in fine Huichol double-cloth woven textiles, and in their embroidery, all stem from nature forms (pl. 163).

Women's Costume

The Huichols, because of their isolation and because of the fact that they are nomadic and live in small ranchos or settlements, are a group which has virtually only one costume—unlike other groups which speak one tongue yet often have quite distinct dress from one settlement to the next. The Huichol women's costume for many years has consisted of a gathered manta skirt with embroidery, a manta blouse, and a large manta quechquemitl. Sandals are sometimes worn.

Quechquemitl. To construct the Huichol quechquemitl two squares about 29 inches each are sewn togeth-

157. Huichol stocks were still in use in Guadalupe Ocotán, Nayarit, in 1937. Although a small Mexican military contingent was sent frequently to abolish this custom, the stocks always reappeared. 1937

er on two adjacent sides, or one rectangle (29 by 58 inches) is folded over to make a square (fig. 10, type No. 1). The corner is left open (a space of 6–8 inches on each side) for a neck opening. Store-bought wool yarn is respun to make fine embroidery thread, used for joining the large squares and for making conventionalized flower, animal, and geometric designs which decorate the *quechquemitl* with absolute freedom of placements and colors. Characteristic is the eight-petaled *toto* flower in prominent view in Plate 163, and many freely spotted unfinished motifs with threads left hanging—believed to assure continuation of life. Cross-stitch and half cross-stitch are used exclusively. Red and black were formerly favorite colors.

In 1937–1938, in some localities, two large red and white bandana handkerchiefs were sewn together to form a *quechquemitl* for everyday wear. Judging from display photographs in the new National Museum of Anthropology this custom is more prevalent now. Before 1900 handwoven wool *quechquemitl* were worn with no blouses beneath, and at times, in the sun or the house, no upper garment was worn.

BLOUSE AND SKIRT. A short, wide, long-sleeved blouse of *manta* is worn under the *quechquemitl*. It is sewn up by hand with a high round neck and vertical tucks across the front (pl. 55). Often it is embroidered with characteristic borders at wrists and shoulders.

The skirt of *manta* gathered into a band is often em-

203

158. This Huichol man is fashioning a sacred "god's eye" (a ceremonial object). At the right we see a "god's chair" containing other ceremonial paraphernalia (pls. 161 & 162). La Mesa, Nayarit. 1937

159. A Huichol woman, the wife of the singer (*cantador*) of the village, with ceremonial arrows in her hair. Rancho El Aire, Nayarit. 1938

160. This Huichol man, with his face painted for the *peyote* ceremony, is carrying a religious painting showing the admixture of pagan and Christian elements. Rancho Las Juntas, Nayarit. 1937

161. The Huichol squash fiesta — with a drum, the "god's chair" containing the god in the shape of a rock crystal tied to a ceremonial arrow in a bloodstained cloth. The drum (center front) is carved from an oak tree and has a top of stretched deerskin. La Mesa, Nayarit. 1937

162. The "god's chair" — showing offerings of fruit, flowers, and incense burner. La Mesa, Nayarit. 1937

163. A Huichol couple in fiesta costume. Alta Vista, Nayarit. 1937

164. A Huichol woman of Las Guásimas, Nayarit, at the Chapalagana River, wears a necklace hung with shells, beads, and beaded earrings. Close about her throat is a necklace made of buttons; and she wears beaded earrings. 1937

broidered around the bottom. Older types tend to have 4–5-inch borders (pl. 163), while 8–10-inch borders are now seen on some skirts in the shops. Respun wool yarn is still used, and garments are hand sewn. An average adult skirt measures 31 inches long by 100 inches in circumference.

JEWELRY, HEAD COVERING, HAIRDRESS, AND OTHER DECORATION. Sometimes the Huichol woman wears a *quechquemitl* over her head under a man's hat. We saw no other head covering. Hair usually is cut in very long bangs across the forehead, with hair either worn loose or held together in back with a twist of a handwoven wool and cotton ribbon tied on top of the head. Ropes of many strings of small blue and white beads (pls. 145 & 164), together with any other type of beads obtainable or in combination with seeds, shells, or buttons, are worn about the neck. Netted beadwork earrings (pl. 145) are characteristic.

Huichol women paint their faces in a masklike fashion with red powdered paint mixed with grease (pl. 145), and often stick the corolla or petals of the sacred *toto* flower, with saliva, to the center of each cheek— "thereby expressing their wishes to the gods" (Lumholtz, 1902, Vol. II, p. 229). Little girls dressed like their mothers in 1937–1938.

Men's Costume

The men's costume consists of a long open-sided shirt, wide straight-sided trousers, a decorative cape, numerous belts and bags (both handwoven and embroidered—pl. 163), sandals, and hat.

SHIRT AND TROUSERS. Formerly the Huichol man wore only a shirt (of the same form as the *manta* one of today), handwoven of dark-brown wool with little embroidery save joining stitches. In 1937–1938 a few of these were still seen, but trousers of *manta* had long since been introduced.

The shirts which we have measured consist of a single selvage-edged strip of store *manta*, about 28 inches wide and 35–41 inches long, with a simply hemmed 10-inch vertical neck slit in the center. Straight sleeves of pieces 22 inches wide and 12 inches long are sewn with a few gathers along the center section of the body of the open-sided shirt. These in turn are gathered into 2-to 2¼-inch closed cuffs. The under side of the sleeve is entirely open. Where sleeves are joined on, there is always an embroidered band (pl. 165), its width depending upon the elaborateness of the *manta* costume.

Trousers are formed of wide straight pieces, 28 inches in circumference by 33–35 inches in length,

with the crotch set in separately. Old style trousers had a bottom border (pl. 163), but today one sees in Mexican shops large parrot, peacock, or other designs above the borders. A few Huichols have been seen in Mexico City with shirts made of flowered blue commercial cotton cloth.

CAPE. The capes we measured were fashioned of 29-inch squares of *manta*. Such a square is doubled to form two triangles, and the half that makes the outside of the cape has a continuous, wide cross-stitch border (red and black), outlined by a 9-inch-or-wider band of bright red flannel. On the fold of the square (pl. 163) about 24 inches apart are sewn two 4-inch twisted cotton cords to be used to tie the cape in front.

Capes are sometimes worn for everyday but are an essential part of fiesta dress. Ceremonial dress may display a cape of feathers as worn by the man in Plate 165 who is dressed in full regalia for a *peyote* ceremony.

Bags, Belts, and Jewelry

Whereas in most Mexican Indian groups the woman has the most colorful, decorative costume, the Huichol man's clothing and adornment far surpasses the woman's. The women are superlative weavers of the men's wide double-cloth all-wool sashes and bags (pl. 166). Sashes are of natural white and black wool in traditional serpent, water-gourd, lightning, and flower patterns with often a discrete line of several warp threads of red near the outer edge. They are often 5–8 inches wide by 120 inches long, including 2½-by-9-inch plaits of diagonal fringe at each end. Belts for small boys may display an animal design (pl. VI b). In addition to one or more wide belts worn at a time, the Huichol man also wears many narrower fine wool or wool-and-cotton belts, and ties about the hips one or more characteristic strings of tiny bags (pls. 97 & 163). Usually seven or nine bags comprise a single string. These bags are 3–4 inches square and have tufts of wool at the lower corners. They are fastened together with twisted tie cords at the end. Some of them are sewn closed, others left open to hold seeds, charms, money, or other oddments. Rarely are these bags handwoven; usually they are of embroidered *manta* (pl. 163). Other tiny single bags and also mirrors are hung about the neck.

Two or more larger bags of natural wool colors are worn hanging at both sides by decorative woven tapes crossing from opposite shoulders. These bags display mythological animals: dogs (pl. VI c), deer, scorpions, double-headed birds, and so on, often with patterns

165. A Huichol man dressed in full regalia for the *peyote* fiesta. His face is painted with a yellow root, and he wears a parrot-feather cape and many belts and bags. Rancho Las Juntas, Nayarit. 1937

166. A Huichol woman weaving a man's double-cloth wool bag. La Mesa, Nayarit. 1937

167. A Huichol man's double-cloth wool bag in dark blue and natural white. The off-center "mountain-lion" design turns into a double-headed bird on the reverse side. A small embroidered neck bag hangs from the handwoven shoulder tape. Guadalupe Ocotán, Nayarit.

168. A Cora woman spinning cotton. Mesa del Nayar, Nayarit. 1938

breaking and changing from one side of a bag to the other (pl. 167). Formerly, when only a shirt was worn, a single fair-sized bag hung in front, holding tobacco, and flint and steel for striking fire, "all of which gave the pouch the necessary weight to hold the shirt in place" (Lumholtz, 1902, Vol. 2, p. 3).

Men as well as women wear earrings and bracelets of netted beadwork in light and dark blue and white with some touches of red. Men's bracelets, particularly, are wider than those of the women.

FACE PAINTING, HEADGEAR, AND HAIR. For the *peyote* ceremony, men's faces are carefully painted with a color made from a yellow root (pl. 165). Hats are distinctive—14–15 inches in diameter, made double of narrow braided straw strips overlapping, with brims slightly turned up. They are trimmed with red felt facings and, on the upper edge, crosses of red felt as well.

The small low crown is decorated on top by a ring of wool-yarn tufting in two or (now) more colors, with a single tuft at the center top. Brims are hung with madrona leaves or copies of their shape (pl. 160) cut out of matchboxes. In Tepic (1963) we found halves of a dried seed pod thorn also being used as decoration.

Formerly all Huichol men had long hair, which was often worn loose or pulled back into a braided knot behind (pl. 163). Otherwise a long sort of bowl cut was usual in 1937–1938 (pl. 97). A more or less conventional haircut is seen more frequently today.

The Cora Indians, found in fairly close proximity to the Huichols, no longer have a distinctive costume. The women, however, spin (pl. 168) and weave very fine bags for the Cora men (pl. 135).

15. Santiago Temoaya, State of México (Otomí)

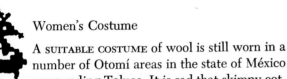

Women's Costume

A SUITABLE COSTUME of wool is still worn in a number of Otomí areas in the state of México surrounding Toluca. It is sad that skimpy cotton ready-made clothing and cotton *rebozos* are taking the place of indigenous dress in that high, severely cold climate. The Temoaya traditional costume consists of an upper garment of wool (the form of which, to our knowledge, is unique in Mexico), a heavy tubular woven wool skirt, a wool and cotton patterned belt, and a cotton blouse. The upper garment may be classed as a cross between a *huipil* and a *cotón*. Even though it is easier and cheaper to buy cotton *manta* for skirts, a woman in such a garment could not survive the cold without blankets. As it is, her wool skirt and upper garment provide covering at night for herself and her baby also.

UPPER GARMENT. The Temoaya women's upper garment comes within the range of the rectangular *huipil* form, with the following variance: instead of being formed of one, two, or three strips, running from back to front, the Temoaya garment (called in Otomí *jhiushu*) is made of four handwoven woolen pieces. It begins as a two-strip *huipil* over the shoulders down to the chest, where the two short webs, with a 12-inch neck opening left between them, are joined to a single rectangle, in front and in back (fig. 8 b). Shoulder pieces

hang out over the arms. The upper part of the garment is 25 inches wide, whereas the single rectangles below measure 19 inches in width. The garment is short, measuring from shoulder fold to bottom usually no more than 24 inches. The sides of the garment are left completely open (pl. 169).

The two shoulder sections in garments we examined were of dark home-dyed red-brown wool, firmly woven on the backstrap loom, with tiny composite warp stripes of bright red wool and white cotton thread occurring every ⅛ inch. The front and back waist sections are usually of the same red-brown color, but always with wider-spaced stripes in slightly different colors. All the *jhiushu* stripes run horizontally in the finished garment. In Temoaya, the common term for this garment is *cotón*—a term ordinarily applied to a rather small men's *sarape*, having a neck opening.

Buttonhole or blanket stitches, varied in depth and arrangement, are used to join the *jhiushu* sections.

The dark reds and browns used in the dyeing of the hand-spun wool for these distinctive garments and for the women's skirts also, are not made from commercial dyes, but from various mixtures of cochineal, and a red fruit of a native tree called *capulin rojo* (red *capulin*) termed *detze* in the Otomí dialect of this region.

SKIRT. The women's wrap-around wool skirt is woven

214

169. A girl of Temoaya, state of México, in costume. (Otomí). 1963

in an actual tube by the ring-weaving technique. The single piece measures 24–26 inches in width by 125–152 inches in circumference. Skirts were seen of red-brown color or of dark blue (anil-dyed), all having equally spaced warp stripes composed of several white threads occurring at 1-inch intervals. The wool tube is sewn onto an upper-hip-to-waist-section of double *manta* some 12–14 inches wide.

Skirts and other women's garments are woven by the women on backstrap looms, but we were told that men also sometimes weave the wool skirts. As usual, skirts are expensive, and the comment about all weaving in 1963 was, "It is very much work." We had the impression that the costume might not endure for long. One girl preferred to have her photograph taken in a new coral-colored store sweater above her wool skirt, but agreed afterward to put on her *jhiushu*. She also wore shoes.

BELT. A very good belt is made in Temoaya of a heavy commercial white cotton thread and home-dyed red and blue wools, in running conventional plant and human figure designs (warp-patterned weave). Reds occur through the center area, blues on the outer edges. Belts measure 2¼–3 inches in width, and 78–102 inches in length, plus 6-inch fringes at both ends (pl. VI a). No *soyate* is used.

COSTUME ASSEMBLING. The assembling of the costume begins with the forming in place of the tubular skirt, first doubled to make three thicknesses on the left side of the wearer from center front to center back.

All remaining cloth length is next pulled forward and laid in pleats across the front, running from left to right (fig. 11 e). Depending on the size of the tubular skirt, seven to twelve deep pleats may be formed. When in place, a 130-inch skirt was observed to form nine pleats across the front (pl. 169).

The long belt is wrapped around the body well below the top edge of the double *manta* strip, leaving about 4 inches of white cloth showing below the belt. The open *jhiushu*, which is short and narrow at the bottom below the wider shoulder section, is easily tucked inside the belt, both in front and in back, after the skirt is formed. A store-bought cotton blouse of miscellaneous character is usually worn under the *cotón*, and during the warmth of the day the *cotón* is not always used. The latter may also be seen at times hanging loose in front and back, with no blouse beneath.

HAIR. The Temoaya woman's hair is worn in two braids down the back. We saw no head covering other than the ready-made *rebozo*. The feet were bare.

Children's Costume

Children were sometimes seen in wool skirts, but usually in *manta* ones. No little girls' *huipiles* or *cotones* were seen when we visited the area in April of 1963.

Men's Costume

Men wore the usual country, small town, or farmer's garb, with various types of *sarapes* (blankets), woven of crude wool in Temoaya by the men themselves.

16. Santa Ana Hueytlalpan, Hidalgo (Otomí)

ALTHOUGH Santa Ana Hueytlalpan is on a paved road only twenty to twenty-five minutes by car from Tulancingo, and not more than two hours from Mexico City, the Otomí women here are still dedicated to weaving to an unusual extent. Aside from their own costumes, they have always woven many articles to sell to other Otomí villages. Belts and narrow white wool skirt strips are made for San Pablito, near Pahuatlán, Puebla; red, curved-weave wool and cotton *quechquemitl* strips are made and sold to Cosquitlán, and also the nearby *barrio* of Grangeño; and embroidered blouses to *ranchos* near Tenango de Doria. Santa Ana women meet with prospective buyers from San Pablito in the Sunday market of Pahuatlán, several hours by bus over a mountain road from Santa Ana. Many women are also seen on market day—Thursday—in Tulancingo.

Santa Ana has an almost entirely Indian population, which shows one unusual feature: those who are conserving custom and costume continue to live in the center of the village, while on the more distant *ranchos* live those who are less conservative. This is the reverse of the usual custom. The village is high, cold, and windy, without trees, and very flat. Most adobe houses are made with partially enclosed patios for protection.

Everywhere are piles of wood for burning. Women find the most sheltered spots close to their houses; here they weave, spin, dye, and embroider. One sees at least one weaver near almost every dwelling, as well as dye pots and warping frames. Young girls spin, or a group of them sit on a bench next to a wall embroidering blouse strips.

Women's Costume

A handwoven *quechquemitl* of wool and cotton, a cotton blouse, a wool wrap-around skirt, and a long, wide, heavy wool belt comprise the costume of the Santa Ana woman.

QUECHQUEMITL. The meaning of the word *quechquemitl* is, *quechtli* (neck), *tlaquemitl* (garment) (Molina, 1944, pp. 89, 134). The Santa Ana example is truly a "neck garment" because it is very small, fitting high and tight about the shoulders (pl. 170).

This and some other Otomí *quechquemitl* of the region are unique in that they are fashioned of two rectangles (fig. 10, type No. 2), but each piece has a curve at one corner of one end. The curve is produced on the loom by using part of the warp as weft (for an excellent description of the so-called "round-shoulder technique" see Christensen, 1947, p. 133). Each Santa Ana woven

217

170. An Otomí weaver and a girl spinning. Santa Ana Hueytlalpan, Hidalgo. 1963

strip has a red wool border 6–8 inches wide (with a few tiny colored stripes, and a white outer edge stripe) along the side of which on the same loom setup is woven the 3–5-inch neck area of white cotton.

The two rectangles are joined together at each end by sections, 3–4 inches wide, of a needle-formed bias darning stitch (pl. 171). When finished and joined, the garment usually measures—from rounded point to rounded point—23–25 inches long by 11–12 inches wide. A few *quechquemitl* entirely of wool were seen, and one old woman showed us a garment much larger than those woven today.

Commercial aniline dye is used for the red wool. Usually raw wool is carded, spun, and dyed by the weavers themselves. Raw wool costs less than factory-bought wool and gives a richer, more varied hand-loomed look to products. When white cotton commercial threads are used, they are often respun to the desired thickness before being employed.

SKIRT. The Santa Ana skirt is woven of dark-blue raw or factory-bought wool. For grown women, the width of this single-web skirt varies from 31–36 inches wide by 132–140 inches long. These skirts weigh as much as three kilos when finished, and are valued from 100 to 200 *pesos* ($8.00–$16.00) at the present time. One informant quoted prices (1963) of 4 *pesos* per kilo for raw wood and 20 *pesos* per kilo for factory-prepared yarn; anil dye costs 8 *pesos* per kilo.

Woven skirt lengths are sewn into tube form. A decorative, handwoven, white cotton tape—½ inch wide—is sewn along the bottom of the skirt when finished. The white edging has four selvages, and sometimes, being miscalculated in length, it falls short of the skirt length, leaving a few inches without edging. This lack of standardization in Indian handwork is common.

BELT. Fine, heavy, red wool belts (pls. 170 & 172), ranging in color from *solferino* to dark red, are a handsome feature in Santa Ana costume. These are woven for home use (pl. VIII) and also to sell to the Otomí women of San Pablito. Belts are 9½ inches wide and about 135 inches long, plus fringes of 3–5 inches. A ⅜-inch blue warp stripe borders the belt on each edge. Those made for San Pablito have a broken red color, resulting from the intentional use of two colors of red yarn. Belts vary considerably in length and width.

COSTUME ASSEMBLING. When the costume is assembled, the cotton blouse is put on first; then the tubular skirt. The skirt is doubled to make three thicknesses across the back after which surplus material is formed

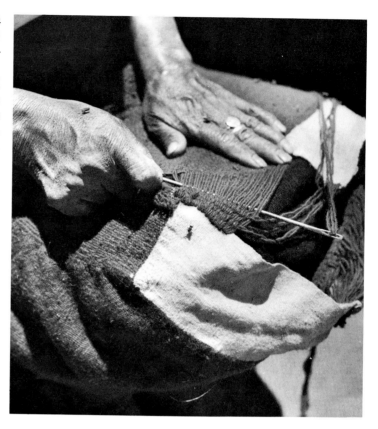

171. This detail shows a woman joining two *quechquemitl* strips with a diagonal darning stitch. Santa Ana Hueytlalpan, Hidalgo (Otomí). 1963

in a number of pleats folded toward the front on the left side only (fig. 11 d-3). About the waist is wound the belt, overlapping very widely to form a belt of exceptional width from waist to hip.

HEAD COVERING, JEWELRY, HAIRDRESS, AND SLEEVE. There are a number of uses of the Santa Ana *quechquemitl* besides that of upper garment. For head covering the *quechquemitl* is sometimes folded to form a jaunty sort of soldier's cap (pl. 173), with points forward and back, to shade the eyes from the sun. Sometimes it is used simply hanging loose over the head, points front or side (pl. 174).

The hair is worn in two braids, with a different color ribbon worked into the end of each (pl. 174).

Commercial cotton *rebozos* are in evidence, but are used for carrying burdens on the back, rather than over the head. Young girls wear many strings of *papelillo*

219

173. This close-up of the same Otomí girl shows one manner of wearing the *quechquemitl* as a head covering. Santa Ana Hueytlalpan, Hidalgo (Otomí). 1963

172. An Otomí girl of Santa Ana Hueytlalpan, Hidalgo. 1963

beads, wisely choosing yellow, silver, blue, and green, to complement the many red elements in their costume. Young girls also wear rings of silver or brass on three fingers of each hand.

A curious pair of full, long sleeves of store-bought cloth, gathered into a narrow cuff and held together across back and chest by tapes, has lately been introduced (pl. 174). These sleeves are commonly put on by young girls out of doors "to protect the arms from the sun." These not only are worn for work in the fields or weaving out of doors, but have been seen in the Pahuatlán marketplace. We saw them worn in the Huehuetla, Hidalgo, market where Santa Ana women sell wool for the Tepehua belts.

A man of Santa Ana, who said the sleeves were for keeping the arms light in color, smiled, "the people here are a little idealistic," perhaps implying that their skins are dark whether covered with the new style sleeves or not. Sahagún says "The Otomí were very gaudy dressers—vain people" (1951–1963, Book 10, p. 178).

Children's Costume

Small girls are not often seen today in total costume, though they may wear tiny *quechquemitl* over their indifferent dresses of store-bought cloth. When girls are 15–17 years old, they put on the complete costume.

Bags

Bags are used for *tortillas* or other produce, and are filled and carried within baskets or *rebozos*. Rectangles 12–25 inches by 15–39 inches are woven of wool, with multicolored warp stripes in one piece. They are folded over and sewn over and over at the sides to form bags with no top finish or hanging cord for carrying—only a simple selvage edge.

Men's Costume

The Santa Ana men's costume shows no distinctive element. Little boys have tiny home-woven *cotones*; and blankets are made for the men.

174. A woman weaving a *quechquemitl*. She wears a *quechquemitl* on her head, and a curious pair of sleeves on her arms. Santa Ana Hueytlalpan, Hidalgo (Otomí). 1963

17. Amatlán de los Reyes, Vera Cruz (Nahua)

 IN A CHARMING tropical setting, twenty-five minutes or less from Córdoba by car, lies the town of Amatlán—which formerly enjoyed considerable wealth from vanilla and pineapples. In those days women made and wore beautiful *huipiles,* and also—which is most unusual—they liked to enlarge their wardrobes by buying *huipiles* from other Indian regions. They were fond of the red *huipiles* from the Chinantla (so different from their own), and of the handwoven, figured white ones possibly purchased in Igualapa, Guerrero. Other signs of wealth were the great chains of coral, and strings of coral alternating with silver coins, worn by the women (pl. 175). Probably very little of this jewelry now remains in Amatlán—so much of it has been purchased by outsiders. During the bonanza period in this town a great deal of gold was worn.

Women's Everyday Costume

In 1939–1940 one still saw Amatlán women wearing their everyday costumes in the market of nearby Córdoba—white store-cloth *huipiles* with blue ribbon trim, and white *manta* or handwoven wrap-around skirts, both skirts and *huipiles* dipped in blueing. In Amatlán, all women wore this costume at home. Today, we understand that even the everyday costume is rarely in

evidence. *Huipiles* were handwoven 40–50 years prior to our visit in 1940, according to informants.

Women's Fiesta Costume

A very fine silk-embroidered *huipil* was formerly worn for festive occasions, with a handwoven white wrap-around skirt.

Huipil. The fiesta *huipil* we obtained is made of imported linen, heavily embroidered with imported silk thread (pl. 175). Although the *huipil* gives the impression that it is formed (as it would have been in earlier years) of three strips of cloth sewn side by side, it is actually made of a single 42-by-70-inch piece of linen, folded in the middle and sewn up the sides, leaving 10-inch arm openings and a round neck opening. The final garment thus measures 42 by 35 inches.

To preserve the visual suggestion of the three separate webs of the handwoven *huipil,* a joining stitch divides the single piece of linen into three sections. This is a 1½-inch satin-stitch band in sections of purple, orange, and red. The center panel is 16 inches wide, and the two side panels 12 inches.

Squared off around the neck are wide satin-stitch bands of solid geometric zigzags in multicolored pure silk thread. In this square yoke section a total of eight colors are counted. From the outer corners of the

222

175. Two women of Amatlán de los Reyes, Vera Cruz, wearing fine old-style *huipiles* and many strings of coins and corals. (Nahua). 1940

square, both front and back, sprout at right angles a mass of eight-petaled star-shaped flowers (a design of Spanish or European origin), referred to in Amatlán as the "design of stars." These spring from elaborate conventionalized stems, carried out in straight running stitch and satin stitch, the latter being called here *punto real*.

Emerging from the wide satin-stitch vertical bands are smaller star-shaped flower patterns, below that, realistic embroidered flowers and leaves. The latter were obviously introduced when modern embroidery pattern sheets appeared in small Mexican towns. Twelve colors are used in the whole garment. A 3-inch dark-blue satin-ribbon band borders the neck and hangs in two 17-inch streamers, center front and back. A great deal of money was once invested in these fine garments, and one hopes that some examples are kept by families today.

In 1940 we found a "new style" fiesta *huipil*—sadly deteriorated—which had pattern book designs in cotton thread on *manta*.

SKIRT. Skirts are called *lia* in Amatlán, and are fashioned of a single handwoven strip of heavy weft faced white cotton 23 by 118 inches. The woven skirt piece is sewn onto a *manta* strip 17½ by 118 inches. As *huipiles* here are always worn loose outside the skirt, the upper *manta* section is not visible under the long *huipil*. Ends of the two-part skirt are sewn together to form a tube. When put on, the skirt is first doubled to make three thicknesses across the back, then on each side the rest of the length is folded toward the front in two pleats (fig. 11 d-2). Skirts hang to below the ankle. A few inferior handwoven skirts were still made in Amatlán in 1940. We were told that better quality skirts were brought in from Ixhuatlán, not far from Orizaba.

BELTS AND FOOTGEAR. We did not see the Amatlán belt, but were told that it was formerly handwoven, and brought from the town of Tequila, and that it was sewn to a *soyate*. No footgear was noted for women.

HEAD COVERING AND JEWELRY. In 1940 the women did not wear and did not remember any special head covering, although some store *rebozos* were used. They wore necklaces measuring 30–40 inches in total length, and containing as many as two hundred or more eighteenth- and nineteenth-century silver coins—each alternating with a coral bead. Red glass beads were substituted when there was a shortage of corals.

Children's Costume

In 1940 we saw one child in a *huipil* and skirt; the rest were in nondescript store-cloth dresses.

Men's Costume

In 1940 one woman about forty-five years old, said she had never seen the old Amatlán men's costume. Men used to wear a suit with full, short, knee-length handwoven white trousers, called *rabones*, that had drawn work near the lower edge, and a fine, decorative, handwoven belt. An outer *cotón* appears from old photographs to have been of fine light-weight wool. We were told that men once wore strings of green beads with silver medals.

18. Cuetzalan, Puebla (Nahua)

CUETZALAN LIES in the northeastern part of the Sierra de Puebla, and the census of 1960 reports a population of 22,418. Formerly entirely Indian, the town proper is now inhabited largely by *mestizos*, and the Indians live outside, within a radius of from one to fifteen kilometers. The town is located on a mountain slope with a sudden drop to the east and the north into the tropics of Vera Cruz. To reach Cuetzalan in 1939, one went from the city of Puebla northward to Zaragoza by train, and by road to Zacapoaxtla, and from thence by horse. Today there is a good road to Cuetzalan, but so far outside influence has not greatly changed the indigenous costume and customs in this region (pl. 176).

Women's Costume

The Cuetzalan woman's upper garment is the *quechquemitl*, of hand-loomed gauze weave or of heavier plain weave in white. A wrap-around skirt of dark-blue wool, white *manta*, or heavy white handwoven material is worn. A blouse, decorative belt, and a large wool turban (*rodete*) topped by an extra *quechquemitl* complete the costume.

QUECHQUEMITL. Cuetzalan *quechquemitl* are of two handwoven types, plus a modern type made of white artificial silk. The woman in Plate 177 is wearing two gauze-weave *quechquemitl*, formed of two handwoven rectangles (made of store thread), 14 inches wide by 28 inches in length, sewn together as in Figure 10, type No. 2. Many variations occur in the gauze weaves. The basic construction is almost always figured gauze bands alternating with plain gauze bands. Sometimes a silky white store thread is introduced for weaving, particularly in the figured gauze areas. The gauze garment is bordered with store-bought or handwoven ½-inch white fringe (pl. 177); and in 1939 hand-made or store-bought lace was often used in the joinings, with a line of colored wool stitching to decorate one edge.

Today, conventional stemlike patterns are often worked in the corners of gauze *quechquemitl* with mercerized store thread in feather-stitching; this device is then decorated with sequins. *Solferino* satin ribbon, 1½ inches in width, is often sewn flat around the neck with a rosette of the ribbon formed front and back, well above the two *quechquemitl* points. In Cuetzalan, *quechquemitl* are worn with points at the center front and back.

The other handwoven *quechquemitl* is of plain-weave, heavy, hand-spun cotton, with a ¾-inch band of wool woven from one to two inches from the bot-

176. The main street of Cuetzalan, Puebla. (Nahua). 1939

177. A man and woman of Cuetzalan, Puebla, in their typical costume. (Nahua). 1939

tom edge. This band is dyed with *elite* (the bark of a small shrub—*Alnus arguta* or *Alnus firmifolio*), and is woven in the round-shoulder or curved-weaving technique (Christensen, 1947, p. 133). Sometimes the front and back points (corners) are decorated with a diamond-shaped motif of vinelike embroidery in wool thread. In some cases, the black, green, red, and gold are home dyed (Cordry, 1940, p. 45).

In October, 1963, this *quechquemitl*—with dark-red wool border—was seen infrequently (Christensen, verbal communication).

BLOUSE. A standard Indian- or *mestiza*-style blouse of store-bought cloth is worn under the *quechquemitl*. The neck and tiny sleeves are bordered with, respectively, a wide and narrow embroidered band of bird, animal, and flower designs in running stitch (pl. 177). Formerly, only black mercerized thread was used here, but today many colors appear in the blouses.

SKIRT. There are three types of skirts seen today in Cuetzalan, all wrap-around and put on in the same manner (Fig. 11 e-2). (1) A heavy black or dark-blue handwoven wool one (pl. 177) has a diagonal weave and sometimes has a narrow border in red at the bottom edge. In 1939 this type of skirt material was woven chiefly in Ahuacatlán and Xochitepec, and sold in Cuetzalan on Sunday market day, but very few were brought in at a given time. Many were woven for individual use in the ranchos. Although in 1939 chiefly older women wore the dark wool skirt, we are told by those who recently attended a fiesta in Cuetzalan (October 1963) that anyone who chooses may wear the dark skirt. (2) The heavy handwoven all-white cotton skirt of a plain or checked weave, is made in the ranchos, and is less expensive than those of dark wool. (3) Now, one sees a predominance of white store-bought *manta* skirts (Christensen, verbal communication) whereas in 1939, *manta* was used only (a) by poorer women; (b) by the women of San Miguel, who had a lower standard of living; and (c) by children. In 1939 some little girls had hand-woven skirts (pl. 178), and none were seen wearing those of dark wool.

Cuetzalan skirts are called *cuelpachuet*. The woven types consist of two lengths, about 19½ by 152 inches. These are sewn together lengthwise, the total skirt then measuring about 39 by 152 inches. This piece is sewn together in tube form. Before being put on the tube is folded lengthwise into four thicknesses. The wearer steps into the folds leaving three thicknesses of cloth across her back (fig. 11 e-2). The skirt is worn at instep length. Depending on the height of the woman, extra cloth may or may not be turned down inside about the waist. All surplus material of the tubular skirt is pulled to the front. One pleat is formed on the right side, and the rest of the surplus is formed into four or five deep pleats, working from left to right (pl. 177). The whole arrangement is then secured by the characteristic Cuetzalan woman's belt.

BELT. The long red wool belts are made in several widths, with a central pattern showing white warp and weft in geometric designs (red warp). The belt examined measures 2¾ inches in width by 65 inches in length, including a fringe occurring only at one end (no *soyate* is used here). Some belts are almost three yards long.

The red belt is adorned, at the fringe end, with a 15-inch (or more) multicolored section of wool-yarn tufts. This design portion consists of two or more rectangles covering the width of the belt, and bordered by two or three rows of tiny tufts in as many as nine colors of wool (pl. VI a). The open center of each rectangle is filled with lace—formerly hand-made, but now store bought. Belts are worn wrapped around over the skirt, the triple-braided fringe tucked in, and the tufted design always worn on one side or across the back. These belts are said to be woven in Xalacapa, but they are decorated in Cuetzalan.

HEADDRESS. Cuetzalan is one of a number of widely distributed Indian areas where the pre-Hispanic great turban, or *rodete*, (pl. 177) is still seen. In modern times these usually are fashioned of wool cords. The method of assembling and the quantities, and colors of wool vary from place to place. Cuetzalan women have used, for many years, a predominance of purple cord, with a few of green. Whereas Indian garments are tending to shrink in size, due to modern pressure, time, and expense (the woven strips of Cuetzalan *quechquemitl* are now, for example, smaller by 4 inches—both in length and in width—than formerly), the *rodete* for fiesta is bigger than ever, piled on the head, not to form a flattish top in accordance with pre-Cortesian *rodetes* seen in archaeological sculpture, but ending in an enormous twist high on one side. In 1939 an extra white *quechquemitl* was neatly arranged on top of a flattish *rodete* (pl. 177) to preserve its color. Today there is no flat space, and the extra *quechquemitl* is simply tucked into the knot and left to hang down behind. This extreme fashion is favored by younger women.

In the Sunday market, the wool cords for these *rodetes* are brought in from Tlatlauqui and are sold in small bunches—one long cord folded four times and tied into a bunch. Each cord measures about 6 yards and is ¼-inch in diameter. In 1939 as many as eighteen were used in a headdress, with fairly equal

PLATE IX. A woman of San Sebastián Zinacatepec, Puebla (Nahua), wearing a fine old *huipil*. 1962

178. The dance of the *quetzales,* showing the extraordinary large paper headdresses trimmed with feathers. Cuetzalan, Puebla (Nahua). 1939

amounts of green and purple. Today about eight times as many of purple are used as of green—up to twenty-four purple and three green. The total cost may be as much as 70 *pesos*.

When the headdress is to be put on, the hair is parted in the middle and brought to the front on each side. Next, all the cords—each of which is doubled four times and arranged with colors mixed, in a long cable tied together in the middle—are laid across the back of the neck, with equal parts brought forward on each side. One side is first twisted with hair; then the other. Then the two are pulled up and tied in two great knots upon the head, with the ends firmly tucked in. Formerly, the mass projected out over the forehead; now it is pulled high on top of the head, with the extra *quechquemitl* tucked jauntily in to fall down the back.

JEWELRY. Some Cuetzalan women have more than one piercing in each ear so that they may wear up to three pairs of earrings. *Papelillo* beads with long ribbon streamers down the back are used. Formerly, corals with small silver coins are said to have been worn, but we saw none in 1939.

Bags

Wide striped brown and white cotton bags are woven in the same patterns and weave as the *mamal* (or infant-carrying cloth), which used to be found in different sizes, and used for various purposes. Large and small bags are used in women's baskets (the large ones are about 12 inches square). The 6-inch bags are used by men for carrying money. All are called *paltil*, and they never have draw strings. When used for carrying money, the bag is twisted into the belt. All bags noted have two wide brown stripes and one white one in the center. Natural tan cotton was formerly employed, or a cinnamon-brown color was achieved by the boiling of a root called *huixtololo* (Cordry, 1940, p. 60).

Children's Costume

Little girls seen in 1939 (pl. 178) were dressed like their mothers, and we are told that in 1963 many still wore the traditional costume.

Men's Costume

Cuetzalan men wear white shirts and trousers—the trousers customarily rolled up below the knees—and a distinctive *cotón*.

COTÓN. There are three types of Cuetzalan *cotones*. One is woven of natural dark-brown wool; the second of dark-blue wool with a small white cotton warp (vertical) stripe as seen in Plate 177; and the third of plain black wool. We know of no special name for the first type, but the second is called *pinto* (of variegated color), and the third, *tiltac* (from the Aztec *tliltic*, meaning black).

These *cotones* have square or round-cut neck openings, and 6-inch sleeves woven apart and sewn on well up under the body of the garment (pl. 177). The sleeves are left open underneath the arm, save for two to three inches near the cuff. Sleeves always hang loose over the shoulders, and arms are never inserted.

In 1939 these various types of *cotones* seemed to be worn without regard to a particular village or rancho, except that in Zacatipan (some two hours from Cuetzalan) the black garment was used almost entirely. In a number of regions in Mexico, wool shirts or *cotones* having sleeves serve without a cotton shirt underneath.

FOOTGEAR. The usual, simple type of men's sandals are seen in Cuetzalan, chiefly a rawhide sole attached to the foot with three sets of thongs. A single thong separates the great toe from the rest, while strands fastened to the sole at the instep are stationary, part passing over the instep and the rest catching over the back of the heel.

BELT. Belts in Cuetzalan are called *xenilol*, and are 6 to 7 inches wide and up to 3 yards long. They are wound twice about the waist and knotted at the left, with the ends hanging. They are fashioned of finely hand-spun, plain-weave, white cotton thread (sometimes store-bought), with a section from 3 to 7 inches long of beautifully worked fringe (made with the aid of needles, and the knotting of weft threads around the warp to form a decorative pattern) at each end of the belt. This knotting technique is commonly called *macramé*. Spottings of multicolored wool embroidery in zigzag bands, and many handmade white cotton tassels finish the ends.

Unadorned belts are sometimes sold in the Cuetzalan market, with long warp threads left hanging for the purchaser to work into decorative ends. One is reminded of the ancient loin cloth, or *maxtli*, which —according to the historian Camargo—was 24 feet long, and had elaborately ornamented ends embellished with fringes, tassels, color, and gold.

19. San José Miahuatlán, Puebla (Nahua)

Women's Costume

THE WOMEN'S COSTUME of Miahuatlán is, in many respects, unique in Mexico today. Women of this town—not far distant from Tehuacán—are seen frequently in the markets of Tehuacán and Ajalpan, where they sell a special bread, *pan de burro*, made in their village. These women go about in full costume (pl. 179), although children and even young girls no longer wear it.

The present costume consists of (1) a *manta huipil* with heavily embroidered transverse stripes, always in dark-red wool with accents of black; (2) a wraparound cotton tube skirt of store-bought black poplin; (3) a wide red wool belt sewn to a *soyate*; (4) an extra *huipil* for a head covering, which—if not used over the head—is often folded over the left shoulder when women are outside their houses; (5) a carrying basket (*tenate*) of palm with *greca* designs, observed in this and other neighboring towns (pl. 187), is carried over one shoulder by its twisted *ixtle* cord. (*Tenates* are made in San Pedro Teotitlán.)

HUIPIL. There have been no handwoven *huipiles* made in Miahuatlán for a good many years. A length of *manta* of approximately 65 inches is cut from cloth varying in width from 35½ to 39 inches. In the four *huipiles* which we examined, the vertical neck slit, when finished with embroidery, measures about 10 inches. This slit is not usually cut in the center of the garment (from front to back), but further toward one end—usually 17 inches from the front bottom edge, and 33–36 inches from back lower edge, making the *huipil* longer in the back than in the front. This open-sided *huipil* is worn inside the skirt and belt in front, but in back is left hanging and bloused outside the skirt, held in by the wide belt (pl. 179).

There are some *huipiles* made here with the front and back of equal length. They measure from 72 to 78 inches. These may be used as upper garments, but are chiefly worn shawl-fashion over the head for church and fiesta. Decoration is usually of type 3 (below), in addition to which large initials in fine black embroidery are often seen below the red embroidery area in front.

Huipil decoration is of three general types. Each of these types has bold horizontal bands of dark-red embroidery, with accents of black, which run across shoulders and chest. These bands vary in width, and are carried out in completely reversible satin stitch, cross-stitch, and deep looped pile stitch resembling hooked-rug work, but showing on the reverse side in a running lozenge design (pl. 181).

231

179. Two Nahua women of San José Miahuatlán, Puebla, in costume. 1962

180. A woman embroidering a *huipil*. San José Miahuatlán, Puebla (Nahua). 1962

181. The reverse side of the *huipil* shown in Plate 180 —
a pile-looped embroidered band. San José Miahuatlán,
Puebla (Nahua). 1962

(1) The oldest type of *huipil*, of which we found
but one example, has no white spaces between embroidered bands. Instead, a solid 15-inch area of 1–
2-inch reversible satin-stitch bands in zigzag pattern
entirely fills the central area of the garment (the neck
slit is in the exact center). Added next to and below
this area, front and back, is a 2½-inch band of deep-
pile embroidery 20 inches long.

(2) The everyday *huipil* now in use (with the short
front) has the same neck finish as the older type—a
firm ⅝-inch-wide combined satin- and buttonhole-
stitch edging. Five decorative bands are standard as
to design, width, and placing (pl. 179). On the shoulder fold is a band edged in black; 2¼ inches below
this band, both in front and in back, is a band of conventionalized plant pattern (in reversible satin stitch)
in red only. Then below the neck slit always occurs
the 4–4½-by-24–25-inch band of thick pile, with its
ends finished in looped fringes. Quite miraculously,

the latter bands are worked pile side out, and when
we asked how the perfect lozenge designs turned up
on the reverse side, we were told—"My hand knows
how" (pl. 180).

(3) An old example of the third type for a young
girl (pl. 182), shows narrower pile bands, the usual
plain band edged in black across the shoulder, and
three intermediate bands of cross-stitch embroidery
in plant and bird designs.

The embroidered bands are so solidly made that
they outlast three or more *huipiles*. The charge for
making the heavy hooked-ruglike bands was 20 *pesos*
for each piece in 1963. Some twelve or thirteen skeins
of commercial yarn are used for each everyday *huipil*,
making the total cost considerable. The preferred yarn
is called *Pato*. The color runs very heavily into the
white of the garment, an effect desired in a good
many Indian communities in Mexico.

Skirt. The black cotton commercial cloth for Mia-

182. A child's old-style *huipil*. San José Miahuatlán, Puebla (Nahua). 1962

183. A Nahua woman of San José Miahuatlán, Puebla, making *tortillas*. 1962

huatlán skirts is sewn up in tube form by a woman in a corner store, who owns a sewing machine and who charged 3.50 *pesos* per skirt in 1963. Four lengths of 42–48 inches are sewn together (the cloth is about 40 inches wide), making a total circumference of about 4⅓ yards. Skirts were formerly of handwoven black wool, but no trace of an example could be found in 1963.

The skirt is put on with triple thickness across the back. The top is folded down inside about 6–8 inches; then all fullness is gathered across the front (fig. 11 e-4). The *soyate* is put on to hold the skirt in place, and the outer red wool belt is wrapped around outside the *huipil* (pl. 183).

BELT. The 5-by-72-inch red wool belt is not woven in Miahuatlán, but is brought in—rarely now—from San Salvador Atoyatempan, Puebla. It is of diagonal weave with a 1-inch warp center pattern carried out in the same red wool. *Soyates* of unusual width (4½ inches) are attached to one end.

HEAD COVERING, HAIRDRESS, JEWELRY, AND FOOTGEAR. There are two ways, at least, for the placing of *huipiles* over the head. For everyday, a *huipil* is turned inside out (showing the lozenge design), and doubled in from both edges to make a rectangle of several thicknesses. This is placed flat over the head, from front to back. When not on the head, this everyday *huipil* is worn folded over one shoulder. A special *huipil*, usually having black initials and fashioned of equal length in front and back, is worn as a shawl over the head for fiesta or church. It is clasped in front by the hands from underneath. Hair is worn down the back in two braids, fastened together at the ends by a longish black cord (pl. 179).

All women who wear the costume also wear a string of black cut-glass beads. Formerly, beads were black jet with small silver coins inserted, and sometimes a large coin hanging at the center front—one we collected had a 1908 silver *peso* as a pendant.

We saw no footgear.

235

Children's Costume

When we visited Miahuatlán (1963) small girls were not seen in costume, and some young women had abandoned the indigenous dress.

Men's Costume

Today old men dress in *manta* clothing or commercial-cotton trousers and shirts, with or without sandals. According to J. Paredes Colín (1921, p. 76), and to one old photograph seen in a San José Miahuatlán corner store, men wore (probably up to 1900) a curious dark wool *cotón* over short white trousers and shirt. This *cotón* seems to have been crossed over the shoulders from back to front in two long strips with a skirtlike section below the waist, all held in by a wide white sash and a belt of leather. The high-necked white shirt with the dark wool crossing high on the chest suggests clerical influence. The man in the corner store (aged about fifty) said his grandfather dressed "that way," and also wore very old-style sandals, with long wide ties of leather wrapped high up the calves of the legs.

20. Altepexi, Puebla (Nahua)

ALTEPEXI is a village of 4,667 inhabitants (*Censo General,* 1960), located near Tehuacán just off the highway that goes southeast to Teotitlán del Camino; it is also on the railway to Oaxaca. The women wear a modification of the true Indian dress. In the general region the *huipil* is worn, but in Altepexi a blouse has been substituted. Some weaving is done, but for the most part on the Spanish treadle loom. Altepexi women are often seen in the nearby market of Ajalpan (market day is Wednesday)—one of the markets where corn is the basis of exchange and little money changes hands (pl. 187).

Women's Costume

The traditional costume still worn by middle-aged and older women consists of a white blouse and a very wide white skirt, both of handwoven material (pl. 185). Most young girls have modified the costume by wearing a very elaborate blouse that wins the approval of Mexico City people and tourists (pl. 184).

BLOUSE. The handwoven, old-style blouse is very full (one example measured 72 inches in circumference around the bottom), gathered into a round neck opening (11-inch diameter), having a 3½-inch vertical slit in the center front. Neck and slit are finished without any band of cloth, but with an elaborate edge (½-inch), consisting of a binding of firm buttonhole stitch, and a band of blanket-stitch with spots of colored embroidery. Black mercerized thread is probably the older style, but some of these blouses are finished in red. An example of the latter type has alternating orange and green spots. A twisted cord of the three colors, with tassels, serves to fasten the neck slit together in front.

The sleeves are short (5½ inches), very fully gathered into a band of the same combination embroidered edge as is described above. The usual square of cloth is set in under the arm, and the shoulder section is made of double cloth—this area is outlined with feather stitching in red or black as the case may be (pl. 185).

SKIRT. Skirts are of handloomed (treadle-loomed) plain-weave, white cloth (of commercial cotton thread) woven 35 inches in width, wider than most backstrap-loom weaving. For the traditional Altepexi skirt, seven widths of 35-inch material, cut in 35-inch lengths, are sewn side by side on a sewing machine—making the longest piece for an unformed skirt we know of. A ¾-inch hem is left at top and bottom, and the whole piece is then sewn together in tube form. The seven

184. Young Nahua girls of Altepexi, Puebla, with traditional *rebozos* and new-style costumes. 1963

widths reduced both ways by hems make a tube about 238 by 33 inches.

Skirts, worn over the blouse, are assembled with each wearing. The whole fullness is first gathered across the front where it can be controlled. Next the belt (of palm) is wrapped securely around the waist in such manner that the fullness is evenly distributed, mainly on the front of the body, and then the outer, narrow belt is wrapped around and fastened. In the process, the upper edge of the skirt is turned down on the outside, and forms a roll under the narrow belt (pl. 185). Skirts are worn quite short—to mid-calf.

BELT. Belts are finely woven of cotton or artificial silk, chiefly by men of the town, on the belt loom in a seated position (pl. 96). This loom has the type of "rigid-heald" used also by the prolific belt weavers of Santo Tomás Jalieza, in the valley of Oaxaca (pl. 186). The firm, neat Altepexi belts measure about 1½ inches wide by 50 inches long. The rep weave contains a ⅞-inch center design section of geometric figures, warp formed: birds, scorpions, human figures, and usually the letters of a name spelled out—"María," for instance.

REBOZO. The white head-covering, a plain-weave *rebozo*, is woven on a treadle loom, and measures 30 by 152 inches, with hand-fashioned ball fringe on the ends—some eighty-six balls to each end. Mildred Stapley (1924, p. 23) says, "we find that Spain true to its oriental heritage remained a land of fringes and tassels . . ." On the other hand, ancient people also used tufts and fringes. Raul D'Harcourt comments (1962, p. 136), "The ancient Peruvians at times made immoderate use of such tassels . . . certain very open network had a tassel applied to each mesh . . ."

The *rebozo* is worn over the shoulders shawlwise (pls. 184 & 187), but more commonly is folded flat over the head, the 30-inch width being divided into thirds. The length is similarly divided, the whole forming a layered cloth about 10 by 19 inches which balances over the head from front to back (pl. 185); the rebozo falls to shoulder length behind, providing ample protection from the sun.

If a woman is in the street or on the road, and is not wearing her head covering in the manner described above, she carries it folded over one shoulder.

Men's Costume

Although there is now no distinctive attire for men in Altepexi, a handwoven costume was used as late as 1900 (from calculations made by talking to a seventy-year-old, whose father died at the age of ninety

185. An old Nahua woman of Altepexi, Puebla, in costume. 1963

and wore the costume). Such a costume was made for us by Concepción Regino, the wife of the aforementioned informant, who remembered the old-style dress of her father-in-law. In Plate 188 the son of this pair poses in the costume. Rather nervous, he made sure that the house doors were closed so no towns-

186. A young belt weaver, using a loom with a rigid heald. Santo Tomás Jalieza, Oaxaca (Zapotec). 1960

187. An old vendor of Altepexi, Puebla, in the nearby market of Ajalpan. (Nahua). 1963

188. The old-style Nahua men's costume of Altapexi, Puebla — no longer in use. In the background of the second view is shown the treadle loom on which the costume was woven. 1963

people would see him. The younger generation considers such costumes a mark of backward provincialism.

SHIRT. Of handloomed white material, the full shirt is gathered into a 1-inch band at the neck with full sleeves gathered into a similar cuff band. No buttons are used, but at the neck and cuff a hand-twisted, white cotton cord with round fringe balls is passed through and knotted.

TROUSERS. Of the same handloomed cloth, trousers are slightly tapered with the crotch set in separately, and with a long narrow tie at the waist. The most distinguished feature of the trousers is the ⅞-inch wide decorative band of *macramé*, in a zigzag pattern worked on the bottom of the trouser legs, and finished with strong buttonhole stitch (also white) on the edge. Whereas the wife of Concepción cut and sewed our costume, after her son had woven the required cloth, it was necessary to take the trousers to a very old man, who did the *macramé* work. He was the only one who still knew how to do it in 1963.

HIP-CLOTH AND BELT. The shirt is worn inside the trousers; over the shirt—about the waist—a curious 45-inch-square cloth is doubled over into a "V", tied center front, and then drawn tightly about the hips. This square cloth is formed of 22½-inch widths sewn to-

242

gether. The whole is outlined with a firm buttonhole stitch in black mercerized thread, and in each corner appears a rather open, large-stitch embroidery motif of three flowers in a pot or vase. The red belt is wrapped about the waist above this cloth.

The belt (9½ inches wide by 120 inches long) was likewise woven on the loom pictured in Plate 188, and is a soft red color formed by a weave of white warp and red weft thread. Every ½ inch there occur two narrow white lines, and then a ⅛-inch white stripe. At the ends of the belt, the cut white warps are twisted to form some 16 fringes 4 inches long. These are to be seen at the back of the wearer—tucked in.

The loom on which the white cloth and the red belt were woven stands behind the young man in Plate 188. The father (pl. 96) is a weaver of women's belts, and the son weaves white cloth and women's white *rebozos*. There are few weavers now in Altepexi, and this family is able to sell to townspeople. The women make the fringe tufts of the *rebozos*, and make baskets and simple pottery to sell in the Wednesday market of nearby Ajalpan and in Tehuacán. Plate 187 shows an Altepexi woman selling foodstuff in Ajalpan.

Footgear

Sandals were seen on some men—leather or tire soles with thongs. The women observed were barefoot.

Children's Costume

Small girls wear variations of the present-day young girl's costume—consisting of heavily embroidered blouses, satin skirts, and the white *rebozo*, often with an apron of store-bought cloth (pl. 184).

21. San Sebastián Zinacatepec, Puebla (Nahua)

ZINACATEPEC is a large town, with a considerable Indian population. It is situated on the paved highway between Tehuacán and Teotitlán del Camino, and has but little left of indigenous dress. In 1963 we found mention of a costume said to have long since disappeared (Paredes Colín, 1921, pp. 155–158). We decided to investigate the matter, and much to our surprise we found that a few old women had kept one or even two beautiful old *huipiles* for two purposes: (1) to be buried in, and (2) for young girls in the family to dress up in. We were able to secure and photograph the noteworthy costume shown in Plate 189, and have found no one—except, of course, J. Paredes Colín—who had, prior to our visit, seen or taken note of this costume.

Women's Costume

Elderly women still wear the old type of ankle-length skirt of finely pleated dark-blue cotton, gathered onto a band. The material is woven on the treadle loom. Some plain *manta huipiles* are seen as upper garments, although we observed that the conservative women sometimes changed to more modern white blouses when leaving their houses. A red wool belt is still used by some. Store *rebozos* serve as head coverings. Younger women wear no part of the old indigenous dress.

HUIPIL. The old handwoven *huipiles* are formed of three strips, with the center strip usually joined to the two side strips with colored ribbon. The sides are sewn together without ribbon in a small overhand stitch, using red silk thread and leaving 12–13-inch armholes. Webs are about 12 by 80 inches, thus making a nearly square *huipil* when assembled. A round neck opening is bordered with ribbon carefully reinforced with hand embroidery.

The white handwoven *huipil* panels (usually of fine hand-spun thread) contain plain-weave areas, broken by a group of heavier white wefts. Some *huipil* strips also have a ¼-inch weft stripe in red silk thread, placed every 3 inches and spaced to frame the white weft stripes (pl. 189).

The center area of the middle panel has a solid embroidered yoke, measuring 11–13 inches down from the shoulder fold in front and back, surrounding the neck opening (pl. 189). The *huipiles* often have a 5-inch open space left in the yoke some 6 inches below the neck, both in front and in back. A piece of the same ribbon which borders the center panel and neck opening is sewn across this space—a piece sufficiently

244

PLATE X. A Chinantec woman of Usila, Oaxaca, painting areas of a handwoven *huipil* with *fuchina* dye. 1964

189. A Nahua woman of San Sebastián Zinacatepec, Puebla, wearing a fine old *huipil* of a style no longer used in the village. The original all silk ribbon has long since worn out and been replaced by modern ribbon. 1962

ong to allow streamers of equal length to hang down some 18 inches. The ribbons display decorative creases fashioned by wrapping the dampened ribbon around a piece of gourd or cardboard, and pressing with a stone. The ribbons fall free when the garment is worn (pl. 189). Bodil Christensen (verbal communication) has seen such ribbons hanging from bead necklaces in Huautla, Hidalgo (Nahua). Decorative creasing of ribbons is to be seen in a peasant costume of Navalcán (Castilla, Province of Toledo) in Spain (Ortiz Echagüe, 1950, pl. 113).

The solid embroidered area about the neck is carried out in a type of cross-stitch resembling French knot technique combined with satin stitch. Rose red predominates with accents of light green, purple, and blue (pl. IX). Only true silk thread has been observed in the few *huipiles* we know from Zinacatepec. Directly below the neck opening one sees an area of diagonal designs, centered with four-petaled patterns within each lozenge in a contrasting color. The outer areas of the whole embroidered section comprise a mass of flower forms, conventionalized in character, and a pair of deer facing left and right. The latter sometimes leave a broken outline on the outer edge of this solid yoke (pls. 189 & IX).

Apparently these *huipiles* have not been made for thirty years or more. One woman of seventy-odd years recounted to us how, from the age of seven, she was made to get up early and spin. If she was lazy, her ears were pulled.

The old-style *huipiles* were worn rolled up about the waist after the skirt and belt were put on, or loose over the skirt (pl. 189).

Skirt. The pleated skirt worn today is of dark-blue cotton treadle-loom cloth made in or near Oaxaca City (30 inches wide with narrow lighter blue weft stripes). Skirts are hand pleated (⅜-inch pleats) in the village by several families who make a specialty of this work. Front and back sections of 3½ yards each are prepared separately. The 30-inch cloth with vertical stripes is sewn onto a 9–10-inch upper section of *manta*, and gathered into a narrow band. The bottom of the skirt is bound with ½-inch reddish-purple store ribbon. One woman in the town makes and sells these skirts. She goes to Oaxaca to secure the *cortes*. She prepares the front and back pieces, and sends them out to be pleated, after which she finishes the final sewing together of the skirts by hand. We were told that a new skirt was valued at 250 *pesos* (1963), about $20.00 in U.S. money—a considerable sum. Such a skirt must be made to last the wearer for a very long time.

The skirt, instead of being tied about the waist, in the usual manner, is tied above the breast—the total skirt length being about 40 inches. The skirt of one unusually short woman measured overall only 32 inches, and it was also tied above the breast.

Belt, Head Covering, and Jewelry. Although the skirt is sewn onto a band and not wrapped around, a belt of red wool is used (some 70 inches long including its 15-inch fringe), attached to a 2-by-70-inch *soyate*. The belt has a warp pattern in heavier red wool through its center section; it is actually 4½ inches wide, but is folded over and sewn together lengthwise, reducing the width by half. We were told that in former times the wool belts were brought from the Mixteca—"But now the men don't come here anymore."

No head covering was seen other than dark-blue cotton *rebozos*. No footgear was noted. The older women wore chains of seeds or corals.

Children's Costume

No child's old-style *huipil* was found. Children wear only nondescript cotton dresses. Sewing machines were noted in many houses, and young girls—with the city of Tehuacán not far away—seemed decidedly clothes conscious, in the modern sense.

Men's Costume

Some older men wore loose *manta* shirts, outside of *calzones* tied in at the ankles. Some *huaraches* were seen. The nice, old husband of the very tiny woman mentioned above was interested in our ages—whereas many Indians tend to lose track of even their own.

22. Hueyapan, Morelos (Nahua)

LOCATED ON THE BORDER of the state of Puebla, in the mountains that lead to the northeastern tip of Morelos and the volcano Popocatépetl—this charming village with its many orchards, cobblestone streets, and unusually well-made adobe houses (some two-storied), retains an indigenous costume.

Hueyapan is a wool-weaving settlement, working only for village consumption. There is an autobus which makes the arduous trip, over a very bad road the last part of the way, to the town. Taking the route, southeastward from Cuautla, one leaves the highway at Amayuca to go north through Zacualpan and Tlacotepec. From Hueyapan, there was in 1964 no further passable road for a car in any direction.

Aside from the fact that but little indigenous dress or handweaving exists today in Morelos, we found an unusual wool carding process in this village. Wool is cleaned by hand, picked apart, and then subjected to further refining and mixing of natural wool colors. This is done by rubbing together (pls. 190 & 191) two dried burrs from a plant the natives call *calum*, that grows "on the mountain." Upon a single burr held in the left hand is placed a bit of brown and a bit of white wool. This burr is somewhat harder than the other one (held in the right hand), which has been softened in hot water. The softer burr is rubbed against the harder one.

This plant is a species of teasel—described in *Webster's Collegiate Dictionary* as follows:

Teasel—(1) Any of the genus *(Dipsacus)* of prickly herbs having blue or lilac flowers in dense, oblong heads, esp. a variety, the "fullers".
Teasel *(D. fullonum)* the flower-head of which is covered with stiff, hooked bracts. (2) A flower-head of the fuller's Teasel, used when dried to raise a nap on cloth.

The above use has been reported, but the Hueyapan use of two single teasels rubbed together for carding and mixing wool colors we have not found previously recorded in Mexico or elsewhere. According to Charles Amsden (1964, p. 35 & pl. 10) the Navaho employed teasels for carding wool "in early times." He describes the "wool card" as "made by clamping a row of burrs to a wooden frame by means of two strips of iron held down by bolts," and says that the device is of Mexican origin, and that the idea probably came originally from Europe, since our own pioneers knew it too.

Lila O'Neale (1945, Fig. 18–g) mentions a "teasel-fan" used by wool weavers to raise nap on blankets. Two sizes of teasel-heads are held "between wood

190. Preparing and mixing natural colors of wool, using two teasels. Hueyapan, Morelos (Nahua). 1963

248

191. A detail showing the teasels being used. Hueyapan, Morelos (Nahua). 1963

strips, the fan measuring from top to bottom 8 in. (Momostenango, Guatemala).”

In Mexico actual wool carding is usually done with a pair of crude boards having short wire bristles and wooden handles.

Women's Costume

The Hueyapan woman's costume consists today of a locally woven skirt, belt, and *rebozo*—all of wool. These are worn with a nondescript cotton blouse, and special sandals woven of *ixtle*. Little girls customarily wear cotton dresses.

SKIRT. The wool wrap-around skirt is woven on the backstrap loom in the village by women for their own use. We saw two types of skirts (1963)—one of dark blue (anil-dyed), and one of natural grey, tan, and dark-brown variegated warps. The latter seemed to be worn by very elderly women (pl. 70). Here the skirt is called *chincuete*, and is woven of hand-spun wool in two strips, each about 24 inches wide, and described to us as being 5 or 7 *varas* in length (a measuring unit of about 33.6 inches). The two strips are sewn together lengthwise, then end to end, to form a tube. As in all Mexican villages today, wool skirts are valued highly and are expensive to produce. The anil for dyeing the blue skirts, we were told, costs 30 *pesos* a kilo, and the requirement for one skirt is at least half a kilo. The wool comes chiefly from the village of Yamacaque, and costs 10 *pesos* a kilo in crude form— one skirt requires at least six kilos, cleaned and carded.

Skirts are put on by first forming a *tabla* or big box pleat about 12 inches wide across the back of the wearer. The long, red wool belt, which has been hanging ready over one shoulder, is thrown across the pleat and held tightly across the back to secure the *tabla* while the rest of the skirt is being arranged. The wearer then forms six or seven pleats from her left side, next to the *tabla*, around toward the front and her right side (fig. 11 g). Finally two pleats are formed on the right side facing front.

We were told that wool skirts are also worn in some neighboring villages, chiefly Alpanocan and Santa Cruz. In the latter a quite different belt, apparently of cotton, is used. This fact is curious, because wool seems to be the only fabric worked in this area. We were particularly interested to discover, during 1963, another region in the state of Morelos having indigenous costume. Before our visit to Hueyapan we believed that the women of Tetelcingo, near Cuautla were probably the only ones in this state still displaying indigenous dress.

BELT. The Hueyapan belt is a heavy, home-woven, red wool belt measuring 3 by 113 inches. This belt has white cotton warps, and a 1¼-inch running center design of a heavier floating red warp pattern bordered by warps of black wool. No *soyate* is used. At one end of the belt, fringes are formed into three 5½-inch braids fastened together.

REBOZO. Although we visited Hueyapan twice during the rainy season and not at all during the coldest months, all the women wore—in the streets—large wool shawls, matching the skirt of blue or mixed brown. These *rebozos*, woven at home, were of finer spun wool than the skirts (pl. 70).

FOOTGEAR. Sandals of *ixtle* fiber, called *ixcatles*, are used by Indian women in Hueyapan (pls. 13 & 70). Pairs are of one size only, and cost the equivalent of 28 cents in U.S. money. These coarsely fashioned, but surprisingly durable, sandals are made in Tepemazolco (or Tepemaxalco), Puebla, and on Tuesday market day in Hueyapan one vendor was seen with many pairs over his shoulder. In Hueyapan we were told that the same sandals are used by women of nearby Alpanocan and Tetela del Volcán, Morelos. We had seen piles of them for sale at a religious fiesta in Amecameca, state of México (also in the vicinity of Popocatépetl) some twenty years before. It is unusual for Indian women to have any standardized footgear. They are far more apt to be barefoot than are Indian men.

Men's Costume

Fine wool *sarapes* are woven in the Hueyapan, in natural colors, without design other than stripes, and are worn by the men over rural type Mexican *manta* clothing.

23. Tetelcingo, Morelos (Nahua)

TETELCINGO is a small, very conservative village about five hundred yards off the Cuernavaca-Cuautla highway. One sees the women waiting at autobus stops or walking along the road wearing an extremely graceful all-blue costume. Before we went there, we were told that the people were difficult and no photographs were allowed. After talking to several shy women (not all are monolingual), we found that some actually wanted them. Pictures were taken on several occasions in 1962–1963, and prints were returned to the people. However, the last time we were met by a furious old woman clutching in her hand the pictures she had been given. She said that they had caused the death of her daughter. A crowd gathered, and the situation was quite unpleasant. A male relative finally appeared who calmed her somewhat after a lengthy and vociferous conversation in Nahuatl. Photos were prohibited in 1964, and at the same time we noticed fewer young women in costume.

About twenty years ago we saw several Tetelcingo women at a religious fiesta in Amecameca, state of México, and noted that the older women wore dark-blue handwoven wool costumes. The younger ones were already dressed in commercial cloth.

Women's Costume

The dark-blue wrap-around skirt and *huipil* of Tetelcingo are of store-bought woolen cloth, formerly imported from England. Those worn today are of three grades (and prices). Three meters (117 inches) are required to make a gala *huipil* and skirt of 55-inch-wide material called *paño de lana* (wool cloth); 33 inches are cut off to make the width of the *huipil*, the 55 inches making the length. This leaves a single skirt length 55 by 84 inches. One price quoted to us for the total required material was 65 *pesos* a meter, or about $15.60 for the costume. We subsequently found that other materials are also used and, therefore, other measurements result—and other costume prices. Materials are purchased in Cuautla.

HUIPIL. The *huipil* is interesting—made in one width, but in some cases having a line of dark, fine running stitch from the neck slit to the bottom (indicating that at one time, when the garment was handwoven, it was made in two strips). When asked what the almost invisible line of stitching was for, the informant replied, *"Es de lujo nada más"* ("only for show"). This *huipil* ordinarily is left completely open at the sides, giving one a glimpse of the belt, but when the wearer is

251

192. Belt loom for ring weaving. Tetelcingo, Morelos (Nahua). 1966

working, the front lower corners of the *huipil* are tucked into the belt (pls. 86 & 192).

SKIRT. The skirt is worn very long—to the instep—and, due to the quality of the material and manner of wrapping, is very graceful. It is sewn into a tube and sometimes has, like the *huipil*, a line of dark-blue handstitching running horizontally to divide the skirt into two parts—as it was divided years ago, when it was handwoven. When the skirt is put on, all extra loom length is doubled down inside at the waist, and the fullness is arranged in three wide folds, reaching well across the back, before the belt is wrapped around (fig. 11 c).

In recent years a lighter-blue cotton skirt is sometimes worn for everyday. Many of these skirts are patched with large squares of cloth, so that one can hardly distinguish the original material.

BELTS. A thick, red wool warp-faced belt, 3 by 103 inches, with a fringe at one end, is attached at the other end to a second narrower, 1½ by 60 inch, less-heavy red wool belt. The first usually has blue warp edges — the smaller one, green or some other contrasting color. This use of two belts of different widths but of the same material is unusual. The wide belt, we were told, lasts ten years, takes the place of the *soyate*, and is wound underneath the narrow one. This is the only handweaving on backstrap loom that is now done in this village (pl. 192).

HEAD COVERING, HAIRDRESS, AND JEWELRY. Usually no jewelry is worn by the women of Tetelcingo, although we were told that a very simple type of silver earring is considered part of the costume. These are purchased in Cuautla. The store-bought cotton *rebozo* may be used on occasion as a headcovering or carrying cloth.

Hair is worn down the back in a single braid. For important fiestas the women dye their hair green with an herb, a custom reminiscent of pre-Conquest times (pls. 86 & V).

24. The Chinantla, Oaxaca (Chinantec)

THE CHINANTECS inhabit a small area in northern Oaxaca called the Chinantla, a word derived from the Aztec word *chinamitl*, meaning an enclosed space. This is appropriate as the Chinantecs are cut off from neighboring groups by natural mountain barriers, except in three spots where the boundary is a river or a plain (Bevan, 1938, p. 9).

The Chinantecs display a great variety of women's costumes, some of the most colorful in Mexico. As Bevan says (1938, p. 81), the finest *huipiles* come from the western Chinantla—Usila, Ojitlán, Mayoltianguis, Tlatepusco, Zapotitlán, Quetzalapa, Zautla, and San Pedro Sochiapan—and we would also particularly add Santa Cruz Tepetotutla (pls. 134 & 193).

From Tuxtepec straight south, the first Chinantec town is Chiltepec, where weaving is not so noteworthy as in the region further west. Valle Nacional, south of Chiltepec, formerly produced *huipiles* with an embroidered folkloric conventionalized floral design which, although delightful, did not have the decidedly Indian design character of the work of previously mentioned villages. Today great deterioration is seen in Valle Nacional design patterns—parrots, peacocks, and modern sample-sheet patterns have taken over.

Unfortunately this important costume area, (the Chinantla) will have to be chiefly represented in photographs, and written descriptions must be minimized in a book of this scope, as there are so very many Chinantec villages with rather similar costumes. In this paper we are confining ourselves principally to the village of San Lucas Ojitlán, with some few comparative comments, particularly in relation to the village of San Felipe Usila.

Women's Costume

The Ojitlán costumes and weaving which we studied and photographed were observed in 1940 in a *rancho* called Choapan (not to be confused with the Zapotec Choapan described elsewhere), populated by a small group of Indians native to Ojitlán, and later in 1965, in Ojitlán proper. In 1964 we visited Usila, and afterward in the non-Indian town of Tuxtepec we saw women from many Chinantec villages passing through for the annual early May fiesta of nearby Otatitlán, Vera Cruz.

The only Chinantec village we know where all costume elements are handwoven is Ojitlán. Parts of the costume are a richly embroidered everyday white *huipil*, an all red fiesta *huipil*, a red striped skirt, a large

193. A Chinantec woman of Santa Cruz Tepetotutla, Oaxaca, in a fine red and white *huipil*. 1943

square red striped headcloth or carrying cloth, and a red striped belt.

In other Chinantec villages, as far as we know, the only handwoven item is the *huipil* (except in Usila which has both a handwoven *huipil* and a handwoven headcloth). Most villages use store-bought cotton *rebozos*, and wear *chiapaneca* (plaid-design) skirt *cortes*. Older Usila women wear the *cortes*, but younger ones now wear flowered commercial cotton skirts. These skirts worry the eye when combined with the very detailed multicolored handwoven *huipiles* (pls. 29 & 194). Usila *huipiles* are the only ones we know in Mexico today that are actually painted in certain areas after weaving is completed (pl. X).

EVERYDAY HUIPIL (OJITLAN). The everyday *huipil* is a soft heavy hand-spun white cotton three-strip

194. A woman of Usila, Oaxaca (who refused to be photographed outdoors), wearing a characteristic *huipil* and handwoven brocaded headcloth. (Chinantec). 1964

195. A Chinantec girl embroidering a *huipil*. Rancho Choapan, Oaxaca. 1940

garment, measuring when assembled 34 inches wide by 36 inches long. Individual strips are 11¼ by 72 inches. Varying areas of gauze-weave stripes alternate throughout with plain-weave areas. The three strips are sewn together with a 1⅜-inch joining stitch in successive sections of red, blue, pink, and orange wool commercial yarns in from ¾- to 1⅜-inch divisions (pls. 40 & 195). Although the sides of some *huipiles* examined were sewn up to leave rather small arm openings (6 inches), occasionally we noticed that the decorative joining stitching stopped some distance below. We were told that this was to facilitate enlarging the openings in case children had to be nursed. The handsome joining stitch is described (O'Neale, 1945, pl. 81, fig. L) as "a common stitch worked into satin-like bands up to 2 in. in width."

The round neck opening is simply bound with black cotton cloth or tape. Embroidered everyday *huipil* decoration seems always to include the large chest, shoulder, and lower-front geometric patterns, which have a decidedly pre-Conquest character—suggesting ancient serpent and lightning motifs. These standardized elements and smaller geometric spots, and conventionalized animal units, are worked in with a needle and red cotton thread. The mechanical count of background warp and weft threads, two white warps crossed by two white wefts, accounts for the even specks of white seen in overall embroidered areas (pl. 40).

FIESTA HUIPIL (OJITLAN). Considered by the Indians to be more desirable is the all red handwoven three-web fiesta *huipil*, having measurements similar to the everyday type, the same web joinings, and usually the same neck binding, but otherwise of different construction and design (pl. 41).

The red plain-weave background (formed with white warps) contains occasional small weft cotton stripes of contrasting colors. A broad band of multicolored geometric pattern forms a border near the bottom of the *huipil*. In the upper half of the center strip are worked bands and rows of solid geometric designs, over which are sewn colored sequins. Around the sleeve opening a white cloth or store-bought lace edge is sometimes added.

In both Ojitlán and Usila, we observed people from the Chinantec town of Analco selling a simplified type of *huipil*—strips whipped together, with no neck opening—which they weave loosely of commercial cotton to sell to Chinantec women who wish to save time and money by using these as a base to embroider on, join together, and complete. The wide red and white areas of the crude, inexpensive Analco *huipiles* may be adapted to the particular style of a number of Chinantec villages.

SKIRT (OJITLAN). In Ojitlán, *huipiles* are often longer than the skirts beneath, and at times no skirt is worn. Handwoven of one-web using red commercial cotton thread (both warp and weft), the plain-weave weft-face skirt is woven in a single width (20 by 90–92 inches). Sewn along its length on one side is a 8- to 10½-inch dark-blue (handwoven or commercial) strip of striped cloth. The red skirt contains 1¼-inch groups of multicolored warp stripes with plain red spaces of similar width between. Skirts are wrapped around with the blue section at the waist. They are worn to mid-calf, and secured with a belt.

BELT (OJITLAN). In Ojitlán proper a handwoven red belt with two groups of multicolored warp stripes was still being woven in 1964 (3¾ inches wide by 67 inches long, including 3-inch twisted fringes at each end). In 1940 in the *rancho* of Choapan the purple cotton treadle-loomed belts of Oaxaca City were being used.

HEAD COVERING, HAIRDRESS, AND JEWELRY (OJITLAN AND USILA). A large squarish cloth formed of two skirt-type woven widths (one examined being 41 by 46 inches when sewn together) is worn over the head by Ojitlán women (pl. 41), with one corner knotted and centered over the forehead. These same cloths also serve as bundle carriers. Sometimes both the center and corners have small spots of colored embroidery. Usila women still wear a handwoven red headcloth with warp and weft colored stripes, the center and corners having multicolored brocaded bird, animal, and geometric designs (pls. 140 & 194).

Ojitlán women commonly wear their hair in two braids, as do older women of Usila. Young Usila girls have a new-style hairdress—very original and truly exotic (pls. 114 & 196).

Tastes in jewelry vary from village to village. Young girls of Ojitlán prefer *papelillo* beads, whereas those of Usila wear masses of opaque vermillion glass beads in longer strings (pl. 114).

Men's Costume

The chief or only distinguishing features of the Chinantec man's costume are said to have been a handwoven red headcloth worn pirate fashion instead of a hat and a red handwoven belt. These items were common in the time of Frederick Starr (1901, p. 170), and were still to be seen in 1940, although at that time many bandana handkerchiefs had taken the place of

196. Two Chinantec girls of Usila, Oaxaca, showing the hairdress. 1964

the woven headcloths. In 1964 in Usila we obtained a fine men's handwoven red headcloth said not to have been used for many years (pl. VI d), and a handsome old-style men's belt (pl. VI b).

Children's Costume

Little girls were seen in Rancho Choapan in 1940 in long narrow handwoven *huipiles* with big tucks near the bottom to allow for growth. Also dresses of store cotton cloth were already being worn at that time. In Usila in 1964 all little girls wore cotton dresses, but before marriage, after a few years of school, almost all were said to revert to native dress. Little boys dress as their fathers do today.

25. Yalalag, Oaxaca (Zapotec)

 YALALAG in Zapotec signifies "tree of copal with leaves." The entomology is *yaga* (tree) plus *yala* (*copal*) and *lag* (leaf), and the town is also called Yagalalag—interpreted as "in the multitude of trees" (de la Fuente, 1949, p. 289). This is a high mountain settlement, 1,678 meters above sea level, exceptionally clean and well organized, and displaying the best qualities of the Zapotecs.

The Tuesday market—seen in 1938—brought Indians in regional dress from many towns, Mixe as well as Zapotec (pl. 52). To reach Yalalag (Villa Hidalgo) in 1938 we went by car from Tlacolula toward the mountains to Santo Domingo. The rest of the two-day journey by horse—with stopover at Santa Catarina—took us over the mountains to Yalalag, which is still not entirely accessible by road—at least in all seasons. In 1938 a number of uniquely painted houses had crosses of clay on the roof ridges (pl. 197). The presence of these decorations meant, we were told, that a few *pesos* had been paid the priest to come and bless the houses.

Women's Costume

The traditional costume of Yalalag consists of a white *huipil* worn outside an open-ended wrap-around skirt —held by a cotton belt with a *soyate*—and a white *rebozo*. Materials used are still largely handwoven. Formerly a large, black wool turban headdress or *rodete* was worn.

HUIPIL. The *huipil*, both for fiesta and everyday, is woven (plain weave) in two 19-inch-wide webs, using commercial white cotton thread. Even in 1938 handspun cotton was uncommon. Webs are about 78 inches long. When strips are joined, a 14-inch selvage neck slit is left; and when folded over and sewn up the sides, the grown woman's garment measures approximately 40 by 36 inches.

Over the shoulders a handsome 12-inch section—of corded white weft stripes in groups of three—makes a contrasting yoke in the otherwise plain *huipil*. The corded yoke stops on the outer edge 3½ inches short of the armhole selvage edge (pl. 48—the girl at the left). This shoulder-area weave, according to I. W. Johnson (1953, p. 253), "is a simple derivation of the technique commonly called 'damask.'"

The bottom edge of the *huipil* is finished with a narrow buttonhole stitch of silk thread in sections of five different alternating colors—about 1¼ inches of each. Just below the neck slit, both in front and in back, there is a 5-inch two-part braid placed horizontally, and consisting of about 115 heavy store-bought artificial silk threads (usually of one color, but sometimes

PLATE XI. A Mixtec Indian family of Santa María Zacatepec, Oaxaca. 1962

197. A decorated house front, dated 1843. Yalalag, Oaxaca (Zapotec). 1938

of mixed colors), with 12-inch tassels hanging from each end (pls. 34 & 48). Until as late as 1927, informants have told us, all-white tassels of cotton thread were predominantly favored. Formerly, this decoration was comprised of fewer threads, and was worked into the cloth in twining technique. Today, however, the braid and tassels are sewn on, a mark of the time-saving methods that inevitably creep in with civilization. Also, if the braid and tassels are removed with each washing of the *huipil* there is no danger of colors running into the white garment. The weaving is still excellent, and in 1963 the variegated finish at the lower edge seemed as good as in 1938.

Fiesta *huipiles*, developed thirty to fifty years ago through outside missionary and school influence (de la

Fuente, 1949, p. 70), have a 3½-inch floral embroidered store-bought cotton strip sewn down the center front (pl. 48). A more traditional type of festive *huipil*—seen in 1940 and before for such occasions as weddings, or mourning—had a wide satin-stitch decorative joining down the center. The sections of changing colors gave the impression of successive squares worked in artificial silk thread. Yalalag *huipiles* are always worn loose, outside the skirt. Some Indians have no extra clothing to change into on journeys by foot to some larger town; but this is not true of the Yalaltecas. In the capital of the state, they wear spotlessly clean garments, and their hair shines with mamey oil.

SKIRT. The Yalalag skirt is woven of cotton in two strips (18 by 116–144 inches each) in a pattern of

198. Selling black pottery from Coyotepec (in the valley of Oaxaca) on market day in Yalalag, Oaxaca. (Zapotec). 1938

narrow tan and white warp stripes. Formerly, natural-tan cotton was employed, but for a number of years commercial dye has been used. Some twenty-five years ago and before that, a finely woven dark-blue wool skirt was worn in Yalalag, particularly by older women, and for very special occasions, weddings, fiestas or mourning. This skirt was woven in one web, 22 by 116 inches, which was sewn to a 14-inch wide piece of unbleached muslin or white cotton cloth. The dark-blue skirt length which we examined has throughout its length six spaced weft stripes (vertical when worn) of ¼-inch salmon-colored wool. This skirt is said to have been worn with the fiesta *huipil* having embroidered "squares," but both now seem to have disappeared from use. All types of wrap-around skirts in Yalalag are worn well above the ankle, with double material across the back and the remaining fullness distributed in the front and secured with a belt (fig. 11 f).

BELT. Formerly, a wide handwoven, white or pink belt was made, but we are told today that almost any length of cloth sewn to a *soyate* will do. Santos Tomás Jalieza figured belts have also been used in Yalalag. We believe that these have been imported in recent years, but reports are varied. Anita Jones (letter, April 5, 1966) reports talking to a Yalalag shop owner in Oaxaca City who says that well-to-do women in Yalalag have always been slow to acquire new (or foreign) items—that they don't go snooping in the big Tuesday market. Instead they expect salesmen to come to their houses. Poorer women, he said, look carefully in the market and if they have the money are quicker to try something new and different.

HEADDRESS. The great turban (commonly called a *rodete* in Indian Mexico) formed of black wool cords is now little used, but is closely associated with the famous Yalalag costume (pl. 48). Among the headdresses of this type in Mexico, this is the most ordered and sculptural. The *rodete* is not formed of loose separate cords, but is pre-fashioned of two joined cord cables, 2 inches in diameter, which are permanently arranged with 20-inch fringes at each end. Some fourteen cords lying neatly side by side are worked diagonally round and round the cable and crossed back again.

Today, the twisted turban is usually prearranged, and placed on the head like a hat. Formerly the great cable of wool was actually twined into the hair of the wearer. According to Julio de la Fuente (1949, p. 73),

the young girl brought the cords directly from back to front where the first crossing was, whereas married women crossed the cables at the back of the neck before bringing them to the front. In Yalalag, when her *rodete* was not well put on, a woman was described as *"airosa"* (giddy). Sometimes a smaller *rodete* was seen on the street in 1938 (pl. 198). Although all Zapotec women, and even little girls, were wearing the traditional *huipil* and skirt, not many *rodetes* were seen in the market or village at that time.

Now, we are told, no young woman under twenty wears the *huipil* and skirt, and the *rodete* is rarely seen in Yalalag, even for fiestas, whereas no costume ball anywhere in the capitals of Mexico is complete without several.

JEWELRY. The famous triple silver crosses of the Sierra Juárez were seldom worn in the village in 1938 (see Chapter 9).

SERVILLETAS AND REBOZOS. Handsome white cotton *rebozos* have long been made in the Yalalag area for home use, and in recent years sold in shops and on the streets in Oaxaca City. In Yalalag, they are folded on top of the *rodete*, or simply folded several times on top of the head (pl. 198).

Rebozos are carried over the arm (pl. 48), draped over the food baskets, or used as carrying cloths. In 1938 the making of *rebozo* fringes was said to require two days for each end. *Rebozo* weaves combine gauze, plain weave and, at times, warp stripes in color. Widths range from 23 to 25 inches, lengths from 75 to 80 inches. Altar cloths and tablecloths are also woven in Yalalag on the backstrap loom. Plate 199 shows work of unusual width for this primitive type of loom. Lila O'Neale (1945, p. 112) states that in backstrap-loom weaving "cloths up to 24 or even up to 27 inches can be woven with a smooth rhythm of movement. Each inch added to the width demands greater effort and more time for the same standard of workmanship."

FOOTGEAR. Formerly, women's sandals were made of finely spun *ixtle* fiber, and were reminiscent of descriptions of the footgear of ancient times. We did not see such sandals worn, but were able to obtain a pair in 1938. According to Julio de la Fuente (1949, p. 69), some old women, as late as the 1940's, were seen wearing sandals from nearby Zoogocho, having the soles of leather and the heel pieces of woven *ixtle*.

In modern times, very good sandals of particularly pliable leather are made in Yalalag for both men and women. They are used also in Mitla, Oaxaca, and are

199. A standing woman weaver of Yalalag, Oaxaca. (Zapotec). 1938

bought by foreigners in Oaxaca City. The upper section (pl. 48) shows the characteristic decoration of cutout designs displaying red velvet.

Children's Costume

Many little girls were to be seen in costume in 1938, but today we are told that in school and on the street no costumes are seen. The children we saw did not use the *rodete* or straw belt of their mothers. Their hair usually fell loose (pl. 34).

Men's Costume

Formerly, a large black felt hat and a garishly striped store-cloth shirt (white ground), worn outside white trousers, was the preferred Sunday costume of Yalalag men. White *manta* clothes were used for everyday.

26. Santiago Choapan, Oaxaca (Zapotec)

THIS IS ONE of the Zapotec towns which "forms a wedge between Mixe and Chinantec areas in eastern Oaxaca" (Bevan, 1938, p. 7), and is particularly famed for the beautiful *huipiles* of its women. Its climate is humid and hot except when *nortes* blow in from Vera Cruz at the end and beginning of the year. Formerly it had a large population, but now it is small and rather lethargic. For example, inhabitants rarely leave their village, whereas other Zapotecs, although they may live in villages as isolated as Choapan, frequently travel to engage in trade or to attend religious fiestas. Coffee today is the chief product and is bought up by outsiders or even by Zapotecs from other villages. Being four or five days of very hard travel over rivers and high mountains from Oaxaca City (one may fly in but only on irregular schedules), the people have no outlet for products and no stimulus to push ahead in any way. They seem to grow only enough for the most meager living. Natural fruits abound, and red cedarwood—cherished elsewhere—is often used here for firewood. They have neither market nor market day. The large, straw-roofed church is in very poor repair; the priest rarely comes—does not like the climate we were told.

Women's Costume

A very few old women in Choapan wear a simple handwoven white cotton *huipil* (woven in the village of Taguí), and the traditional red gathered skirt (of *chiapaneca* material brought in from Oaxaca City), and heavier red-striped headcloth. The rest wear skirts and blouses and are termed *"civilizada no india"* (de la Fuente, 1947, p. 170). In January, 1964, and March, 1965, we made visits to Choapan. We found but an occasional old woman who still owned one of the famous white multipatterned gala *huipiles*, which have not been made for many years; and one of the triple crosses, of which there used to be many in Choapan.

HUIPIL. The old white cotton patterned "weft-warp open-weave" (I. W. Johnson, verbal) gauze *huipil* is made of two webs, each measuring 20 by 76 inches. The two strips contain many horizontal rows of bird, animal, human figure, and flower motifs. Woven designs are so intricate that we were told it might take as much as four months to finish one-half of a *huipil*. Design rows vary in width from 1½ to 5 inches, and are separated by narrow stripes in plain weave, or by gauze-weave areas in geometric patterns (pls. 200 & 201).

200. A Zapotec girl from Santiago Choapan, Oaxaca, wearing very old jewelry and one of the most extraordinary *huipiles* of Mexico. 1941

201. One of the old Zapotec *huipiles* of Santiago Choapan, Oaxaca, desired by all collectors and now almost impossible to find.

When the strips are joined together a 12-inch neck slit is left. The garment we examined (40½ by 38 inches) contained a ½-inch inset of handmade lace from the neck slit to the bottom, both in front and in back. The selvage-edged neck opening is reinforced with white scalloped buttonhole stitch. To ensure long wear and perhaps for modesty's sake, the upper part of some old Choapan *huipiles* are lined with white store-bought cloth from the neck slit outward for some 12 inches, and 12 inches down from the shoulder, front and back. Outer edges of this inside lining are carefully sewn in cut hemmed points, so as to make the yoke as inconspicuous as possible behind the patterned open-work *huipil*. At the bottom of each garment is a plain-weave area varying in adult *huipiles* from 4½ to 9½ inches wide, broken only by gauze-weave stripes.

We were told that only one woman is still alive in Choapan who knew how to weave the *huipil "de labor"* many years ago. The next to the last woman to weave one died twenty-five years ago, informants said.

SKIRT. The Choapan skirt is gathered into a band at the waist—not wrapped around—and is made of the *chiapaneca corte* of Oaxaca City, which is all red cotton with two groups of from three to seven black pin stripes having plain spaces between. The pattern which has two groups of five vertical pin stripes was seen in Choapan, and also the one with groups of three. Anita Jones (letter, August 31, 1965) reports having seen *chiapaneca cortes* with groups of seven pin stripes being woven by an enterprising Zapotec in Yalalag, to be sold in the Choapan area no doubt. These *cortes* measure approximately 31 by 110 inches.

Worn rather short, Choapan skirts have a decorative bottom border of ribbon (usually bright green) cut out and hemmed by hand in points, with lines of yellow and blue rickrack braid (pl. 81). No belt is used (1967). Formerly an upright-loomed all-red Oaxaca City belt was worn. *Huipiles* are worn outside the skirt pulled up about the waist, where the material is first pulled to the back, and crossed, and the ends brought forward and tucked in at each side (pl. 200).

In former times, we were told, for *misa* (mass) the *huipil* was worn differently. It hung free over the skirt and the lower plain border in front only was folded neatly upward under the large silver cross and held thus with the two hands of the wearer.

HEADCLOTH. A square of red cotton handwoven cloth with alternating black and white warp pin stripes makes the distinctive Choapan headcloth. The material is very firmly woven in 24½-inch widths, cut off the loom into squares and hemmed by machine on the two sides which are not selvage edged. This material was formerly made in the village but, is at present brought in by traders from the Zapotec village of Comaltepec. So few women wear the costume that demand for headcloths is slight.

As seen in Plates 124 and 200, when it is worn one side of the square is folded back a few inches across the top of the head and is caught center front under the roll of hair which encircles the head.

In Oaxaca City, in the private collection of María Luisa B. de Audiffred, we were shown a very old silk headcloth from Choapan, but we could find no trace of any like it in the village.

JEWELRY. At the Oaxaca Indian State Fair of 1941, two girls of a delegation of six from Choapan wore rather extraordinary jewelry. One girl (pl. 200) wore two large silver crosses hanging to waist length on strings of corals, and opaque red-glass trade beads and ribbon from which hung at each side two very old reliquaries. From a separate ribbon in the center hung another one—large and very rare, with egg and dart moulding and a silver gilt frame.

The second girl wore one large cross and a necklace of corals alternating with tiny silver roosters, combs, coins, and pomegranates, bringing to mind the fact that the Navajo Indian "squash blossom" in silver originated from the pomegranate brought from Mexico.

27. Santo Tomás Mazaltepec, Oaxaca (Zapotec)

In 1942 it was a common and dramatic sight in Oaxaca City to see women from Santo Tomás Mazaltepec running with short rhythmic steps, balancing on their heads incredibly high piles of *tortillas* wrapped in cloth. These striking figures were from a village southwest of Etla in the valley of Oaxaca. They came with whole families in picturesque ox-carts which are now disappearing from all paved roads in this valley.

Women's Costume

Several very full, gathered skirts and half-skirts of store-bought cloth, a *huipil* (no longer handwoven), and a complicated series of belts comprise the costume of Mazaltepec women—with a dark, store-bought *rebozo* for head covering.

The drama of these figures in 1942 was due largely to the number (four or five) of their enormously full, gathered skirts, and belts of the largest circumference we know in any Mexican Indian costume (pl. 203). In 1965 we still saw these women, but the costume was modified. The belts were largely the same, but the skirts were less full and fewer of them were worn at a given time. Today *huipiles* are often left at home and blouses are worn, which will not inspire the laughter or disdain of the "city people."

Huipil. In 1942 the commercial-cloth *huipil* (one width) preserved the aspect of the handwoven one formerly used, by a wide tuck down front and back over each shoulder, sewn with a running stitch in colored thread and dividing the garment into three sections. In 1965 we found this tuck to have largely disappeared.

The center of the *huipil* consists of a ribbon-formed yoke varying from 8–12 inches wide by 12 inches from front to back. In its center a very small, round neck opening is cut. The three to five ribbons 1½ inches wide, running from front to back (pl. 202), may be of one color or alternating colors—pink, red, and yellow are favorites. Ribbons are joined with multicolored feather-stitching combined with narrow, patterned store tape. The neck opening is sewn securely with an inconspicuous running stitch.

Free-style multicolored embroidery runs as a border around the ribbon yoke for gala *huipiles*. In 1942 some delightful folkloric patterns could be seen, such as star-like flowers on stems done in chain stitch. These sprang from small vases between which in the center front was

203. A group of smiling women by an organ-cactus fence. Two girls in the background wear half skirts as head coverings. Santo Tomás Mazaltepec, Oaxaca (Zapotec). 1944

202. The costume of Santo Tomás Mazaltepec, Oaxaca, with the outer skirt tucked up on both sides. (Zapotec). 1944

a pink heart surrounded by big roosters and little people holding hands. Sometimes in front or center back, below the yoke, occurred an embroidered cross, a motif not often found on women's garments (pl. 202). (See Chapter 38, on Huistán men's costume.)

SKIRT. A series of 25-inch waist to ankle-length, full, gathered skirts are worn. These have from four to six tucks near the bottom edge, usually sewn with red machine stitching. First is put on the underskirt of *manta,* which is from 6 to 8 yards in circumference. Over this is worn, across the back of the wearer, a 4-yard half-skirt of *manta* or other white cloth. Over this, in front, is worn a final half-skirt made of white or colored cloth, plain or patterned. When we went to the village again in 1965, bright orange front half-skirts or aprons were much in vogue.

Outer skirts for fiesta wear are often tucked up over and into the belts on each side (pl. 202), showing to advantage the skirt beneath (which in 1942 was sometimes pink).

BELT. Over the skirts which are gathered into cloth tapes, an unusually heavy 2½-by-120-inch *soyate* is wound about the waist, followed by two 17-by-127-inch dark-purple cotton sashes with 9-inch twisted fringe at the ends. The outer sash is folded lengthwise and sewn into a long tube and the second sash is folded also (though not always sewn) and is pulled through inside the first one. This long double belt (four thicknesses) is wound over the *soyate* and securely tucked in, making a great tire about the waist (pls. 202 & 203).

Most *soyates* are 2–3 by 56–70 inches. The special ones used in Mazaltepec are made in the village. The diagonal-weave cloth sashes are usually purchased in the Oaxaca market, although we were told that some were formerly woven in the village.

HEAD COVERING. Cotton store-bought *rebozos* are worn over the head in various fashions typical of Oaxaca, particularly the one which brings the *rebozo* forward from behind the head, where it is crossed over the forehead, and tossed back to hang down behind. In the village, and probably in the fields, one of the half-skirts may serve as head covering (pl. 203), an unusual custom according to our observations.

Children's Costume

Little girls were dressed like their mothers, though in long sleeved blouses, in 1940. Women and children were barefoot, and some wore *papelillo* beads.

Men's Costume

We saw nothing distinctive in the men's costume.

28. Tehuantepec, Oaxaca (Zapotec)

 THE TOWNS OF Tehuantepec and Juchitán in the Isthmus of Tehuantepec have long been leaders in women's fashion for a number of Indian settlements. Their influence spreads not only to Zapotec towns and villages but also into Huave, Mixe, and Chontal terrains, and into the villages of the Oaxaca Zoques (San Miguel Chimalapa and Santa María Chimalapa). In these outside areas, the fashions of the two large Isthmus towns are considerably modified. Often some indigenous elements of the area are retained. Examples of this are several Mixe villages within the Tehuantepec district, namely Coatlán, Guichicovi, and Mogoñé. Mogoñé *huipiles* have but two simple vertical shoulder stripes (pl. 206), quite unlike those of Tehuantepec and Juchitán.

Tehuantepec women are to be seen everywhere, and their presence is generally felt throughout southern Mexico. Extremely confident, capable and business-minded, they buy and sell at fiestas and fairs as far away as Tuxtla Gutiérrez, Chiapas, and Oaxaca City. It is not an uncommon sight to see a Tehuana sweeping along the Paseo de la Reforma in Mexico City.

Women's Costume

Only the old women's costume here shows clearly its Indian origin. The showy Tehuana dress, admired everywhere for costume balls, is a far cry from its true beginnings. Once the Tehuana wore the wrap-around skirt (commonly called *enredo*), no upper garment, and a thin, handwoven lacelike *huipil* as a head covering. Today the costume consists of a skirt (two types), a *huipil*, and a head covering for special occasions only —the "large *huipil*" or *huipil grande.*

The special dignity and excellent carriage of the Tehuana may be attributed partly to the fact that she never carries burdens on her back—only on her head, be it water jar, wooden tray, basket, or gourd. Associated with the Tehuana are the large ripple-edged flower-lacquered gourds, from 1 to 1½ feet in diameter, purchased from Chiapa de Corzo, Chiapas. These are sold in the square in Tuxtla Gutiérrez during the June "Corpus" fair and are called *jicalpextles.* They are used every day in the Isthmus but particularly for the "fruit-throwing" ceremony, during which the gourds are borne piled high with candy, toys, and fruit, all to be thrown into the crowd.

EVERYDAY HUIPIL. Through comparison of photographs from sixty-five years ago and twenty-five years ago with today's styles, we know that in Tehuantepec the *huipil* fashioned of commercial cloth, always more or less to waist length and called *huipilili* (little *huipil*), has been used since before 1900. For a grown woman a

273

204. Three seated Zapotec girls of Tehuantepec, Oaxaca. 1940

straight piece of cloth (and lining), 20–22 by 40–42 inches, is folded to make a squarish garment with a round neck cut on the center fold. Sides are sewn up leaving small arm openings of 5–6 inches. In 1898, Frederick Starr says (1901, pp. 148–149), *huipiles* were of "light cotton print stuff bought in the market." This is still the case, although in 1963 dark-colored velvets had been introduced for everyday.

Dark-purple or red cotton cloth with a white polka-dot or white repeat flower motif has always been popular, and was formerly imported from Manchester, England. Today all the cloth used is of Mexican manufacture, including—of course—the cheaper loosely woven small polka-dot cottons used for *huipil* linings (dark colors also).

1898 photos show a few bands of machine embroidery, bordering the lower edge, though some garments had no ornamentation whatsoever. Twenty-five years ago the everyday cotton *huipil* had developed a wide band of elaborate geometric design (pl. 204), embroi-

dered in "a solid pattern by crisscrossing superimposed lines of chain stitching done on a special Singer sewing machine" (Covarrubias, 1947, p. 249). The thread was "lemon yellow and red for the purple huipils, yellow and black for the red ones." The design and width of bands are subject to change and fashion. New, more elaborate designs are constantly being introduced. Another type of decoration is accomplished with a special hook (pl. 209).

Finished *huipiles* of the cotton type, with machine chain stitching, which we measured in 1940 were 22 by 19 inches. In 1963 the style was for snugger fitting, slightly narrower *huipiles*.

Old women wear simpler ones today, often of dark purple or black sateen or velvet, with lines of black stitching or black ribbons sewn on.

EVERYDAY SKIRTS. As late as 1898 most Tehuanas all still wore the wrap-around skirt, either of purple cotton, thread dyed with *caracol*, or of striped cotton woven as now on upright looms. These seem, from old photographs, to be very similar to wrap-around skirts still used by older women (pl. 205). Very few shellfish-dyed skirts are owned today. The present purple ones are chiefly imitation.

A photograph in Frederick Starr's *In Indian Mexico* (1908, p. 40) shows two women walking by the Tehuantepec market. One wears the traditional wrap-around skirt, but the other wears a gathered plain-colored cotton skirt with a very wide white ruffle (*olan*), indicating that styles had already begun to change.

Wrap-around skirts are formed of two lengths, each 20 by 90–98 inches, sewn side by side to form a piece 40 by 90–98 inches. This piece is wrapped around with no pleats and secured with a cloth belt; its only "give" being the open end which, in the Isthmus, usually terminates toward the left side of the wearer or in front (pls. 205 & 206).

These *cortes* (2 lengths) cost 30 *pesos* (about $2.20 in U.S. money) in the Tehuantepec market in 1963. Commonly we saw only one woman each day from Juchitán selling them. These red skirts have ¼-inch weft stripes of either yellow, white, or blue occurring every 3–4 inches. In Tehuantepec proper any of these colors may be seen, but in many of the influenced Indian regions mentioned earlier, one particular colored stripe is preferred. These are the skirts most used; but another type has a ⅛-inch combination stripe of 2 yellow, 2 black, 2 yellow weft threads, alternating every 2½ inches with a 2 thread yellow stripe.

205. Two women in gathered skirts and one elderly woman in an old-style wrap-around skirt. The steps of the church are visible in the background. Tehuantepec, Oaxaca (Zapotec). 1940

206. Mixe women vendors of Mogoñé, Oaxaca, selling fruit and vegetables at a railroad stop. They wear the wrap-around skirt materials of Juchitán, and simplified *huipiles* of the Isthmus of Tehuantepec. 1941

207. A street in the outskirts of Tehuantepec, Oaxaca. (Zapotec). 1941

208. Girls going up steps. Tehuantepec, Oaxaca (Zapotec). 1941

Another type of everyday skirt came in during the first decade of this century for girls and young women. Over a full white underskirt was worn a long full gathered skirt of bright patterned or plain-colored store cloth edged at the bottom with a white cotton ruffle (pls. 204 & 208). Widths for the ruffle vary—8 inches was the rule in the 1930's and 1940's. Nearby Juchitán has always worn a wider ruffle—up to 16 inches—and has been somewhat scornful of those of Tehuantepec. In fairly recent years, skirts with ruffles of the same material as the body of the skirt have begun to appear.

Today most Tehuanas wear for everyday a long gathered or gored skirt without ruffles of any kind. In 1963 a few white ruffles were seen on the street worn by middle-aged women wearing all black costumes—probably for mourning (pl. 207).

EVERYDAY HEADDRESS AND FOOTWEAR. For everyday wear, wide satin ribbons are braided into the hair, and the braids in turn are wrapped around the head with a bow in front. Older women use black ribbons and a black shawl. Many younger Tehuanas go barefoot in the streets or market, and wear ready-made *rebozos*. Today, many store-bought shoes or sandals are seen.

FIESTA COSTUME. Gala costumes are made of satin or velvet (*huipil* and skirt matching, not contrasting as in everyday dress), and often cost hundreds of *pesos*. Both parts of the fiesta costume are decorated with large flowers (probably copied from imported shawls) done in multicolored silk or artificial silk thread (pl. 211). Some costumes have elaborate geometric bands instead of flowers, but the freer flower patterns are preferred. For some types of embroidery, cloth is stretched horizontally on a frame (pl. 209). A costume examined, made in the early 1930's, showed that the flower-patterned garments were sometimes executed with combined machine chain-stitch and hand satin-stitch embroidery.

The ruffles that finish the lower edge of gala skirts are made of four to five yards of starched finely pleated lace, laborious to prepare, and often soiled in dusty streets while coming and going from the many rounds of fiestas so enjoyed in Tehuantepec. These ruffles are only worn once before the arduous process of relaundering, starching, and pleating by hand must be repeated.

Formerly, gold jewelry was seen in quantity in the Tehuantepec region. The Tehuanas proverbially wore their entire savings in the form of heavy gold necklaces and earrings of gold coins. U.S. gold pieces, and English and Guatemalan coins dating from the famous prosperous days of the Tehuantepec railway were used. Today much jewelry is made of Mexican silver pieces, gold dipped.

The most spectacular Tehuana garment, the *huipil grande* or "large *huipil*," is really a glorified *huipil* in form but is not worn as a blouse. Of straight-cut colored, unstarched lace, the body of the *huipil* is 28 by 32 inches. When folded over, this piece makes a garment 28 by 16 inches. The neck is cut round, some 10 inches in diameter, and edged with starched white lace, 3½ inches wide sewn in 1-inch box pleats. The unusable 4½-inch arm openings are edged with ribbon, and a 7-inch-wide starched pleated white lace ruffle. At the bottom of the garment, edged first with colored ribbon like the sleeve, is a starched and pleated lace ruffle, varying from 7 to 12 inches depending upon the cost and the fashion.

Around 1900 *huipil grande* ruffles were very wide (Starr, 1908, p. 40), although the rest of the costume was far simpler. The geometric decoration appeared to

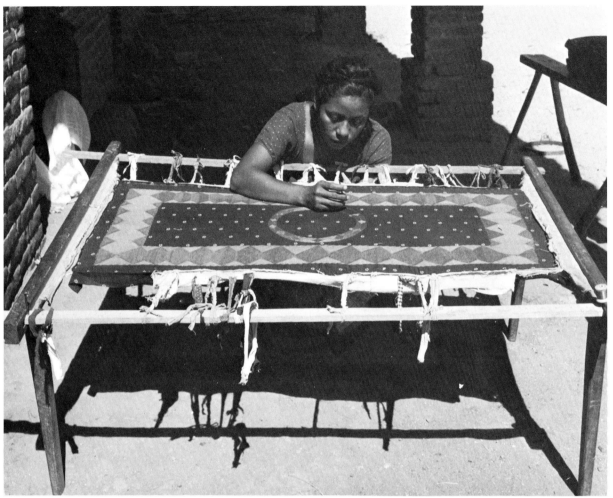

209. Embroidering a *huipil*. When the embroidery is completed the round neck opening will be cut out and the garment folded and sewn up the sides, leaving arm openings. Tehuantepec, Oaxaca (Zapotec). 1940

210. A girl wearing a *huipil grande* for church. Tehuantepec, Oaxaca (Zapotec). 1940

211. The fiesta costume, showing the *huipil grande* as worn for gala occasions. Tehuantepec, Oaxaca (Zapotec). 1940

a small degree soon after, but the lavish flower embroidery developed much later.

The *huipil grande* is worn two ways. For church, the neck opening is worn around the face and under the chin (pls. 205 & 210), framing the face. The rest of the garment falls down over the shoulders with the tiny sleeves hanging one in front and one in center back.

For all other fiesta events, the *huipil grande* is worn with the wide starched ruffle thrown back over the head, the ruffle falling backwards from the forehead and left to ripple down over the shoulders and back where hang the collar and sleeves (pl. 211).

The *huipil grande* like the similar garment of the Zoques (called *huipil de tapar*), was probably once the only upper garment worn. A color plate in Linati (1956, pl. 11) shows a young woman in 1828 wearing a wraparound skirt and a transparent *huipil grande* with nothing worn underneath. At that time there was no ruffle on the lower edge of the garment—only the small one framing the face. The *huipil* was adopted by both Zoques and Tehuanas for propriety after 1850. The Zoque *huipil de tapar* and small upper garment were still made of handwoven gauze on the outskirts of Tuxtla Gutiérrez, Chiapas as late as 1940 (pl. 250); but no actual date has been established tracing the Tehuana costume to its Indian beginnings. Spanish or foreign influence crept in very early.

In the 1900's, before the Revolution, the ruffle of the "large *huipil*" was of gold fringe (Covarrubias, 1947, p. 262). Such garments were still kept in families in the 1940's, and were worn for weddings only.

Almost no examples of the *huipil grande* were seen on the street in 1939 and 1941 (two visits), and none at all in 1963 except for two girls walking with an older woman, all obviously dressed to attend some special ceremony in the middle of the day.

Children's Costume

Formerly when dressed to leave the house, little girls wore dresses exactly like their mothers'; at home they wore only scanty underdrawers. Today, although some Tehuana clothes are to be seen, skimpy modern cotton dresses are, alas, all too common. Many young women have given up the traditional dress—a great loss of distinction. Also they now favor permanents and short hair (we heard a report that in a Tehuantepec hotel, a Tehuana waitress was seen pinning on braids in the morning to give local color with the required costume).

In 1941 little boys were seen nude or nearly so at home, and in the streets near their own houses (pl. 212).

Men's Costume

Although nothing distinctive is seen in the Tehuantepec men's dress today, some old men may still be seen with white cotton trousers that cross over in front, legs narrowing toward the ankles; full white shirt, pleated at the back and worn loose; and locally made sandals. Occasionally an old straw hat with high-peaked crown is still worn, and a few of the old heavy felt hats with silver cords—a memory of better days.

212. Boys standing on a pottery kiln. Juchitán, Oaxaca (Zapotec). 1941

29. San Sebastián Peñoles, Oaxaca (Mixtec)

In 1963 WE WERE able with difficulty to reach the high mountain village of San Sebastián Peñoles—through Etla, north of Oaxaca, and Zautla to the west. From Zautla we climbed in an old army jeep high over the mountains for many hours by a road that was almost impassable. The people of Peñoles, except for a few families, do not live in the village but in *ranchos* distributed over a large radius in the surrounding mountains. The town itself consists of a church, a school, a municipal building, the houses of a few Indians, and that of an American linguist who is recording the Peñoles dialect of the Mixtecan tongue. There is no real market or market day.

In Peñoles there was evidence of a former silk industry. Borah mentions that in the sixteenth century Peñoles was one of the silk-raising centers (1943, pp. 67–68). Most of the industry was conducted at altitudes between 1,500 and 2,300 meters—Peñoles being 2,000 meters. We were shown a few mulberry trees near the river which runs past the village. The people said that there used to be hundreds of trees and that everyone worked silk and raised silkworms. Widespread spraying—a national program that has virtually made malaria a thing of the past—affected the silkworms. Natives said that the mulberry trees and the silkworms had died. We found a number of carrying bags with silk stripes—greatly prized—and some men's sashes—obtainable but valued very highly.

An old woman (pl. 213 left), who no longer wore the costume (probably because her daughter had married a Spaniard and gone to live differently in a larger town), still had a large quantity of silk cocoons, and showed us the process by which silk was prepared. She boiled the silk with ashes—this changes the color of the cocoons from yellow to white—(pl. 214), pulled the mass apart in small handfuls when dry, and spun it (p. 215). She used a painted clay spindle from Jamiltepec in southern Oaxaca, whence come almost all the spindles used in both the Mixteca Alta and the Mixteca Baja for cotton or silk spinning.

Women's Costume

The Peñoles woman's costume consists, today, of an open-sided *manta huipil* and a handwoven wool skirt. Belts are purchased in Oaxaca City; no footgear was seen, and for head covering only the dark cotton *rebozo*.

HUIPIL. No one here could tell us when women stopped weaving and wearing a handwoven *huipil*. The white commercial cloth *huipil* used today is a 75-inch length of material, 40 inches or more in width (often pieced). The cloth is folded over, and a vertical

213. The new and old Mixtec woman's costume of San Sebastián Peñoles, Oaxaca. 1963

neck slit of some 11 inches is cut in the center. Along the sides of this slit, a length of 1¼-inch store-bought ribbon is sewn flat. At the end of the slit, front and back, is sewn a small tab of the same ribbon. Six or more rows of chain-stitched zigzag lines are neatly embroidered up and down the side ribbon lengths, covering and reinforcing the ribbons (pl. 216). Several colors of mercerized commercial thread are used. Often loose 3-inch variegated threads hang from the square-cut ribbon tabs, front and back. *Huipiles* are worn, as are those of Santa Catarina Estetla, inside the skirts (pls. 216).

SKIRT. Skirts are called *mantas* in Peñoles. Weavers here are wool workers, although formerly the region was a well-known silk-raising area. The heavy wool skirts and excellent blankets comprise the chief weaving output at the present time.

Two 21-inch webs, approximately 150 inches in length, are woven of hand-spun wool, the black warp thread alternating with one of light natural wool. Each strip has, on both selvage edges, a solid black ¾-inch warp stripe (pl. 216). Strips are joined lengthwise with the same dark natural wool, and are not sewn in tube form.

Skirts are worn over the *huipil* doubled down several inches inside at the top, depending on the size of the skirt and height of the woman. All fullness is handsomely arranged into as many as four or five high standing wide box pleats across the center back (pl. 216; fig. 11 h).

BELTS AND HEAD COVERING. The belts which hold this tremendous weight are purchased at market stalls in Oaxaca City, and come from the belt-weaving town of Santo Tomás Jalieza (pl. 95). The preferred width

214. Doña Alberta preparing the silk cocoons before spinning. San Sebastián Peñoles, Oaxaca (Mixtec). 1963

215. Doña Alberta spinning silk. San Sebastián Peñoles, Oaxaca (Mixtec). 1963

216. The front and back views of a San Sebastián Peñoles, Oaxaca, woman's costume, showing the Santo Tomás Jalieza belt used here, and the manner of wearing the skirt. (Mixtec). 1963

217. A Mixtecan woman exerting the considerable force necessary in weaving a patterned woolen blanket. A deer's head is carved on the end of one of her loom sticks. San Sebastián Peñoles, Oaxaca. 1963

218. A pre-Conquest Coxcatlán Cave textile from near Tehuacán, Puebla (150 A.D.). Courtesy of R. S. MacNeish.

of these patterned wool and cotton belts is 2¾ inches; the preferred colors are red and white with small borders of yellow and green. The length must be at least 60 inches, but the longer the better (a matter of price). One end is sewn to a heavy 3-by-65-inch *soyate* (pl. VI a).

Only cotton *rebozos* from Oaxaca City were seen as head coverings. There was no distinctive jewelry, and no footgear. The hair was worn in two braids.

Men's Costume

BLANKET. Splendid wool blankets having no neck slit are wrapped around the body—Navaho Indian style—by the Peñoles men. All-wool hand-spun blankets are made by women for local consumption only. These handsome blankets can sometimes be seen in the streets of Oaxaca City, but they are not woven for tourist trade. It is, in fact, difficult to persuade a Peñoles Indian to sell his *cobija* (blanket).

Twill weaves in natural-wool colors and lozenge patterns distinguish these bankets, which are made in two webs. Measurements are 20–25 inches in width by 70–75 inches in length for each strip; striking warp borders in combinations of orange, red, and dark brown edge each width. Also, colored weft stripes are sometimes worked into the lozenge weaves. Great strength is demanded for the use of the heavy blanket loom, with the constant shifting of three heddles (pl. 217) needed to weave lozenge patterns. At either end, for reinforcement and for decoration, a narrow weft stripe in red and orange is put in with the fingers by a twining technique. We have seen this feature only in present-

288

day blankets from this area, but have noted the identical treatment at the ends of a striped textile, dating from 150 A.D., found as a mummy wrapping of "an adolescent" (MacNeish, 1962, fig. 3) in Coxcatlán Cave, near Tehuacán, Puebla (pl. 218).

BELTS. Handwoven belts are still made for men and boys of cotton or wool with warp stripes. Formerly, belts were woven of cotton with silk stripes dyed with *fuchina* (commercial purple dye), or with *cochineal*. The strong *fuchina* purple used here was never firmly set, and its color spreading through the weaving seemed to be admired. One fine old men's belt which we examined measured 15 by 106 inches plus 5 inches of unworked fringe at each end, and contained many silk stripes, both warp and weft.

Bags

Bags were woven formerly of white cotton with raw-silk *fuchina*-dyed warp stripes which show stamped onto background areas by a process of dampening and folding (pl. 219). They commonly measure up to 19 by 24 inches. After many washings, the purple in Peñoles sashes and bags becomes a lavender color indistinguishable from shellfish-dyed hues. Mr. Max Saltzman has verified our belief that shellfish dye had not been used (letter, January 9, 1964).

On market day in Oaxaca City one may still see some fine large *fuchina*-striped wool bags used by vendors of small fruits from this general area in the Mixteca Alta. We obtained such a bag from a woman of Santiago Xolotepec.

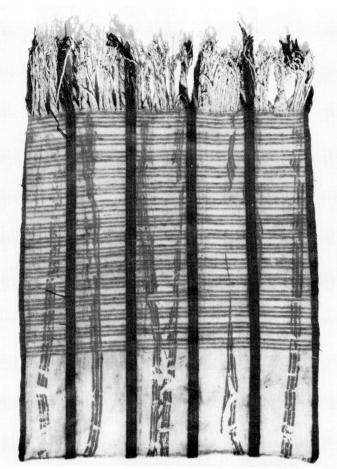

219. A Mixtec cotton bag showing color stamping between the *fuchina* silk stripes. San Sebastián Peñoles, Oaxaca.

30. Santa Catarina Estetla, Oaxaca (Mixtec)

 AT THE DECEMBER 1941 Indian State Fair in Oaxaca City, we were tremendously interested in the group from Estetla because of the women's costume, which had several unusual features, and was apparently unknown—or unnoticed—until that date. In 1963 we were able to reach the Mixteca Alta settlement of Peñoles, and to make contact with Estetla (also in the district of Etla) which is several hours beyond, by foot over a very difficult stony river bed.

We stayed in a hut on a hillside near Peñoles, and could look down toward the river and footpath far below, where the people from Estetla passed carrying fruit and fowl to sell in the distant Oaxaca City market. Among thirty women who passed, only three wore old-style skirts, and one a *manta huipil*. The remainder wore miscellaneous cotton dresses and straw hats or *rebozos*.

Women's Costume

The earlier indigenous women's costume consisted of a heavy but finely woven cotton *huipil*, a wool wrap-around skirt, a wool and cotton belt with *soyate*, a half gourd as head covering, and two stiffly bound braids (pl. 84). Between 1941 and 1963, one of the most noteworthy costumes of Oaxaca had vanished, even though

the village is exceedingly inaccessible. Only a few skirts and the custom of wearing the half gourd on the head remain. During the years 1941–1944, women and girls were commonly seen in Oaxaca City on market day. Although they wore *manta huipiles* rather than their fine handwoven ones, they were easily distinguished by the heavy purple wool that bound their braids.

HUIPIL. In 1941 the beautiful *huipiles* (pls. 84, 220, & 221), worn by the Estetla delegation, were highly regarded in the village. They were awarded a prize for one of the best costumes at the Indian Fair. With difficulty we secured a costume (now in a museum), and in 1963, and again in 1965, we were able to rescue two other *huipiles*—exceedingly old, soiled, and obviously destined for prompt oblivion.

The old *huipiles* obtained in 1963 and 1965 are of exactly the same vintage as those seen in 1941. The *huipil* is formed of three handwoven white cotton webs. The outside panels measure approximately 12-inches in width, and the center one 14 by 76 inches. The weave contains 3 inches of heavier weft stripes alternating with 2 inches of plain weave. Each panel is bordered on each side with ½-inch purple warp stripes. These stripes, in spite of the age of the *huipiles*, are of fairly intense color. Estetla purple *huipil* threads examined

220. Fine old brocaded *huipiles* no longer made or seen today. Here they are worn by Santa Catarina Estetla delegates at the Oaxaca Indian State Fair. (Mixtec). 1941

The center panel contains a solid 24-inch area of beautiful, fine, geometric, single-faced brocaded motifs —12 inches in back and 12 inches in front of the shoulder fold. This decorative yoke consists of 15 horizontal rows of fish-bone, zigzag, triangle, 8-pointed star, or flower motifs, each separated by an ⅛-inch purple weft stripe, with three such stripes at the yoke terminal, front and back.

Most designs are carried out in broken areas of yellow-orange, lavender, blue-green, and faded Indian-red (probably vegetable dyed) silk thread (possibly wild silk). Because of the single-faced technique, designs are barely visible on the reverse side of the cloth, and the outer edges of the brocaded motifs are "more visible than color within the units" (I. W. Johnson, 1954). Mrs. Johnson explains, "Brocading weft taken from one shed to another in the following way; colored ridges of change from shed to shed gives outline to design."

At the 1941 Fair, we observed and had demonstrated the manner in which the open sided Estetla *huipiles* were worn (the same holding true for the *manta huipiles* of Peñoles). (1) The bottom front of the *huipil* is turned up about 8 inches and pulled evenly from each side to the back (before the skirt is put on), where corners are knotted underneath the back panel. (2) Next, the back is turned up 8 in., and each side pulled to the front, where corners are tied at the waist, center front. After the skirt and belt are put on, folds from each side of the back panel of the *huipil* fall outside over the top of the skirt, on either side toward the front (pl. 84).

SKIRT. The Estetla open-ended wool wrap-around skirts are, in appearance, almost identical to those of nearby Peñoles, San Mateo Tepantepec, and Huitepec, and are not seen to our knowledge elsewhere. The Estetla skirts we examined have been somewhat smaller than those of Peñoles, but there are usually a number of sizes woven in all wrap-around-skirt villages, the size depending upon the age of the wearer and the condition of her pocketbook.

Here, the wool chosen for skirts is of a brown tone, rather than the blacker natural wool favored in Peñoles. The weave is identical, but the solid-colored border of each of the two strips is ⅝ inches as compared to ¾ inches in Peñoles. The Estetla strips examined measured 18 by 106 inches, making a skirt of 36 inches from waist to above the ankle (several inches of which are turned in at the waist). Skirts were woven by women

221. Winners in a dance contest — the "wedding dance" of Santa Catarina Estetla, Oaxaca — at the Indian State Fair. 1941

by Mr. Max Saltzman (letter, January 9, 1964) were found not to contain the shellfish dye used chiefly in more southerly coastal regions of Mexico. Quite possibly a combination of brazilwood, cochineal and/or *fuchina* was used.

The three strips are sewn side by side to form a garment, when folded over, of about 38 by 38 inches. The sides are left entirely open. The 9-inch neck slit is of special interest, because it is not cut but is woven with selvage edges vertically in the center of the middle *huipil* strip, a technique termed the "kelim slot."

PLATE XII. Two Mixtec girls of Jamiltepec, Oaxaca, in fiesta *huipiles*. 1965

(who in 1965, still wove blankets), and are arranged for wearing in the same fashion as those of Peñoles, although Estetla skirts are worn somewhat shorter.

BELT. The Belts, like those of Peñoles, are woven in Santo Tomás Jalieza near Oaxaca City (pl. VII a), and purchased in the Oaxaca City market. They are worn attached to a *soyate.*

HEADGEAR AND JEWELRY. *Papelillo* beads were worn by the Estetla women at the Fair in 1941. Three of the delegation wore home-made sandals with thongs next to the big toe, and laced leather strips over the insteps. The two braids of hair were so tightly bound with purple wool that they seemed to spring out in a curve behind each ear like horns. They were, in fact, called *cuernos* (horns). Barbro Dahlgren de Jordan (1954, p. 128) points out several pre-Hispanic Mixtecan hair arrangements from the Codex Nuttall. One of the five heads portrayed clearly shows the ancient origin of the Estetla *cuernos.* In Peñoles some informants told us that a few old women of Estetla still wear their braids tightly bound with purple cords, but others said that no one wore them anymore.

Men's Costume

In 1941 men wore black felt hats and *sarapes,* and carried *ixtle* net bags. Some handwoven cotton *tortilla* bags were observed having purple stripes of silk, as in Peñoles.

31. Santa María Zacatepec, Oaxaca (Mixtec)

ZACATEPEC, a town of 7,401 inhabitants (census 1960), is in a state of transition. We first visited this village before the new highway passing through here from Tlaxiaco to the coast was finished (1961) and as the hostelries were full of road workers, the Presidente Municipal gave us a room in which to stay. Most of the members of the *ayuntamiento* wore the regional costume, but we found that there was already some dissension among the townspeople as to what effect the road was having. The road will undoubtedly facilitate medical treatment and bring certain other advantages, but will also make the people self-conscious about wearing their unique costume.

Men of Zacatepec are called *tacuates* (as are also the Mixtecs of Ixtayutla, Oaxaca) a term which may well have its origin in the Nahua word for serpent, *tlalcóhuatl* (Gutierre Tibón, 1961, p. 189).

Women's Costume

The Zacatepec women's costume consists of a rather long *huipil*, either handwoven or of *manta*, and a wraparound skirt not commonly worn. We saw no head covering (1941, 1961, 1965). Our observations of December 1941 were made during the Indian State Fair in Oaxaca City.

HUIPIL. *Huipiles* of Zacatepec and of Amusgos, the town to the south on the highway, are rather closely allied in design and form—although weavers of *huipiles* are undoubtedly more numerous in Amusgos than in Zacatepec. Zacatepec weaving tends to revolve around the elaborate men's costume, whereas in Amusgos, weaving for men is now almost a thing of the past.

Today, in Zacatepec, one commonly sees women dressed in *manta huipiles*, with little or no decoration, and it is said that many *huipiles* for fiesta are purchased from Amusgos women, although some are still woven here. At the 1941 Fair, three-web *huipiles* worn by women of this delegation were handwoven, heavily brocaded and embroidered, and worn long to the instep. Animal designs, scarcely used to our knolwedge in Amusgos, occurred in *huipiles* of Zacatepec together with a free, more primitive and less stereotyped approach to design, compared with the regular crisp brocaded designs of Amusgos *huipiles*. In the Amusgos brocaded *huipil* (pl. 240), designs are carefully followed through without change across each unit.

Today, Zacatepec *huipiles* (pl. XI) whether homewoven or purchased from Amusgos weavers, seem strongly influenced by them. Modern realistic flower embroidery patterns are being introduced into the work of both neighboring villages. In Zacatepec only two family groups wanted to be photographed in their best

294

222. A young woman spinning cotton. She works in the cool interior of an airy round bamboo-walled house. Santa María Zacatepec, Oaxaca (Mixtec). 1962

array, but we visited one exceedingly interesting and active weaving family. Within the cool round house (pl. 222), with soft light entering between bamboo slats, a young girl and a child were spinning white cotton. The mother (unfortunately not seen in the photo) was winding thread on a large warping frame (*urdi-*

dor). Thread was being prepared for the weaving of a man's costume. The actual weaving would probably be done outdoors in stronger light.

In 1941 Zacatepec *huipiles* were distinctly longer than those of Amusgos, but now that many *huipiles* are purchased from Amusgos, lengths seem modified. One

223. Two Mixtec men (*tacuates*) of Santa María Zacatepec, Oaxaca, in Oaxaca City. 1941

characteristic which still holds in *huipiles* actually woven in Zacatepec is the 1–2-inch red woven warp (vertical) stripe on the outer edge of the center *huipil* web. Amusgos *huipiles* have ribbon or simply decorative stitching.

SKIRT. We saw no skirts worn for everyday in 1961, but at the Indian Fair in 1941 Zacatepec women wore the same dark-blue skirt used by Amusgos women, and made in Sayultepec—an hour on horseback from the large town of Cacahuatepec. One skirt seen at the 1941 Fair had added around the bottom edge a series of embroidered animals. Zacatepec skirts came to below the ankle, but they barely showed under the long *huipiles.* Judging from our visit to the village in 1961 and 1965, skirts are not used for everyday, although *huipiles* are shorter in length than before.

HEAD COVERING AND JEWELRY. We have seen no head coverings in Zacatepec. Hair is worn twisted about the top of the head. Necklaces of coins and miscellaneous beads were worn at the Fair.

Little Girls' Costume

Ordinarily store-cloth dresses are worn by little girls for everyday, but *huipiles* are owned for better wear (pl. XI).

Men's Costume

A handwoven men's costume comparable to the Huichol men's costume and the Tzotzil and Tzeltal costumes of Chiapas is still woven and worn in Zacatepec. Elsewhere in the Mixteca Baja are to be found handwoven shirts, and sometimes trousers of natural-tan cotton or *caracol*-dyed stripes; but few costumes we know in this area may be compared to the spectacular one of Santa María Zacatepec. In the state of Oaxaca only that of Ixtayutla might run a close second. The now extinct Zapotec costume of San Bartolo Yautepec may be found today only in collections—likewise those of the Chontal area.

SHIRT. Extraordinary and unique, the body of this garment is formed of a plain-weave single white strip measuring 19 by 113 inches. Some garments of handspun thread and a few of natural-tan and white warp stripes still exist, but the majority of the costumes are woven today of commercial thread. This long piece is folded unevenly from front to back, before the neck is cut. More material is given to the back of the garment than to the front. The example measured was 59 inches in back and 54 inches in front, from the shoulder fold. To make the neck opening, a T-cut is made, a 6–7-inch

vertical slit from the center fold down the front, and a centered cross cut, totaling about 6 inches on the shoulder fold. The two flaps are folded back (pl. 223) and hemmed with a running stitch in red thread.

Sleeves are simply formed of two rectangles measuring 15 by 19 inches. These are attached along the shoulder, well underneath (1¼ inches in the shirt proper, centered on the shoulder fold, and are sewn with a running stitch in red or other color. The sides of the long shirt are left entirely open, and the sleeves are sewn up for only 2 inches at the wrist.

Shirt decoration consists of (1) a double band of elaborate 1-inch–wide drawn work straight across the shoulder fold on either side of the neck executed in a checkerboard effect of ¾-inch sections of yellow, red, green, and purple mercerized embroidery thread. (2) With the same colors, a 3–4-inch single row of drawn work often occurs, placed horizontally some 3–4-inches below the front neck point. (3) Massed about the neck are many rows of tiny embroidered animal, insect, and bird motifs in multicolored thread (fig. 18). As many as 190 figures may be worked in this front embroidered section. (4) On the back side of the shoulder fold occur three or four rows of these same designs, running horizontally across the entire 19-inch cloth width. As many as 27–28 separate little figures occur in each row, some not more than ¼-inch square. Satin stitch, running stitch cross-stitch, and chain stitch are used to draw and carry out these convincing small motifs, a dozen or more and many variations of each (produced by varying use of stitches and colors). Alternating with each creature motif is a pre-Hispanic appearing double-headed bird looking left and right (fig. 18) from the top of an architectural pyramid of four cubes.

TROUSERS. Zacatepec trousers are of enormous dimensions, formed of four lenghs of straight material seamed together without crotch or gusset. Each piece measures 16 by 38 inches, 2 inches of the length being turned down at the top to form a wide hem, through which a 75-inch draw string of hand-twisted white thread is run from a center front slit. The sides and center front seams are joined with a herringbone stitch in red thread. Trouser legs on the inner side are sewn up for only the lower 9 inches, leaving 28 inches from crotch to waist. Trouser legs are bordered at the bottom edge with one or more rows of drawn work matching the shirt decoration previously described. Some four rows of scorpions, dogs, horses, birds, or other designs border the lower edges of the trousers.

BELT. Men's belts, 13½ inches wide by 146 inches

long, of plain-weave red cotton striped with blue are handsomely finished at the ends with twisted cords caught together in multicolored tassels of cotton thread. The wide red and blue stripes vary from 2½ to 3 inches. The warps of the belt are white with 1 inch of red warp on each outer edge. Even when the collector is able to secure a costume, very rarely will the Indian part with his belt.

COSTUME ASSEMBLING. Zacatepec trousers, when put on, are rolled over and over at the top, until the garment reaches only to midway between knee and hip—in other words, the trousers are worn very short. The shirt is put on next, with the long front and back panels hanging free. Then the long belt is wound about the waist and the front and back panels are brought up, tucked in generously over the belt, and left to form long pouches hanging almost to trouser length. The front one is used as a carrying bag (pl. 223).

It is said that in earlier years the panels of the shirts of *caciques* were even longer than those of today, and that the back panel was borne like a train by a *topil* (helper of the *cacique* or elder in the village), and that the *mestizos* laughed and called the *caciques* the "ones with tails." A photograph of an elderly *tacuate* (Basauri, 1940, Vol. II, p. 292) shows the front and back of his shirt held in by a belt, but hanging loose to ankle length.

Two other young men in the same photograph have front panels tied up into pouches with the back panel left long.

HAT. Between the years 1941 and 1961 the characteristic hard black-felt Zacatepec hat with its straight brim and medium-low round crown (pl. 223) seems to have disappeared. This hat was reminiscent of the Chiapas Zinacantán (Tzotzil) village elders' hat, hung with colored-ribbon streamers. The ribbons on the Zacatepec hat were attached in a bunch in the center top of crown, with part of the ribbons falling free to the shoulders in center back, and part drawn through a hole in the hat brim on the wearer's right side, falling close behind the right ear. In 1936 handwoven cotton ribbons were reported to have decorated these hats.

Tibón states that one old man in Jamiltepec, an important town in the Mixteca Baja, still knows how to make the black felt hats of Zacatepec, but that when he dies no one else will know how (1961, p. 194).

Small Boys' Costume

We saw boys 4–8 years old with shirts of the same pattern as the men's, but with the front and back panels proportionately shorter and hanging free. No belt and no trousers were worn, and boy's costumes had less embroidery.

32. The Mixteca Baja

THE ENTIRE REGION of southwestern Oaxaca, inhabited largely by Mixtecs (and *mestizos*), is erroneously but popularly known as the Mixteca Baja (Lower Mixteca). There is considerable negroid population on the coast proper, and the Mixtec towns are inland. The Pacific is visible from Jamiltepec at its higher points—some five hundred meters above sea level.

The correct meanings of the terms "Mixteca Baja" and "Mixteca Alta" are clarified by Alfonso Caso (1965, No. 70/71, p. 5, Spanish text). He says that the area of Oaxaca concerned can be divided into three regions: Lower Mixteca, where the states of Oaxaca and Puebla join, and where some Mixtecs and Popolocas still live; the Higher Mixteca, the sierra country; and the Coastal Mixteca, the latter bordered on the north by the Higher Mixteca, and on the south by the Pacific Ocean. The terms used here which particularly pertain to Indian costume are the "Higher Mixteca (Mixteca Alta)" and the "Coastal Mixteca," known erroneously today as the "Mixteca Baja."

The area commonly called the Mixteca Baja still contains great variety in costume, and much excellent weaving, in spite of acculturation. Examples of change are the following. In Jamiltepec on New Year's Day, 1965, we attempted in vain to talk with men (pl. 224)

who had come in their unique costumes from the distant village of Santiago Ixtayutla, in the same district. The whole idea of contact with us was incomprehensible to them, as was our interest in and admiration of their brocaded costumes. Some carried extra handwoven clothing, but none would show or sell a single textile. We are told, however, that this year (1966), at the fourth Friday of Lent fiesta of Huaxpaltepec, on the highway between Jamiltepec and Pinotepa Nacional, things had changed. At least one man from Ixtayutla approached foreigners (Mexican and other tourists) with textiles for sale. In the interim, Mexicans of the region had made the two-day trip to this village by horse from Pinotepa de Don Luis, to make contacts and purchase *huipiles* (pl. IV c), and other textiles (pl. 92) for collectors. The quality of work is less fine than formerly, and we are told that commercial embroidery cotton is being used for the large purple areas and brocaded designs, instead of cochineal-dyed natural silk, formerly obtained only at certain fiestas and brought from San Miguel Peñasco in the Mixteca Alta.

Jamiltepec

As to costume, Jamiltepec, which seemed to us more conservative than Pinotepa Nacional, was already changing in 1963. Susana Drucker (1963, p. 50) gives

224. A man from Ixtayutla, Oaxaca, wearing a brocaded costume. He and his companions wear their trousers in small tight rolls at the bottom edges, a feature characteristic of Ixtayutla men's dress. Market day, Jamiltepec. (Mixtec). 1965

225. Two girls wearing embroidered *huipiles* and brocaded skirts. Jamiltepec, Oaxaca (Mixtec). 1965

226. Mother and daughter of Mechoacán, Oaxaca (Mixtec), weaving and spinning. 1965

the following reasons for the discarding of the indigenous costume: (1) departure from their own village;
(2) nature of their employment; (3) marriage with
one wearing *mestizo* clothing.

Women's Costume

The women's costume consists of a handwoven three-
web *huipil* and handwoven white skirt. The *huipil* has
distinctive embroidery in artificial silk about the neck
(pl. XII) and wide ribbons at web joinings. It is worn
about the shoulders, and over both head and shoulders.
For brides, the head is put through the neck opening,
but armholes are not used. Only when burial takes
place is the garment actually put on—a custom in many
Mixteca Baja villages.

For everyday wrap-around skirts some *manta* is now
used, but there are three types of handwoven skirts still
in use: (1) a two-web heavy white skirt with colored

embroidery joining; (2) the distinctive Jamiltepec skirt
(pl. 225); (3) the striped *posahuanco* skirt—from Nahuatl *cosahuanqui* (Drucker, 1963, p. 26)—which is
used daily in many villages of the area, but is worn in
Jamiltepec only for ceremonial occasions. Types (1)
and (2) are rectangles, and measure overall approximately 42 by 56–66 inches. They are worn rather short,
and wrapped with no fullness—sarong fashion. The
brocaded skirts (2) are not seen ordinarily except for
Mass. All women on the streets and in the market keep
their white garments notably clean; vendors at the market stand in front of their wares, and do not usually sit
on the ground. Jamiltepec belts are described in Chapter 8.

Men's Costume

The men's hand-spun, handwoven, and hand-sewn
white flaring shirt and rolled up trousers are disappear-

227. A man and wife, seen outside the house where the wife has been spinning. Mechoacán, Oaxaca (Mixtec). 1965

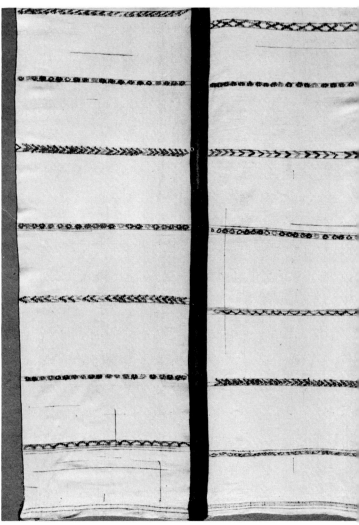

228. A fiesta *tralla* from Mechoacán, Oaxaca. The garment was used to cover the upper part of the body as in Plate 227. (Mixtec).

ing from Jamiltepec—as are the sashes, which are woven by women with the ends knotted and embroidered by men (pl. VI b). Our *malacatero* (spindlemaker) friend (pl. 11) told us that he formerly engaged in this work, and that he had been the *maestro* (teacher) of the specialty of men's belt decoration.

Mechoacán

Women's Costume

Mechoacán is one of the few villages we have visited where women at home still go about, completely un-self-consciously (1965), with no upper garment of any

302

kind (pl. 226). Very handsome two-web rectangles (pls. 227 & 228) are woven for upper garments (termed *trallas*) to be worn for special occasions or outside the village. They measure approximately 39 by 65 inches.

The *posahuanco* (striped skirt) is worn to the instep in this village. We noted, however, that more convenient short skirts resembling those of Jamiltepec type (2) were worn for bathing in the river near the town. For the most part blue Jamiltepec belts were noted here. The *posahuanco*, as seen in Plate 226, is folded down outside over the belt.

Men's Costume

The typical men's costume is more enduring in Mechoacán than in the larger, more accessible town of Jamiltepec. Handwoven natural-brown cotton is used for shirts, and often for trousers, although white is also used (pl. 227). Special sashes are still worn.

Tetepec

In Tetepec (not visited), much further inland and without a road, women wear a unique upper garment (*tralla*) which has one armhole (pl. 142; fig. 8 k & 1). The rest of the garment goes about the shoulders and over the chest. The lower closed end of the double rectangle forms a carrying pocket. The Tetepec skirt is the *posahuanco* which is purchased from weavers of Pinotepa de Don Luis or from those of Huaxpaltepec.

Huaxpaltepec

Huaxpaltepec is a small *posahuanco* skirt-weaving center just off the highway between Jamiltepec and Pinotepa Nacional. Here a simple rectangular *manta* cloth is worn as upper garment to cover the head and shoulders. On the outskirts of the village we saw older women wearing only their *posahuancos* even though their huts were located close to the highway.

Huazolotitlán

Huazolotitlán is further off the coastal road on the southern side. Here, as in Pinotepa Nacional, aprons with bibs are worn with the *posahuanco*. Some interesting matters regarding hairdress are seen in this village (pls. 82 & 83), and a few old wedding *huipiles* (pl. 147) may still be found. For everyday the usual *manta* rectangle is used as a head or shoulder covering.

Pinotepa Nacional and Pinotepa de Don Luis

Pinotepa Nacional has communication by air from Oaxaca City, and by road from Tlaxiaco and from Acapulco.

A large Indian population inhabits the outer edges of the town, while *mestizos* engage in business and live in the center. Pinotepa de Don Luis has but a few *mestizos* and is much smaller—a truly Indian village. To reach it one must travel north and east by jeep on a narrow, bad road.

Although different in many details, the costumes worn in both Pinotepas and in a number of related villages are essentially the same. The women wear the handsome *posahuancos* (pls. 131 & 230) and, for everyday, large handwoven or *manta* squares or rectangles, here termed *huipiles*, for upper garments. Between 1962 and 1965 the apron with bib appeared in Pinotepa Nacional; it is worn by young girls. Older women have not adopted the apron, and go nude above the waist in their houses (pl. 229).

Women of Pinotepa Nacional wear a red and purple wool belt (pl. VI a) which differs from the red and white patterned wool belt worn in Pinotepa de Don Luis. Both belts came from the Mixteca Alta and are worn with *soyates*. Women of the former village double their skirts down inside before putting on the belt, whereas in the latter village the skirt is folded down at the top over the belt. (pl. II).

The fiesta *huipil* of Pinotepa Nacional is woven in three webs joined with ribbon (pls. 230 & 231). The round neck opening is bordered with the same ribbon solidly embroidered in chain stitch with multicolored minute animals, birds, flowers, and insects. Four larger motifs of double-headed birds are often embroidered outside the ribbon area, in front, in back, and on the shoulders. Very old *huipiles* do not have this last feature.

For marriage the *huipil* is put on with the head through the neck opening, but the armholes are not used. When some older informants put on the *huipil* for us, they turned the garment sideways. Others wear the garment with the neck opening centered in front. Both fashions must have been used at some time. Perhaps the manner of wearing this garment is dictated by age, rank, or social status. Today we are told that the young girl wishes to be married in a blouse, with a silk scarf for the head.

We believe that an important matter regarding pre-Conquest women's upper garments must be subsequently studied. Viewing some clay figures and codice drawings, we believe that garments thought to represent *quechquemitl* may represent the *huipil* put on in the manner of Plate 231. Folds are not commonly shown in codex drawings, nor in clay and stone figures

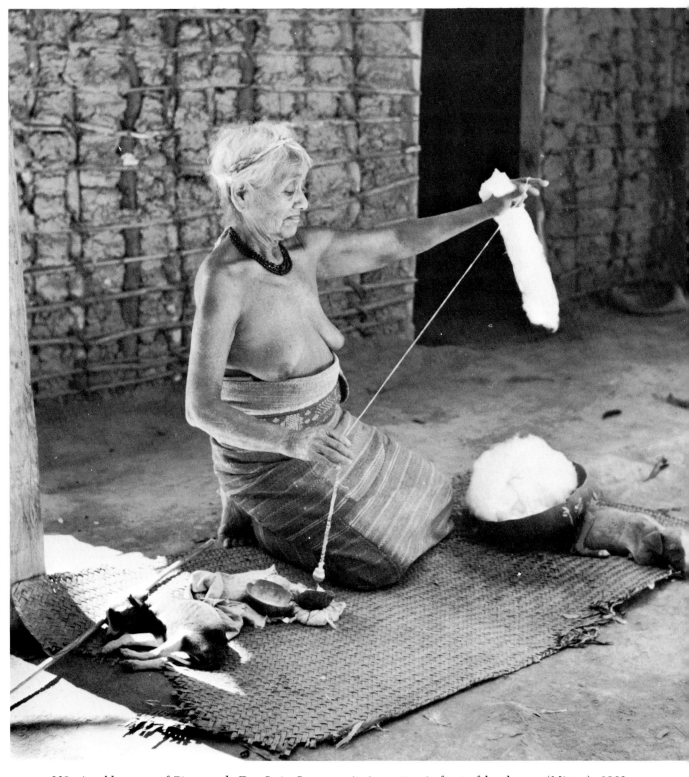

229. An old woman of Pinotepa de Don Luis, Oaxaca, spinning cotton in front of her house. (Mixtec). 1962

231. A woman of Pinotepa Nacional, Oaxaca, in a plain-weave wedding *huipil*. (Mixtec). 1965

230. A young Mixtec woman of Pinotepa Nacional, Oaxaca, wearing a typical skirt, an old white brocaded wedding *huipil*, silver cross, and hair cords with tassels (*tlacoyales*). 1965

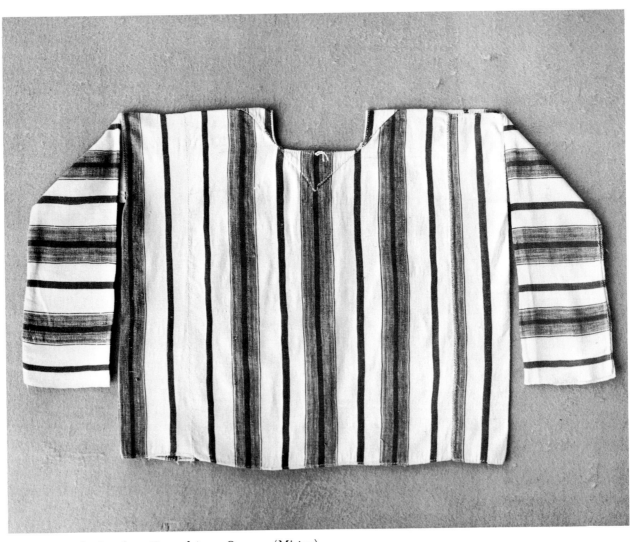

232. A man's shirt from Tetepelcingo, Oaxaca. (Mixtec).

—only the overall shapes or forms, so that ancient garment constructions can easily be misconstrued.

We went to the religious fiesta (third Friday of Lent) in Igualapa, Guerrero, and took note of eight or ten women of Pinotepa Nacional as they purchased the much desired finely woven *huipil* strips sold there by women of the villages of Chacalapa and San Cristóbal. Although they weave themselves, they admire and purchase this weaving, which they say is fashioned of more finely spun thread.

Some twenty to fifty years ago, at the same fair, Pinotepa women purchased very beautiful sets of three *huipil* strips, containing all-over brocaded white designs (pls. 42 & 230), and a few *huipiles* fashioned of this material have still been treasured in Pinotepa Nacional, Pinotepa de Don Luis, and Huazolotitlán. We have

long been trying to determine the source of these now rare old *huipiles*, kept by a few old women in Pinotepa Nacional from the time of their grandmothers. None of the many, many informants we questioned could tell us more than that the strips were purchased long ago, and in Igualapa. We first thought that the forebears of the present Chacalapa weavers must have produced this rare and excellent fabric. At this moment, however, signs point in another direction—to San Esteban Atatlahuaca in the Mixteca Alta. It seems strange indeed that this fine thin cloth should have been woven in a high cold area.

Pinotepa de Don Luis, which is the biggest skirt (*posahuanco*) weaving center, still makes some expensive skirts with shellfish-dyed purple stripes. Today, however, much new commercial thread from textile

306

factories in the city of Puebla, and from Cuernavaca, Morelos, has come into use. Different combinations of stripes are woven for different villages, all fashioned of three strips called *piernas* (legs).

According to informants San Pedro Jicayán and Chayuco skirts contain more red, and can thus be distinguished. Ixtayutla skirts have no purple, only red stripes on a blue ground. Rectangular upper garments for everyday are formed of two white squares separated by red ribbon, in San Pedro Jicayán, Ixtayutla, and San Juan Colorado. Hairdress, belts, and jewelry vary everywhere, as do fiesta and wedding *huipiles*.

A single color photograph (pl. XIII) will display a good number of the differences, and with this we must leave the fascinating Mixteca Baja. At the New Year's market in Jamiltepec (1965) we see a group of women looking at a skirt which is for sale. Facing the camera at the lower left we see a little girl from Jamiltepec, who wears a fragment of the typical white brocaded skirt of this village. The bare-shouldered woman behind the child is considering purchasing the spread-out skirt which we are told contains the particular stripe pattern preferred by women of San Pedro Jicayán. The buyer does not wear the same skirt but she told us after she made her purchase that she had only recently gone to live in Jicayán. Above the prospective buyer we see the skirt seller, who is from the *posahuanco*-weaving village of Pinotepa de Don Luis, as is the woman opposite her, holding one edge of the skirt. The women in the background are casual onlookers enjoying the proceedings. Their hairdresses suggest those of Huazolotitlán. However, the woman whose skirt with red stripes is partially visible may be from Jicayán, Chayuco, or Atoyac, where red stripes are favored.

Men's handwoven fiesta costumes from a number of inland Mixteca Baja villages contain a variety of colored stripes, some wider and some narrower. Shirts with very wide stripes, like that shown in Plate 232, are sometimes worn with plain white trousers, either handwoven or of *manta*.

Some little girls of Mixteca Baja villages still may be seen in indigenous dress (pl.131).

33. San Andrés Chicahuaxtla, and San Juan Copala, Oaxaca (Trique)

Of the five Trique towns—Santo Domingo Chicahuaxtla (now called Santo Domingo del Estado), San José Chicahuaxtla, San Martín Itunyoso, Copala, and San Andrés Chicahuaxtla—all but Copala (district of Juxtlahuaca) are in the district of the big Mexican market town of Tlaxiaco, where there is a huge Saturday market, bringing Indians from many Mixtec and Trique villages.

We visited the Trique village of San Andrés Chicahuaxtla first in 1943 (pl. 233) and again in 1961. The town is located on the very crest of the Sierra Madre, from which on a bright clear day the Pacific Ocean may be seen, perhaps seventy-five miles away. However, it is commonly enveloped in a heavy cold mist which sweeps up from the coast at night. Round houses, some 24 feet in diameter have roofs thatched with palm— "Laid on in several layers from below, one overlapping, the edges being trimmed so as to present several well defined concentric circular lines" (Starr, 1901, p. 145). Our first trip, on horseback, was arduous compared to the ease with which one may now reach the town from the new road to the coast that passes not far away. Today the village is somewhat transformed by a new "Centro de Salud" building near the market. Three or four Trique girls have been trained in nursing and hygiene in Oaxaca City, and are now back in San Andrés working under health officials who appear at designated intervals. At last report these girls still wore their indigenous dress.

We spent Christmas Day, 1964, in the *mestizo* town of Putla, Oaxaca, an important market and religious center. It is located on the new highway about a third of the distance from Tlaxiaco to Pinotepa Nacional. Many Trique Indians came into Putla, particularly from San Andrés Chicahuaxtla, Copala, and Santo Domingo del Estado. In this chapter we will deal only with the costumes from the first two of these villages as they are the more distinctive.

San Andrés Chicahuaxtla

Women's Costume

The women's costume of San Andrés Chicahuaxtla consists of a *huipil*, skirt, belt, and blanket. Sometimes a half gourd is worn on the head.

Huipil. The San Andrés Chicahuaxtla *huipil* is handwoven on the backstrap loom. There are two types of weaves (1) a plain weave of medium weight; (2) a white gauze weave with plain white weft stripes, the latter being particularly characteristic. The woman's *huipil* which we examined is fashioned in three strips, joined together and folded over with a round neck

PLATE XIII. New Year's Day in Jamiltepec, Oaxaca. Skirts brought in for sale from Pinotepa de Don Luis (Mixtec). 1965

233. A view of the village of San Andrés Chicahuaxtla, Oaxaca. (Trique). 1943

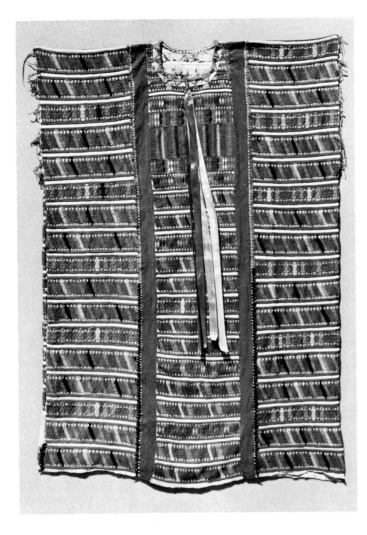

234. A Trique *huipil*. San Martín Itunyoso, Oaxaca.

opening cut in the center of the middle strip. The outer strips are 11 inches wide; the center strip 15 inches wide; the finished garment 37 by 40 inches. The center section is edged with 1½–2-inch dark-blue or red woven cotton warp stripes (pl. 235). We have seen woven stripes bordering center webs in Trique *huipiles* only in San Andrés Chicahuaxtla and San Martín Itunyoso (pl. 234); Copala *huipiles* are joined with either ribbon or plain whipping stitches. Many Mixtec *huipiles* from the area have woven red stripes of various narrower widths—San Miguel Chicahuaxtla, Santo Tomás Ocotepec, Yosonicaje (pl. 143), and Santa María Cuquila; but, except for that of San Andrés Chicahuaxtla, we have seen only one wide blue woven stripe in the whole area—in a *huipil* of Santa María Yucunicoco.

Below the ribbon-edged neck, which is overlaid with continuous points of contrasting colored ribbon, are five or so long ribbons hanging loose down the center back. Three inches below the neck, front and back, is worked a solid 3-inch-wide band of zigzag brocading in red, orange, yellow, and green commercial wool yarn. The rest of the entire *huipil*, in all three sections, is weft banded with ½-inch-wide brocaded bands chiefly in red (rosettes, zigzags, squares) occurring every 1½ inches throughout. These bands alternate with 1¼-inch gauze white background sections each having three heavier white weft stripes. *Huipiles* here are left open down the side to within about 7 inches of the bottom (pl. 235).

Trique (and Mixtec) *huipiles* are more heavily decorated today than in 1900 and shortly before (Starr, 1899, pl. XXXI), probably because colored commercial yarns and less expensive embroidery cotton thread are very tempting, whereas before they were not easily obtainable. San Andrés Chicahuaxtla *huipiles*, though otherwise beautifully made, all have one characteristic weakness or fault in workmanship—the "join" or *remate* is loosely and carelessly executed. See the torn area near the bottom front edge of the *huipil* in Plate 91.

As seen in Plate 235, the *huipil* is often worn hanging loose, but also is seen bunched up about the waist, used as a sort of bundle carrier. When *huipiles* hang loose no skirt is visible except at the sides where *huipiles* are very open.

SKIRT. A strange fashion in the high, misty, cold climate, is the skimpy San Andrés Chicahuaxtla wraparound skirt worn only to knee length (as in no other Indian group we have observed in Mexico) (pl. 235).

A heavy, dark-blue, cotton single strip (measuring 26 by 62 inches) comprises the whole of this garment. Varied small warp stripes of white and red embellish the skirt. The strip is wrapped around, with no pleats or fullness, and with the final end folded in 2 or 3 inches. Skirts have the same badly woven *remate* (finished edge) as do the *huipiles*.

BELT. The belt used to fasten the abbreviated skirt in this Trique village is purchased in the Tlaxiaco market. It is made in Santo Tomás Jalieza, the town in the valley of Oaxaca which furnishes belts for many Zapotec and Mixtec villages also. A great variety of widths and color combinations are made. The San Andrés Chicahuaxtla Indians favor a narrow 1¾-inch-wide dark-red cotton belt with a simple black warp design. No *soyate* is used.

235. In the market — a cold day in San Andrés Chicahuaxtla, Oaxaca. (Trique). 1943

BLANKET. Diagonal-weave black-and-white blankets (all wool), with wide transverse end stripes, are said to be used solely by the women of San Andrés Chicahuaxtla (men's blankets being somewhat different). These blankets according to Starr (1901, p. 144) were made around 1900 in Yolomeco. Today, we are told that the same blanket is now made in San Miguel el Grande near Chalcatongo. The blankets are woven in two 21-inch widths joined in colored blanket-stitch sections of pink, orange, and green commercial yarn. Final blankets usually measure about 42 by 72 inches. Tranverse end stripes are made of black or white (and sometimes today of colored) commercial yarns. In cold weather blankets are wrapped around the shoulders often doubled to one strip width (pl. 91).

HAIRDRESS AND COMBS. Hair is worn in two braids. Characteristic combs for the hair are made from a number of bamboo strips placed side by side, bent double, tied, and wrapped with colored bands of fiber. These same combs are used in weaving, to pull down weft threads, and to tighten and straighten out tangled yarn. Described by Frederick Starr in about 1900, these combs were still to be seen when we visited the village in 1943 and again in 1961.

Servilleta

Handwoven cloths are used here instead of the bags found in many Indian villages. Such cloths are made in two strips, each having a blue or red warp stripe on one edge only. When the two rectangles are sewn together to form a square, the two stripes are joined together down the middle (pl. 98). Strips have weft bands of red and variegated brocading, reminiscent of the *huipil* weaving done here. *Servilletas* of Santo Domingo del Estado are identical. San Martín Itunyoso *servilletas* have the same construction, but the weft stripes are very wide and closely spaced as they are in their *huipiles* (pl. 234).

Soft palm baskets or *tenates*, carried on the back and fastened by a cord across the front above the chest, are also used for carrying bundles (pl. 235).

Children's Costume

The little girl's costume in the authors' collection, purchased in San Andrés Chicahuaxtla in 1961, consists of a tiny *huipil* (15½ by 21 inches), a skirt (16 by 27 inches), and a miniature Jalieza belt (1¼ by 50 inches).

Mens' Costume

We observed no distinctive men's costume in San Andrés Chicahuaxtla, other than an occasional long handwoven belt with transverse brocaded stripes like both *huipiles* and *tortilla* cloths, (*servilletas*). In 1941 villagers were still wearing large, quite high-crowned, black felt hats with white bordered brims. These were purchased in Tlaxiaco—which town, together with Tlacolula in the valley of Oaxaca, formerly furnished distinctive hats for many different villages.

San Juan Copala

Women's Costume

All parts of the Copala women's costume are handwoven—*huipil*, skirt, and belt. Bags are used instead of *servilletas* for carrying *tortillas*.

HUIPIL. The Copala *huipil* is a heavily brocaded white cotton garment of the general style of San Andrés Chicahuaxtla, with, however, no gauze-weave areas (in examples we have seen) and with somewhat wider horizontal brocaded bands at closer intervals (pls. 90, 236, 237 & XIV), red predominating. The total width of the *huipil* is about the same (12–13–and 12-inch webs), about 37 inches. Finished Copala garments as a whole are longer (43–48 inches) than those of San Andrés Chicahuaxtla, and are sewn up the sides about half-way.

The brocaded chest band, front and back, is wider (4–5 inches) on the Copala *huipil*. Six or seven colors of cotton embroidery thread are used with only small spots of colored wool in the horizontal stripes. Some Copala *huipiles* are woven with natural-tan cotton hand-spun thread instead of white. *Huipiles* are worn either loose or rolled up at the waist.

SKIRTS. Two types of skirts were observed in Copala, both ankle length. One is a dark-blue, heavy, two-strip cotton tube with red horizontal stripes (warp stripes). The strips, when joined, make a skirt 37–44 inches long by 76–78 inches in circumference. Evenly spaced stripes (pl. 237) are massed in the center of each woven web. Stripes for young girls' skirts are narrower, and closer together than those for married women—so we were told. See Figure 11 b-1 for the manner of arranging this skirt. A black wool skirt is also used in Copala. Both types usually have a handsome multicolored wool embroidery joining stitch. We noted in Putla that the vertical *randa* was often worn center front in the black wool skirts. Skirts are probably secured either with a Jalieza belt or with one of similar design woven in the Mixteca Alta. *Soyates* are used.

HAIRDRESS AND JEWELRY. In Copala the hair is worn

236. A Trique group from San Juan Copala, Oaxaca, at the Oaxaca Indian State Fair, showing the manners of wearing and the usages of the *huipil*. Oaxaca City, Oaxaca. 1941

237. A Trique group from San Juan Copala at the Indian State Fair. Oaxaca City, Oaxaca. 1941

in one braid in the center back, with about 6 inches falling loose at the ends. With this simple hairdress, young girls use many colored plastic combs and other plastic hair ornaments. Some young girls have several very long ribbons near the end of their single braid, falling to the bottom of their *huipiles* and hanging loosely. They wear many strings of yellow and white *papelillo* beads, sometimes also having multicolored ribbon streamers. Very large shiny earrings seem to be in vogue.

Children's Costume

Many little girls in Copala were seen in long *huipiles,* tiny ones often without skirts.

Men's Costume

The men of Copala wear strong-colored artificial silk or cotton shirts. In 1964 we also saw fine red striped belts folded double and sewn over (pl. VI b), and worn knotted at the center front with ribbons hanging. We noted in 1941 that men at the Indian State Fair wore these belts with no ribbons and knotted at the side. Colored shirts had not yet been inroduced (pl. 237).

Tortilla Bags

Copala uses firmly woven red cotton bags in many sizes with a variety of tiny warp stripes in a number of colors, and with twisted fringes (pl. 238).

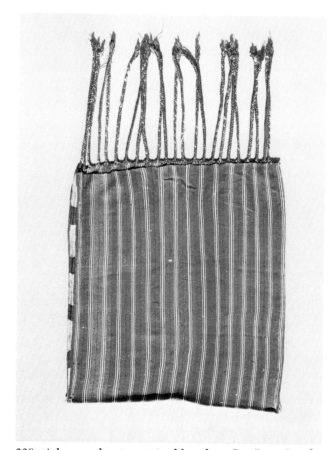

238. A large red cotton striped bag from San Juan Copala, Oaxaca. (Triique).

34. Amusgo Villages of Oaxaca and Guerrero

THE AMUSGO AREA lies in the south of Mexico, midway between Oaxaca City and Acapulco, and Amusgo villages are located in both the states of Oaxaca and Guerrero. The area has for its western boundary the Camino de Ometepec Tlapa, and to the east it is more or less bounded by the new road from Tlaxiaco to Cacahuatepec. The latter actually runs through the village of San Pedro Amusgos, Oaxaca, although the Indians dwell away from the highway, and the women continue (1964–1965) to weave and wear their well-known fine *huipiles*.

This linguistic group lives in ten villages, only two of which are in Oaxaca—Amusgos and Ipalapa. The remaining eight are centered about Xochistlahuaca and Cozoyoapan, which lie side by side and actually constitute one settlement. The commercial center for all the Guerrero Amusgos is the important, largely non-Indian town of Ometepec.

Amusgo women are renowned for superlative *huipil* weaving. The weavers of Amusgos, Oaxaca, and Xochistlahuaca, Zacualpan, Minas, and Cochoapa in Guerrero are all excellent, although we found the women of Cochoapa—located nearest to Ometepec—to have largely abandoned their native costume and weaving. As far as we know, the weaving of material for men's and boys' clothing exists today only in Cozoyoapan.

Women's Costumes

In the above-mentioned weaving villages fine to heavy three-web cotton *huipiles*, white or natural-tan, are worn; these *huipiles* are usually hand-spun and have considerable brocaded decoration. Skirts vary from village to village. Those of all the Guerrero Amusgos we saw in 1965 were of colored store-bought cotton cloth, contrasting oddly with their beautiful *huipiles*. Women of Amusgos, Oaxaca, ordinarily use no skirt, but for gala occasions they wear a wrap-around handwoven one from Sayultepec, Oaxaca.

HUIPILES. A detailed description of the average *huipil* of Amusgos, Oaxaca, follows, with comments on points of difference with those of Guerrero villages.

Among the Amusgo *huipiles* we have studied, the three webs are apt to be of equal width (12–15 inches), except in the *huipiles* of Minas, Guerrero (pl. 241). The latter are the only Amusgo *huipiles* we know today having woven red warp 1¾-inch bands on either side of the center strips. In a 1941 and a 1965 example the center web is 16 inches wide, the outer ones 13½ inches. Amusgos web lengths are 70–80 inches long, many with hems—indicating that looms have been set up to hold two or three lengths at one time.

Xochistlahuaca *huipiles* (pl. 239) are worn some-

316

PLATE XIV. Two women of Copala, Oaxaca (Trique), in the market of Putla on Christmas day. 1964

what shorter than those of Amusgos, where a skirt is not commonly worn (pl. 240). Because no skirt is worn, Amusgos village textiles are a little heavier on the whole than the thin weaves of Zacualpan, or the lace weaves of Xochistlahuaca. Necks are round and finished with colored or black cloth or ribbon cut in points, and hand sewn with embroidery stitches. *Huipil* webs are joined with a variety of decorative blanket stitches. Ribbon is often used between webs in *huipiles* of the village of Amusgos (although the sides may be sewn with embroidery stitches). A fine Cochoapa *huipil* has ribbon joinings only, but most Guerrero examples were without ribbon.

Amusgos, Oaxaca, *huipiles* tend to have solid brocaded yokes 15 inches or more down from the shoulder fold both in the front and in the back of the center panel (pl. 240). Guerrero *huipiles* do not have this; instead, they have an elaborate 5–7-inch-wide brocaded band across the center panel a few inches below the neck opening.

Certain eight-petaled conventionalized flower shapes (pls. 136 & 240), and varieties of zigzag vine patterns predominate in the old traditional Amusgo designs, whatever the village. Red, which used to be the dominant color throughout the area, now seems to predominate only in Minas *huipiles*. Other villages employ four to six colors of commercial embroidery thread in woven brocaded design elements.

Below the solid central design yoke or wide band, and throughout the side panels, occur horizontal repeat patterns in evenly spaced rows. Except in Xochistlahuaca *huipiles*, where more elaborate wider design bands occur (pl. 136), variations of eight-petaled flower patterns are used. *Huipiles* of Guerrero (Minas, Zacualpan, Cochoapa) border all design rows with red weft stripes, or contain red stripes between the design rows (Minas). Minas and Zacualpan *huipiles* may have heavier white weft stripes spaced at intervals as well.

Huipiles of Amusgos, Oaxaca, may have red weft borders for their horizontal brocaded rows, but usually do not, a fact which distinguishes them from Guerrero *huipiles*. The chief distinction characterizing Amusgos village *huipiles*, however, is the solid central brocaded yoke.

Some older women of Amusgos, Oaxaca, still prefer rather heavy *huipiles* of natural-tan hand-spun cotton, with striped and design areas entirely in white or red brocading. In *huipiles* of tan cotton were seen only the best old designs. No ribbon was used between strips. A little color appeared in the blanket-stitch joinings of

239. A woman and children of Xochistlahuaca, Guerrero. (Amusgo). 1965

317

240. Beautiful brocaded *huipiles* of Amusgos, Oaxaca. (Amusgo). 1962

241. A fine Amusgo *huipil* from Minas, Guerrero, brocaded only in red. Although this example dates from about 1940, garments from Minas are still excellently woven.

the strips and the buttonhole stitch worked in triangles around the neck and the 6-inch armholes (the old-style neck finishing of this village is no longer common).

One new *coyuche huipil* which we examined measured 47 inches wide, putting it in the "very broad" *huipil* classification (which allows the garment to reach between elbow and wrist)—the classification given by Lila O'Neale in relation to Guatemalan *huipiles* (O'Neale, 1945, p. 112). Very broad *huipiles* are unusual in Mexico, but *huipiles* are more often than not

wider than they are long. This particular *coyuche huipil* measured 47 by 42 inches.

Amusgos village *huipiles* fall usually to mid-calf. Girls in early or mid-teens dressed in their best *huipiles* (pl. 240) to near ankle length would bear out the idea that garments are made longer for young girls to allow for growth. We saw only handwoven *huipiles* being worn even for everyday use in 1961, and when we approached any of the neat round bamboo and mud houses (pl. 242), all the female members of the family

242. Round houses in the well-swept village of Amusgos, Oaxaca. (Amusgo). 1962

243. A *huipil* weaver of Amusgos, Oaxaca. (Amusgo). 1962

—down to the tiniest—seemed able to run indoors and quickly don fresh sparkling *huipiles*. Many women in Amusgos were weaving, or could show us a loom with a *huipil* in the making (pl. 243). All Amusgos village *huipiles* which we have seen were worn falling free, not rolled up about the waist.

SKIRTS. When dressing in their best clothes to be photographed, girls of Amusgos, Oaxaca, did not wear skirts (pl. 240), although for fiestas and ceremonials older girls and women use one of heavy anil-dyed dark-blue cotton, hand-loomed. The wrap-around skirt measures 46 by 83 inches, and consists of two 23-inch widths sewn together. These skirts have a series of red and mauve warp stripes breaking up the blue background, both stripes being edged with a ⅛-inch red stripe, then ¾-inch of blue background, and a ¼-inch mauve stripe. In the center of both skirt divisions a 1-inch mauve stripe is bordered in ⅛-inch red. When worn, skirts here are arranged with a large inverted box pleat in the center front. We have not seen what belt is used.

At the 1941 Indian State Fair, the Amusgos delegation wore these skirts very long; their toes barely showed. *Huipiles* of mid-calf length left in view some 10–12 inches of skirt. See Chapter 31 which describes an identical skirt, used in Zacatepec and made in nearby Sayultepec.

Of Guerrero Amusgo skirts only that of Xochistlahuaca is distinctive (pl. 78).

HEADDRESS AND JEWELRY. Commonly no head covering or footgear is seen in Amusgos, Oaxaca. Xochistlahuaca women weave nice *servilletas*, but we did not see them worn on the head (Ometepec, 1965). In 1941 at the Oaxaca Indian State Fair women of Amusgos wore almost no jewelry. In 1962 many of them wore a single string of red cut-glass beads.

Women of Amusgos, Oaxaca, wear their hair in a single braid down the back, but in the Guerrero Amusgo villages hair is apt to be worn wound about the head in a cooler fashion.

Children's Costumes

Many little girls of varying ages, even very young, are dressed in miniature *huipiles*, particularly in Amusgos, Oaxaca (pl. 240).

Men's and Boys' Costumes

Nonbutton shirts and white cross-over trousers were seen on men in Amusgos, Oaxaca. No handwoven materials were observed. Some men wore store-bought shirts. In Cozoyoapan, Guerrero, a very individual all-white men's handwoven costume (shirt and trousers) is still being made, though the custom is disappearing. A wide straight-sided long-sleeved shirt is gathered high about the neck into a narrow band with a 6-inch slit down the center front (no buttons). Trousers are cut with a separate crotch and long ties that cross in front. The legs are fashioned narrowing toward the ankle, a characteristic feature of handwoven trousers in the southern areas of the Pinotepas and in Jamiltepec. Most indigenous men's trousers in Mexico are not cut to shape, but are fashioned of straight pieces (Huichol, Nayarit; Ixtayutla, Oaxaca; Huistan, Chiapas, for instance).

The unique feature of the Cozoyoapan costume is the open-weave diamond-patterned rectangles across the shoulders, front and back, below the shoulder seam, with the same decorative band around the wide cuffs of the shirt and at the bottom of the trousers. A loom displaying this unusual decorative weave within plain weave material may be seen in the National Museum of Anthropology, Department of Ethnology.

35. San Mateo del Mar, Oaxaca (Huave)

"They have today but four villages, San Mateo del Mar, Santa María del Mar, San Francisco del Mar, and San Dionisio del Mar. Ixhuatan mentioned by Orosco has long been abandoned" (Starr, 1901, p. 163).

We first visited San Mateo del Mar in 1940. At that time there was no automobile road, and we traveled by ox-cart from Tehuantepec. Now a very old autobus makes the trip. The people said that they were from "San Mateo *del Mar Vivo*"—"San Mateo of the live sea," the ocean, as distinguished from the long, narrow, shallow, salt lagoons which they call the "*mar muerto*" or "dead sea." In Tehuantepec, when we had asked in 1940, no one seemed to know of the old Huave *huipil* with shellfish-dyed designs, which we had read about in "Notes upon the Ethnography of Southern Mexico" (Starr, 1900–1902, p. 164). We found that a good many fine examples still existed in San Mateo, but by now they have almost all completely vanished.

Although the Chontals have always collected and used *Purpura patula pansa* dye (Gerhard, 1964, p. 181), the Huaves have also collected it for their own use, probably in small quantities. Francisco de Burgoa (1934, Vol. II, p. 406) mentions shellfish-dyed *huazontecas* for skirts. San Mateo del Mar used to be called Huazontlán, and Hans Gadow says (1908, p. 162), "They have one industry, which is probably quite peculiar to them, namely, the weaving of small pieces of cotton cloth, *huatz*—which they dye with the juice of the *Purpura patula*, a marine shell which is common on the rocks."

These descriptions indicate that the Huave women once wore shellfish-dyed purple skirts, handwoven belts, and no upper garments—except on ceremonial occasions. The famous hand-spun, handwoven Huave *huipil* with shell-dyed brocaded plant and animal designs was no doubt worn for special occasions, or folded over the head as protection from the sun. When the Huaves began having more contact with the nearby Zapotecs and needed upper garments for trips to the Tehuantepec market, they ceased wearing their own dress, and the commercially minded women from Juchitán and Tehuantepec found still another outlet for their cheaply made *huipiles* and skirts. Materials for the latter are woven in quantity on treadle looms, and sold over a wide area in the state of Oaxaca.

Zapotecs from Juchitán carry on regular trading with San Mateo, exchanging corn, bread, chocolate, fruit, *zacate*, modern *huipiles*, and skirts for eggs, fish, shrimp, and iguanas.

323

244. The church of San Mateo del Mar, Oaxaca, during a windstorm. Our hosts fed us cold food because the wind made the lighting of fires in or near their thatched homes hazardous. (Huave). 1940

245. Weaving a large red and white Huave *servilleta*, while the man of the house rests in his hammock. San Mateo del Mar, Oaxaca. 1940

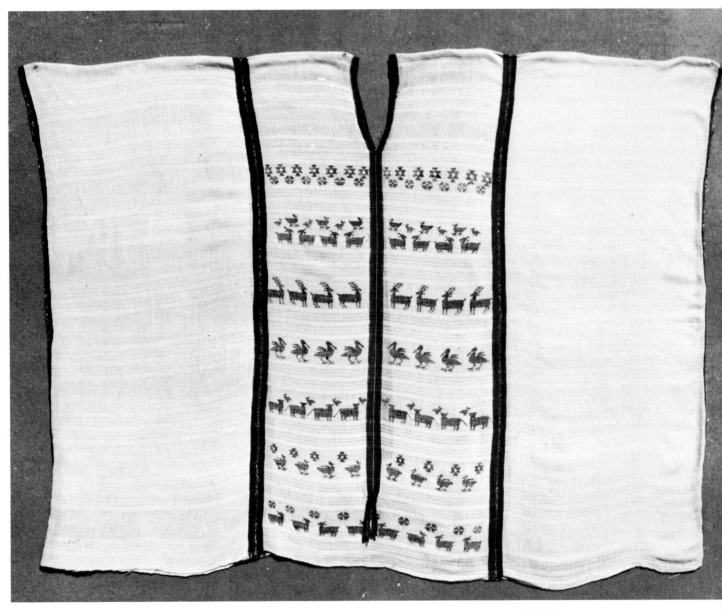

246. An old Huave *huipil* from San Mateo del Mar, Oaxaca, with shellfish-dyed purple brocaded designs.

Women's Costume

The Huave women's costume, observed both in 1940 and 1963, is essentially the same as that worn today by some conservative old women of Tehuantepec. It consists of a Juchitán-woven wrap-around skirt and a *huipil* made of commercial cloth. A piece of white commercial cotton cloth is used to cover the head.

MODERN HUIPIL. The conservative Huave women do not wear Tehuantepec or Juchitán *huipiles* (which have elaborate bands with geometric patterns). The Huave *huipil* is specially made for them in Juchitán of a single piece of commercial dark-blue cotton cloth (lined with a cheaper, often polka-dotted cotton) folded over to make a garment approximately 23 by 20 inches. The sides are sewn up leaving small armholes, and a round neck opening. Decoration consists of five or seven bands (each ¾ inch) of solid yellow and red machine chain-stitch embroidery (three red, two yellow). Alternating bands run side by side vertically over each shoulder from back to front, and across the bottom, front and back, 2 inches above the lower edge. In 1940 the stripes were more modest (pl. 245). The round neck has a 1½-inch band of running and crisscross chain stitching in red and yellow. In the San Mateo market in 1963, such a *huipil* cost us 18 *pesos* ($1.50).

For mourning, and for everyday also, old Huave women were seen in *huipiles* of the same form, made of dark purplish cotton or velvet (the latter a new style), having several bands of black ribbon, instead of machine embroidery.

OLD HANDWOVEN HUIPIL. The fine, old-style three-strip, white *huipil* hand-spun and handwoven, has not been worn as an upper garment or head covering for many years, and it is no longer woven. Data concerning the two examples we measured follows: *Huipil* strips—(1) 9, 12, 9 inches wide and 50 inches long; (2) 11, 13, 11 inches wide and 60 inches long. The garments, when assembled, measured (1) 30 by 25 inches, (2) 35 by 30 inches.

All *huipil* webs were of plain white weave with heavier weft stripes at intervals, and all were edged on both sides with a ¾-inch shellfish-dyed purple warp (vertical) stripe. The center strip contained an additional ½-inch purple center stripe, on which the 10-inch neck slit was cut. Neck slits were sewn in overhand stitch with red or purple thread. The weaving of the center strip involved a particular technique (seen only in two other *huipiles* in Mexico, to our knowledge, those of Mazatlán and Acatlán, Oaxaca (Mixe). In San Mateo the center purple stripe stops some 5 inches from the bottom of the *huipil*, ending in a 3–4-inch fringe. Below this point, the white background (having been woven with floating warps) is again worked without break or change in both warp and weft (pl. 246).

The center panel on the front side of the garment contains brocaded rows (usually five or six rows) of animal, shell, plant, and bird designs, worked in purple thread (very rarely in white) dyed with shellfish dye (pl. 246). These designs are very well copied from nature, and tremendously in keeping with the life and setting of these people, who live on and near ocean and lagoons. Their terrain is sandy, unadapted to agriculture. They live by fishing, and the produce of their domestic animals.

The horizontal rows of brocaded figures 1–2 inches wide (fig. 17) are worked into plain-weave areas between heavier white weft stripes. Only one example seen (in the collection of I. W. Johnson) has a few purple brocaded figures in the side panels on the front of the *huipil*, near the bottom of the garment. All other *huipiles* have had brocaded elements only in the front center section. Usually the top design row consists of

two rows of conventionalized shell or flower patterns —not easily recognized as such, being the only rather abstract representations among otherwise realistic patterns (fig. 17, 2nd row). This first row is often placed down from the shoulder fold about 7 inches, a slight distance below the neck slit.

In 1940, we saw a few old women wearing the old *huipiles* for church, but today probably very few of them exist outside of textile collections. It is from these few old garments that the beautiful designs may be recorded. The curious mode of wearing the old *huipil* for ceremonial occasions was demonstrated to us in 1963 (pl. XV). After putting her head through the neck slit, the wearer turned the garment around, leaving the brocaded side to fall down her back, and pushed the rest softly up about her throat, giving the impression of a cape, her arms free, and the armholes not used.

A few rather poorly made *huipiles* of the old style have come to light in the last few years, and we believe it probable that someone tried to interest modern Huave weavers in their making. These *huipiles* are coarsely woven, the brocaded designs ungainly, large, and poorly executed, although the purple threads of one such garment, when examined by Mr. Max Saltzman were found to be shellfish-dyed.

HEAD COVERING. The women of San Mateo, since 1900 or before, have been recognized away from home by a white cloth about a yard square (often now a bath towel), tied pirate fashion over the head. Formerly a handwoven headcloth with *caracol* stripes was worn, but not even one was to be seen in 1940. A report in 1949 states that for "All Saints Day," November 2, red skirts with blue stripes were observed, and some Tehuana headdresses (*huipiles grandes*), but that no *caracol* brocaded handwoven headcloths appeared (Cook and Leonard, 1949, p. 503). In 1940 hair style was described as follows—two braids twisted low about the forehead and tucked in. In 1963 ribbons in the braids prevailed in Tehuantepec-Juchitán style.

SKIRT. *Caracol*-dyed wrap-around skirts were formerly used in San Mateo, and dark-blue or white handwoven ones were commonly worn into the 1930's. Today, the women wear—as previously explained—the Juchitán upright-loomed red skirts, favoring the *corte* which has ¼-inch weft blue stripes (vertical when worn) placed every 3 inches or so. (There are a number of stripe variations in these red skirt lengths, each used chiefly in some particular locality—as far away as San Juan Cotzocón [Mixe] and Acatlán [Mixe], Oaxaca.)

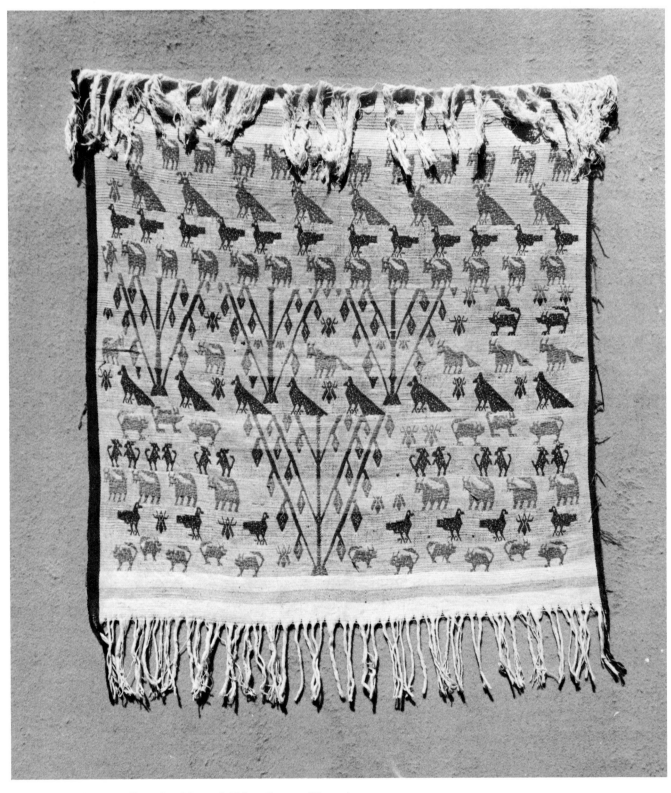

247. A *servilleta*. San Mateo del Mar, Oaxaca (Huave).

BELT AND JEWELRY. Today San Mateo belts are of white store-bought poplin, but twenty-five years ago handwoven belts were used to secure the women's wrap-around skirts. They were of white cotton, 5 inches wide, having small groups of black weft strips and a white fringe.

Necklaces of fish vertebrae were formerly worn in San Mateo, but at the present time strings of small, red glass beads are chiefly seen.

Children's Costume

In 1940 many little girls were seen in regional dress, but today a skimpy cotton frock is more usual. Women and children are almost always barefoot.

Servilletas

The pride of San Mateo Huave weavers, since the days of the fine old *huipiles,* are the charming *servilletas* made by many weavers (pl. 149, 245, 247). Large white squares—often 26 inches and sometimes 31–32 inches square—are solidly worked with bands of weft-brocaded animal, bird, and plant motifs; usually, today, in red commercial thread, formerly in shellfish-dyed purple thread. Some backgrounds are of natural-tan cotton (*coyuche*) or a deeper tan obtained from brazilwood used as dye.

Servilletas have many uses. When they wrap a bundle, the wrong side is left out; when they are spread on the ground with *tortillas* or other merchandise, the right side appears on top. Some cloths are used for home altars, some are used ceremonially, folded in the left hand under a gourd containing *atole* (a corn drink) (Cook and Leonard, 1949, p. 464).

Men's and Boys' Costume

Men are seen in red or white cotton shorts when working in the country, or near the water. Not long ago, men and boys wore only breechcloths when fishing or at home. Frederick Starr (1901, p. 164) says that not long before his trip to San Mateo in 1898, men went in only breechcloth and headcloth to Tehuantepec. Now, for church or fiesta, or to go to Tehuantepec, dark trousers are preferred, with a silk shirt and black felt city hat.

Formerly, a hand-spun handwoven shirt and trousers were used, the shirt with no buttons, but a small neck slit and a 1-inch hand-sewn stand-up collar. The short wide shirt (27 by 22 inches) had one patch pocket and straight-cut sleeves, and was fringed at the bottom. The sides were slit up 4 inches. The trousers, wide and straight legged, with the crotch sewn in, were of the same plain-weave material and were pleated into a double narrow band at the waist. One free end of this band (32 inches long) was left to be wrapped around the body and tied with a 4-inch fringed end hanging.

At one time, these men's clothes are said to have had brocaded bands of figures worked in purple shellfish-dyed thread. One suit was seen (in a collection) having inferior red designs. These garments, however, had not actually been used by a Huave Indian; they had never been worn. In photographs from 1900 we see no trace of design work in men's clothing, although in some related areas there most certainly have been some. A Tehuantepec Zapotec told us he once saw a man in brocaded costume at the Fiesta of Corpus Christi in San Mateo many years ago.

Men of the village formerly wove and wore heavy wool striped jackets of natural-white with brown or blackish wool, for cool evenings. These lacked sleeves, had fringe at the bottom edge in front and back, a cut and bound vertical slit neck, and were sewn up the sides to leave comfortable 8-inch arm openings. The garments were fashioned of a single woven web, approximately 25 by 58 inches before folding.

According to Starr (1901, p. 164) Huave men formerly shaved the forepart of the head, and men of office wore a red headcloth. The men's old-style belt was "red with narrow blue lines marking them off into checks."

36. Tuxtla Gutiérrez, Chiapas (Zoque)

AFTER CHIAPAS was invaded by the Aztecs in 1482 and 1484, the Zoques, Mames, and Quelenes began to pay tribute to the Aztec emperor Ahuitzotl in cotton, clothing, colored plumes, and so forth. When the Spaniards arrived the Zoques were submissive. Adjacent to Tabasco, they were the first to come in contact with the conquerors (Sánchez, 1915, pp. 96–97). The Zoque Indians of Chiapas are to be found today in villages in the departments of Tuxtla, Mezcalapa, Pichucalco, and Simojovel. There are three Zoque settlements in the state of Oaxaca and several in Tabasco.

In 1940 there was a considerable Zoque population living in the outskirts of the capital of Chiapas, Tuxtla Gutiérrez, who still appeared in indigenous dress, observing old customs. Some of their dwellings were of distinctive Zoque construction: vertical poles lashed together with vines, daubed with mud inside and out, and then whitewashed (Cordry, 1941, p. 26).

Women's Costume

The old type of Zoque costume consisted of a short, fine, hand-spun, handwoven white cotton *huipil;* a dark-blue handwoven, cotton wrap-around skirt, and a special *huipil* (*huipil de tapar*) which was worn on the head.

Even in 1940 the regional folk costume of nearby Chiapa de Corzo—popularly used also by some of the *mestizo* population of Tuxtla—was beginning to be worn by most younger Zoque women (a blouse with wide flounce of net or lace, and a bright-colored skirt of silk or cotton). At the time of our visit, there were but a few elderly Zoque weavers, and even some old women were buying simple blouses instead of waiting for *huipil* strips to be finished. A type of checked cloth from Comitán, woven on the treadle loom, was being purchased for skirts also, but some old women wore the indigenous Zoque costume. It is very doubtful that there are any Zoque weavers left near Tuxtla Gutiérrez. Twenty-five years ago there were very few, and none of the daughters of middle-aged weavers were interested in learning the craft.

Informants told us that the greatest change in the costume came with "the Revolution," when no one could procure dyes or cotton, and that not many women resumed weaving afterward. They also pointed out, as do Indians in many parts of Mexico, that it now costs less to purchase clothing than to weave it. They admit, however, that there is no comparison in comfort or length of wearing time. Also older Zoque women said they did not wish to lose their group identity.

HUIPIL. The handwoven *huipil* (pl. 248; fig 8 e) is

330

248. A Zoque woman in an old-style costume with the *huipil de tapar* arranged for every day use. Tuxtla Gutiérrez, Chiapas. 1940

249. An old Zoque woman resting in her house. Tuxtla Gutiérrez, Chiapas. 1940

made of two strips fashioned of fine hand-spun thread, each strip measuring about 9 by 36 inches. Strips are sewn together by hand to form one rectangle 18 by 36 inches. No neck slit is left as is usual when there are center selvages. Instead the closed rectangle is folded to make a *huipil* 18 by 18 inches, and a round, fairly large neck opening is cut and bound with a ⅛-inch strip of black cotton cloth. Such a neck opening is far cooler than a vertical slit would be. The sides are sewn up to leave a 5-inch armhole which is edged with a 1½–2-inch gathered frill of store-bought or handmade white lace, or with a white cotton ruffle with a running design in black cross-stitch referred to as *contado* (counted). Motifs are flowers, birds, and animals.

Huipil weaves are combinations of gauze, plain-weave, and heavier-weft stripes. The heavier stripes are put in with heavier commercial white thread which contrasts with the creamy hand-spun cotton. When the material is washed, an attractive seersucker effect is obtained, because the hand-spun thread contracts more than the commercial thread areas. The plain-weave spaces are incredibly fine, some better *huipiles* counting up to seventy-five warp and sixty-four weft threads to the square inch (Cordry, 1941, p. 77). We were told it took about one week to weave a coarse *huipil* and considerably longer for a very fine one.

In Tuxtla, when we were there, some old women went about their work in their houses nude above the waist (pl. 249), saving their *huipiles* for the street.

SKIRT. The skirt, commonly called a *costal* (bag or sack), was handwoven of cotton thread dyed with indigo (pl. 248 & fig. 12). The thread was not hand-spun. The skirt was made of two strips, sewn together lengthwise and at the ends to form a cylinder. Two sizes were made for grown women: the entire cloth for the large skirt (two strips joined lengthwise) measured approximately 64 by 125 inches, and was wider than any skirt we know, except, perhaps, a very old-style skirt of San Bartolomé de los Llanos. The smaller Tuxtla Zoque skirt was 50 by 78 inches before it was sewn in tube form.

The plain-weave material has woven into it very narrow lighter-blue warp stripes, usually three groups to a strip, placed at slightly varying distances apart. The strips are sewn together both horizontally and vertically with decorative buttonhole or blanket stitch in colored silk or mercerized store threads in as many colors as the owner can afford, colors being changed about every inch or so.

HEAD COVERING. The finest Tuxtla weaving was found in the *huipil de tapar* (pl. 250), a garment of the same general form and dimension as the *huipil grande* of Tehuantepec (worn also as head covering but fashioned of commercial materials).

The Tuxtla *huipil de tapar* is woven in three strips appxoximately 12 by 43 inches, making the finished garment 36 by 21½ inches. Strips are sewn together with an exceedingly fine silk joining stitch in sections of several light colors—lavender, blue, yellow, and so on. The neck opening has a ruffle of 2-inch lace, and is bound with black cotton and bordered with several rows of fine silk chain stitch. The tiny 4-inch sleeves (never used as such) have ruffles of 6-inch lace and borders of the same chain stitching. This garment, unlike the Tehuantepec *huipil grande*, has no ruffle on the bottom edge.

There are three ways of wearing the *huipil de tapar*. (1) The fashion for church is seen in Plate 250. (2)

PLATE XV. A Huave woman of San Mateo del Mar, Oaxaca, showing how the old *huipil* with shellfish-dyed stripes and brocaded animals was worn. 1963

250. Dressed for church in a finely woven *huipil*, a *huipil de tapar*, and gold and coral jewelry. Tuxtla Gutiérrez, Chiapas (Zoque). 1940

That of old women (*priostas*) is the same as for church except that the sleeves are folded on top of the head. (3) For everyday the garment is folded over and placed casually on the head (pl. 248).

Store-bought cotton *rebozos* were commonly used in 1940.

HAIRDRESS AND JEWELRY. The hair of Zoque women may be worn loose or in two braids, in which are twined ribbons. Braids are sometimes crossed at the neck and brought to the top of the head and fastened.

Necklaces of large old corals with gold filigree beads were worn and highly prized as heirlooms. A gold rosary (pl. 250) was formerly an important item in the fiesta costume with a chain of corals, gold beads, and gold coins. Hardly any of these more valuable items were still to be found in 1940. All Zoque women we saw were barefoot.

Men's Costume

The Tuxtla Zoque men's costume (fig. 16) formerly consisted of a white handwoven shirt and trousers, a handwoven belt, a large flat hat and short over-trousers of leather. In 1940 the flat hat was no longer seen; instead a market hat of straw was used.

SHIRT AND TROUSERS. The old hand-spun round-neck nonbutton shirt was woven of a single width on the same loom used for the woman's skirt. Of same width as the smaller skirt (25 inches), it was worn short— well above the waist. Sleeves were formed of long straight pieces.

Straight-cut trousers of the same material were worn beneath short leather trousers, the latter having been borrowed from Spanish dress. Even in 1940 we found it almost impossible to obtain a pair. They were made of brown leather with appliquéd designs in black and cream leather. The buttons on the side pockets were made from Mexican and Guatemalan coins.

BELT AND HAT. Old-style belts were 6 by 84 inches, a dark-blue warp with narrow weft stripes of red, purple, and white. To the fringe at the ends of the belt were tied small tassels of colored silk threads. Few such old handwoven belts survived in 1940. A belt of netted string in red or multicolored stripes from Comitán de las Flores, Chiapas, had largely replaced the old, already much treasured, Tuxtla belt.

Market straw hats of the high-crowned type, formerly worn in the Isthmus of Tehuantepec, were worn by the Tuxtla men, in 1940, on top of bandana handkerchiefs tied over the head. Sometimes the latter alone was used. A simple leather sandal was worn.

37. San Bartolomé de los Llanos, Chiapas (Tzotzil)

THE WOMEN of San Bartolomé are among the most famous weavers in Chiapas. Their work in former times was especially admired by Zoque women of Tuxtla Gutiérrez. There was trade between the two areas and a similarity of costume—due to the warm climate of both localities, as compared to the high, cold San Cristóbal de las Casas region. Raw cotton came to Tuxtla from San Bartolomé, and Zoque women bought one kind of all white *huipil* strips from this village. Because of the different climate the costume of San Bartolomé does not resemble that of other Tzotzils, of Chamula or Zinacantán, for instance.

We were told in 1940 that the Zoques had not woven brocaded figures in their white *huipiles* for a very long time, and that therefore they liked to buy figured strips, referring to them as *huipiles* with *hombrecitos* (little men). At that date only a few old Zoque *huipiles* from Ocozocoautla were seen with brocaded designs (Cordry, 1941, pp. 78–80) (pl. 47).

Women's Costume

Fine, handwoven, short white *huipiles*, embroidered wrap-around skirts, and white *servilletas* brocaded in multicolored wools, for use as head coverings and *tor-* *tilla* cloths, comprise the costume of women of this famous weaving center. In 1940 very fine, long, handwoven, red hair ribbons were used.

HUIPIL. Woven of fine, hand-spun thread, the very short *huipil* is fashioned in one piece, folded, with a round neck. The latter is bound in ½-inch wide black cloth or store ribbon, with two short ends to mark the front of the garment. *Huipil* lengths are usually about 20 by 28–30 inches (fig. 8 c). When folded over and sewn up the sides—leaving a 4–5 inch arm opening—the garment measures 20 by 15 inches, often so short that the bare midriff is exposed above the skirt. *Huipiles* are richly adorned with as many as twenty-eight to thirty rows of raised brocaded figures—sometimes entirely in white on white, at other times with a row of the brocading worked in brilliantly colored store-bought yarns across the shoulder and chest. Around the arm opening, a band 1–2 inches wide of zigzag, multicolored wool brocading occurs. Designs are variations of dot, diamond, zigzag, and fishbone patterns, with human figures hand-in-hand, and bird or plant motifs.

Sometimes a wide, plain, horizontal band of red weft runs around the *huipil* chest section (pl. IV b), with a brocaded design row in multicolored wool running through its center. The lower edge of such a *huipil* has

335

251. A girl of San Bartolomé de los Llanos, Chiapas, with a brocaded *huipil, servilleta,* and embroidered skirt. (Tzotzil). 1940

a 1½-inch section of plain red weft, on top of which rests a continuous row of multicolored brocaded birds. We believe that similar weaves are found around Cobán, Guatemala.

SKIRT. In 1940 San Bartolomé wrap-around skirts were of heavy dark-blue handwoven cotton—two strips sewn lengthwise and joined end to end to form a tube. Sizes varied considerably. Strips of one young girl's skirt measured 21½ by 70 inches. The best women's skirts were tremendously large in dimension, although somewhat smaller than the similar old Zoque skirt. We are told that today store-bought blue cloth has taken the place of the handwoven anil-dyed cloth.

Both vertical and horizontal skirt joinings are emphasized by 1–2-inch bands embroidered in over-and-over stitch in colored wool and artificial silk—three yellow wool threads, three *solferino* silk threads, three green wool, three *solferino* silk, three blue wool, and so on, alternating. The point where both joinings intersect (worn over the left hip) is further decorated by a large, curled fernlike, multicolored motif in chain stitch. Along the bottom and top edge of the skirt is a multicolored embroidered wave-patterned border running along on either side of the vertical tube joining, and stopping some 15 inches from the join. Spotted above the wave pattern, and resting upon it, are bird and flower motifs usually alternating. Handwoven skirts had in addition a number of curious 5–6-inch-long narrow black snakelike motifs placed horizontally, and at random, in background areas.

This skirt (pls. 71 & 251) is put on in the general manner of the Zoque skirt of Tuxtla Gutiérrez or Copainalá, with a *bolsa* (bag) formed of extra material on the right front side. From photographs seen of present-day San Bartolomé women, we would judge that the store-cloth skirts now worn are reduced in size.

SERVILLETA. *Servilletas* are made of many sizes and for many uses in San Bartolomé, and are very colorful. Often 15–30 inches square, with white weft rib stripes, these cloths are woven of heavier, more serviceable weight than the fragile *huipiles.* Rows of brocaded dots in many colors of wool, with some of artificial silk, characterize these *servilletas.* The design spots are arranged in rows, covering the entire square. Some old-style (1902) *huipiles* from San Martín Jilotepeque, Guatemala, characterized by dotted background areas (O'Neale, 1945, Fig. 86), seem closely related.

Servilletas are placed on top of the head, corners turned under, for protection against the sun or as buffers beneath burdens carried on the head (pl. 251). They are also used to carry *tortillas,* to cover baskets, and so on (a volume could be written on the decorative bags and cloths made in Mexico for the indispensable *tortilla*).

HAIRDRESS. In 1941 a special handwoven hair ribbon

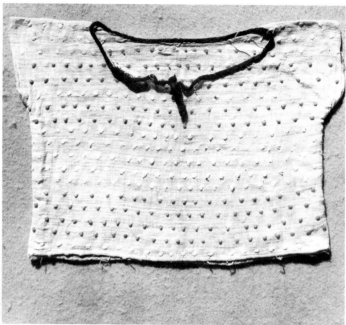

253. A *huipil* for a small child. San Bartolomé de los Llanos, Chiapas. (Tzotzil).

252. A group of young Tzotzils of San Bartolomé de los Llanos, Chiapas. 1940

was made in San Bartolomé of red cotton, in plain weave. A long band, 2½–3 by 90 inches, had in its exact center a 6-inch multicolored brocaded section, which was placed to be seen across the lower back of the head between the two hanging braids. The long ends were braided into the hair on either side, and left to hang down the back. Toward each end of the band a brocaded wool area of the woven hair ribbon was looped to show at the ends of the braids.

Little Girls' Costume

All little girls in 1941 were dressed like their mothers (pl. 252). We examined one tiny *huipil*, for a baby—one of the few Mexican Indian baby garments in the authors' collection that is entirely fashioned by hand (pl. 253). A miniature of a grown-up *huipil*, made with great care, it is formed of one handwoven web 13 by 18 inches, folded over to form a garment 9 inches long.

The traditional narrow black ribbon binds the neck opening. For decoration, tiny brocaded polka dots in rows cover the cloth entirely—all dots are of pink, with one single dot of green and one of purple, placed at random in Indian fashion.

Men's Costume

SHIRT. Formerly (probably still to some extent), San Bartolomé men wore handwoven brocaded shirts (pl. 254), cut in one piece with a V-cut neck, and having handwoven, plain-cloth sleeves set in. Sometimes the men's shirts had fringe at the bottom edge. An uncut shirt strip which we examined measured 23 by 40 inches, making a garment 23 inches wide and 20 inches long. Shirts were worn short and loose, leaving the midriff bare above the trousers.

TROUSERS. The trousers of San Bartolomé men were of heavy handwoven white material, with red figure "8"

337

254. Tzotzil musicians of San Bartolomé de los Llanos, Chiapas. 1942

brocaded elements placed at intervals over the entire cloth. The trousers were gathered into the waist, full about hips, and very narrow at the ankle (pl. 254), giving them a curious Oriental look.

BELT. The belt which holds the San Bartolomé trousers is of handwoven red cotton, with multicolored brocaded designs at both ends.

HEADDRESS. To finish this striking costume, the men wore large, very heavily brocaded, handwoven red cotton kerchiefs on the head, tied in the back (pls. 125 & 128). One example, at hand, measures 45 by 48 inches, and contains a large solid center square of multicolored brocading. Throughout the elaborate headcloth, with its bird and zigzag patterns, six or seven colors are used. A second, larger cloth—similarly composed—measures 43 by 60 inches. Both examples were fashioned of three woven strips, the center one twice the loom width of the outer webs, and containing most of the multicolored brocaded work. For ceremonial purposes a second one of the same cloths may be seen about the neck, as in Plate 128.

Boys' Costume

Little boys, in 1941, wore shirts like their fathers' woven of hand-spun thread with rows of brocaded figures.

38. Some Tzotzil and Tzeltal Villages in the Highlands of Chiapas

THERE ARE fourteen Tzeltal, and twenty-eight Tzotzil communities (Villa Rojas, 1962, p. 55). Each community consists of a head town (*cabecera*), having church, authorities, and small stores, surrounded by smaller settlements and *ranchos*.

San Cristóbal de las Casas is the principal center where Indians of many of these villages go to sell their products, and to buy the few things they can. The Indians are vendors of *carbón* (charcoal), wood, *ocote* (torch pine), and vegetables which they have raised or bought in warmer climates to resell. In the picturesque Calle Real are shops owned by *ladinos* (mestizos) who buy textiles, bags, and baskets from Indians to sell to other Indians who do not make these particular items themselves.

The Indians of the large Tzotzil town of Chamula are the chief producers of many of these items. The men make hats (pl. 255), bags, *caites* (high-backed sandals), musical instruments—even furniture, which is destined for *ladino* households. The women weave belts *sarapes, cotones,* and other wool items for a number of villages, in addition to the woolen garments needed for their own families.

In deference to the book *Chiapas Indígena*, by Gertrude Duby (1961), with its fine photographs, the complete costumes of only a few villages of this area will be touched upon here. These are described and photographed as we saw them during a stay in San Cristóbal de las Casas in 1940. Apart from this, a few outstanding textile examples from other villages are represented in some of the plates.

Since our visit there has been much improvement in the status of the Indian of this region. The Departamento de Protección Indígena and the Instituto Nacional Indigenista have done much to cause the distrustful Indian to feel his Mexican citizenship; to open new roads; to build schools and medical stations; and to help in agriculture. Also redistribution of the people of some localities, villages, and *ranchos* has been officially organized, because of extreme erosion of land in this area. This erosion has caused the able Indians of Chamula to become productive in other crafts, as has been mentioned.

Chamula (Tzotzil)

Women's Costume

The women's clothing of Chamula consists of five elements, all of wool with black wool predominating, al-

340

255. Two Tzotzil men of Chamula, in San Cristóbal de las Casas, Chiapas. 1940

256. A Chamula, Chiapas, girl with a pottery bowl. (Tzotzil). 1940

though lighter, natural wool colors are also used. The costume parts are a wool *huipil*, skirt, belt, cape, and headcloth. All but the belt have a feltlike appearance. We have not visited the village, but are told that washing and beating creates this feltlike look. As one nears the area of San Cristóbal de las Casas by road from Tuxtla Gutiérrez, one may see women of Chamula tending sheep and spinning in open country some distance from their homes.

HUIPIL. The *huipil* is handwoven of very heavy black grey, or white feltlike wool in three strips, and has a small square-cut neck opening carefully finished with blanket stitch and rows of multicolored chain stitching in mercerized thread. Arm openings (6–7 inches) are finished with an identical treatment. One *huipil* examined measured 30½ inches wide, each strip a different width—9½, 13½, 9, respectively. This *huipil* had a narrow grey stripe running warpwise (vertically) ev-

ery 2 inches. *Huipil* length from the shoulder fold measured 26–28 inches. At the center, both in front and in back, about 5 inches below the neck, were two large home-dyed red wool tassels with some threads left free and others finger-twined. *Huipiles* are worn both inside and outside the skirt.

Rarely seen today is the fiesta *huipil*, also of wool with a very deep yoke of multicolored brocading. We have been told by a native of Chamula that feathers were formerly used in the decorative areas of some fiesta *huipiles*.

BELT. A wide red wool belt is worn in Chamula 7¾ by 114 inches, including two ends of 38 inches each consisting of cords with tasseled ends. This belt is of the type seen in Plate VI a, except that the dark stripe is narrower in the San Juan Chamula belt. The same plate shows the woman's belt of Larrainzar, which is woven in Chamula.

SKIRT. The two-web wrap-around tube skirts are usually of heavy black wool with a narrow light-grey stripe every 2 inches or so. Two adult Chamula skirts which we examined had rather widely divergent measurement weight, and thickness. Not much attention is given to making both webs the same width. The first skirt had webs measuring in width 16½ inches and 17½ inches by 60 inches in circumference. The second had webs measuring in width 13½ inches and 16 inches by 76 inches in circumference.

When worn the skirt is formed into an inverted box pleat at the center front, with the right side lapped over the left (fig. 11 b-3). Whether the *huipil* is worn inside or outside the skirt, a number of inches at the waist are folded over, and looped down over the wide heavy red wool belt.

HEADCLOTH. Chamula headcloths are usually black (sometimes grey), and often of a less heavy weave than the skirt and *huipil* but still feltlike in appearance. The example at hand measures 19 by 48 inches and has hand-spun corded tassels of *solferino* wool at each corner. The headcloth is worn folded lengthwise, and doubled flat on top of the head, projecting out over the forehead (pl. 256).

CAPE. The cape is fashioned of a rectangular woven piece, usually of black wool, and is used as an additional garment over the *huipil*.

Men's Costume

For everyday, in Chamula, a knee length, light-tan or white wool *cotón* is worn by the men, tied about the waist with a long piece of leather which serves as a belt (pl. 255). Under this are worn short, tight *manta* trousers and shirt having red machine stitching. A black *cotón* is worn for special occasions. Chamula men wear a white cotton headcloth, which shows quite low beneath their straw hats (pl. 255). They weave hats as they walk. They used to carry burdens in high square crates and walk with a staff.

Children's Costume

The Chamula children still dress as their elders do, although lighter-colored wool is often employed for garments of little girls.

Tenejapa (*Tzeltal*)

Women's Costume

Huipil. The Tenajapa *huipil* is usually made of plain white, heavy cotton weave, similar to men's trouser material from this village. In the example studied, commercial, not hand-spun, thread was used. Formerly very wonderful hand-spun heavily brocaded *huipiles* were made here, and some few may still be woven in the village. The *huipil* we were able to examine was simpler—woven in two webs, each 17 by 54 inches, making the garment when folded at shoulders 34 inches wide by 27 inches long. Some Chiapas *huipiles* are shorter than they are wide, a characteristic also of Guatemalan *huipiles*. Tenajapa *huipiles* are left entirely unsewn down the sides, and a 10-inch selvage neck slit is left open in the sewing together of the two strips. On either side of the 10-inch neck slit, a vertical 1-inch zigzag brocaded section borders the neck—a solid zigzag pattern in red, orange, purple, and pink store wool yarn. Across the shoulders run two brocaded bands in geometric lozenge pattern, with red predominating. Some plain white handwoven wool *huipiles* are worn (pl. 257), also open down the side and having a spot of embroidery at intervals along the arm opening.

Skirt. Tenajapa women wear a blue wrap-around cotton skirt with white lines, made in San Cristóbal de las Casas on the treadle loom. Two horizontal strips are sewn lengthwise, and joined with a decorative stitch in varying colors. Such skirts are used by many Chiapas villages—San Andrés and Oxchuc, for example.

Carrying Cloth. A heavy white wool blanket with groups of three small black stripes at 4-inch intervals is used as a cape and carrying cloth.

Belt. A wide white belt with a number of dark warp stripes is worn in Tenajapa. The measurements

257. Buying and selling — a Tenajapa woman in San Cristóbal de las Casas, Chiapas. (Tzeltal). 1940

258. A Zinacantán, Chiapas, baby's garment. (Tzotzil).

343

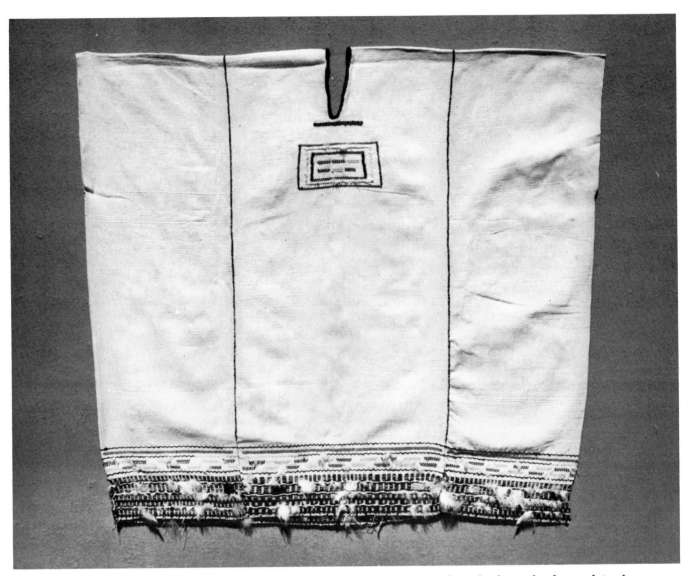

259. A Zinacantán, Chiapas, wedding *huipil*, with feathers spun into the thread in the lower border, and in the pre-Conquest-type rectangular design below the neck opening. (Tzotzil).

are not known. The upper edge of the skirt left to fall or stand above the belt (pl. 257) must be doubled down considerably inside, as the decorative join of the skirt webs occurs well above the hips.

Tortilla bags

Formerly, in the days of hand-spun weaving and superb brocading, the bags from Tenejapa were famous.

Men's Costume

HAT AND TROUSERS. Tenejapa men wear straw hats having peaked crowns, with ribbons hanging a few inches over the hat brim. Trousers are short, made of white handwoven cotton cloth, with straight legs and no gusset. They are formed of four 13-inch selvage-edged pieces sewn together by hand, and gathered in with a cord of *pita* run through. Near the bottom, a 2½-inch band of quite solid brocading in red wool with orange, green, and purple accents occurs—an overall pattern of zigzag and lozenge shapes. The weft-woven border is placed ¼ inch above the lower edge of the woven cloth.

COTÓN AND BELT. A black and white warp stripe

344

260. Tzotzil musicians and officials of Zinacantán, Chiapas, in Tuxtla Gutiérrez. 1942

261. Tzotzil men of Huistán, Chiapas, visiting in Tuxtla Gutiérrez. 1942

wool *cotón*, made in Chamula, is worn in Tenejapa, commonly with no cotton shirt beneath. A cotton belt woven in San Cristóbal—whitish background, with a blue-lined check (suggestive of dishcloth material)—is worn outside the *cotón* (Duby, 1961, pl. 7).

ALFERECES' (OFFICIALS') COSTUMES. For ceremonial occasions officials and their helpers have magnificent costumes (Duby, 1961, pl. 80). Two shirts and two trousers are worn, the underneath handwoven brocaded garments showing at the cuff, and also through slits up the calves of the leg. A wonderful long wide-striped cloth with brocaded ends is worn by officials over the right soulder. For other occasions, a black *sarape* and long *rosario* (rosary), with cross and medals hanging, are used.

Zinacantán (Tzotzil)

People from Zinacantán go to San Cristóbal to sell corn and salt. They are very independent, making everything they use except the men's high-backed shoes and some women's skirts. Also, their distinctive checkered kerchiefs used as headcloths or neck kerchiefs are woven in San Cristóbal.

Women's Costume

HUIPIL. For everyday in Zinacantán a handwoven white cotton *huipil*, with pink embroidered joining stitch between webs and around the neck, is used. For weddings, a special, heavy, handwoven white cotton *huipil* is worn, having a lower border, 5–8 inches wide, of three or four colors of brocaded wool in running weft lines and broken patterns. In this border are several white lines of specially spun thread in which feathers have been spun. A pre-Conquest-style 3½ by 6½ inch rectangle (pl. 259) is worked in colored wool below the neck slit of the three-web garment, both in front and in back. A smaller rectangle inside the outer one is fashioned of spun white thread (with feathers). This same feature occurs in both *huipiles* we have examined. Neck slits of both are buttonholed with bright green wool, not used elsewhere in the garment. The overall measurement is 37 by 41 inches. We were told that the wedding *huipil* was worn over the everyday costume.

SKIRT. In 1940 we found that three types of skirts were being used in Zinacantán: (1) the blue treadle-loomed cotton skirt woven in San Cristóbal de las Casas; (2) a skirt handwoven in the village (details not known); (3) a skirt of black wool with a white hair stripe, bought in San Cristóbal and woven in Chamula. On this last skirt the stripes seemed closer together than on skirts worn in Chamula—to differentiate one village from the other.

SHAWL AND BELT. The Zinacantán shawl is of white wool with pinkish stripe; and the wide belt is of red wool.

Men's Costume

TROUSERS AND COTÓN. The men wear very short wide trousers which flare at the sides, and a shortish shirt with a round neck. These men are chiefly recognized, however, by their outer garments, or *cotones,* which may be of three distinct types: (1) a pink and white candy-striped cotton *cotón*; (2) a *cotón* very similar to (1) but made of wool; (3) a long black wool garment worn by officials (pl. 260).

KERCHIEF AND HAT. Zinacantán men wear a 24-inch square kerchief of blue and white, small-checked cotton cloth loomed in San Cristóbal, with large pink wool tassels at each corner. Special flat-topped straw hats are worn, with wide, straight brims and hanging ribbons. Hats are woven with a dark stripe near the outer edge of brim.

SHOES. Zinacantán men wear very high-backed shoes (*caites*), made in Chamula, for fiestas, and less high-backed ones for everyday (pl. 126).

ALFERECES' (OFFICIALS') COSTUME. Zinacantán men of office, with long staffs (pl. 260), wear long red hand-woven head sashes, with ends hanging down the back under their special flat black felt hats, with red bands and narrow green ribbons hanging. They also wear a long black wool *sarape*-like garment with fringe around the bottom edge. It is trimmed at the neck with red flannel piping. Strips of cloth for this colored reinforcement are purchased in San Cristóbal de las Casas. The long black garment reaches to the top of their high-backed *caites*.

Huistán (Tzotzil)

Women's Costume

In 1940 Huistán women wore a plain handwoven white cotton or *manta huipil,* a dark-blue San Cristóbal treadle-loomed skirt (having no white line), and a white cotton shawl with a 1-inch dark-blue border; ¾-inch red-wool handwoven tapes were twisted *rodete*-like in the hair. We saw two types of belts worn: one of heavy natural-colored wool with red and black warp stripes

347

(3 by 125 inches), and one of red-check wool as used on Huistán men's hats.

Men's Costume

The Huistán villagers wear one of the most distinctive men's costumes still to be seen in Mexico—comparable to that of the *tacuates* of Zacatepec, Oaxaca, or the Huichols of Nayarit and Jalisco. The costume consists of white handwoven shirt and trousers, a wide red cotton belt, and a curious, very small, specially woven straw hat (pl. 261).

SHIRT. The shirt is a white handwoven slit-necked loose-sleeved garment, fashioned of four-selvaged pieces, with seams in center front and back. The finished garment is about 32 inches wide by 34 inches long. The straight sleeves are 8 by 18 inches (16 inches in circumference). A little delicate embroidery occurs below the neck slit on gala costumes, the design elements being a cross and flowers in subdued colors.

TROUSERS. Huistán trousers have extraordinary dimensions. The two legs are each 60 inches in circumference by 35 inches in length. The trousers have a draw cord at the top, and no crotch or gusset. When worn (over the shirt) the great width of each leg is pulled up at the side—a little toward the front—and looped over the belt.

BELT. An 18½-by-136-inch red cotton sash with occasional black and white warp stripes is wrapped around the waist, to hang down below the knees on each side of the body.

COTÓN AND HAT. A black and white striped Chamula-made wool *cotón* covers the cotton clothing, and a small round flat-brimmed, low-crowned hat is worn jauntily.

Huistán men, when away from their own village, seem aways to appear in tattered overlaid clothing. Even at an Americanista Congress in 1942, the Huistán delegation was cleanly but poorly dressed (pl. 261). When at home we understand that handsome unmended garments are worn, at least for ceremonial occasions (Duby, 1961, pl. 70; and from hearsay). We have been told that this curious custom of appearing in patched clothing is caused by the Huistán men's pride in their women's ability to mend their clothes.

Men of office (*autoridades*) (Duby, 1961, pl. 73) seem not to wear hats, but special handsomely striped, double, rather stiff, handwoven bands around the head —perched far back. Such personages also wear the very high-backed *caites*.

WORKS CONSULTED

Ajofrín, Francisco de
1964 *Diario del viaje que hizo a la América en el siglo XVIII.* 2 Volumes. Vol. 2. Instituto Cultural Hispano-Mexicano, A.C. México, D.F.: Talleres Tipográficos Galas de México, S.A.

Amsden, Charles Avery
1964 *Navaho Weaving: Its Technique and Its History.* Chicago: Rio Grande Press.

Aveleyra Arroyo de Anda, Luis
1964 *Obras selectas del arte prehispánico.* Consejo para la Planeación e Instalación, Museo Nacional de Antropología. México, D.F.: Museo Nacional de Antropología.

Basauri, Carlos
1940 *La población indígena de México. Etnografía.* 3 Volumes. Vol. 2. Oficina Editora Popular. México, D.F. Secretaría de Educación Pública.

Beals, Ralph L.
1943 *The Aboriginal Culture of the Cáhita Indians.* Ibero-Americana 19. Berkeley and Los Angeles: University of California Press.
1945 *The Contemporary Culture of the Cáhita Indians.* Smithsonian Institution, Bureau of American Ethnology Bulletin 142. Washington, D.C.: U.S. Government Printing Office.

Bennett, Wendell C., and Robert M. Zingg
1935 *The Tarahumara: An Indian Tribe of Northern Mexico.* Chicago: University of Chicago Press.

Bevan, Bernard
[1938] *The Chinantec: Report on the Central and South-Eastern Chinantec Region.* Vol. 1. México, D.F.: Instituto Panamericano de Geografía e Historia.

Beyer, Hermann
1965 *Mito y simbolismo del México antiguo.* Carmen Cook de Leonard (compiler, translator). El México Antiguo, Vol. 10. Sociedad Alemana Mexicanista. México, D.F.: Talleres Gráficos de Librería Madero, S.A.

Borah, Woodrow
1943 *Silk Raising in Colonial Mexico.* Ibero-Americana 20. Berkeley and Los Angeles: University of California Press.

Borbolla, D. F. Rubín de la
1963 "Arte Popular de México," in *The Popular Arts of Mexico,* pp. 2–9. Artes de México, Edición Especial de la Revista, Instituto Nacional Indigenista. Mexico City, Editorial Helio.

Brandomín, José María
1955 *Toponimia de Oaxaca.* México, D.F.: Imprenta Camarena.

Burgoa, Francisco de
1934 *Geográfica descripción.* 2 Volumes. Publicaciones del Archivo General de la Nación, Secretaría de Gobernación. México, D.F.: Talleres Gráficos de la Nación.

Cano, Gastón M. D.
1960 "*The Seri Indians of the Sonora Coast.*" Tucson, Arizona: College of Liberal Arts, School of Nursing, Univ. of Arizona. Mimeographed.

Caso, Alfonso
1959 *The Aztecs: People of the Sun.* Lowell Dunham (translator). Norman: University of Oklahoma Press.
1960 *Interpretación del Códice Bodley 2858.* Sociedad Mexicana de Antropología. México, D.F.: Editorial Libros de México, S.A.
1962 "Los ideales de la acción indigenista," in *Los centros coordinadores indigenista,* pp. 7–13. Instituto Nacional Indigenista. Edición conmemorativo en ocasión del XXXV Congreso Internacional de Americanistas. México, D.F.: Instituto Nacional Indigenista.
1964 *Interpretación del Códice Selden 3135* (A. 2). English text, pp. 55–100. Jacinto Quirarte (translator). Sociedad Mexicana de Antropología. México, D.F.: Editorial Libros de México, S.A.
1965 "The Mixtec Region," in *Oaxaca.* Artes de México. Año XII, 70/71, pp. 33–34. México, D.F.: Fotocomposición, S.A., Offset Multicolor, S.A.

Chimalpopoca. See Galicia Chimalpopoca, Faustino.

Christensen, Bodil
1947 "Otomí Looms and *Quechquemitls* from San Pablito, State of Puebla, and from Santa Ana Hueytlalpan, State of Hidalgo, México," in *Notes on*

349

Middle American Archaeology and Ethnology, Vol. 3, pp. 122–142. Carnegie Institution of Washington, Division of Historical Research. Cambridge, Massachusetts: Carnegie Institution of Washington. Offset.

1953 "Los Otomíes del Estado de Puebla," in *Huastecos, totonacos y sus vecinos,* pp. 259–268. Ignacio Bernal and Eusebio Dávalos Hurtado (editors). Revista Mexicana de Estudios Antropológicos, Vol. 13. México, D.F.: Sociedad Mexicana de Antropología.

Cicco, G. de, and F. Horcasitas
1962 "Los cuates: un mito chatino," in *Tlalocan,* Vol. 4, No. 1, pp. 74–79. México, D.F.: La Casa de Tláloc.

Códice Borgia (facsimile). See Seler, Eduard, 1963.

Columbia Encyclopedia
1954 2nd Edition, 10th Printing. New York: Columbia University Press.

Cook, Carmen, and Don Leonard
1949 "Costumbres mortuorias de los indios huaves: un viaje," in *El México Antiguo,* Vol. 7, pp. 439–513. México, D.F.: Editorial Cultura, T.G., S.A.

Cordry, Donald Bush, and Dorothy M.
1940 *Costumes and Textiles of the Aztec Indians of the Cuetzalan Region, Puebla, Mexico.* Southwest Museum Papers 14. Los Angeles, California: The Southwest Museum.
1941 *Costumes and Weaving of the Zoque Indians of Chiapas, Mexico.* Southwest Museum Papers 15. Los Angeles, California: The Southwest Museum.

Covarrubias, Miguel
1947 *Mexico South: The Isthmus of Tehuantepec.* New York: Alfred A. Knopf.
1957 *Indian Art of Mexico and Central America.* New York: Alfred A. Knopf.

Dahlgren de Jordán, Barbro
1954 *La Mixteca: su cultura e historia prehispánicas.* Colección Cultura Mexicana. México, D.F.: Imprenta Universitaria.
1963 *Nocheztli. Economía de una región: la grana cochinilla.* Nueva Biblioteca Mexicana de Obras Históricas, No. 1. Dirigida por Wigberto Jiménez Moreno y Antonio Pompa y Pompa. México, D.F.: José Porrúa e hijos, sucs.

Davis, Mary L., and Greta Pack
1963 *Mexican Jewelry.* Austin: University of Texas Press.

Davis, Russel
1961 "The *Quechquemitl* with a Twist." Centro de Investigaciones Antropológicos de México, Boletín 12. México, D.F. Mimeographed.

D'Harcourt, Raoul
1962 *Textiles of Ancient Peru and Their Techniques.* Seattle: University of Washington Press.

Dockstader, Frederick J.
1964 *Indian Art in Middle America.* Greenwich, Connecticut: New York Graphic Society.

Drucker, Susana
1963 *Cambio de indumentaria.* Colección de Antropología Social. México, D.F.: Instituto Nacional Indigenista.

Duby, Gertrude
1961 *Chiapas indígena.* Dirección General de Publicaciones, Universidad Nacional Autónoma de México. México, D.F.: Talleres Gráficos de Librería Madero, S.A.
1965 Letter, August 16.

Edwards, Emily
1966 *Painted Walls of Mexico: From Prehistoric Times until Today.* Austin: University of Texas Press.

Emory, Irene
1966 *The Primary Structures of Fabrics.* New York: The Spiral Press.

Enciso, Jorge
1947 *Sellos del antiguo México.* México, D.F.: Imprenta Policolor.

Florentine Codex. See Sahagún, Bernardino de

Foster, George M.
1940 *Notes on the Popoluca of Veracruz.* Instituto Panamericano de Geografía e Historia, No. 51. México, D. F.: Instituto Panamericano de Geografía e Historia.
1960 *Culture and Conquest: America's Spanish Heritage.* Viking Fund Publications in Anthropology 27. New York: Wenner-Gren Foundation for Anthropological .Research, Inc.

Frazer, Sir James G.
1963 *The Golden Bough,* 3rd Edition. Part I, Vol. I. New York: Macmillan & Co., Ltd., Saint Martin's Press.

Fuente, Julio de la
1947 "Los zapotecos de Choapan, Oaxaca," in *Anales del Instituto Nacional de Antropología e Historia,* Vol. II (1941–1946), pp. 143–205. Secretaría de Educación Pública. México, D.F.: Talleres Gráficos de la Editorial Stylo.
1949 *Yalalag: una villa zapoteca serrana.* Serie Científica, No. 1. Museo Nacional de Antropología, Instituto Nacional de Antropología e Historia, Secretaría de Educación Pública. México, D.F.: Imprenta Nuevo Mundo, S.A.

Gadow, Hans
1908 *Through Southern Mexico.* London: Witherby and Company.

[Galicia Chimalpopoca, Faustino (translator)]
1947 *Relación de los tributos que daban todos los pueblos.* Biblioteca Aportación Histórica. México, D.F.: Vargas Rea.

Gamboa, Fernando
1963 *Masterworks of Mexican Art, from Pre-Columbian Times to the Present.* Catalogue 565. Los Angeles, California: Los Angeles County Museum of Art.

García Cubas, Antonio
1876 *The Republic of Mexico in 1876.* George F. Henderson (translator). México, D.F.: La Enseñanza.

Gay, José Antonio
1950 *Historia de Oaxaca.* 3rd Edition. 2 Volumes (each in 2 Parts). Vol. 1. Biblioteca de Autores y de Asuntos Oaxaqueños. México, D.F.: Talleres V. Venero.

Gerhard, Peter
1964 "Shellfish Dye in America," in *Actas y Memorias, XXXV Congreso Internacional de Americanistas, 1962.* 3 Volumes. Vol. 3, pp. 177–191. Instituo Nacional de Antropología e Historia. México, D.F.: Editorial Libros de México, S.A. Reprint.

Griffen, William B.
1959 *Notes on Seri Indian Culture, Sonora, Mexico.* Latin American Monographs 10, School of Inter-American Studies, University of Florida. Gainesville: University of Florida Press.

Guiteras-Holmes, Calixta
1961 *Perils of the Soul: The World View of a Tzotzil Indian.* New York: The Free Press of Glencoe, Inc.

Hald, Margrethe
1962 *An Unfinished Tubular Fabric from the Chiriguano Indians, Bolivia.* Monograph Series Publication No. 7. Stockholm. The Ethnographical Museum of Sweden.

Hendrichs Pérez, Pedro R.
1945–
1946 *Por tierras ignotas.* 2 Volumes. Vol. 1. México, D.F.: Editorial Cultura.

Johnson, Irmgard Weitlaner
1953 "El *quechquemitl* y el *huipil*," in *Huastecos, totonacos y sus vecinos*, pp. 241–257. Ignacio Bernal and Eusebio Dávalos Hurtado (editors). Revista Mexicana de Estudios Antropológicos, Vol. 13. México, D.F.: Sociedad Mexicana de Antropología.
1954 "Chiptic Cave Textiles from Chiapas, Mexico," in *Journal de la Société des Américanistes*, n.s. Vol. XLIII, pp. 137–147. Paris: Musée de l'Homme. Reprint.

1954 "A Santa Catarina Estetla, Oaxaca, huipil." MS. in possession of I. W. Johnson.
1960 "Un *tzotzopaztli* antiguo de la región de Tehuacán," *Los Anales del Instituto Nacional de Antropología e Historia*, Vol. XI (1957–1958), pp. 78–85. Instituto Nacional de Antropología e Historia, Secretaría de Educación Pública. México, D.F.: Talleres Edimex, S. de R.L. Reprint.
1965 Letters, August 4, October 14.
1966 Letter, undated.
1967 Letter, February 14.

Johnson, Irmgard Weitlaner, and José Luis Franco C.
1967– "Un *huipilli* precolombino de Chilapa, Guerrero,"
1968 In press.

Johnson, Jean B., Irmgard Weitlaner Johnson, and Grace C. Beardsley
1962 "Industrias y tejidos de Tuxpan, Jalisco, México," *Los Anales del Instituto Nacional de Antropología e Historia*, Vol. XIV (1961), pp. 149–217. Instituto Nacional de Antropología e Historia, Secretaría de Educación Pública. México, D.F.: Talleres Edimex, S. de R.L. Reprint.

Jones, Anita
1965 Letters, August 31, October 20.
1966 Letters, April 5, April 19.
1967 Letter, March 10.

Kelemen, Pal
1965 "Folk Textiles of Latin America," in *Textile Museum Journal*, Vol. 1, No. 4 (December, 1965). Washington, D.C.

Kelly, Isabel, and Angel Palerm
1952 *The Tajín Totonac. Part I, History, Subsistence, Shelter and Technology.* Smithsonian Institution, Institute of Social Anthropology Publication 13. Washington, D.C.: U.S. Government Printing Office.

King, Mary Elizabeth
1966 *Village Costumes of Guatemala and Mexico.* Catalogue, March 1–September 16, 1966, Textile Museum. Washington, D.C.: Textile Museum.

Krickeberg, Walter
1933 *Los totonaca.* Secretaría de Educación Pública. México, D.F.: Talleres Gráficos del Museo Nacional de Arqueología, Historia y Etnografía.

Kroeber, A. L.
1931 *The Seri.* Southwest Museum Papers 6. Los Angeles, California: The Southwest Museum.

Leonard, Don
1955 *General Information about Anthropological Exploration of the Lacandón Jungle: Ethnology.* Preliminary report. México, D.F.: Centro de Investigaciones Antropológicas de México. Mimeographed.

Linati, Claudio
1956 *Trajes civiles, militares y religiosos de México (1828)*. Universidad Nacional Autónoma de México. México, D.F.: Imprenta Universitaria.

Lumholtz, Carl
1902 *Unknown Mexico*. 2 Volumes. New York: Charles Scribner's Sons.
1904 "Decorative Art of the Huichols," in *Memoirs of the American Museum of Natural History*, Vol. III, pp. 279–327. [Anthropology II (part III).]

MacDougall, Thomas, and Irmgard Weitlaner Johnson
1966 *Chichicaztli Fiber: The Spinning and Weaving of it in Southern Mexico*. Archiv für Völkerkunde: 20, pp. 65–73, pls. I–VI. Vienna: Museum für Völkerkunde.

MacNeish, Richard S.
1961 *First Annual Report of the Tehuacán Archaeological-Botanical Project*. Phillips Academy. Andover, Massachusetts: Robert S. Peabody Foundation for Archaeology.
1962 *Second Annual Report of the Tehuacán Archaeological-Botanical Project*. Phillips Academy. Andover, Massachusetts: Robert S. Peabody Foundation for Archaeology.
1964 Letter, March 31.

Mangelsdorf, P. C., R. S. MacNeish, and G. R. Willey
1964 "Origins of Agriculture in Middle America," in *Handbook of Middle American Indians*, Vol. 1, pp. 427–445. Robert Wauchope (general editor). Austin: University of Texas Press.

Massey, William C., and Caroline M. Osborne
1961 "A Burial Cave in Baja California." *Anthropological Records* 16, No. 8. Berkeley and Los Angeles: University of California Press. Photolithographed.

Matthews, Washington
1884 "Navajo Weavers," in *United States Bureau of American Ethnology Annual Report 3* (1881–1882) pp. 371–391. Washington, D.C.: U.S. Government Printing Office.

McGee, W. J.
1898 "The Seri Indians," in *Bureau of American Ethnology Annual Report 17*, Part 1, pp. 1–344. Washington, D.C.: U.S. Government Printing Office.

Mendizábal, Miguel Othón de
1946–
1947 *Obras completas*. 6 Volumes. México, D.F.: Talleres Gráficos de la Nación.

Miller, Walter S.
1956 *Cuentos mixes*. Biblioteca de folklore indígena. México, D.F.: Instituto Nacional Indigenista.

Molina, Alonso de
1944 *Vocabulario en lengua castellana y mexicana*. Colección de Incunables Americanos, Vol. IV. Madrid: Ediciones Cultura Hispánica.

Montoya Briones, José de Jesús
1964 *Atla: etnografía de un pueblo náhuatl*. Instituto Nacional de Anthropología e Historia, Departamento de Investigaciones Antropológicas 14. México, D.F.: Instituto Nacional de Antropología e Historia.

Morgadanes, Dolores
1940 "Similarity between the Mixco (Guatemala) and the Yalalag (Oaxaca, Mexico) Costumes," in *American Anthropologist*, n.s. Vol. 42, pp. 359–364.

Motolonía, Toribio de
1950 *Indians of New Spain*. Elizabeth Andros Foster (translator and editor). The Cortés Society. Berkeley, California: Bancroft Library.

O'Neale, Lila M.
1945 *Textiles of Highland Guatemala*. Carnegie Institution of Washington, Publication 567. Richmond, Virginia: The William Byrd Press.
1948 "Textiles of Pre-Columbian Chihuahua," in *Contributions to American Anthropology and History*, Vol. IX, No. 45, pp. 95–162. Carnegie Institution of Washington, Publication 574. Richmond, Virginia: The William Byrd Press.
1949 "Basketry," in *Handbook of South American Indians*. Julian H. Steward (editor). Bureau of American Ethnology Bulletin 143, Vol. 5, pp. 69–138. Washington, D.C.: U.S. Government Printing Office.

Orchard, William C.
1929 *Beads and Beadwork of the American Indians*. Museum of the American Indian, Heye Foundation, New York. Lancaster, Pennsylvania: Lancaster Press, Inc.

Ortiz Echagüe, José
1950 *España: tipos y trajes*. 8th Edition. Madrid: Editorial Mayfe.

Osborne, Lilly de Jongh
1935 *Guatemala Textiles*. Middle American Research Series Publication 6. New Orleans: Tulane University.
1965 *Indian Crafts of Guatemala and El Salvador*. Norman: University of Oklahoma Press.

Paredes Colín, J.
1921 *El distrito de Tehuacán*. México, D.F., Tipografía Comercial "Don Bosco."

Parsons, Elsie Clews
1936 *Mitla: Town of the Souls*. University of Chicago Publications in Anthropology, Ethnological Series. Chicago: University of Chicago Press.

Paso y Troncoso, Francisco del (compiler)

1905 *Papeles de Nueva España*. 2nd Series. *Geografía y Estadística*, Vols. IV, V, VI. Madrid: Sucesores de Rivadeneyra.

1950 *Xilotepeque. Relaciones del siglo XVIII relativas a Oaxaca* (tomada del Legajo 99, Sección de MSS. del Instituto Nacional de Antropología e Historia). México, D.F.: Vargas Rea.

Peñafiel, Antonio

1903 *Indumentaria antigua mexicana*. México, D.F.: Oficina Tip. de la Secretaría de Fomento.

Pozas, Ricardo

1959 *Chamula: un pueblo indio de los altos de Chiapas*. Memorias del Instituto Nacional Indigenista, Vol. VIII. México, D.F.: Ediciones del Instituto Nacional Indigenista.

Recopilación de leyes de los reynos de las Indias

1943 3 Volumes. Madrid: Gráficas Ultra, S. A.

Redfield, Robert

1930 *Tepoztlán: A Mexican Village*. Chicago: University of Chicago Press.

1962 *A Village That Chose Progress: Chan Kom Revisited*. University of Chicago Publications in Anthropology, Social Anthropology Series. Chicago: University of Chicago Press.

Robelo, Cecilio A.

1904 *Diccionario de aztequismos*. Cuernavaca: Imprenta del autor.

Roth, H. Ling

1934 *Studies in primitive looms*. [3rd Printing]. Yorkshire, England: F. King and Sons, Ltd.

Sahagún, Bernardino de

1951–
1963 *Florentine Codex: General History of the Things of New Spain*. Arthur J. O. Anderson and Charles E. Dibble (translators). Monographs of the School of American Research and The Museum of New Mexico. No. 14 (Books 2, 3, 5, 7, 8–11). Santa Fe, New Mexico: The School of American Research and The University of Utah.

Saltzman, Max

1963 "The Identification of Colorants in Ancient Textiles," in *Dyestuffs*, Vol. 44, No. 8, pp. 241–251. New York: National Analine Division, Allied Chemical Corporation.

1964 Letter, January 9, with report of dye analysis of some Mexican Indian textiles from the Cordry collection.

Santamaría, Francisco J.

1959 *Diccionario de mejicanismos*. Méjico: Editorial Porrúa.

Schurz, William Lytle

[1959] *The Manila Galleon*. [2nd Edition]. New York: E. P. Dutton and Company, Inc.

Séjourné, Laurette

1962 *El universo de Quetzalcóatl*. México–Buenos Aires: Fondo de Cultura Económica.

Seler, Eduard

1963 *Comentarios al Códice Borgia*. 2 Volumes and Facsimile. Mariana Frenk (translator). México–Buenos Aires: Fondo de Cultura Económica.

n. d. *Collected Works of Eduard Seler*. Vol. 3, Parts 3–4. Anonymous translation. Mimeographed.

Spence, Lewis

1923 *The Gods of Mexico*. New York: Frederick A. Stokes Company.

Spratling, William

1960 *More Human than Divine*. México, D.F.: Universidad Nacional Autónoma.

Stapley, Mildred

1924 *Popular Weaving and Embroidery in Spain*. New York: William Helburn, Inc.

Starkie, Walter

1957 *The Road to Santiago: Pilgrims of St. James*. London: John Murray.

Starr, Frederick

1899 *Indians of Southern Mexico: An Ethnographic Album*. Chicago: printed for the author by the Lakeside Press.

1900,
1902 "Notes upon the Ethnography of Southern Mexico," Parts I and II. *Proceedings of the Davenport Academy of Natural Sciences*, Vol. VIII, pp. 1–98, IX, pp. 1–109. Davenport, Iowa: Putnam Memorial Publication Fund.

1908 *In Indian Mexico*. Chicago: Forbes and Company.

Start, Laura E.

1963 *The McDougall Collection of Indian Textiles from Guatemala and Mexico*. Occasional Papers on Technology, No. 2. Pitt Rivers Museum. Oxford: University of Oxford.

Thompson, J. Eric S.

1961 *The Rise and Fall of the Maya Civilization*. 5th Edition. Norman: University of Oklahoma Press.

Tibón, Gutierre

1961 *Pinotepa Nacional*. México, D.F.: Universidad Nacional Autónoma de México.

Torquemada, Juan de

1943 *Monarquía indiana*. Facsimile edition. 3 Volumes. Vol. II, Book 10. México, D.F.: Editorial Salvador Chávez Hayhoe.

Toscano, Salvador, Paul Kirchoff, and Daniel F. Rubín de la Borbolla
1946 *Arte precolombino del occidente de México.* México, D.F.: Secretaría de Educación Pública.

Tozzer, Alfred M.
1907 *A Comparative Study of the Mayas and the Lacandones.* Archaeological Institute of America. New York–London: The Macmillan Company.

van der Post, Laurens
1961 *The Heart of the Hunter.* London: The Hogarth Press.

Velasco, Alfonso Luis
1891 *Geografía y estadística del Estado de Oaxaca de Juárez. Geografía y estadística de la República mexicana,* Vol. IX. México, D.F.: Oficina Tip. de la Secretaría de Fomento.

Villa Rojas, Alfonso
1962 "El Centro Coordinador Tzeltal–Tzotzil," in *Los centros coordinadores indigenista,* pp. 51–68. Instituto Nacional Indigenista. Edición conmemorativo en ocasión del XXXV Congreso Internacional de Americanistas. México, D.F.: Instituto Nacional Indigenista.

Williams García, Roberto
1963 *Los tepehuas.* Xalapa, Veracruz: Universidad Veracruzana, Instituto de Antropología.

Yturbide, Teresa Castello (dibujos), and Carlotta Mapelli Mozo (texto)
1965 *El traje indígena en México.* Instituto Nacional de Antropología e Historia. México, D.F.: Secretaría de Educación Pública.

Zingg, Robert Mowry
1934 *The Huichols: Primitive Artists.* Germany: n. p. Report of the Mr. and Mrs. Henry Pfeiffer Expedition for Huichol Ethnography.

INDEX

Revolution: influence of, on costumes, 330

ribbing: on *huipil*, 75

ribbons: distinctiveness of, 11; on *huipiles*, 13, 56, 62, 68, 72, 73, 75, 77, 87, 222, 224, 244–246, 278, 283, 297, 301, 317, 327, 335; on *quechquemitl*, 13, 225; flowered, 13, 56; on necklaces, 18, 56, 156, 161, 162, 246, 269, 315; as serpent symbols, 43; on skirts, 114, 269; as hair ties, 115, 118, 119, 125, 210, 278, 315, 327, 335, 336–337; on men's belts, 163, 315; on hats, 166, 298, 344, 347; on Mixtec upper garment, 307. SEE ALSO rosettes, ribbon

rickrack: used on *huipiles*, 13, 56, 87; used on skirts, 114, 269

rings: discussion of, 151; Otomí girls', 221

ring-weaving: loom used in, 32; of Mayos, 34; for belts, 139; of Otomís, 216; of Nahuas, 252

rigid-heald: of belt loom, 239

rivers: serpent as symbol of, 43

rock crystal: 8, 206

rodete: of Zapotecs, 18, 125, 263, 265; used in spinning, 27; on figurines, 95, 130; of Huastecs, 125; in codices, 125; materials used for, 125; of Nahuas, 228–230; styles of, 263; *rebozo* worn on, 263; Tzotzil hairdress compared to, 347

Rome: costumes of, 11

roosters: as necklace ornaments, 269; in textile designs, 271

roots: face paint made of, 211

rope: used as belt, 135–136

rosarios: pendant crosses as, 155; Zoque, 170, 334; Tzeltal, 347; SEE ALSO cross

rosette, ribbon: on *huipiles*, 56, 310; on *quechquemitl*, 225. SEE ALSO ribbons

round-shoulder technique. SEE curved weave

ruff: at waist of skirt, 101, 105. SEE ALSO ruffles

ruffles: on blouses, 91; on skirts, 278; on *huipiles*, 278, 280, 332

Ruiz, Don Felipe: 162

running stitch: on *huipiles*, 224, 251, 270; 326–327; on skirts, 253; on shirt hem, 297

sacrifice: and weaving, 5–6; symbolism of, 43; and weaving picks, 47, 48; in Sun-Moon-Bird legend, 49. SEE ALSO religious ceremonies

St. George: and Santiago, 156

St. James. SEE Santiago

saints, Christian: costumes for, 12, 87; and rain ceremonies, 27; on medals, 156; on reliquaries, 158

Salamanca, Spain: cross from, 155, 157

San Agustín Tlacotepec, Oaxaca: 137, 247

San Andrés, Chiapas: skirts of, 343

San Andrés Chamula, Chiapas (Tzotzil). SEE Larrainzar

San Andrés Chicahuaxtla, Oaxaca (Trique): *huipiles* from, 41, 52, 308, 310, 312; skirts from, 101, 103, 105, 310; children's costumes of, 101, 312; hair styles in, 118, 312; blanket garments of, 132, 134, 308, 312; belt of, 136, 310, 312; *servilletas* of, 142, 143, 145, 312; market in, 311; men's costume of, 312

San Andrés Teotilalpan, Oaxaca (Cuicatec): women from, opp. i; cotton beating in, 27; weaving pick from, 45; *huipiles* from, 56, 65, 69, 70; Chinantec traders in, 69; skirts from, 109; hair styles in, 118

San Antonio Castillo Velasco, Oaxaca (Zapotec): 140, 142

San Antonio de la Isla, México: 115

San Antonio Palopo, Guatemala: 44

San Bartolomé de los Llanos, Chiapas (Tzotzil): sale of cotton in, 25; religious beliefs in, 42; *huipiles* of, 50, 52, opp. 100, 335–336; blindness among weavers in, 73; skirts from, 103, 104, 109, 110, 332, 336; hair styles in, 118; 336–337; head coverings of, 130, 163; 164; *servilletas* of, 145, 336; men's costume of, 166, 171, 337–339; weaving in, 335; children's costume of, 337, 339; musicians of, 338

San Bartolo Otzolotepec, México, 167

San Bartolo Yautepec, Oaxaca (Zapotec): *huipiles* from, 58, 62; skirts from, 109; men's costumes of, 163, 168, 297

San Cristóbal, Guerrero: 306

San Cristóbal de las Casas, Chiapas: spindle-making centers near, 31; sheep raising in area of, 100; costumes in area of, 110; skirts from, 110, 343, 347; Tzeltal men's costume in, 168; climate of, 335; as trade center, 340; Tzotzil men in, 341; weaving in, 343; mentioned, 342

sandals: pre-Hispanic, 9; women's, 9, 10, 250, 263, 265, 278, 293; men's, 163, 164, 168, 170, 230, 236, 243, 280, 334, 340. SEE ALSO *caites*

San Dionisio del Mar, Oaxaca: 323

San Esteban Atatlahuaca, Oaxaca (Mixtec): brocade weaving in, 66; double-headed bird on textile from, 180; wedding *rebozo* from, 181; *huipil* strips from, 306

San Felipe del Progreso, México (Mazahua): 90–91, 118

San Felipe Usila, Oaxaca. SEE Usila, Oaxaca

San Fernando, Chiapas: 25

San Francisco Cajonos, Oaxaca (Zapotec): Jamiltepec spindles in, 31; silk belts from, 139; sleeve belts of, 142

San Francisco Chapantla, Hidalgo: *quechquemitl* from, 95, opp. 164, 180, 184

San Francisco del Mar, Oaxaca: 323

San José Chicahuaxtla, Oaxaca (Trique): 308

San José Miahuatlán, Puebla (Nahua): *huipiles* from, 65, 172, 231–234; skirts from, 101, 107; commercial cloth used in, 111; hair styles in, 118, 235; belts in, 136, 139, 231, 235; men's costume of, 166, 171, 236; head coverings of, 231, 235; jewelry of, 235; children's costumes of, 235, 236

San Juan, Guatemala: loom rattle in, 44

San Juan Bautista fiesta: of Mayos, 198

San Juan Chamula, Chiapas. SEE Chamula, Chiapas

San Juan Colorado, Oaxaca (Mixtec): skirts from, 105; belts in, 137; *servilleta* from, 145, 150; bags of, 150; men's costume of, 168; upper garment of, 307

San Juan Copala, Oaxaca (Trique): SEE Copala, Oaxaca

San Juan Cotzocón, Oaxaca (Mixe): costumes of, 16, 130; *huipil* from, 58; skirt from, 327

San Juan del Río, Querétaro: 91

San Juan Guivini, Oaxaca: 50

San Juan Mazatlán, Oaxaca. SEE Mazatlán, Oaxaca

San Juan Mixtepec, Oaxaca: 140

San Juan Numi, Oaxaca: 137

San Juan Yalalag, Oaxaca. SEE Yalalag, Oaxaca

San Lucas Ojitlán, Oaxaca. SEE Ojitlán, Oaxaca

San Luis Potosí, state of: 12, 90

San Martín Itunyoso, Oaxaca (Trique): *servilletas* in, 142, 143, 312; *huipiles* of, 310, 312; mentioned, 77

San Mateo del Mar, Oaxaca (Huave): *huipiles* in, 12, 41, 68, 189, 326–327, 329, opp. 332; hair styles in, 118; head coverings in, 134, 327; *servilletas* of, 145, 189, 190, 328, 329; jewelry of, 153, 329; skirt of, 327; belts of, 329; children's costume of, 329; men's costume of, 329; fiesta in, 329

San Mateo Tepantepec, Oaxaca: 292

San Miguel, Puebla: 228

San Miguel Chicahuaxtla, Oaxaca: 59, 310

San Miguel Chimalapa, Oaxaca (Zoque): 273

San Miguel el Grande, Oaxaca: 312

San Miguel Metlatonoc, Guerrero. SEE Metlatonoc, Guerrero

San Miguel Mitontic, Chiapas: 51, 52

San Miguel Peñasco, Oaxaca. SEE Peñasco, Oaxaca

San Pablito, Puebla (Otomí): *quechquemitl* from, 86, 87, 91, 94, 95, 180; skirts in, 101, 105, 107, 217; hair styles of, 115; 118; *servilletas* of, 145; belts in, 217, 219; mentioned, 105

San Pablo, Nayarit: dance in, 199

San Pablo Güilá, Oaxaca: 139

San Pablo Yaganisa, Oaxaca (Zapotec): 114

San Pedro Acatlán, Oaxaca. SEE Acatlán, Oaxaca